Y0-BDL-812

THE MUSIC OF MALAYSIA

The Music of Malaysia

The Classical, Folk and Syncretic Traditions

PATRICIA MATUSKY
and
TAN SOOI BENG

SOAS Musicology Series

ASHGATE

© Patricia Matusky and Tan Sooi Beng 2004

All rights reserved. No part of this publication may be reproduced, stored in a retrieval system or transmitted in any form or by any means, electronic, mechanical, photocopying, recording or otherwise without the prior permission of the publisher.

Patricia Matusky and Tan Sooi Beng have asserted their moral right under the Copyright, Designs and Patents Act, 1988, to be identified as the authors of this work.

Published by
Ashgate Publishing Limited
Gower House
Croft Road
Aldershot
Hampshire GU11 3HR
England

Ashgate Publishing Company
Suite 420
101 Cherry Street
Burlington, VT 05401-4405
USA

Ashgate website: http://www.ashgate.com

British Library Cataloguing in Publication Data
The music of Malaysia : the classical, folk and syncretic
    traditions. – (SOAS musicology series)
    1. Music – Malaysia – 20th century – History and criticism
    I. Matusky, Patricia II. Tan, Sooi Beng III. University of
    London. School of Oriental and African Studies
    780.9'595

Library of Congress Cataloging-in-Publication Data
Muzik Malaysia. English.
    The music of Malaysia : the classical, folk, and syncretic traditions / Patricia
Matusky and Tan Sooi Beng.
        p. cm. – (SOAS musicology series)
    Includes bibliographical references (p.), discography (p.), videography (p.),
    and index. ISBN 0-7546-0831-X (hardback : alk. paper)
        1. Music–Malaysia–History and criticism. I. Matusky, Patricia Ann. II. Tan,
Sooi Beng. III. Title. IV. Series.

ML345.M28 M8913 2003
780'.9595–dc21

                                                                    2002027782
ISBN 0 7546 0831 X

Printed and bound in Great Britain by MPG Books Ltd, Bodmin, Cornwall

Table of Contents

List of Figures and Table

Figures

Table

List of Plates

List of Musical Examples

The Authors and Contributors

Authors

Patricia Matusky is an ethnomusicologist and has taught for several years, including posts at the Universiti Sains Malaysia in Penang (1978-79, 1981-82 (Fulbright-Hays Lecturer in Music) and 1994-97 (Associate Professor), the University of Malaya in Kuala Lumpur and the LaSalle-SIA College of the Arts in Singapore. Her degrees are Bachelor of Music, Master of Arts (Library Science), and Doctor of Philosophy in ethnomusicology from the University of Michigan (Ann Arbor, USA), and Master of Arts in musicology from Hunter College of the City University of New York. Her doctoral field research focused on music of the Malay shadow puppet theatre (*wayang kulit*) from the state of Kelantan (1975-76), while her continuing research involves Malaysian musical instruments, folk and classical Malay music in Peninsular Malaysia and music in Sarawak. Her publications include articles on the folk music in Malaysia in international journals, and a book entitled *Malaysian Shadow Puppet Theatre and Music: Continuity of an Oral Tradition* (Kuala Lumpur: Oxford University Press, 1993 and Penang, The Asian Centre, 1997). She has contributed articles on folk and classical music of Malaysia in the *Garland Encyclopedia of World Music* (1998) and in *The New Grove Dictionary of Music and Musicians* (2001).

As a principal author in this publication project, she formulated the basic concept of the book and wrote on folk and classical music of the Malays and the indigenous groups in Sarawak.

Tan Sooi Beng is an ethnomusicologist and Associate Professor in the Music Department of the Universiti Sains Malaysia in Penang. Her degrees are the Bachelor of Arts from Cornell University (USA), Master of Arts from Wesleyan University (USA) and Doctor of Philosophy in ethnomusicology from Monash University (Australia). Tan Sooi Beng planned and originally chaired the Bachelor of Arts degree in music at the Universiti Sains Malaysia. The research for her doctorate degree focused on the history and development of music in the *bangsawan* theatre (Malay opera) of Malaysia from the 19th through the 20th centuries. Her continuing research includes the popular music of Malaysia, current issues in traditional and contemporary music, and music education in Southeast Asia. Her publications include several articles and a book entitled *Bangsawan: A Social and Stylistic History of Popular Malay Opera* (Singapore, Oxford University Press, 1993 and Penang, The Asian Centre, 1997).

Tan Sooi Beng proposed the idea of this book as a resource for information on traditional music and the analyses of folk, classical and syncretic music. She is also a principal author in this project, writing about syncretic music, Chinese music, and popular music in Malaysia.

Contributors

Mohd. Anis Md. Nor is a professor of ethnochoreology and ethnomusicology at the Culture Centre of the University of Malaya in Kuala Lumpur. His degrees are the Doctor of Philosophy in Southeast Asian studies and ethnomusicology from the University of Michigan (Ann Arbor, USA), the Master of Arts in the field of dance ethnology from the University of Hawaii at Manoa and the B.A. (Honours) from the University of Malaya. Among his specialized areas of study and research are the zapin dance and music, dance traditions among the Malayo-Polynesian societies in Southeast Asia and Polynesia and the development of new traditions through contemporary performances. For this project Mohd. Anis contributed articles on the music in the *randai* theatre, the *zapin* dance and the *caklempong*.

Jacqueline Pugh-Kitingan holds the Bachelor of Arts Honours from Monash University (Australia) and the Doctor of Philosophy in ethnomusicology from the University of Queensland (Australia). Since 1982 she has lived in Sabah with her family. She has carried out music research among many ethnic groups in Sabah including the Kadazan Dusun in Tambunan and Penampang, the Lotod Dusun in Tuaran, the Tatana Dusun in Kuala Penya and the Iranun and Bajau communities. Since 1986 she has worked as the music specialist in the Ministry of Culture, Youth and Sports in Sabah and currently is on the anthropology faculty of the Universiti Malaysia Sabah. Jacqueline Pugh-Kitingan has contributed the information on the folk music of Sabah in this book.

Hajjah Fakhariah bte. Datuk Lokman holds the Diplomas in Piano and Voice (ALCM, LLCM) and the Graduate Diploma (GLCM) from the London College of Music (1979) and the Master of Music in Education

(1990, Indiana University, Bloomington, Indiana (USA). She is Associate Professor and Lecturer in the Music Department of the MARA Institute of Technology (Kuala Lumpur), and is currently carrying out studies for the Doctor of Philosophy in ethnomusicology at the Universiti Sains Malaysia in Penang. She has produced a practical study entitled *The Development and Piloting of a Method of Teaching Basic Qur'anic Arabic Reading Through Music Rhythms.* In this book Fakhariah has contributed information for the discussion on *zikir, nasyid* and *kompang*.

The section on nobat music is based on the research and writings of the late Ku Zam Zam Ku Idris, a former Associate Professor in the Academy of Malay Studies at the University of Malaya in Kuala Lumpur. Other contributors include Ang Bee Saik, lecturer and administrator at the Kolej Damansara Utama in Penang who wrote about the *menora*, and Margaret Sarkissian, associate professor at Smith College, USA on whose work the section about the music of the Portuguese community of Malacca is based.

Preface and Acknowledgements

This book records the history, appreciation and analysis of folk, classical and syncretic music genres found in Malaysia. It was first published in the Malay language in 1997 and was especially written for specialists in music including music teachers in elementary and secondary schools, lecturers and students in the teachers' training colleges and universities, ethnomusicologists, cultural anthropologists, and the interested public who have some background in music. The scope of the Malaysian music genres discussed is comprehensive and stresses the major genres that reflect the aesthetics of a multicultural society.

In addition to the indepth discussion and analyses of the various music genres, this work categorizes the various types of music in Malaysian society and provides an overview of the development of music in the country. The historical development of Malaysian music encompasses a discussion of folk, classical and syncretic genres as well as popular music and contemporary art music. The analyses of the music are illustrated with examples transcribed mainly from original field recordings.

This book is the result of field investigation that was carried out by a number of researchers over many years. The background and professional qualifications of these scholars is given in the section Authors and Contributors.

The principal authors of this work, Patricia Matusky and Tan Sooi Beng, express their sincere appreciation to the many people and several institutions who made this book possible. The authors give many thanks to the contributors of some of the materials used in this book, Dr. Mohd. Anis Md. Nor, Dr. Jacqueline Pugh-Kitingan, Fakhariah binte Lokman, the late Ku Zam Zam Ku Idris, Ang Bee Saik and Margaret Sarkissian for their contributions on specific music topics. The authors also express immeasurable thanks to Noriah binte Abdullah who advised on translation of Arabic texts and the Jawi script and who edited the Malay text of the first version of this work, to Goh Hung Meng who prepared the illustrations of musical instruments and other drawings, to Dr. Ghulam Sarwar Yousof who loaned his recordings of theatrical music from Kelantan for transcription purposes, to Razak Abdul Aziz who always gave his advice and opinion on the music analyses and other technical matters and who gave permission for use of excerpts from his scores, and to Sunetra

Fernando who also gave permission for use of excerpts from scores of her works for *gamelan*. Many thanks are also in order to the students in the Music Department at the Universiti Sains Malaysia, Norlida Mohd. Jalaludin, Toh Lai Chee, Soon Yean Wan, Joyce Yeoh, Kweh Seok Bin and others, who provided photographic and other information for the production of this book.

The Universiti Sains Malaysia in Penang supported a short-term grant (1994-96) for the field research necessary to complete this work. Over the past years other institutions have also sponsored field research for the principal authors and contributors, especially the University of Malaya and the MARA Institute of Technology in Kuala Lumpur.

To all persons who have given their time for consultation and cooperation in the preparation and completion of this study many, many thanks are extended.

Finally, the authors express their highest appreciation to all the musicians of the folk, classical and syncretic music genres who have given permission to record their music and performances over the past many years. This book is dedicated to those musicians without whose musical performances, knowledge about their art forms and generosity this book would not have been possible.

Patricia Matusky, Michigan, USA
Tan Sooi Beng, Penang, Malaysia

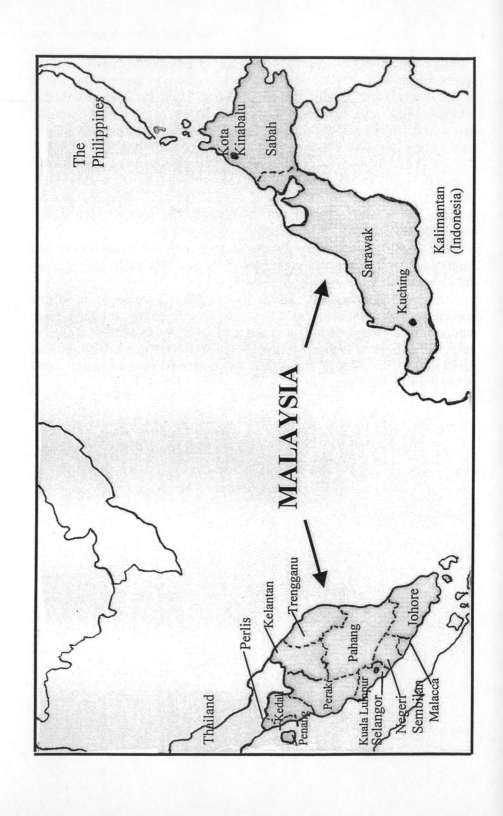

Introduction

Malaysia lies in the heart of Southeast Asia and comprises two noncontiguous regions referred to as West (or Peninsular) Malaysia and East Malaysia (or Sabah and Sarawak) on the north coast of Borneo. With territories on the Malay Peninsula and also on the island of Borneo, the country is unique in that it spans both the mainland of Southeast Asia and the Malay Archipelago.

The Malay Peninsula is about 500 miles (800 km) long and 200 miles (325 km) wide. It is particularly characterized by a central range of high, densely forested mountains (up to 7000 feet [2000 m] in elevation) contrasting with coastal lowlands that are densely populated on the mid- and south-west side of the mountains and heavily farmed on the northwest and east sides.

The East Malaysian states of Sabah and Sarawak on Borneo's northwest coast encompass an even larger area, about 670 miles (1075 km) long and 240 miles (385 km) wide. The coastal lowlands of Sabah and Sarawak give way to a hill and valley region and then to densely forested mountains (with elevations of 4000 to 7000 feet [1200 to 2000 m]). Mount Kinabalu (13455 feet [4101 m]), in the state of Sabah, is the country's highest point. Many rivers, large and small, flow from the central mountainous core in both West and East Malaysia. The rivers and their deltas have served as the main places where villages, towns and cities have taken shape and where culture has been nurtured by the local inhabitants.

Malaysia's equatorial climate fosters dense tropical vegetation with a great variety of flora and fauna, including elephants, tigers, leopards, orangutans and rhinoceros. In addition, one of the most varied bird populations in the world may be found in Sabah and Sarawak.

The people, society and political economy

Malaysia has often been noted as a meeting place of peoples from all parts of Asia and, in fact, from nearly all parts of the world. The Straits of Malacca, along the Peninsula's west coast, is one of the major sea lanes of the world and over the centuries has seen the arrival of a great diversity of people on the Malay Peninsula.

Today the Malays are the most numerous and politically important group among the citizens of this country. Minor differences in dialect, physical characteristics and, to some extent, culture may be seen among the Malay communities in the north and south of the Peninsula. Nevertheless, the Malays as a whole share a common culture, an Austronesian language (the Malay language, called *Bahasa Malaysia*, the national language of the country) and they are predominantly Muslim.

In East Malaysia the ethnographic picture becomes more complex. The Malays in Sabah and Sarawak are a coastal-dwelling minority, while the indigenous inhabitants constitute dozens of ethnolinguistic groups speaking mutually unintelligible Austronesian languages. These indigenous groups include, in Sarawak --- the Iban (the largest group), Bidayuh, Melanau, Kayan, Kenyah, Kajang, Kelabit, Penan, Bisayah, Murut and others; in Sabah --- the KadazanDusun (the largest group), Bajau, Murut, Kedayan, Orang Sungei, Bisaya, Sulu, Tidong and so on. Most of these groups in both states are Christian or practice their traditional animist religions; however, the Malays, Melanau and Bajau are mainly Muslims.

The Malays, the indigenous peoples of Sarawak and Sabah and the aborigines of Peninsular Malaysia [*orang asli*] are known as *bumiputera* [sons of the soil]. They make up about 63 per cent of the total population of 21.7 million, with the orang asli the smallest at about three percent of the bumiputera group.[1]

Another major ethnic group in the country is the Chinese who comprise about 26 per cent of the citizenry. Most Chinese in Peninsular Malaysia migrated from southeastern China in the 19th and early 20th centuries. The main dialects spoken among them are Hokkien, Cantonese, Hakka and Hainanese, and today most are also Malay speakers (the medium of education in the public school is the Malay language). The Hokkien and Cantonese communities are dominant among the Chinese on the Peninsula, while the Hakka and Fuchou (Hokchiu) speaking Chinese are the majority in East Malaysia. A small number of Chinese families trace their arrival on the Malay Peninsula to the 16th century or earlier and are known as the *Baba* or *Nonya* Chinese (also, Straits Chinese). This group has uniquely mixed some aspects of Malay culture such as dress, music and language with Chinese customs, manners and religion. The Baba live mainly in Malacca, Penang and Singapore. The larger Chinese community ascribes to Buddhism, Taoism or Christianity while also practicing or acknowledging Confucian moral precepts. The Chinese Malaysians are mainly an urban-based group operating the majority of shops in towns and cities throughout the country. However, dating from the 18th century and the onset of substantial Chinese migration from southeast China, a significant number were also important in running the agricultural estates and, by the late 19th century, the tin mines on the Malay Peninsula.

The people of South Asian heritage make up the next largest group in Malaysia. About seven per cent of Malaysians are of South Asian descent from different parts of South Asia. About 80 per cent of the South Asians are Tamils whose forefathers originally came from Tamil Nadu (south India). Other smaller groups include the Malayalees from Kerala (south India), the Punjabis, Bengalis, Pathans and Sindhis from north India, and the Singhalese and Tamils from Sri Lanka. The descendants from south India are mainly Hindu, while those from north India are Muslims, Sikhs or Christians. The Singhalese of Sri Lanka are mainly Buddhists. A small number of Indian Muslims known as *Jawi peranakan* were the offspring of early Indian traders who married Malay women.

The linguistic map of Malaysia becomes thicker with several Dravidian languages (Tamil, Telugu, Malayalam) and Indo-European languages (Punjabi, Bengali, Pashto and so on) spoken among the South Asian peoples. Many of the Tamil-speaking South Asians migrated to Malaysia mainly to care for the rubber plantations that were established from the 19th century onward. From the late 19th and into the 20th centuries many Indians from the sub-continent also worked in the Malayan civil service under British administrators, while others held occupations providing services in the towns and developing cities, mainly on the west coast of the Peninsula. In particular, the Punjabis were brought by the British to serve in the armed forces, while the Bengalis were employed as sepoys.

Others who hold citizenship in this country constitute about 3 per cent of the population. These include Thais, Javanese, Eurasians and Arabs. The remainder of the population consists of non-citizens, comprising East Asians, Europeans, West and South Asians, North and South Americans and so on.

Of all the indigenous peoples of Malaysia, the Malays and many of the native peoples of Sabah and Sarawak come from hierarchical societies with a ruler (a sultan among the Malays) or chief, nobility and commoners. Among some of the East Malaysian groups slaves were also common at one time, while other groups such as the Iban of Sarawak maintained egalitarian communities. Today Malaysia is a constitutional monarchy with a figurehead king (sultan), an elected parliament and a prime minister chosen from the majority party (to date this has always been the majority Malay political group).

Traditionally, the Malay commoners and the indigenous ethnic groups of Sabah and Sarawak were (and still are) the farmers of Malaysia. Many farm holdings are small and typically allow for subsistence farming with any extra produce sold at a central village or town market. Paddy, or wet-rice farming, is typically found in West Malaysia, with irrigation schemes provided for the farms through state and federal projects such as the KADA and KEMUBU projects in the north of Peninsular Malaysia.[2] In East Malaysia, although paddy may be found, swidden agriculture is more typical with hill rice [*padi bukit*] cultivated as the staple crop. Along the coastal regions fishing is a major occupation.

With the beginning of colonization by the British in the late 18th century on the island of Penang, the patterns of subsistence agriculture began to change. The British introduced the plantation system to the Malay Peninsula and by the late 19th century the cultivation of rubber, and then oil palm, became significant. Eventually, large rubber and oil palm plantations were established by multinational firms, and the small, local farm holders also planted rubber as a cash crop. While both large and small rubber holdings were important as one segment of the economy, many Chinese migrated to Peninsular Malaysia to work the mines in the rich tin fields on the west coast of Peninsular Malaysia. At one time Malaysia was the world's leading producer and exporter of natural rubber and a main producer of tin. Since the 1950s the government has carried out programs to clear forested areas, replant the areas with rubber and oil palm and establish housing and other facilities in order to resettle mainly poor Malay families to these areas to cultivate the crops and to improve their economic status.[3]

The year 1969 is an important watershed in contemporary Malaysian political economy.[4] Following the 1969 riots, policies for 'restructuring society' and the 'inculcation of loyalty to the nation' were introduced beginning in 1971, and the medium of instruction in former English language national-type schools was changed to Bahasa Malaysia. The New Economic Policy (NEP) was implemented in 1970. This policy emphasized the creation of a Malay commercial and industrial community, the encouragement of bumiputera participation in urban activities and the establishment of new growth centers. The policies that favored the Malay community strove to create equality between the rural Malays and the urban-based Chinese who have been seen to control the economic wealth in the country.[5]

As it was believed that progress for Malays would come via industrialization and urbanization, the government began a program of intense industrialization in the 1970s such as the setting up of free trade zones in specific states to attract export-oriented manufacturing industries. Over the past several decades thousands of Malays have migrated from their villages and farms to work in the cities where large-scale industries are based. This massive migratory pattern may be witnessed during the local Muslim holidays when vast numbers of people travel back to the villages to celebrate the religious occasions with family. The unsuspecting non-Malaysian traveler will find that not an empty seat is available on an airplane, train, taxi or other mode of transportation during these times.

Malaysia experienced rapid economic growth in the 1980s and 1990s and became a flourishing country in Southeast Asia with a growing industrial base in the automobile, computer chip, petroleum, and other commodity-based industries. Coinciding with the economic boom and industrialization, Dr. Mahathir, the Prime Minister of Malaysia, launched the *Wawasan 2020* [Vision 2020] in 1991. The main objective was to push Malaysia to become a Newly Industrialized Country (NIC) by 2020 and to mark Malaysia's position in the world. The vision called for a Malaysia that is not only developed in economic matters but also in political, spiritual and cultural dimensions.

To symbolize Malaysia's aspirations to the world, modern icons have been constructed. Kuala Lumpur, the capital of Malaysia, has some of the world's tallest buildings such as the KL Tower and the Petronas Twin Towers. The high-tech multimedia super corridor, an area stretching from Kuala Lumpur to several miles southward, is touted to become the hub of information technology in the region. Within this context the performing arts, and particularly music, have experienced radical changes in their traditional settings and in their relatively new urban modern setting.

Music in Malaysian society and culture

Even though Malaysian culture is multi-ethnic, the existing musical genres found in the country reflect the specific ethnic groups concerned, namely the Malay, Chinese, Indian, Dayak, KadazanDusun, Portuguese, Eurasian and other groups. There has not been a substantial assimilation of musical styles among the various ethnic groups, and the distinctions in music genres and styles among at least the Malay and other indigenous peoples, Chinese, and Indian communities are still very clear.

In general, music in Malaysian society may be categorized as classical, folk, syncretic, popular and contemporary art music. Sometimes the characteristics of these categories overlap. Still, these five terms are useful in organizing and understanding the musical world in this Southeast Asian country.

Types of Music in Malaysia

Classical music Both classical and folk music emerged during the pre-Colonial period. Classical music[6] is associated with the urban areas or with the royal courts and palaces. The music has a theoretical/historical base and a defined repertory that is learned by the musicians. The performers are trained in a structured way over a long period of time, and the process of formal training is sponsored by the aristocratic classes or, today, by government agencies. The concept of professionalism is recognized among the performers. Traditional classical music is usually known by only a part, usually the educated part, of the society. In Malaysia, as in other parts of the world, the classical music that develops in the urban or palace context often derives its inspiration and even its basis from the folk music traditions of the villages. This is so in the shadow puppet theatre and other traditions in Malaysia (see, for example, the *wayang kulit Kelantan* [Kelantanese shadow play] *and wayang Melayu* [Malay shadow play] discussions in the following chapters). The main genres of Malaysian classical music are discussed in this book, genres such as the *joget gamelan*, *wayang Melayu*, and *nobat*.

Folk music In contrast to classical music, folk music[7] is usually found in villages and farming regions where a writing system may or may not be known, and where many people function mainly in an oral tradition. Music training is not systematic and a knowledge of music history and theory is usually not known. If there is a training process in learning to play musical instruments, it is by rote method. Concepts of professionalism sometimes exist in the Malaysian folk music traditions and are defined by the process of training within an apprenticeship system. Furthermore, a repertory of music is usually not consciously specified or realized within the folk music tradition, and it or its style changes very slowly over long periods of time.

The folk music of a given society is an expression of the ordinary people, and it does not easily change when compared to other types of music. The existence of folk music depends upon the agreement and support of the entire community from which it comes and, hence, it strongly reflects the basic values and norms of that community. Many genres of folk music are described and analyzed in this book in the chapters concerned with music for theatre, dance music, percussion ensembles, vocal and solo instrumental music, and social popular music.

Although there are differences between folk and classical music, in practical terms some genres appear to exist in both categories. For example, in Peninsular Malaysia there are some genres of music that existed in the past in both the rural and palace contexts, genres such as *makyung, wayang kulit Melayu, tarinai* and *zapin*. In the discussion of these musical genres both the folk and the classical musical features are made apparent.

Syncretic music   Syncretic music (or acculturated music) in Malaysia is heard in both urban and rural settings. Syncretic music emerged during the post-Portuguese period (16th century). It developed rapidly after British intervention following exposure of the local multi-ethnic population to foreign kinds of entertainment such as the talkie, European and American operetta and vaudeville, Parsi theatre and Chinese opera that toured Malaya then. In this category of music, local elements from both folk and classical traditions are combined with foreign elements from Arab, Persian, Indian, Chinese and Western musical and theatrical sources. In Malaysia this music exists in the form of vocal, dance and theatrical music such as the *ghazal* [love songs], *dondang sayang* [repartee singing], *lagu Melayu asli* [original Malay songs], *zapin, inang*, and *joget* [dance music], *boria* [comic skits and singing], *keroncong* [a vocal and instrumental genre] and *bangsawan* [Malay opera]. Several types of syncretic music are discussed within the topics of theatre, dance, percussion and social popular music in this book.

Popular and contemporary art music   Both Malaysian popular music and contemporary art music are essentially Western-based music combined with some local elements.

Malaysian art music was first composed by musicians of Malaysian Radio and Television in the 1960s and 1970s. Like art music traditions around the world, Malaysian art music has a theory and exhibits a high degree of refinement and professionalism. It is composed by highly trained individuals and is written using mainly Western notation. The audience for art music is not large, and consists mainly of those educated in the tradition.

Popular music, also, has a Western theoretical base and is often notated, but it changes very quickly and in a short period of time, and much of it is highly ephemeral. Malaysian popular music is commercial, it is disseminated through the mass media and in live performances in pubs, restaurants, clubs and open-air venues. It usually has a very large audience of people from all levels of society.

In effect, the syncretic music that spread to many parts of the country through the bangsawan theatre and the joget dance halls in the early decades of the 20th century was the first 'popular' music in Malaysia. Many foreign musical features combined with local elements in this type of music, and it was disseminated through the mass media including recordings, radio, books and printed music. In addition, this music has always been very flexible in terms of change and the assimilation of elements such as musical instruments, melody, texture, scale, themes, lyrics, and performance practice, all of which originated from many different sources. In these two categories musical elements are often borrowed from external, that is, non-local, sources. The music is usually found in an urban setting where the accessibility to many foreign elements is quite easy. Malaysian art and popular music are further discussed in the final chapters of this work.

Common characteristics of the classical and folk arts

Today, both the palace or classical arts and the folk arts in Malaysia are known as the 'traditional arts'. Even though the classical and folk arts developed in different strata of society and their historical development varies, they share some of the same characteristics that are often adapted in syncretic, popular and contemporary art music:

First, the different genres of classical and folk performing arts are found in specific regions of the country. They developed in particular regions and sometimes are not widespread throughout the country. Namely, the *wayang kulit Kelantan* [Kelantanese shadow play], *makyung* [Malay dance drama], *menora* [southern Thai dance drama] and *tarinai* [dance] are performed in the north states of the Peninsula, while the *tumbuk kalang* [mortar and pestle percussion instrument] and *caklempong* [gong-chime ensemble] are limited to the southern state of Negeri Sembilan. The hanging gong ensembles are found only in Sabah and Sarawak.

Another similarity is that the performances of theatre, music and dance take place not only for the entertainment of people but also for ritual purposes, especially in the past. Formerly, the folk arts had strong ties to religious ceremonies. For example, the *wayang kulit*, *sumazau* dance and *magarang* music were performed to give thanks to the rice spirit after the harvest season, while the *makyung*, *main puteri* [healing ritual] and aborigine ritual songs accompanied by stamping bamboo tubes were often performed to heal the sick. The performances of theatre also took place as a sign of thanks and propitiation to otherworldly powers, which could bring destruction to the crops and danger to mankind. Because of this belief, the special ceremonies to 'open the stage' [*buka panggung*] take place before the beginning of each performance. Nevertheless, it must be acknowledged that today many of the traditional arts such as wayang kulit, tumbuk kalang and the hanging gong ensembles are performed only for entertainment and no longer have a ritual function.

In addition, the performances of both the folk and classical arts have a social function. Members of the audience mingle informally during the performances of wayang kulit, makyung, *mek mulung* [a regional Malay dance drama] and other presentations. They sit or stand around the stage that is, in effect, a 'theatre-in-the-round', and they talk and eat while they watch the performance. In Sarawak, performances usually occur in a social meeting place, on the veranda [*ruai*], of the longhouse. The village folk socialize as they listen to the music of the *antan* and *lesung* [mortar and pestle], gongs or bamboo instruments. The performance develops concord and harmony among the members of the society.

The stories used in the folk arts are handed down from one generation to another in an oral tradition. The stories of the shadow puppet theatre are based on the Indian epics, the *Ramayana* and the *Mahabharata,* as well as local legends, while the makyung and mekmulung stories are Malay folk tales. Romantic love, comedy, war, fantasies and the triumph of good over evil are important elements in a given story. Dialogue, declamation, movement, singing and instrumental music are combined in each performance. Among some groups in Sarawak, such as the Kajang, Kayan and Kenyah peoples, cultural heritage is associated with the cultivation of rice and is handed down in an oral tradition from parent to child, especially from mother to daughter.

Just as in oral tradition in other countries, formulae, mnemonics or schemata that are known by the actors and the audience are used in dialogue and in stories of folk theatre.[8] Certain stock characters (such as 'refined' and 'coarse' types) and specific episodes (such as a garden or palace scene) are also formulaic tools used in classical and folk theatre. The formulae are very important in dialogue because scripts or texts are not written down. They help the actor to organize ideas and materials for spontaneous composition on the stage. The actors improvise plot, dialogue and character movement by using the formulae.

Like the building of a dialogue, character, or story using formulaic structures, certain formulae are also used in the musical repertory, the rhythm of the music and the lyrics of the songs. A specific piece is played to accompany the walking movement of a character, to pick flowers and to exhibit a given situation such as battle, happiness or sadness in folk theatre. Each piece is associated with a unique rhythmic pattern or formula. In order to learn and create the rhythmic pattern of a given piece, mnemonic syllables that represent the drum timbres such as 'cak', 'dong', 'duh' and 'ting' are vocalized. Formulae are also used in the lyrics and melody of a *pantun* [poetic verses] and in the long narratives that are sung in Sabah and Sarawak.

Four types of musical forms are usually found in classical and folk pieces:

1.   The first musical form is based on a cyclical time unit that is called a gong unit [*gongan*]. The gong unit is a special type of colotomic unit that consists of a cyclical temporal/rhythmic pattern, which is repeated and marked by the lowest-pitched gong of an ensemble, usually the *tetawak ibu* [lowest gong tone]. This gong unit is divided binarily (based on multiples of two), and is based on a 2-beat stress unit with the strongest stress on beat 2. Each gong unit is tied to the next gong unit at the sound of the lowest gong tone or tetawak ibu. This type of gong unit and musical form is usually found in the music of the shadow puppet play, the makyung and the gamelan.

2.   The second type of musical form is also a colotomic unit that is repeated and marked by a gong. However, this colotomic unit is not subdivided binarily and in some pieces the gong tones provide punctuation at the ends of the rhythmic patterns regardless of their length. It is found in several pieces of music in the tarinai and mekmulung repertories.

3.   The third type of musical form is strophic, which is found in vocal music such as songs accompanied by the tumbuk kalang mortar and pestle, in *dikir barat* pieces, the asli, inang and *branyo* song repertories, and in the singing of *zikir* and *kompang* pieces.

4.   The fourth kind of form is iterative, that is, a specific melodic motif is repeated with variation such as that seen in much of the solo instrumental music of Sabah and Sarawak and in the music of the aborigines (*orang asli*) of the Peninsula.

In terms of musical instruments, although variation is found from one ensemble to another, many of the same musical instruments appear in the folk and classical ensembles. These include knobbed gongs of various types and sizes that are hung or placed horizontally in a wooden rack (*tetawak*, *tawag*, *gong agung*, and so on); single-headed, goblet-shaped drums (*gedumbak*), double-headed, elongated barrel drums (*gendang*), single-headed narrow-frame drums (*rebana* and *kompang*), 3-stringed instrument (*rebab*), quadruple-reed instrument (*serunai*), and concussion and stamped bamboo and wood instruments (*kecerek*, *kesut*, *goh*, *togunggu* and others).

A musical texture that is polyphonic and overlapping is found in folk and classical music. A piece usually consists of several unique strata of sound: a melodic layer that is sung and played heterophonically with a melody instrument; a rhythmic layer with a specific pattern played in an interlocking style by drums; and the gong unit or colotomic layer which is played by bronze instruments.

Furthermore, in Sabah and Sarawak, rudimentary harmony is also used. Examples are the music of the *sompoton* and *keluri* mouth organs and the *sape* plucked lute, all of which produce a drone with the melodic line. Additionally, the singing of narratives among the Kajang people of Sarawak use a counter melody which is sung simultaneously with the main melody as in the *wa* narrative.

Many folk and classical pieces use scales with five, six or seven pitches with a focus on five of the pitches. These five pitches form pentatonic scales that are used in much of the traditional music in Peninsular Malaysia. Most of these scales have intervals that are wider than half or whole steps.

Similarities can also be seen in terms of rhythm. All folk and classical music use mainly duple meter. As in the music of the *gendang silat* [music for martial arts], kompang, wayang kulit and makyung, the drums are played in an interlocking style to produce resultant rhythmic patterns. It must be remembered, too, that in Sabah and Sarawak gongs and bamboo tubes are also played in an interlocking style.

In addition, several genres of music such as wayang kulit, makyung, gamelan, gendang silat and tumbuk kalang use rhythmic patterns that carry great stress or accent at the end of the patterns or phrases. These kinds of rhythmic patterns may be described as 'end-accented'. In contrast, other genres like the music of the gong ensembles, the kulintangan and engkerumong ensembles, stamped bamboo ensembles, vocal music and several other types of instrumental music in Sabah and Sarawak, use rhythmic patterns in which the most stress occurs on the first beat of the pattern.

Finally, foreign elements, such as those from other regions of Southeast Asia, the Middle East and India have influenced the development of the Malaysian folk and classical arts in terms of stories used as well as musical style. An example is the use of the Indian epic, the *Ramayana*, in the stories of the Kelantanese wayang kulit. In addition, we find the use of highly ornamented melodies and heterophonic style between a solo singer and the rebab, showing the connection between the music of the makyung and certain styles of Islamic music from the traditions of the Middle East.

The musical elements in Malaysian classical and folk music from sources in Southeast Asia are no less important. For example, we find the use of the gong unit as the basis of musical form, the performance on drums in an interlocking style and the beating of bronze gongs in many forms of folk and classical music. We see then, from ancient times, that the classical and folk arts have been open to outside influences. Over the centuries foreign features have combined with local elements to produce a style which is unique and has become the traditional arts of Malaysia

The state and culture

The year 1969 not only marked significant changes in Malaysian political economy, but it signaled radical transformations in culture as well. The State began to centralize cultural activities and played an important role in the direction of development of the traditional arts. The government prioritized the creation of a national and common culture for the purpose of national unity. A national culture policy was based on the promotion of cultures indigenous to the region, the incorporation of elements from other cultures that were deemed suitable, and Islam as an important element. A network of State and District level offices of the Ministry of Culture, Youth and Sports was created to promote the traditional arts and research in indigenous culture.   Radio and television programs were to foster national unity, and workshops about the nationalized Malay forms were held for school children.[9] Selected Malay folk arts were streamlined, promoted as the traditional arts[10] and were performed at local state functions and at shows for tourists.

With the launching of Vision 2020 in 1991, performances with representative dances from all the states have been organized by the Ministry of Arts, Culture and Tourism to promote the country's cultures and traditions to local and foreign tourists. These shows are also extravagant spectacles of ethnic diversity and unity to stage the new 'global Malaysia' to the world – a Malaysia which is technically advanced, yet rooted in its own cultural identity where all the various ethnic groups live in harmony.[11]   Theatricalized performances of heritage are also produced in the new state-of-the-art national theatre, *Istana Budaya* [Palace of Culture], conveying messages of modern statehood, technological development and national identity.

Paradoxically, as traditional music and theatre are transformed into spectacles to captivate urban and foreign audiences, there has been a decline of traditional theatre and music troupes in the rural areas where they originated. Whereas in 1970 there were a hundred-odd *wayang Kelantan* (Kelantanese shadow play) troupes, today there are only a handful left. It has been suggested that one of the reasons for this decline is criticism from purists and orthodox Muslims. To the Islamic purists, traditional Malay theatre forms are *haram* [forbidden] because they are performed for spiritual occasions including healing. They contend that spirits are invoked during performances and idolatry is promoted on stage by humans and puppets (see further, wayang kulit Kelantan and makyung in Chapter 1).

More importantly, rural performers cannot compete with national spectacles funded by the State. They also cannot make a living from traditional performances as the younger generation are captivated with pop music promoted by transnational companies, which have vast resources to launch massive marketing campaigns involving satellite television, compact discs, digital video discs and other means of merchandising

Notes

1   All population figures are based on 1997 estimates, *Malaysia 2000, Official Yearbook*, Department of Information, Kuala Lumpur.
2   The MUDA and KEMUBU irrigation schemes are run by the MUDA Agricultural Development Authority (MADA) in Kedah on the west coast and the KEMUBU Agricultural Development Authority (KADA) in Kelantan on the east coast of Peninsular Malaysia.
3   The large programs of this type were carried out by FELDA (Federal Land Development Authority). See further Andaya, Barbara Watson and Andaya, Leonard A., *A History of Malaysia* (London: Macmillan Education Ltd., 1982), pp. 283ff.
4   See Kahn, J. and Loh, F. (eds), *Fragmented Vision, Culture and Politics in Contemporary Malaysia* (Sydney: Allen and Unwin, 1992) for a critical analysis of social, cultural and political developments in contemporary Malaysia.
5   The Malaysian government's New Economic Policy (NEP), begun in 1970, was designed initially as a 25-year policy to ensure economic growth and eliminate poverty (aimed mainly at the poor rural Malays), and also to restructure society so that the distinction of race with economic function would also be abolished. See further, Andaya, A *History of Malaysia*, pp. 282ff. In 1991, the NEP was replaced by the New Development Policy (NDP), which focuses on the development of a *bumiputera* commercial industrial community and the private sector as an important player in the restructuring of the economy.

6   In a classical tradition a writing or notation system is taught in schools, in religious places of worship (a mosque or temple), and in other centers of government such as the palace of a king. Usually found in an urban or suburban setting, communication is carried on both verbally and in writing and the latest in technological advances are known and used among the members of the society. Theories and histories are known and documented in the society. This tradition normally exhibits refinement and professionalism in the arts and other fields, and the importance of social, political and economic institutions is stressed. This type of culture and society may experience fast or even sudden changes, and the importance of the creative ability of the individual in the society is highly valued.   See further, Robert Redfield, *Peasant Society and Culture* (Chicago & London: University of Chicago Press, 1959), pp. 69-104; and 'The Folk Society' in *Human Nature and The Study of Society*, Margaret Park Redfield, ed. (Chicago & London: University of Chicago Press, 1962), pp. 231-253.

7   Folk music is handed down by word of mouth in an oral tradition in the small towns, villages and rural areas. Existing in a rural environment, communication is carried on mainly orally even though a system of writing may be known among the members of the society. Thus, history is usually not written down but is recorded orally, and an awareness of theory is less clear because of the dominance of the oral tradition.   The personal relationships and behavior patterns of members in the folk culture are maintained and controlled by laws or sanctions agreed upon by those members.   In addition, this kind of society undergoes changes very slowly over a long period of time.   Cooperation, work and interaction done in a communal way is another characteristic which is special in the folk culture and often in folk music.

8   A. B. Lord, *The Singer of Tales* (New York: Atheneum, 1976), Walter J. Ong, *Orality and Literacy: The Technologizing of the Word* (London: Methuen, 1982), and Amin Sweeney, *Authors and Audiences in Traditional Malay Literature* (Berkeley: Center for Southeast Asian Studies, University of California, 1980).

9   See Tan, Sooi Beng, 'The Performing Arts in Malaysia: State and Society' for a discussion of the laws and restrictions on cultural activities, censorship rules created after 1969 and the responses of different ethnic groups in Malaysia, *Asian Music* 21(1), 1990, pp. 137-171.

10   See Tan, Sooi Beng, *Bangsawan, A Social and Stylistic History of Malay Opera*, Singapore: Oxford University Press, 1993 for an analysis of how the bangsawan, a popular commercial theatre (which combined Malay, Western, Indian, Chinese, Javanese and Middle Eastern elements) was gradually Malayized in the 1970s and 1980s.

11   Since the 1990s and Vision 2020, a movement toward the creation of a *Bangsa Malaysia* [Malaysian race] has rested on the cultural identities of all ethnic communities.   An account of the transformation of the *boria* theatre of Penang into a cultural spectacle and an icon of modernity was presented by Tan Sooi Beng in a paper presented at the World Conference of the International Council for Traditional Music, Rio de Janeiro, July 5-11, 2001.   See Also M. Sarkissian, *Albuquerque's Children: Performing Tradition in Malaysia's Portuguese Settlement* (Chicago and London: The University of Chicago Press, 2000), pp. 159-160,   for a comparison between government-sponsored troupes and local troupes performing at the Portuguese settlement in Melaka.

Chapter 1

Music of the Major Theatrical Forms

The different styles of the various forms of traditional theatre in Malaysia reflect the regional characteristics of dramatic productions found throughout the country. This chapter offers an overview of the setting and background of the major theatrical forms such as the *wayang kulit* shadow puppet play, the *makyung* and *mekmulung* dance dramas, the *bangsawan* Malay opera, the *randai* dramatic presentation and the Chinese opera. However, the discussion here focuses mainly on the music that accompanies each of these genres.

In Malaysia, the music for nearly all the major theatrical forms is played by percussion-dominated ensembles. An orchestra or ensemble using a predominance of percussion instruments is important throughout Southeast Asia, and in Malaysia this type of ensemble usually features gongs and drums with only one melody-producing instrument. For example, the ensembles for the Kelantan shadow puppet play, the mekmulung dance drama, the *tarinai* dance music, and the *gendang silat* music for martial arts use a number of drums and gongs, while only a single *serunai* provides the melody. Likewise, the orchestras for the makyung dance drama and the *main puteri* healing ritual consist of specific drums and gongs and only one 3-stringed *rebab* which carries the melody. The *randai* orchestra consists of gong-chimes and drums with the *pupuik* reed pipe, while the Chinese opera orchestra also features various drums, gongs, wood blocks and stringed instruments.

All the orchestras and ensembles for the major theatrical forms are essentially chamber ensembles. These small Malaysian ensembles contrast greatly with the large orchestras found in Southeast Asia such as the Javanese *gamelan* from Indonesia or the *pi phat* and *mahori* bands from Thailand. Although the Malaysian ensembles are small, they still feature struck percussion, both idiophones and membranophones, and usually one wind or stringed instrument, which provides the melody in the music.

The bangsawan orchestra, which has existed only since the late 19th and early 20th centuries, is a mixture of traditional and modern orchestras because it developed using traditional instruments such as the *gendang*, *rebana* and gong along with musical instruments originating from the Western, Arab and Indian worlds. The bangsawan orchestra preceded the modern Malaysian orchestra, notably the RTM Orchestra (*Orkes Radio Televisyen Malaysia* [orchestra of the Radio and Television of Malaysia]) and the orchestras which play the *lagu asli* social dance repertory today.

Shadow puppet theatre

The shadow puppet play (*wayang kulit*) is an ancient form of traditional theatre in Malaysia. The stories are told by a puppet master (*dalang*) who manipulates the puppets (called *wayang*) which are seen in shadows projected on a screen. In this very old form of theatre a small ensemble plays the music to accompany the movement of the puppets and the events in the stories. In Malaysia there are four types of shadow puppet play, each with a specific name and distinctive style. These are the *wayang kulit Jawa* (also called the *wayang kulit purwa*; the Javanese shadow puppet play), the *wayang kulit gedek* (or simply *wayang gedek*; a mixture of Thai and Malay folk styles of shadow puppet play), the *wayang kulit Melayu* (also called *wayang Jawa*; the Malay court form of shadow puppet play) and the *wayang kulit Kelantan* (also called the *wayang kulit Siam*; the Kelantanese folk shadow puppet play).

Wayang kulit Jawa

The *wayang kulit Jawa*, also known as the *wayang kulit purwa* [ancient shadow puppet play], originated in Indonesia and is performed today by the descendants of Javanese immigrants who settled in the southern state of Johore (and formerly in the state of Selangor) many decades ago. In Malaysia this form of shadow play still maintains the basic features of the wayang kulit purwa of Indonesia, including the use of the stories and characters from the *Mahabharata* epic and the musical accompaniment of the Javanese *gamelan*. The gamelan in this shadow play includes singers as well as xylophones, metallophones, and knobbed gongs just as in Indonesia.[1]

Wayang kulit gedek

The *wayang kulit gedek*, performed in the northern peninsular states of Perlis, Kedah and Kelantan, is called *nang talung* in Thailand. This type of shadow puppet play originated in southern Thailand and features small-sized, flat leather puppets. In Malaysia the wayang gedek is performed by Thai and Malay peoples using a mixture of the Thai and Malay languages or just the southern Thai dialect, depending upon the audience. The stories feature local tales and episodes from the *Ramayana* epic (called the *Ramakien* in Thailand). The style of performance, music and puppet design show a distinct mixture of southern Thai and Malay traits including the small orchestra of drums, knobbed gongs, cymbals and bowed stringed instruments. In former times the wind instrument called *pi* or *pi Jawa* (a quadruple reed shawm) was included in this ensemble, and it is still often featured in the wayang gedek orchestra in Malaysia. However, today in southern Thailand the bowed lutes called *saw oo* and *saw duang* (originating from the *huqin* family of Chinese bowed lutes) are preferred in place of the pi.

The drums in this ensemble include the *klong that*, *thon* and *klong khaek*, similar to the Malay *geduk*, *gedumbak* and *gendang*, respectively (see Wayang kulit Kelantan, below). A small pair of finger cymbals (called *ching*) and the gong-chime called *mong* (two knobbed gongs placed horizontally in a wooden box) are also used.

Wayang kulit Melayu

The *wayang kulit Melayu*, also called *wayang Jawa*, is strongly influenced by the wayang kulit purwa of Indonesia. In the 19th and 20th centuries this type of shadow play developed under the patronage of the sultan and existed as entertainment mainly for the aristocrats connected to the palaces of Kelantan and Kedah. In earlier times it was also performed in the Malay Sultanate of Patani. Today this Sultanate no longer exists, but the location of the former kingdom is in present-day southern Thailand.

The stories of the wayang kulit Melayu focus on episodes of the *Mahabharata* epic, and the form and design of the puppets are nearly identical to the style of puppets from Java in Indonesia (Plate 1.1). During World War II this type of shadow puppet theatre was not performed; but after the war years it was revived as entertainment for villagers without the patronage of the sultans. By the 1980s experienced puppet masters were difficult to find and the wayang kulit Melayu, today, is rarely performed.

The orchestra consists of several bronze gongs including a pair of large, hanging gongs called *tetawak*, a single knobbed horizontal gong called the *mong*, and a set of six or more small horizontal gongs called the *canang*. In addition, a pair of *kesi* cymbals, a pair of elongated barrel, double-headed drums called *gendang* and one 2-stringed *rebab* are used.

The rebab exhibits a mixture of Malay and Javanese features using only two strings as in the Javanese form, but with the body construction of the Malay rebab. A specific musical repertory existed for this type of shadow play, but today only a few pieces are still known.

Wayang kulit Kelantan

The wayang kulit Kelantan is a form of folk theatre that is also referred to as the *Wayang kulit Siam*. It is the most popular and widespread form of shadow puppet play and is traditionally found in the states of Kelantan, Trengganu, Kedah, and formerly in Perak and Pahang. This type is also performed by Malays in several provinces of southeastern Thailand. Today the main purpose of a performance is entertainment. But in past times performances occurred for ritual purposes, such as for the fulfillment of a vow, the initiation of a student puppeteer or for paying respect to one's teacher.

In the past, the state of Kelantan was considered to be the stronghold of Malay performing arts where shadow play, dance drama and other performing arts genres originated and flourished. However, during the past many years with the fundamentalist Islamic-based political party, Parti Islam Malaysia (PAS), dominating the state government of Kelantan, the usual village performances of wayang kulit and other traditional arts have been banned in the state (Cf., makyung). Interestingly, this situation has led to the flourishing of shadow play and other traditional arts in the urban centers of the country outside of the state of Kelantan. The traditional arts are taught, for example, in the universities and in the National Arts Academy in Kuala Lumpur as well as in the public schools especially in the urban and suburban areas. Such is the case with the wayang kulit Kelantan.

The trunk or main story of the Kelantanese shadow play is based on the *Ramayana* epic. The Malay version of this epic is known as 'The Story of the King Rawana' (*Cerita Maharaja Rawana*). The main characters include the prince Rama, his brother Laksamana, his wife Siti Dewi, the king of the demons Rawana, Hanuman the White Monkey, Rama's main warriors as well as ogres, country bumpkins, animals and so on. The two major clown characters, known as Pak Dogol and Wak Long, function as the clown-servants to Rama. These two characters have their origins in Malay culture from Kelantan and do not appear in the Ramayana. In other Malaysian states and in southern Thailand these two clown characters are known by other names, but their physical resemblance is strikingly similar from one region to another. The most prominent and popular shadow play stories today include Malay folk tales, the Panji stories and new local stories created by the puppet masters.

The newly created tales are often based on topics of timely interest and sometimes incorporate political, economic and social issues and events in the country or in the city or town where the performance is taking place. When local and national elections take place the puppeteers have been known to campaign for the candidate or party of their choice with performances incorporating events relative to the election at hand. The puppeteers need to be clever and witty, telling interesting stories to hold the attention of their audiences, and although the stories may be new, the new characters are usually still played using the traditional puppets and musical pieces. The same pattern of dialogue or monologue followed by puppet movement accompanied by music still holds true in the performance of new stories. Over the past three decades some puppeteers have experimented with new puppet characters, creating cowboys, contemporary local heroes and heroines and new villains. The recently deceased, well-known puppeteer, Hamzah Awang Amat, even created a whole new set of puppets to be used in performing tales from Islamic literature. His stories and puppets were used for a time in performances on university campuses, but never became widely used outside of the academic context.

Performance practice

The wayang kulit Kelantan is performed on a stage comprising a small hut-like building raised about one meter above ground level, with a white screen making up one of the walls of the hut and an electric lamp hanging near mid-screen inside the hut. The *dalang* [puppeteer] operates the puppets between the lamp and the screen (see Plate 1.2), while the musicians sit behind the puppeteer to provide musical accompaniment upon cue from him.

Several nights are required to perform one entire tale. According to customary practice, a special ceremony called the *Buka panggung* [opening the stage] is required on the first night of a performance. This ceremony is performed by the dalang who offers prepared foods, a *kenduri* [feast], to other worldly beings.[2] All the musical instruments and puppets are bathed in the smoke of burning incense by the puppet master who, at the same time, prays for a beautiful voice, pleasing sounds from the instruments, and the inspiration to tell a clever and enjoyable story for the evening.

After the opening ceremony, the orchestra plays both old and new pieces to fill in the time until the dalang arrives at the stage. At the appropriate time the deputy puppet master, known as the *dalang muda* [young or deputy puppeteer], takes his seat before the screen to begin the prologue to the shadow play that is called the *Dalang Muda*. This prologue contains nine different musical pieces and dramatic episodes which are still used to teach new musicians and would-be puppeteers the techniques of playing the musical instruments, singing, dialogue, narration, and the performance of several basic pieces in the shadow play repertory.

The first part of the Dalang Muda prologue consists of four pieces that are performed to ensure a successful performance as well as a safe and undisturbed performance venue. The usual pieces used are i) *Maharisi* [piece for the character of that name], ii) *Dewah Panah Turun* [the descent of the godlings with bows and arrows], iii) *Dewa Panah Perang* [the battle of the godlings with bows and arrows], and iv) *Dewa Panah Berjalan* [walking by the godlings with bows & arrows] (also called *Hulubalang* [the piece for warriors]). The second part of the prologue introduces several main characters from the root epic. This part consists of five episodes and pieces which are entitled v) *Seri Rama Keluar* [Prince Rama emerges] (played with the gedumbak drum), vi) *Hulubalang Seri Rama* [Prince Rama's warriors], vii) *Menyembah* [paying homage], viii) *Berkhabar* [giving news], and ix) *Seri Rama Masuk Istana* [Prince Rama enters the palace].

At the end of the prologue the deputy puppeteer is replaced by the main puppet master who performs the story for the evening lasting some three to four hours. During the story, the puppeteer uses instrumental music (drawing on a repertory of some 35 pieces) to accompany the manipulation and movement of the puppets, and vocal pieces to convey mood, information and so on.

The musical instruments

The orchestra for the Kelantan shadow puppet play is a small ensemble consisting of 10 instruments, which are usually played by 8 to 10 musicians. During a performance the musicians sit on the floor of the stage behind the puppeteer, and although various seating arrangements are possible among the musicians, the two gedumbak drummers and the shawm player usually sit directly behind the puppeteer.

Idiophones The idiophones called *tetawak*, *canang* and *kesi* appear in pairs (each pair featuring two different pitches or timbres).

The tetawak is a bronze knobbed gong with thick walls, a deep rim, and a diameter of about 40 to 70 centimeters. A pair of tetawak is hung from a wooden rack or from the roof beams of the hut-like stage for the shadow play (Figure 1.1). When hit on the knob with a padded beater, the largest gong provides the lowest pitch (called the *'tawak ibu'* [mother tawak]), and the smaller gong has a slightly higher pitch (called the *'tawak anak'* [child tawak]). The tuning of these gongs is not standard from one set to another, but the interval between the pitches is usually about a major third or sometimes as large as a perfect fifth. The standardization of these two pitches, as well as the pitches on the *canang* gong-chime (see below), is not of primary importance in the music.

The canang consists of two small knobbed gongs, 15-20 cm in diameter, placed horizontally in a wooden rack or box (Figure 1.2). These gongs are light in weight with a narrow rim and, today, usually made of iron or other metal. The two gongs are hit with a pair of padded wooden sticks producing two different pitches: one high and the other low, called *'canang anak'* and *'canang ibu'*, respectively. The tuning of these two gongs is also not standard from one set to another, and the interval between the two pitches may range from a major second to a sixth.

The kesi are cymbals made of bronze or iron, with a diameter of about 10 centimeters (Figure 1.3). Each cymbal has a cup-like protruding center section with a small hole in the middle that enables two cymbals to be connected with a thick string running through the hole. The second pair of cymbals is nailed to a wooden board. The player strikes one pair of cymbals onto those attached to the wooden board, obtaining two different timbres: a ringing, resonant sound and a damped, muffled sound. In most pieces these two timbres are played in unison with the canang, the ringing timbre played with the canang anak (high pitch) and the damped timbre with the canang ibu (low pitch). Similar small hand or finger cymbals are found in various sizes throughout Asia, including neighboring southern Thailand where these small cymbals are known as *'ching'* and are found in the *menora* (southern Thai dance drama) and *nang talung* (large puppet theatre) ensembles.

Membranophones The three kinds of drums used in the Kelantan shadow play ensemble are called the *gedumbak, gendang* and *geduk*. These drums appear in pairs, in large and small sizes called *'ibu'* ([mother], large size) and *'anak'* ([child], small size), or alternately *'bapak'* ([father], large size) or *'adik'* ([younger brother], small size). All of these drums are made from the wood of the jackfruit tree.

The body of the gedumbak is carved in the shape of a goblet with a long, hollow foot (Figure 1.4). A single head of dried goatskin is attached to the goblet-shaped body with rattan laces, while small wood wedges (inserted between the laces and the body) are used to tighten the laces and tune the drum. It is held horizontally on the player's lap and one hand strikes the drum head while the other hand closes and opens the end of the foot to obtain specific timbres of sound. The basic timbres are used to create specific rhythmic patterns for the various tunes in the repertory.

A mnemonic system includes at least four different timbres, which are vocalized by the gedumbak player as 'dong', 'duh', 'cap', and 'ting'. The timbre 'dong', for example, is played when the drum head is struck in the center with one hand while the foot or base end of the drum is left open (a variant of this timbre, 'duh', occurs using the same playing technique but the hand remains on the drum head after impact). If the foot is closed with one hand and the drumhead is struck in the middle, then the timbre 'cap' is produced. The timbre 'ting' is produced with the fingers of the player's hand striking the edge of the head while the foot is closed. This instrument may be considered a pillar drum in the ensemble, for it is used to play the basic rhythmic patterns for more than half the tunes in the repertory. Drums of similar construction are found in other parts of Southeast Asia and the Middle East, including the *thon* goblet drum of Thailand and the *tombak*, *darbuka* or *darabukka* of the Middle East.

The gendang is double-headed with an elongated, barrel-shaped body (Figure 1.5). Like the gedumbak, this drum also appears in two sizes called 'anak' and 'ibu'. The drumheads are made from goatskin, or the larger head may be made from cowhide. These skins are attached to the body with rattan laces or, today, with thick nylon rope, which is tightened to tune the drumheads so that they will produce certain timbres when hit with the player's hand or fingers. In shadow play music the drum is held horizontally and the drum heads are struck with the player's hands, while in other genres of traditional Malay music the drum heads may be struck with a wooden stick or a light rattan beater. The drum timbres and mnemonic syllables for the small gendang are 'cak' and 'ting', while the large gendang produces the sounds 'pak' and 'duh'.

The geduk is a short, double-headed barrel-shaped drum (Figure 1.6). The two drumheads are made of cowhide which are attached to the body with glue and wood pegs. Two long, bamboo sticks are attached to one side of the body and extend beyond the body to form feet on which the drum rests. These feet allow the instrument to be propped upright with one drumhead facing the player. Using a pair of wood sticks to hit the drumhead, the geduk player uses different drumming techniques, depending upon the kind of rhythmic pattern to be played. For example, to play drum rolls the arm is bent naturally at the elbow and the player uses a supple wrist and hand motion to hit the head with the sticks (see further

Matusky, 1993 and 1997). There is no mnemonic system used in learning to play this drum. The geduk always accompanies the movements of battle and other violent or strong action in the drama. The rhythmic patterns that reflect these kinds of puppet movements are the loud drum rolls and triplet figures, which alternate with loud drum strokes on the off-beat. Sometimes hemiola is also found in these rhythmic patterns.

Aerophone   The quadruple-reed shawm in the Kelantan shadow play ensemble is called the *serunai* (Figure 1.7). Like the drums and gongs, this instrument also appears as a pair in two different sizes (referred to as 'ibu' and 'anak') ranging from 40 to 50 centimeters long. Although the size is not standard from one set to another, usually the serunai ibu is about 10 centimeters longer than the small-sized instrument. The Malaysian serunai features a reed made of four thin layers of dried palm leaf usually from the *lontar* [palmyra] tree.[3]

When the instrument is blown the entire reed is inserted into the player's mouth while the lips rest against a lip-disk (Plate 1.3). In this way, the reeds are not controlled by the player's lips and are free beating reeds. The serunai player uses a continuous or circular breathing technique so that when the air in his lungs is nearly depleted, he continues to blow air through the reeds (using air in his puffed cheeks) and at the same time

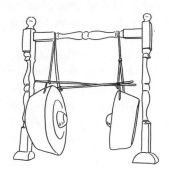

Figure 1.1 *Tetawak*

Figure 1.2 *Canang*

Figure 1.3 *Kesi*

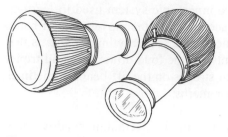

Figure 1.4 *Gedumbak*

Figure 1.5 *Gendang*

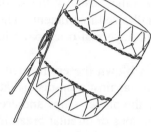

Figure 1.6 *Geduk*

Figure 1.7 *Serunai ibu/anak*

refills the lungs with air inhaled through his nose. Using this playing technique, the melody played on the serunai usually never stops until a piece comes to an end.

This type of folk shawm is found in several forms in the Middle East, northern India and Southeast Asia. It is called *surnay* or *surnaya* in Iran, *zurna* in Turkey while in Thailand it is known as the *pi chawa*. In Southeast Asia this instrument is often times the only melody instrument in the percussion-dominated ensembles that accompany theatrical performances.

Kelantan shadow play music

The repertory of the Kelantan shadow puppet theatre consists of about 35 pieces, including overture music, pieces to set the mood of a scene and other pieces to accompany puppet movement of various kinds.

The pieces may be grouped into several different categories. There is music for the appearance of specific characters (examples are the tunes entitled *Seri Rama*, *Pak Dogol* and *Maharisi*), pieces for giving news (the sung pieces entitled *Berkhabar* or *Khabar Dan Dayang*), pieces which reflect daily activities such as bathing, sleeping, letter reading and so on, pieces for battle (for example the piece called *Berperang*), and pieces to specify mood or special intention. Usually the pieces to depict a particular mood or intention are sung by the puppet master with instrumental accompaniment by the orchestra.

Texture and Form   The polyphonic texture of the pieces in the repertory is made up of at least three important layers of musical sound. These are the melodic lines played by the serunai or sung by the puppeteer, the drum rhythmic patterns, and the gong unit that is played by the bronze instruments.

The form or structure in each piece of shadow play music is determined and defined by the colotomic unit or gong unit in the music (Matusky, 1993 and 1997, pp. 40ff). The gong unit is a time unit marked at its end by the lowest gong tone in the orchestra. In the shadow play ensemble the lowest-pitched gong is the tetawak ibu, which is struck on the last beat of each gong unit. In very old traditional music (such as the wayang kulit, the makyung dance theatre and the tarinai dance music), in which the gong unit serves as the basis of musical form, the total number of beats in the given colotomic unit is based on multiples of two beats. Hence, the basic gong units in the repertories of these ancient music genres may consist of 4- , 8- , 16- , 32- , 64-beats and so on (there are no 2-beat gong units).

Several features are important in defining this type of colotomic unit. First, all gong units are cyclical and are repeated throughout the given pieces in the repertory. These gong units are chained together, so that the tetawak ibu marks the end of one specific gong unit and, at the same time, also marks the beginning of the next gong unit that immediately follows it (see Example 1.1).

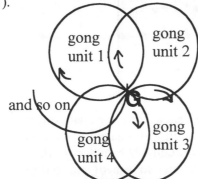

Example 1.1 Concatenated gong units. (G = point of concatenation)

Furthermore, the structure or form in a gong unit is defined by certain gong tones that are played on specific beats in the gong unit. The internal gong tones are played on certain beats as a result of the subdivision of gong unit that occurs in a binary way. The gong unit is first divided in half (in a 16-beat gong unit, for example, gong tones occur on beats 8 and 16), then into quarter segments (the 16-beat unit is further subdivided with higher gong tones on beats 4 and 12), then eighths (with even higher gong tones on beats 2, 6, 10 and 14) , and so on.

Another important feature in the gong unit is a 2-beat stress pattern, with a weak stress on the first beat followed by a strong stress on the second beat. In all gong units these two beats of weak and strong stress are repeated so that the appropriate number of beats are obtained for each different gong unit (that is, a gong unit of 4, 8, 16 or 32 beats, and so on). In wayang kulit music this short 2-beat stress pattern is played on the canang gong-chime, and sometimes it is vocalized using the syllables 'ding-Dong'. The first beat 'ding' is a weak stress and is played by the canang anak (high pitch), while the second beat 'Dong' is a strong stress played by the canang ibu (low pitch) (see Example 1.2 below). Usually the kesi cymbals are also played simultaneously with the canang, marking the weak beat with a ringing timbre and the strong beat with a damped timbre.

a) 8-beat gong unit (the musical form for the pieces *Berjalan* [walking by refined characters], *Pak Dogol* [the piece for the character by that name], *Berperang* [battle music] and so on.

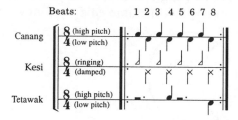

b) 16-beat gong unit (the musical form for many different pieces, including *Bertukar Dalang* [changing the dalang], *Binatang Berjalan* [animals walking], *Orang Darat* [country bumpkins], *Memburu* [hunting], *Sang Kaki* [piece for the character so named] and so forth.

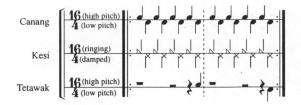

Cyclical representation of the gong units

a) 8-beat gong unit   b) 16-beat gong unit

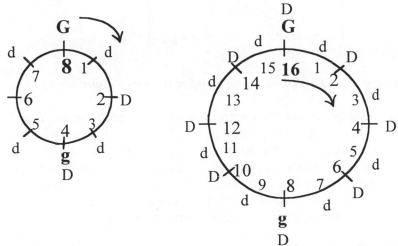

Example 1.2   The basic 8-beat and 16-beat gong units in shadow play music.

In this musical system the basic 8-beat gong unit has undergone a process of expansion so that each beat in the 8-beat unit has doubled to result in a 16-beat gong unit having the same form as the original colotomic unit. The canang and kesi still mark the weak and strong beats in the 16-beat gong unit, while the high tetawak gong tone is played on beat 8 and the low tetawak is played on the beat 16, the last beat, of the gong unit. The above examples show the 8-beat gong unit (Example 1.2a) and the 16-beat gong unit (Example 1.2b) with the specific instruments played on each beat.

A gong unit used for the ending cadence in a piece is 8-beats long, but has high gong tones on beats 4 and 6, thus differentiating it from the 8-beat colotomic unit noted earlier.

A final example of a gong unit is 32-beats long (see Example 1.3).

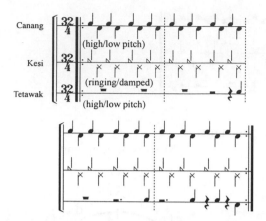

Example 1.3 The 32-beat gong unit for the piece *Hulubalang*.

In this long gong unit the canang and kesi still mark the weak and strong beats of the 2-beat stress pattern, as noted earlier. The tetawak anak carries the task of specifying the form of this gong unit. To do this, the high-pitched gong is struck on beats 16, 24, 28 and 30, while the tetawak ibu is played only on the last beat (that is, beat 32). This particular structure is the form and basic gong unit for the pieces entitled *Hulubalang* [warriors] and *Hulubalang Menyembah* [the warriors pay homage].

Rhythm   The drums in the shadow play ensemble produce specific rhythmic patterns for each piece.   Generally all rhythmic patterns in the musical system are resultant rhythmic patterns, which are obtained from an interlocking style of playing the drums.   In this performance style two or more drummers simultaneously play different rhythmic patterns that combine to form one complete or 'resultant' pattern.

In nearly all the pieces in the shadow play repertory, the gedumbak drum is used to play a specific rhythmic pattern.   At the same time, the gendang anak (small size drum) is used to play another rhythmic pattern, which compliments the gedumbak pattern.   Thus, in many pieces of the repertory these two drums produce the complete resultant rhythmic pattern.

Just as in the gong units, the drum rhythmic patterns also feature end-accented rhythms.   The stress that is the strongest usually appears at the very end of the rhythmic pattern.   The length of the drum rhythmic pattern is usually the same length as the complete, half or quarter length of the given gong unit. Consequently, the drum rhythmic patterns usually consist of 4- or 8-beat patterns that are repeated to fill the time of the specific gong unit in a given piece.

These rhythmic features may be seen in the Examples 1.4a and 1.4b. In the piece *Pak Dogol* (Example 1.4a) the gedumbak and gendang anak produce specific 4-beat rhythmic patterns that combine to give a complete resultant rhythmic pattern for the piece. Because the piece *Pak Dogol* is based on an 8-beat gong unit, the 4-beat resultant drum pattern is played twice in the time of one complete gong unit (Matusky, 1993 and 1997, pp. 52-9).

a) *Pak Dogol*

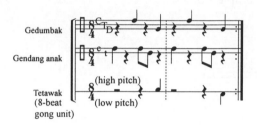

b) *Bertukar Dalang*

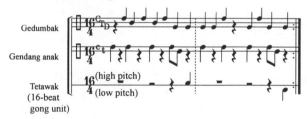

Example 1.4 Resultant rhythmic patterns for: a) the piece *Pak Dogol* and b) the piece *Bertukar Dalang*. (Key: C, T, D = timbres 'chak', 'ting' and 'dong' on the gedumbak; c, t = timbres 'chak' and 'ting' on the gendang anak)

Scales and Melody The melodies in the shadow play pieces are played on the serunai or sung by the puppeteer. The three types of pieces used, in relation to the drama, are those for specific activities, pieces to give news, and pieces to relate specific thoughts or moods. A given piece (that is, the melody, gong unit and rhythmic pattern) for a specific activity such as bathing, letter reading, picking flowers, lullaby or sleeping may consist of the same melody, gong unit and rhythmic pattern, but is given a specific name and lyrics according to its dramatic function. The pieces used to give news in certain contexts are entitled Berkhabar and Khabar Dan Dayang, and the pieces to convey ideas or mood are simply called *menyanyi*, or 'sung pieces'.

In general, the shadow play pieces are based on three kinds of scales, that is, pentatonic, hexatonic and heptatonic types. Although these three scale types may be identified in the repertory, in the hexatonic and heptatonic scales there is usually emphasis on 5 specific pitches which may be considered a 'pentatonic core' within the larger scale system. Almost all these scales contain intervals that are larger than a semitone or whole tone (for example, some scales include the interval of a third). A sampling of these scales is given below in Example 1.5.

Heptatonic scale

Hexatonic scale

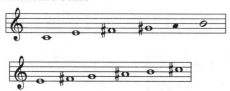

Pentatonic scale (anhemitonic)

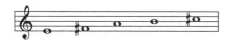

Example 1.5 Typical scales in shadow play music. (Matusky, 1993 and 1997, pp. 65-6)

The melodies in the shadow play piece are improvisatory in nature and still exist today in an oral tradition (they are not written down). Consequently, the same or similar melodic phrases and contours may be found in different pieces. For example, very similar melodic phrases are found in the pieces entitled *Bertabuh* [piece to signal the opening of the shadow play], *Berperang* [piece for battle] and *Menghendap* [crouching in ambush], while other like phrases are found in the pieces *Dewa Berjalan* [godlings walking], *Bertukar Dalang* [changing the puppeteer], *Sang Kaki* [piece for the character so named] and *Menggali* [piece for digging].

Most melodic lines in the shadow play repertory feature conjunct melodic motion. The melodies consist of long sustained pitches sung or played without vibrato that contrast with fast-moving melodic motifs using quavers, semiquavers and triplets. Incorporated into the fast moving passages are motifs using many types of melodic ornaments as shown in Examples 1.6a and 1.6b.

The puppeteer vocalist and the serunai player produce long melodies which, as noted above, contrast the sustained vibrato-less tones (so-called 'dead tones') with melodic motifs that are highly ornamented and fast-moving. The typical melodic lines feature repeated, sustained pitches early in the phrase while the long melismas generally occur at the end of the phrase. Hence, the singing style is mainly syllabic near the beginning of the phrase, but is melismatic at the end of the phrase.

The melismatic passages are embellished with melodic ornaments. As shown in Example 1.6, the melodic ornaments may consist of a portamento to a beginning pitch (see Example 1.6a, bar 1) or between two or more different pitches (the same example, bars 1-2), the acciacatura (bar 1), and the glottal stop (bar 2). The serunai player also executes similar ornaments such as the appogiatura, the cambiata and the trill (Example 1.6b, bar 2).

In an instrumental piece the serunai player imitates the vocal style of the singer by using sustained vibrato-less notes (see Example 1.6b, bar 2) followed by passages filled with melodic ornaments similar to the vocal ornaments. The serunai player also uses fast moving notes such as the 16th and 32nd notes along with triplet figures (as in Example 1.6b, bar 2).

With the highly ornamented melodic lines, the lively resultant rhythmic patterns and the system of repeated, concatenated gong units, the music for the wayang kulit Kelantan is rich in musical sound and resources. The system of concatenated gong units allows a piece to be rendered in a very short time span or a long one, depending upon the requirements of the puppet action at any given moment in a story. Furthermore, the highly percussive nature of this music along with the air-piercing sound quality of the Malay serunai melodies makes it appropriate for performances in its traditional outdoor venue. It is a music well suited to accompany the actions and moods of the dramatic aspects of the shadow play stories, and reflects a folk music tradition rich in indigenous Malay elements.

a) excerpt from the vocal piece *Menyembah* [paying homage]

b) excerpt from the instrumental piece *Binatang Berjalan*

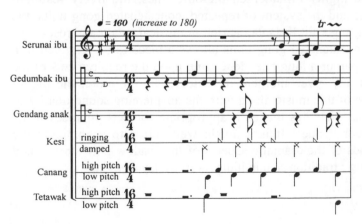

Example 1.6 Melodic ornaments in the shadow play melodies.

Plate 1.1 The *dalang* [puppeteer] and puppets in a *wayang kulit Melayu* performance.

Plate 1.2 The *dalang* at work in a *wayang kulit Kelantan* performance.

Plate 1.3 The *serunai* player in the *wayang kulit Kelantan*.

Dance theatre

Human characters and not puppets perform the traditional theatres known as makyung and mekmulung. These two forms use dialogue, dance, and vocal and instrumental music to present a story.

Makyung

The makyung has been noted as an ancient Malay form of theatre as witnessed in legends, myths and by its close ties to the traditional healing ceremony called the *main puteri*. In addition to the oral myths and legends, written sources have attested to the development of the makyung in the rural areas of Patani and Kelantan from the 19th through the 20th centuries. By the early 20th century the makyung theater was found in both rural and urban settings throughout Peninsular Malaysia, in Medan and in the Riau-Lingga islands of Indonesia (Ghulam-Sarwar Yousof, 1983 and 1986).

In the early 20th century this form of theatre was given royal patronage by the court of Kelantan which established a 'theatrical village' known as the *'Kampung Temenggong'* in the town of Kota Bharu. This theatre was supported and patronized by His Highness Temenggung Ghaffar from the Kelantan palace at that time. But the royal patronage did not last long, and just after the 1920s the patronage and support ceased. Although the makyung originated in the rural regions as a folk tradition, through its years of royal patronage the music, dance, costumes and other theatrical aspects were refined because of the constant opportunities for practice and performance in the Kampung Temenggung.

Today the makyung exists as folk theatre that is performed for entertainment among the common people. However, over the past several years a serious decline in the number of able makyung performers and musicians has occurred. The recent past (2000) saw the passing away of one of makyung's highly esteemed singers/actresses, Katijah Awang, and although many of her children and other relatives are still deeply involved in the art form, it remains to be seen if the makyung will survive in 21st century Malaysia.

In the 1980s and 90s, with the fundamentalist religious political party taking the reigns of government in the state of Kelantan (the former stronghold of the makyung) nearly all of the traditional performing arts, including the makyung, have not been allowed to flourish (see also, Introduction, and wayang kulit Kelantan in this chapter). The authorities in the state government have not deemed it suitable for women to be on stage, and the art form itself has been seen to be strongly tied to rituals that invocate the spirit world, especially in the connection of the makyung to the main puteri healing ritual. However, the importance of this art form as well as the Kelantanese shadow play, the bangsawan and other Malay forms is witnessed in the teaching of these theatrical-musical genres at institutions of higher learning in the country today, including the National Arts Academy in Kuala Lumpur. As noted in the earlier discussion of Kelantanese shadow play music, in the end, the makyung may find its place of nurture and development in the urban areas of the country and not in its home state of Kelantan.

Sometimes the makyung is found in the context of a high ritual performance. A good example is the *sembah guru* [paying homage to one's teacher] ceremony and performance in which a student, who is ready to go on stage as a principal, performs certain rites within the context of a performance itself (see further Ghulam Sarwar Yousof, 1976). The main structural elements of the makyung also sometimes combine with the main puteri healing ceremony for the expressed intention of healing a sick person. Here a shaman (*bomoh*) or the main actress (the Pak Yong character), serving as the shaman, takes the lead in communicating with the spirit world to discover the root of an illness. Although main puteri ceremonial elements become dominant in the performance, the music used is still that of the makyung.

In the villages the makyung, as ritual theater, is performed on a stage at the ground level, but for entertainment, especially in the urban areas, it is performed on a raised stage several feet above the ground for ease of viewing. A roof covers the floor area and the acting area [*gelanggang*] is located in the middle of the floor. The musicians and the actors serve as the chorus as they sit at the edge of the floor (the chorus is called the *'jong dondang'* among makyung actors). Because the makyung theatre has no walls the audience can view a performance from all sides as a theatre-in-the-round.

The original story in the makyung dramatic repertory is called the *Dewa Muda*, which is a Malay folk tale. The story *Dewa Muda* along with about 12 other tales comprise the dramatic repertory. Several of these stories are also performed in other local theater forms such as the wayang kulit, menora and the bangsawan. The stories focus on folk heroes, heroines and their fantastic adventures, and are told using dialogue, singing and dance by the characters along with the accompaniment of vocal and instrumental music (Ghulam Sarwar Yousof, 1976). Some of the especially important roles are the *Pakyung* and *Pakyung Muda* (the king and prince), the queen or *Makyung* and the princess or *Puteri Makyung*, the old and young clown-servants known, respectively, as the *Peran Tua* and *Peran Muda*, and the astrologer or expert of some kind called *Tok Wak*. In the 20th century, and still today, all principal roles are taken by women who dress according to the role played. However, before the 1920s men played the roles of the *Pakyung* and *Pakyung Muda* and not women.[4]

Performance practice

The makyung performance begins with an opening ceremony called the *Buka Panggung* [opening of the stage] with prayers, offerings of food and the consecration of the musical instruments and other items.[5] Immediately following the official opening is the performance of several pieces before the story itself actually begins. These pieces each have a special function and serve to introduce the characters or carry out some other special purpose. For example, the actors and actresses come onto the stage with the accompaniment of the piece called *Pakyung Turun* [the king descends], an instrumental piece. This piece is followed by a ritual song and dance called the *Menghadap Rebab* [paying homage to the rebab], which salutes the musical instrument called the *rebab* (Plate 1.5).

The opening section of the performance continues with the pieces entitled *Sedayung Makyung* and *Sedayung Pakyung*. These two pieces are performed to introduce the Makyung and Pakyung characters. Another piece entitled *Ela* is performed by the Pakyung character to introduce the character he will play in the story for the evening.

All of these pieces (except the *Pakyung Turun*) also involve specific dances, which are performed by the main singer along with the members of the chorus (the *jong dondang*). This group of sung and danced pieces comprises a fixed opening, which is performed each time a makyung performance takes place. A given story takes several nights to complete and, before its continuation from night to night, the fixed opening of sung and danced pieces is repeated. From a repertory of some 30 named tunes the actors and actresses use the various musical pieces and dances that are appropriate at specific times in the unfolding of the drama.

Makyung musical instruments

Makyung music is performed by a small orchestra consisting of a pair of gendang drums, a pair of tetawak gongs and one 3-stringed rebab. Additional instruments such as the serunai, canang and the geduk drum are sometimes borrowed from both the wayang kulit Kelantan and the Thai *menora* ensembles to play instrumental pieces for special purposes such as the dance piece entitled *Tari Ragam*.

Tetawak and *gendang* The tetawak and gendang in the makyung orchestra are identical to those instruments found in the shadow play ensemble (see Figures 1.1, 1.5, and Plate 1.6).

Rebab The 3-stringed rebab plays melody in makyung music. This bowed lute belongs to the chordophone family of musical instruments (Plate 1.4). It has a triangular-shaped wooden body, and its front (or face) is covered with a membrane from the lining of the cow's stomach that has been cleaned and dried. A small knob called the *susu* (nipple) made from bee's wax is attached to the upper left side of the face and serves to dampen the sound. The back side of the body is covered with cloth and colorful yarn. A thick, rounded wooden neck extends from the body and is attached to it by a long, thin wooden spike placed vertically inside the body (hence this instrument is often called a 'spiked fiddle'). At the lower end of the spike and at the base of the body another thick peg is attached and serves as a 'foot' on which the instrument rests when it is played. The rebab is completed by a head piece (*kecopong*) located at the upper end of the neck. This head piece is carved in the bamboo shoot (*pucung rebung*) design and painted, while the very top of the head piece is finished off with a removable finial.

The three metal strings on the instrument are attached to the bottom of the body and stretched over a small wooden bridge (called *pacat* [grass leech]), located near the front upper middle part of the body. From the bridge the strings run along the neck and are attached to three lateral tuning pegs. The pegs are turned to tighten the strings. The placement of the strings is secured with thick cotton string tied around the neck just below the tuning pegs. The three strings are tuned (from the lowest to the highest) at the intervals of a Perfect 4th and a Perfect 5th or in two Perfect 4ths. The actual register and pitches of the open strings depend on the vocal range of the singer.

The metal strings of the rebab are bowed using a wooden bow with nylon strings that are tightened by the player's hand as he holds the bow (today the nylon replaces the original strings made of coconut husk fibers).

Makyung music

The makyung musical repertory consists of 'drummed' or instrumental pieces (*lagu paluan*) and sung pieces (*lagu nyanyian*). The instrumental pieces are played for a number of specific activities including the *Pakyung Turun* to accompany the actors and actresses onto the stage at the beginning of a performance, the piece *Barat* which usually accompanies a traveling scene in a story, and the piece entitled *Sang* or *Penyudah* played to conclude a performance.

Most makyung pieces, however, are vocal and are performed for specific purposes and scenes in a given story. For example, the piece entitled *Ela* is sung to give news, while the piece *Mengulit Raja Nak Tidur* is played for sleeping or other scenes of an intimate nature. For sad scenes the pieces *Jembar* or *Mengambul* may be played, and for extended walking scenes the appropriate pieces are *Timang Welu* and *Kijang Emas*.

Plate 1.4 *Rebab* bowed lute and player in a *makyung* performance.

The sung pieces called *Sedayung Makyung* and *Sedayung Pakyung* are used often in many different situations. It is believed that the piece *Sedayung Pakyung* is associated with extraordinary power (magical power) and this piece is used especially for character transformations in a given story.

The most important piece, however, occurs at the very opening of a performance. It is entitled *Menghadap Rebab*, and is performed by the entire troupe to salute and honor the rebab. In the lyrics of this piece, the imagery of the natural environment, kingship and many other aspects of rural Malay culture unfold through the voice of the lead singer and the melodic lines of the rebab. The analogy of the human voice to the rebab bowed lute becomes clear in the duplication of melodic lines in heterophonic texture between these two parts (that is, the voice and the bowed lute).

Texture and musical form   Makyung music is polyphonic and, like the Kelantan shadow play music, consists of three basic layers of sound. These are the melody that is played on the rebab or sung, the percussive rhythmic patterns by the gendang drums, and the gong unit played on the tetawak gongs.

In the makyung musical system the tetawak gongs produce the layer of sound that is the basis of formal structure and time organization. This musical part is the colotomic unit (or gong unit). It is identical to the gong unit found in the Kelantan shadow play music, but is played using only the two tetawak hanging gongs.

Just as in the shadow play music, the total number of beats in a given gong unit is based on a 2-beat unit or a multiple of the 2-beat unit. Several examples of the gong unit are discussed in the earlier discussion of the Kelantan shadow play music. For example, the 8-beat gong unit (Example 1.2 above) defines the form for the makyung pieces entitled *Tari Ragam* and *Barat cepat*. Aside from the 8-beat forms, the pieces *Sedayung Pakyung* and *Sedayung Makyung* are based on 16-beat and 32-beat gong units, respectively, with identical form or structure as illustrated in Examples 1.7a and b.

The musical forms of the gong units for the two *Sedayung* pieces in Example 1.7 are signified by the tetawak ibu gong tone (low pitch, written as G in the circle representation) and the tetawak anak gong tone (high pitch, g). The tetawak anak gong tone marks the specific beats within the gong unit, while the tetawak ibu tone marks only the final beat of the unit.

a) *Sedayung Pakyung*

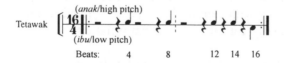

b) *Sedayung Makyung*

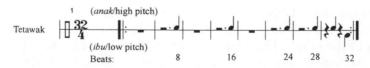

Cyclical representation of the gong unit for *lagu Sedayung Pakyung*

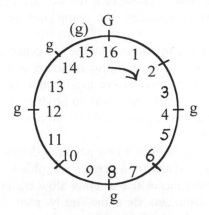

Example 1.7 Colotomic (gong) units for the pieces a) *Sedayung Pakyung* and b) *Sedayung Makyung*.

In this music system a given piece consists of several gong units that are chained together. The point of concatenation from one gong unit to the next is the last beat of the unit, so that the low gong tone (tetawak ibu), sounding out on the last beat of the gong unit, signifies the end of one unit as well as the beginning of the next one. The dual role of the tetawak ibu gong tone, as a marker of the end and the beginning of the gong units, underlies the notion that the gong unit is a cycle in time. The fact that all makyung pieces actually start on a beat within the gong unit and never at the very beginning of the unit also supports this premise.

In the two *Sedayung* pieces, as in all makyung music, a given gong unit with a particular musical form is repeated several times, but the total number of repetitions is determined during the performance of the piece and not before. The repetition of the gong unit depends on the singer's part and the information or news (through the text and lyrics) to be conveyed at a particular time and situation in the drama. Because of this, the colotomic unit, regardless of its length, may be repeated two, three or more times in one piece.

Rhythm Within the time framework of a given colotomic unit, the two gendang drums are used to play specific rhythmic patterns for each piece in the makyung repertory. These two drums are played using the interlocking playing technique described in the above section on Kelantanese shadow play music. Just as noted earlier, the two gendang produce four different timbres of sound, which are vocalized by the players using the mnemonic syllables 'cak', 'ting', 'duh' and 'pak'. These four timbres are used to play the resultant rhythmic patterns produced by using the interlocking performance style.

In makyung music the basic rhythmic patterns are generally four or eight beats long, but sometimes 2-beat rhythmic motifs are also found. These short patterns are the standard percussive motifs and the rhythmic phrases in the repertory that combine in various way to produce the resultant rhythmic patterns of the makyung pieces (see the rhythmic phrases noted by letters in Example 1.8).

The rhythmic patterns played by the two gendang drummers mark out the running beats in the gong unit and in the entire polyphonic texture of the music. Nearly all the makyung pieces use a rather slow tempo, and the rhythmic patterns played by the drummers show the steady main down beats in the music. Also, in nearly all the rhythmic patterns of makyung pieces the density of the drum strokes and timbres increases near the end of the rhythmic patterns (see samples, Example 1.8a-c).

As noted earlier, the rhythmic patterns in makyung tunes are structured according to the time framework of the colotomic unit for each individual piece. Hence, a rhythmic pattern of 8 beats in length has an accompanying colotomic unit of 8 beats, a 16-beat pattern has a colotomic unit of 16 beats and so on (see Example 1.8a-c, rhythmic pattern and gong unit). Generally the low, deeper drum timbres occur on the strong beats of the gong unit, while the high timbres are played on the weak beats. The internal structure of the 4-beat (or longer) rhythmic phrases may be arranged in various ways and three possibilities are outlined in Example 1.8.

The rhythmic patterns notated in Example 1.8 are the basic patterns used by the players for improvisation of the given pieces. In the process of improvisation, the two players may add ornaments (additional timbres) and modify the original pattern by substituting other timbres or rests on certain beats. But, the final beat (beat 8) is usually a rest (silence) and is usually not modified. In a rendition of the piece the drummers may improvise to produce rhythmic patterns that are very different from the basic pattern, but they eventually return to the original, basic pattern.

Another important feature in these rhythmic patterns involves the prolonged or sustained beats as distinguished from the usual, regular downbeats in the established tempo. As shown in Example 1.8c and 1.10, beats 1 and 3 of the rhythmic phrase *A* are sustained in duration at the discretion of the singer. Often on beat 3 the singer takes the liberty to sing a lengthy textual phrase using a melismatic melodic passage. At this point in the piece the makyung singer is able to show off her skill and vocal ability by improvising a highly ornamented and melismatic melodic line.

a) *Barat cepat,* 8-beat gong unit

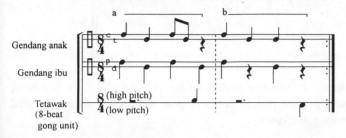

b) Sedayung Pakyung 16-beat gong unit

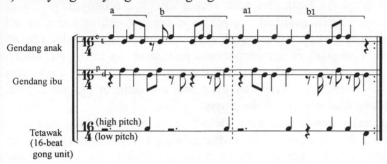

c) Sedayung Makyung, 32-beat gong unit

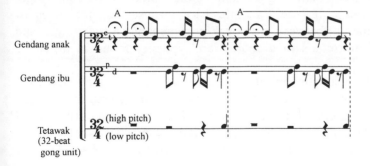

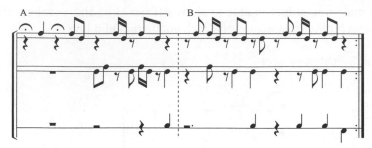

Example 1.8 The basic rhythmic patterns played on the two *gendang* drums for the pieces *Barat cepat, Sedayung Pakyung* and *Sedayung Makyung*.

Melody The melodies in makyung pieces are performed by a solo singer or by the rebab player. Both the solo singer and the rebab player, who accompanies the singer, perform complex and ornamented melodies in all the sung makyung pieces. The vocal and rebab parts are usually played simultaneously and produce a heterophonic texture in the music. In effect, the two players simultaneously perform the same basic melody each with his or her own variations. The variations that are sung or played depend upon the skill and discernment of the player.

The performance of a sung melody with the accompaniment of a bowed lute (or other instrument) in a heterophonic style is found in various genres of music in the Islamic world from North Africa to the Middle East. This style of performance and texture is found, too, in makyung music. A heterophonic texture is also found in the makyung chorus music when several singers in the chorus sing the same, basic melody while each singer simultaneously varies it (see Example 1.9). These two instances of heterophonic texture, a) between a musical instrument and a solo singer, and b) between several singers in a chorus, are typically found in makyung music.

Other characteristics in makyung melodies involve pitch and scale, intervals, melodic contours, and melodic ornaments. In general the melodic contours are characterized by descending lines, or a combination of ascending and descending lines. The melodic range is usually rather narrow, regardless of whether the melody is played by the rebab player or sung by the solo vocalist.

The scales in makyung tunes range from 4- to 7-tone patterns (see Example 1.10). Nearly all of the scales are based on a core set of pitches along with semitonal and microtonal neighboring pitches and inflections. Sometimes the interval of an augmented 2nd is featured in a makyung scale along with neighboring pitches that consist of whole or semitones.

As illustrated in Example 1.10, whenever very important lyrics are sung by the solo singer, the core pitches and a syllabic singing style are used along with conjunct melodic motion (movement of pitches by whole or semitones) (see Example 1.10, beats 3, 14-16). However, near the end of a melodic line and text phrase, when meaningless syllables such as *'lah'*, *'gak'*, and *'weh'* are sung, the melodic line features melisma and very dense ornamentation (see Example 1.10, beats 11-12, 28-29). In this example several types of melodic ornaments are used including the cambiata (beats 4 and 18), the trill (beat 6), the appogiatura (beats 11, 21), the portamento (beat 11), the glottal stop (beat 31a) and a downward release of the pitch (beat 14). The use of these melodic ornaments and chromatic pitches produce a melodic line, which is extremely active and volatile.

Yet another important characteristic of makyung music, shown in Example 1.10, is that the gong unit in a given piece functions as a guide or framework for the performance of melodies (and for the drum rhythmic patterns, too). This function of the gong unit involves the entrances of the chorus and the solo singer, the occurrence of melismatic and syllabic singing styles and the occurrence of the dance movements in a given piece. For example, in the piece *Sedayung Makyung* the complete gong unit of 32 beats guides the chorus and soloist to begin and conclude their respective parts on beat 32.

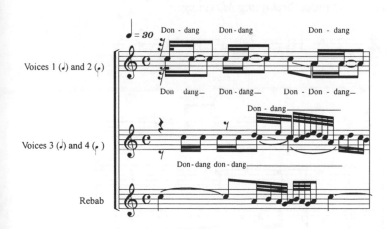

Example 1.9 Heterophonic texture performed by several singers in a
***makyung* chorus (from *lagu Sedayung Makyung*).**

In Example 1.10 the chorus in the previous gong unit (shown as beats 30a, 31a and 32a) sings only up to the final beat of the gong unit (beat 32a). From this point onward the Makyung character begins her solo part. Hence, it is at the last beat of the gong unit where the shift from chorus to soloist and from soloist to chorus occurs. The change between the chorus and soloist never happens within the quarter segment or the middle of the gong unit. At these final beats in the unit (beats 32a and 32) it is also clear that the solo and chorus parts usually overlap, providing continuity in the music from one gong unit to the next.

Scale for the piece *Sedayung Makyung*:

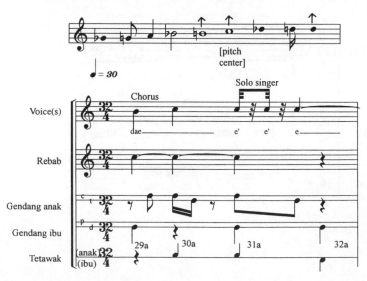

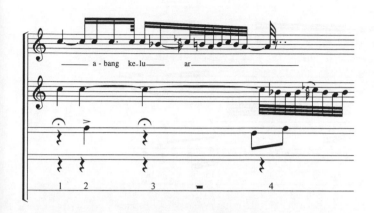

itu lah-bang weh—— ka - lau   ja——— ngan   nak la—ma,

ka-lau la

hor—— ha - ri—— ma-suk da-lam is - ta—— na—— lah——

Example 1.10 Excerpt from the piece *Sedayung Makyung*, illustrating the scale and one complete gong unit of 32 beats.

Plate 1.5 *Makyung* actresses performing the *lagu Menghadap Rebab* [salutation to the *rebab*] at the beginning of a performance.

Plate 1.6 *Makyung* drummers and gong player in a village ensemble (the stage is at ground level).

Mekmulung

Like the makyung, the mekmulung is traditional dance drama featuring dialogue, singing, dancing and instrumental music. However, it is found only in the state of Kedah, and although its origins are unclear, the actors in this theater form refer to the region of the former Patani Sultanate as its place of origin. Today performances of the mekmulung theater are limited to a troupe in the area of Kampung Wang Tepus in north Kedah. There is no formal apprenticeship system for the actors or musicians, but the young members in the troupe learn the music and stories in a rote method from the experienced players. Today this theatrical form is performed only by men who take both male and female roles in a given story.

The mekmulung is staged in an open, roofed hut-like structure at ground level. The shape of the stage is almost the same as that used for the makyung, but the mekmulung stage is smaller, the roof is pointed at the center and the back wall is made of plaited bamboo. The musicians sit at the back edge of the stage while the center space serves as the acting area. The main actor takes the role of the *pak mulung* (the king in a given story), and the younger actors play roles such as the prince or princess. The clown-servants are played by four experienced actors who wear red masks that cover only the upper part of the face and head. The princesses and clown-servants also join the musicians as members of the chorus.

The mekmulung is usually performed as entertainment, presenting Malay folk stories. Among these, the most important tale is entitled *Dewa Muda*. Just as in the makyung theater, specific musical pieces are played to accompany certain activities or situations in a given story, such as music for traveling, for giving news and so on.

As a standard opening or introduction, the mekmulung performance begins with instrumental music called *Pembukaan* [the opening piece]. This tune is usually followed by the piece *Bertabik* [greeting] to welcome the audience. The greeting piece is sung by a soloist and the chorus in responsorial style with the accompaniment of drummed rhythmic patterns (see Example 1.11). At the end of this piece the prince and princess characters enter the stage. The standard opening continues with pieces entitled *Puteri Nak Bangkit* (a salutation to the musical instruments by the prince or princess), *Puteri Berjalan* (a dance by the prince or princess), and the piece *Pakmulung Nak Bangkit* (the first song and dance number by the pakmulung character). At the conclusion of this standard opening, the main story for the evening begins.

The musical instruments

The mekmulung ensemble features the *rebana* drum. The main rhythmic pattern in a given piece is played by two drummers on two large rebana drums called *'rebana ibu'* or *'gendang ibu'* (Figure 1.11). Two small size rebana drums, called the *rebana penganak* and the *rebana peningkah* (or, alternately, the *gendang penganak* and *gendang peningkah*) produce a specific rhythmic pattern and the running beat in the music, respectively (Figure 1.12). One or two knobbed, hanging gongs (Figure 1.8) and several pair of bamboo clappers (*kecerek*) (Figure 1.9) are also used. The main melody is played on the serunai (Figure 1.10). Some characters sing solo songs and the musicians serve as the chorus whenever needed in the drama.

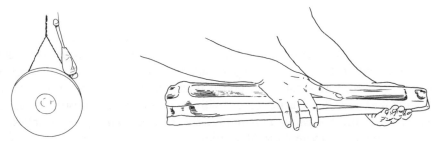

Figure 1.8 Small gong   **Figure 1.9 *Kecerek***

Figure 1.10 *Serunai*   **Figure 1.11** *Rebana ibu*

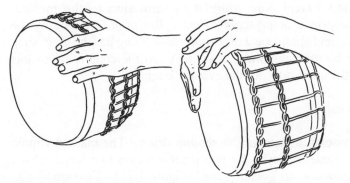

Figure 1.12 *Rebana penganak* and *peningkah*

Idiophones   In the mekmulung ensemble the musical instruments that function as markers of time are the gong and the kecerek. The hanging bronze knobbed gong is medium in diameter (about 20-25 centimeters), and is hit on the knob with a padded stick. Any pitch may be used.

The kecerek consists of two bamboo sticks struck together. Each stick is about 30-35 centimeters long and several pairs are usually used in a given ensemble.

Membranophones   The drums in the ensemble are referred to as 'gendang' (a term usually referring to the elongated, barrel drum) but actually they are the rebana drums --- the single-headed frame drums made of jackfruit wood. The body is a narrow wooden frame, and the two drum sizes used are the *rebana ibu* (large size) with a diameter of about 50 to 60 centimeters, and the *rebana penganak* and *rebana peningkah* (small size) with a diameter of about 25 to 30 centimeters.

In the construction of the rebana the goat hide is attached to the body with rattan laces which are tied from the hide to a thick rattan brace located at the base end of the body. Several wood wedges are inserted between the rattan brace and the body to tighten the drumhead. To make the drum head even more taut before playing another rattan brace is pressed inside the drum between the goat hide and the edge of the wooden body.

Each rebana is played by a single player who strikes the drumhead with both hands. Just as in playing other rebana drums, certain timbres are produced when the drumhead is struck in specific ways. For example, striking the drumhead in the center produces a sound which is low and resounding (called 'brom' or 'dung' by the players), while striking the head near its edge produces a high and sharp sound (called 'cak' or 'tak'). Using these timbres the rebana players drum out specific rhythmic patterns for each different piece in the mekmulung repertory.

Aerophone The main melody of a piece is played on a wind instrument called the serunai. The serunai is cone-shaped and the reed is made of four layers of dried palm leaf. This somewhat short version of the serunai is not as large or ornate as found in the east coast variety, but the playing method is similar to the serunai from Kelantan.

Mekmulung music

Like other traditional Malay music, mekmulung pieces are characterized by three distinct layers of sound, that is, a resultant rhythmic pattern, a melody and a repeated colotomic unit.

As shown in Example 1.11, a piece to welcome the audience, the rebana peningkah player drums out the running beat, while the other two rebana parts provide the interlocking resultant rhythmic pattern (24 beats long in this case). The small, knobbed gong repeats the simple 4-beat colotomic unit throughout the piece with a gong tone on every fourth beat. Above these parts the chorus and soloist sing a simple melody in call and response style as they welcome the audience to the evening's performance.

In some pieces the kecerek concussion sticks are added to the colotomy, usually punctuating every other beat in the music. Unlike other genres of Malay music, the colotomic units in mekmulung pieces are usually very short (4 beats, for example) and do not necessarily signify musical form or other structure in the music.

a) basic rhythmic pattern and melodic line

Example 1.11 Excerpt from the piece *Bertabik* from the *mekmulung* theater.

The mekmulung vocal melodies are often very simple and static, using 3- and sometimes 4-tone scales. In contrast, the serunai melodies are based on heptatonic scales, but using a pentatonic core of whole steps, half steps and 3rds. Just as in the wayang kulit music noted earlier, passages of long, sustained notes contrast strongly with ornamented melodic passages of trills and fast moving quaver notes. The introductory sections of pieces feature a serunai passage in free rhythm, but when the drums, gong and kecerek enter, the rhythm becomes measured and steady, in duple or quadruple time, throughout a piece.

Randai

The *randai* is a traditional dance and theatrical form of the Minangkabau people. It incorporates dance movements, singing, instrumental music, story and acting. Today randai is identified with Minangkabau communities throughout Indonesia and Malaysia.

This theatrical form developed through a number of successive influences and in several stages. The word 'randai' implies a circle or circle-like formation around a particular location. It was derived from the action of a group of people surrounding a particular area as if searching the grounds for something while moving in toward the center of the circle. The randai dance is analogous to such movements and group formations. Other sources of the randai were oral storytelling and the martial art called *pencak silat* (Mohd. Anis Md. Nor, 1986).

Oral storytelling was the forerunner of randai. It was the most popular form of entertainment among the Minangkabaus, and through it Minangkabau folklore was handed down orally from one generation to the next. Storytelling was and still is a professional art and only performed by professionals called *penglipur lara*. The storytelling among the Minangkabau people is referred to as *kaba* of which there are two main kinds: the narration of love stories and romances known as *batalerek*, and stories depicting the heroic deeds of the Minangkabau legendary hero Si Tongga Maget Jabang, known as *basijobang* or *basitongga*. The stories were narrated in the form of songs and were usually accompanied by a rebab. Taking several nights to complete a single story, the storytelling sessions were considered a special entertainment in the Minangkabau large community house (the *rumah gadang*). They were the most popular form of entertainment before the advent of the randai. The storyteller, the focus of attention, would usually sit at the edge of a circle of listeners, and it was through his mastery of language and good memory that entertaining stories of educational value were delivered to the audience.

The young boys who went to stay at the small family prayer house (*surau kaum*) were familiar with the stories, songs, and the poetic art of the storyteller. Often these stories were used to boost their morale for their future travelling (*merantau*) mission. In the meantime, they would be taught the art of self defense (*pencak silat*) by the older members who stayed at the family prayer house and by the returned travelers who were still bachelors. As a means of encouraging and maintaining their interest in the pencak silat, tunes from the oral storytelling tradition were sung as an accompaniment for the martial art practices. A variety of dances involving the martial arts gestures were also taught to the young men at the family prayer house, and specific songs from the oral storytelling tradition accompanied these dances. The dances, performed in a circular formation and accompanied by the songs from the repertory of the storyteller, came to be known as randai.

As this form of dance theater developed throughout the 20th century, acting became a required element in randai performances emphasizing good memory, skill in vocalization, and a mastery of impromptu dialogue with poetic flavor. Over the years some performers became good dancers and others became good actors, and in some instances a performer functioned both as an actor and a dancer. In the past, female characters were impersonated by male actors and were not required to dance with the rest of the performers. They were to remain outside the circle of dancers and would present themselves in the center of the circle only when required for a particular episode in the story. However, by the 1970s, females were allowed to act and dance in all randai performances, and this change brought even greater popularity to this dance theater form.

Randai performance

The randai performance today includes several basic elements: the introductory and concluding processions of the actors, dances, songs, story, acting and dramatic text. The musical procession introduces and accompanies the entire cast of performers into the arena, while a procession out of the arena marks the end of a performance. The songs accompanying the dance movements function as prologues to the respective dramatic scenes, while scenes enacted during the end of a dance sequence constitute the theatrical segments of a major story.

Traditionally, randai was performed in an open space in front of the large community house, the *rumah gadang*. Today it is performed in many places, ranging from specially erected stages to soccer fields, school halls and community centers. The audiences view the performances from any area they choose, since randai continues to be performed in a circular formation.

The performers are introduced into the performing area by a group of musicians walking in a procession. Led by the musicians, the dancers/actors walk single file into the performing area. Once these performers are introduced, the musicians leave the area and sit among the audience. At the end of a performance, the musicians again enter the performing area and lead the dancers/actors out in a procession. This formally marks the end of an evening's performance.

The randai ensemble

The traditional instruments used by the musicians are the *caklempong pacik* that consists of five knobbed gongs, a *katindiek* or *adok* drum, and a reed instrument called the *pupuik* or *serunai*. In all there are five musicians, three for the caklempong pacik, one drummer, and one serunai player. Today sometimes only the caklempong pacik is used.

Idiophone The caklempong pacik consists of five small knobbed gongs, each gong measuring about 14 centimeters in diameter.

One of the players holds a pair of the gongs in the left hand and a beater in the right hand, a second player does the same (Figure 1.13). A third player holds only one caklempong gong along with a beater. In a typical caklempong tuning, the first pair of gongs have the approximate pitches *c* and *e*, while the second pair are approximately *d* and *f*. The single caklempong is tuned close to the pitch *a*. Thus, a scale of one possible caklempong pacik would be:

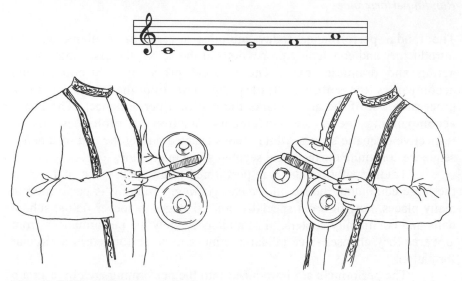

Figure 1.13 *Caklempong pacik*

Figure 1.14 *Katindiek*

The pair of caklempong, which produce a continuous melody, is referred to as the *dasar*, while the second pair of caklempong which provides a simple 2-note phrase is called the *paningkah*. The single caklempong gong plays a part called the *anak*.

Membranophones   The katindiek in the randai ensemble is a double-headed, barrel-shaped drum (Figure 1.14). The drum heads are made of goat skin and are attached to the body with rattan laces. The drum is held in a horizontal position and the drum heads are struck with the player's hands.

The adok is a single-headed frame drum similar in shape to the rebana or *kompang*. It is held upright on the floor or on the player's lap and struck with the hands.

Aerophones   The serunai, sometimes called the pupuik, uses a double reed and has four finger holes. The reed is made from dried palm leaf. Just as in other shawms in Malaysia, the serunai in the randai is played using a circular (or continuous) breathing technique so that when a melody begins the sound is continuous to the end of a piece.

The pupuik gadang is a wind instrument made of a coconut palm leaf rolled up in the shape of a cone. It is a single reed instrument blown from the pointed end of the cone.

The music

There are four different melodies played on the caklempong pacik in a randai performance. They are entitled *Parambahan, Tetarak Lapan, Cak Din-Din* and *Tigo-Tigo*. A randai group may choose any one of these pieces for the introductory and concluding procession in a performance.

The piece *Parambahan* is played by only one pair of caklempong gongs. The melodic phrase of this piece is 8-beats (or 2-bars) long and is repeated over and over in an iterative fashion.

In contrast, the entire caklempong (five gongs) is used to play the other pieces of the repertory. The part in the music referred to as the *dasar* [lit., base, foundation] carries the main melody, while the *anak* [lit., child] and the *paningkah* [lit., accompanying] parts provide an underlying accompaniment consisting of short rhythmic/melodic phrases that are played in an interlocking style. The piece *Tigo-Tigo* in Example 1.12 shows the main melody and the two interlocking parts. In this example it is also clear that each part (dasar, anak and paningkah) begins at a different time interval so that none of the instruments begin in unison. This technique of staggered entrances is characteristic of nearly all caklempong pacik pieces.

a) the piece *Tigo-Tigo* showing the *dasar*, *anak* and *paningkah* parts

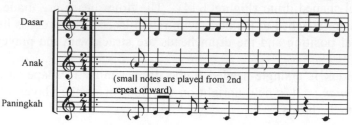

Excerpt from *Akademi Seni Karawitan Indonesia dan Sekolah Menengah Karawitan Indonesia*, Padang Panjang, Sumatera, Indonesia.

b) the resultant melody for *Tigo-Tigo*

Example 1.12 Excerpt from *Tigo-Tigo* for the *randai*.

As can be seen in Example 1.12b, the interlocking nature of the parts results in a composite or resultant melody that incorporates harmony. The common harmonic intervals in this piece are thirds (and sixths), fifths and a strongly contrasting interval, the major second. The melody is structured in a short 2-bar phrase that is repeated with some variation throughout the piece.

The dance movements in the randai are accompanied by songs that vary from region to region or from group to group. The songs are recognized by their melody, but the lyrics change to satisfy the story line. The entire repertory of melodies is divided into two types: (i) melodies for pleasant and elated moods, and (ii) melodies for melancholy (*ratok*) sentiments. Establishing the appropriate sentiment for a particular scene in the story is done through the type of song used. At the conclusion of a song and dance sequence the sentiment is established and the dramatic scene with dialogue continues.

The songs are usually sung monophonically, led by the main singer who is also the lead dancer. Two examples of typical songs sung in the randai, both melancholy and non-melancholy styles, are shown in Example 1.13a-b.

a) *Lagu Suaian* (melancholy [*ratok*] piece)

b) *Lagu Situjuah*

Example 1.13 *Randai* **vocal pieces.** (Mohd. Anis Md. Nor, 1986)

Scales   The vocal pieces may use 5- , 6- , or 7-tone scales that are modal in nature. The melancholy melody entitled *Suaian*, for example, is based on a heptatonic scale whose interval structure is like the mixolydian mode. However, in this case the pitch center of the piece is the second pitch of the scale.

In contrast, the *Situjuah* melody sounds similar to a diatonic major scale (the pitch center, however, is the third scale degree). The melodies are usually simple in structure and conjunct in motion, which makes them easy to perform and suitable to accompany the dance movements, especially since the dancers are also the singers.

Rhythm and Form   The rhythm of both the instrumental and vocal pieces is usually duple (or quadruple) which is compatible with the rhythmic structure of the dance phrases.

The processional pieces *Parambahan* and *Tigo-Tigo* are structured in 2-bar (or 4 or 8-beat) phrases, while the vocal pieces also tend to be structured in 2- or 4-bar phrases. An exception is the melancholy melody *Suaian* (Example 1.13a), which is organized in 3-bar phrases. In all the pieces, however, the melodies are symmetrical and balanced.

Each piece is in two main parts, *AB*, (see Example 1.13), the second part being twice the length of the first.

In general, the instrumental and vocal pieces in the randai use duple meter with 4- or 8-beat melodic phrases sung monophonically. The melodies are unornamented and are easy to sing, while the melodic lines are usually balanced and repeated with some variation. The interlocking style of playing on the caklempong pacik produces short resultant melodies that are repeated throughout a piece.

Opera and musical theatre

Bangsawan

The *bangsawan* or Malay opera is a form of theatre which appeared at the end of the 19th and beginning of the 20th centuries. With colonization by the British during that time, the Malay Peninsula experienced many socio-economic, political and cultural changes. Cities developed on the Malay Peninsula with inhabitants of many different races, and new forms of entertainment emerged. The local population was exposed to a wide range of non-indigenous cultural activities such as the silent film, commercial theatrical performances by touring European and American operetta, revue and vaudeville as well as Chinese opera and Parsi troupes.

The bangsawan or Malay opera appeared during these early times as a result of the influence of the Parsi troupes from Bombay, which traveled widely in Southeast Asia. The Pushi Indera Bangsawan of Penang was the first professional troupe formed by Mamat Pushi, a rich Parsi who lived in Penang.

The term 'bangsawan' referred to the stories and characters that mainly concerned the Malay royalty. Each bangsawan performance consisted of one or more stories accompanied by songs and 'extra turns' (song and dance) which were performed during the set changes. The performance took place on a proscenium stage in a hall, large tent or in an entertainment park. On the stage there were backdrops (*tirai latar*), curtains (*jalar* or *drop sin*), painted flats (*kota bam* or *said wing*), and the valance curtain (*kening*) and crown (*mahkota*) where the name of the troupe was shown (Plate 1.7).

The bangsawan was different from folk and classical theatre because it was commercial in nature. It was not performed for ritual ceremonies, but rather it was entertainment for both city dwellers as well as rural communities. Each show was advertised through the newspaper, radio, handbills and leaflets. As commercial theatre, bangsawan troupes visited cities in Peninsular Malaysia, Singapore, Sumatra, Java and Borneo throughout the year. This commercial theatre attracted audiences, actors and entrepreneurs from all races and social strata, and by the 1920s and 30s, bangsawan had become the popular theatre in Malaya. Its songs and dances became the hits of the day. The famous bangsawan groups managed by these entrepreneurs included Dean's Opera, Nooran Opera, Wayang Tap Chow Thong, Pushi Indera Bangsawan and Wayang Kassim.

Plate 1.7 *Bangsawan* characters in a performance of the fairy tale *Shamsir Alam*.

To attract theatre-goers of a multi-ethnic population, the bangsawan stressed a great variety of styles. Malay, Arab, Chinese, Indian and Western stories and tunes were performed. Several of the popular stories included *Laksamana Bentan* (a Malay story), *Laila Majnun* (an Arab story), the Chinese tale *Sam Pek Eng Tai*, the Hindustani *Puteri Bakawali* and the Western (or Classical) tale of *Hamlet*. The backdrops and sets that depicted palaces and gardens in Malaya, India, the Middle East, China and the West were used. When the extra turns were performed, tunes and Western dances such as the tango, rumba and waltz were the usual featured items by a female chorus, but Malay songs and dances such as the *asli*, *inang*, *joget* and *zapin* were also presented. As is evident from the following discussion, bangsawan music was extremely flexible and highly adaptable, using musical influences from Western and other countries.[6]

The musical instruments

Three types of instrumental combinations were used in the bangsawan. The first was the Malay orchestra that exemplified the Western dance orchestra. This ensemble consisted of musical instruments such as the violin, trumpet, trombone, saxophone, flute, clarinet, piano, guitar, bass, drum, maracas, wood block and tambourine. It was used to accompany the Western (Classical) stories and those from the Middle East. This Malay orchestra was the forerunner of the Orchestra of Radio and Television Malaysia, which accompanies television and radio singers today.

The second type of ensemble, similar to that for the social dance known as the *ronggeng*, consisted of the violin, accordion, rebana and gong (see Chapter 5 --- Ronggeng). This ensemble was used for the presentation of Malay and Javanese stories. The bangsawan musicians often exchanged the accordion with the piano, the rebana with the Western drum set and the gong with the double bass. This ensemble could also be enlarged by the addition of more violins, the bass, trumpet and other instruments. The rebana was the earliest Malay drum in the bangsawan (see mekmulung in this Chapter).

The harmonium and tabla made up the third ensemble that was used in Hindustani stories. The harmonium is a small reed organ introduced to India by religious missionaries in the 19th century. The musician plays a keyboard with one hand while pumping the bellows on the instrument with the other hand. The tabla, a membranophone, consists of two types of drums: (i) the tabla or small drum made of wood with a high pitch, and (ii) the baya or drum a little larger than the tabla with a low pitch and made of clay or nickel. Each type of drum has a circular patch of paste on its drum head to tune the instrument. The drumhead is made of goat skin and is attached to the body with goat hide laces that are tightened with wooden dowels (Cf. Chapter 5).

The number of musical instruments used in a given performance would be based on the number of available players. Generally the trumpet, trombone and other instruments could be excluded from the Malay orchestra if the players were not available. Sometimes only a piano was used. The bangsawan orchestra was different from the folk and classical theatre orchestras because it was continually undergoing changes and incorporating new musical instruments.

The musical repertory

Just as in the folk and classical traditional theatre genres, specific tunes are used for specific dramatic situations or characters. For example, a song of fate (*lagu nasib*) is performed for a scene of separation from a loved one, ill luck or a sad event, a song for a garden scene (*lagu taman*) occurs whenever the queen or maidens dance in the garden and a song for a dialogue (*lagu cakap*) is performed when the king, queen, princes or ministers converse with one another. A song for a street scene (*lagu strit*) underlines a character walking through the streets, while a song for a genie or fairy (*lagu jin*) accompanies a scene with a genie character and a song for fighting (*lagu perang*) is performed for a battle or a violent scene.

Each song is associated with specific musical elements such as the rhythmic pattern and tempo, which helps the audience recognize a scene, character or situation in a story (see Table 1). For example, a fast waltz (the piece *Donau Walen*) is used as a song for dialogue, and a slow waltz (the piece *Penceraian Jula Juli dengan Sultan*) is used as a song of fate in a classical or Arabic story. A slow *asli* tune, the piece *Puja Kamati Darsha Alam* for example, is played as a song of fate, and a fast *asli* number, such as the piece *Che Wan Gayah*, is used in a garden or street scene or for dialogue in Malay and Javanese stories. In general, a slow tempo indicates sadness and a fast tempo depicts happiness.

From its beginnings, the bangsawan musical repertory was different from that of the traditional theatre forms because new melodies were always created for songs using specific rhythmic patterns and tempos needed in particular scenes. As in film and Western theatre, the themes of songs were created for each new story. Even the waltz, tango, foxtrot, quickstep, march and other rhythmic patterns played by Western bands, Western theater groups, and on recordings and radio were introduced (see the discussion on rhythmic patterns in bangsawan pieces below).

The music

Basically, bangsawan pieces combine Malay and Western musical elements, but some features of Chinese, Indian, Middle Eastern and Javanese music are also included. According to the bangsawan experts, the Malay songs are used in Malay stories, the Middle Eastern songs occur in Arab stories, Javanese tunes in Javanese stories, Hindustani pieces in Hindustani stories, classical pieces in Western stories and Chinese pieces in Chinese tales.

Table 1.1 The Relationship between Dramatic Situations/Characters and Rhythmic Patterns/Tempos in the *Bangsawan*

DRAMATIC SITUATION / CHARACTER	RHYTHMIC PATTERN / TEMPO		
	Classical stories	Arab stories	Malay/Javanese stories
Song of fate (*lagu nasib*)	slow waltz, slow foxtrot	slow *masri*, slow *asli*	slow *asli*
Song for a garden scene (*lagu taman*)	slow waltz, fast waltz, foxtrot, quickstep	*inang/masri*	*inang, masri,* fast *asli*
Song for dialogue (*lagu cakap*)	fast waltz	fast waltz, *masri*	fast *asli, inang*
Song for a street scene (*lagu strit*)	march, quick-step, foxtrot	march, quick-step, foxtrot, *masri*	fast *asli, inang*
Song for genies (*lagu jin*)	march, quick-step	march, quick-step	none
Song for a battle (*lagu perang*)	march	march	*joget/inang*

Scales In general diatonic major and minor scales are used in bangsawan pieces. However, other scales are also introduced, for example:

(i) the Chinese pentatonic scale for Chinese pieces

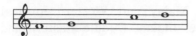

(ii) a mode similar to *Hicaz* for Middle Eastern pieces

(iii) a mode similar to *pelog pathet nem* for Javanese pieces

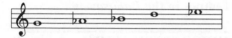

Texture and Melody There are two types of texture in bangsawan pieces.
1.   linear texture (a melodic line and a percussive pattern which are independent, and harmony is not stressed).
In the piece *Hiburan Raja Ahmad Beradu* (a Malay piece, see Example 1.14), there are several layers of music. First, the violin, piano and voice each produce independent melodies. Although the violin and high register of the piano play the same basic melody as the vocal part, improvisation occurs with ornaments such as the turn (bar 5) and the trill (bars 6 and 8). Specific melodic phrases called *patahan lagu* are also played in unison on the violin and piano (as illustrated in bar 8). The singer improvises the rhythmic pattern and the melodic line and, as shown in Example 1.14, the melodies in stanzas 1 and 2 are different.

Example 1.14 Excerpt from the piece *Hiburan Raja Ahmad Beradu*.

As can be seen in Example 1.15, the singer embellishes the melody with ornaments such as (i) a portamento from one tone to another (bars 4 and 5), (ii) vibrato on a sustained note (bar 5), (iii) trill (bar 12), (iv) appogiatura (bar 14), and (v) mordent (bar 13). In addition, a nasalized voice is used in the performance of the piece.

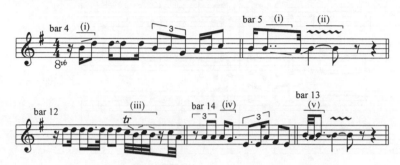

Example 1.15 Melodic ornaments in the piece *Hiburan Raja Ahmad Beradu.*

At the same time, the low register of the piano and the rebana play the *asli* rhythmic pattern from the *ronggeng* repertory:

Although triads are played by the piano on scale tones 1 and 5, these triads do not function harmonically but rather as ornaments.

2.   homophonic texture (melodies accompanied by triads and harmony).

In the piece *Penceraian Jula Juli dengan Sultan* (a classical or opera piece, see Example 1.16), harmony and key changes occur. The stanzas 1 and 2 are in the key of *A* minor and stanzas 3 and 4 in *A* major. The vertical triads I, IV and V are used throughout the piece. In stanza 1 the trombone and piano play in parallel major 3rds and 6ths, and arpeggios are a characteristic feature in the instrumental parts.

Example 1.16   Excerpt from the piece *Penceraian Jula Juli dengan Sultan* (stanzas 1 and 3).

Rhythm   As shown in Table 1 above, various rhythmic patterns are associated with particular dramatic situations and characters. The rhythmic patterns are usually repeated cyclically throughout a piece, including the examples given below in Example 1.17 (for a detailed explanation of the rhythmic patterns, see Chapter 5 --- Ronggeng).

Malay pieces
(i) the *asli* rhythmic pattern

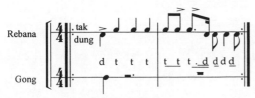

(ii) the *inang* rhythmic pattern

(iii) the *joget* rhythmic pattern

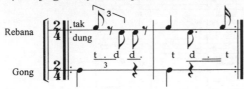

Middle Eastern pieces

(i) the *masri* rhythmic pattern
   (similar to the rhythmic mode *Masmudi Kabir*)

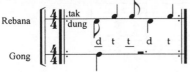

(ii) the *zapin* or *gambos* rhythmic pattern

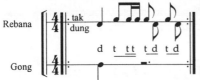

Classical pieces

(i) the waltz rhythmic pattern

(ii) the tango rhythmic pattern

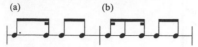

(iii) the foxtrot rhythmic pattern (duple meter with 4-bar phrase, tempo
about 30 to 40 bars per minute), or quickstep (with a tempo of 50 or
more bars per minute)

Quickstep (*Lagu Taman/Kayangan* [song for a Garden/Heavenly scene])

(iv) the march rhythm in 4/4 meter with a loud, repeated pattern

Excerpt of 'Colonel Bogey' (as whistled by Mat Arab)

Hindustani pieces
(i) the *barshat* rhythmic pattern (similar to the tala *dadra*)

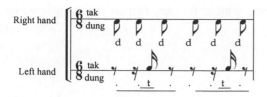

Javanese pieces
Keroncong and stambul pieces were used (see Chapter 5 - Keroncong).

Chinese pieces
(i) ragtime (syncopated melody with an non-syncopated bass line)
   Shanghai Street

Example 1.17 Standard rhythmic patterns used in the *bangsawan*.

Musical Form Most bangsawan pieces are in strophic form in which the melody of each stanza is repeated with different text. Usually a chorus part is inserted between each of the stanzas. Most texts consist of a 4-line verse in the form of the traditional *pantun* and *syair*, with each line of text associated with one melodic phrase (see Examples 1.16 and 1.17 above).

   In general the characteristics of bangsawan music clearly show that it is different from the music of traditional theater because the bangsawan combines elements from the music of Malay, Western and other cultures. The Malay elements consist of the use of the Malay vocal style, heterophony, the cyclical nature of the rhythmic patterns and the use of the texts of the pantun and syair. In contrast, the elements of harmony, and the constant use of Western musical instruments are clearly the Western influences. The features from other countries include the Chinese, Arab, Javanese and Indian scales or modes and rhythms.

   The bangsawan began to decline during the post-World War II period. The Malay intelligentsia created a new form of theatre called *sandiwara* with more realistic stories that could more readily express the mood of anti-colonialism and national consciousness. Bangsawan also lost its following to the Malay film, which, in fact, filmed the bangsawan as well as contemporary stories.

Boria

Another kind of syncretic theatre and music that is popular in Penang is known as *boria*. Although it is believed that the boria originated in Persia and was brought to the Malay Peninsula by south Indian soldiers, it has been adapted and developed by the Malays of Penang.

Early in this century the boria was found all around Penang, but today it is performed only in certain areas of the island. For example, one can hear and see boria during National Day, at the annual Penang Festival and at the Exposition sites with the aim of developing the tourist industry. Competitions of boria groups are also held from time to time.

According to various sources, in the middle of the 19th century the boria, which involved only vocal pieces and dances, was brought to Penang by Muslim Indian soldiers. At that time the boria was performed by the soldiers for 10 days during the month of *Muharram* in remembrance of the events of the *Karbala* and the mourning of the death of Hussein r.a.[7] Later it was performed in Penang by the local inhabitants, better known as the *Jawi Peranakan*, that is, Indians who married local Malay women. This theatrical form was then adapted to the local tastes and needs of the community.

In the villages the boria is often performed on a stage made of a wooden platform raised about one meter above the ground. Usually this stage does not require any sets or props, but the performers sometimes use small hand props. The participants enter the stage from the rear where the musicians are seated during the performance, while a space at the front of the platform is the performing area. Whenever the boria is held for a state celebration, a stage in a hall is usually used, but stage props and sets still are not needed.

The costume used in the boria performed in the villages is usually the normal street wear of the performers, or a costume appropriate for the story being performed. However, in a staged performance in a hall or on television the costumes consist of colorful uniforms worn by all the performers.

In the early history of the boria only men acted all the parts, both male and female, in a given story. But, since the 1950s female boria groups began to emerge. Today there are mixed gender troupes, and in these troupes the men do the acting and the women do the singing. The boria performers may be amateur or professional. The amateurs are usually youth groups from the various political parties in the country, or school and college groups. On the other hand, the professional troupes consist of several experienced actors who are acknowledged to be skilled in improvising dialogue. The professional troupes tend to be stable with a given group of actors and singers who stay together for a long time.

Today the stories presented in a boria performance focus on social issues of the day, or themes associated with the reason or purpose for the performance. Sometimes Chinese or Indian stories are presented, and even stories from films are enacted on the boria stage.

Performance practice

A performance is divided into two segments: (i) a comic story or comedy sketch, and (ii) a song and dance section. The two segments feature the same story or theme.

The comedy sketch is usually acted by 10 to 14 actors. The role types in this part consist of several village people and the headman of the village or a professional person like a doctor or a government worker. The theme of the story is presented in a comic sketch with slapstick comedy and improvised dialogue. A small band plays instrumental music to accompany the story and to produce sound effects whenever needed.

The second part in the performance consists of songs and dances that occur a number of times. This part is presented by a solo singer and a chorus consisting of about 30 to 40 people (smaller groups use 10-12 people). The members of the chorus also dance and they are referred to as the *kelasi* or sailors, while the solo singer or lead singer is known as the *tukang karang*. The tukang karang carries a baton, while the sailors hold a flag and two pairs of umbrellas (Plate 1.8).

The *tukang karang* stands on the stage before a microphone and the chorus/dancers stand in rows behind him. Instrumental music by the band starts off the song and dance routines. After the short band introduction, the tukang karang sings the first verse of the song lyrics, which is structured in four lines of text with a set rhyming scheme of some kind. For example, the first verse might have a rhyming scheme outlined as *a,a,a,a*, while the second verse might follow with the scheme *b,b,b,b*. The theme of the verse would be the same as the theme of the earlier comic sketch. The verse sung by the tukang karang is accompanied by the band and, at the same time, the chorus members begin to move in unison dance steps and routines.

Plate 1.8   The *tukang karang* lead singer (foreground) and the 'sailors' chorus in a *boria* performance. (Photo by Toh, L.-C.)

When the tukang karang finishes his first verse, the chorus/dancers repeat the lyrics and melody of that verse while dancing to the rhythm of the tune. Then the tukang karang sings the second verse of the piece while the chorus members continue the dance routine. The tukang karang and the chorus alternate through some 12 to 20 verses of the piece. The theme of the song lyrics focuses on the main story in the boria performance.

Musical instruments

The performance of a story and the vocal tunes along with dance in the boria is accompanied by a band that usually sits at the back area of the stage. Providing popular entertainment, this ensemble usually consists of various musical instruments that adapt to audience tastes and western popular music trends.

In former times, the ensemble included the violin, *gambus* plucked lute, *marwas* hand drums, Indian *tabla*, accordion, gendang, cymbals and harmonica (Kementerian Kebudayaan, Belia dan Sukan, *Boria*, 1980, p. 6). In the 1950s, with the popularity of rock n' roll, modern Western instruments such as electric guitars and the drum set became popular. Electric keyboards were introduced in the 1960s, and by the 1990s synthesizers often provided the accompaniment. Additionally, the asli or ronggeng ensemble comprising the violin, accordion, rebana and gong often accompany joget, inang and zapin songs that are sung in present-day boria

Form, Melody and Texture The music for the boria is syncretic and combines Western, Malay, Indian and other musical elements and instruments. In the early twentieth century, the strophic form, with variations of the same melody sung to different stanzas, were used. But, since the 1950s, different melodies are usually employed by the tukang karang and sailors to accompany each stanza. Each song has an elaborate introduction and ending to accompany performers as they enter and leave the stage.

The melodies chosen for the introduction and ending as well as the tukang karang and sailor parts are adapted to popular music trends. Sometimes Malay or Western popular songs are performed. With the use of the synthesizer in the 1990s, many different kinds of arrangements are produced by boria musicians. The melodies are often in the diatonic major-minor scales and the basic chords on I, IV and V are played by the piano/keyboard and guitar (see Example 1.18).

Rhythm Popular Latin American rhythms such as the cha-cha, slow rumba, mambo and foxtrot are common in boria, but the traditional asli, inang, joget and zapin rhythms are also popular (see the excerpt in Example 1.19).

As a form of entertainment focusing on specific kinds of stories and timely social issues, the boria is still quite popular in the Penang Malay community. Being highly syncretic in nature, it includes the use of a set performance structure, local themes, local poetic forms, popular Western dance music, and a band that features Malay, Western, Indian, Arab and other musical instruments.

Example 1.18   An excerpt of *Sambutan Dewi Bunga,* by the *tukang karang,* in a boria performance. (Boria of the Batu Lanchang Elementary School (Penang), arr. 1996 by Ahmad Ramli, for synthesizer, transcription by Toh, L.-C.)

Example 1.19 *Zapin* **rhythm accompanying** *boria asli* **[original** *boria***].**
(transcription by Toh, L.-C)

The Chinese opera and Po-te-hi (hand puppet theater)

Today various types of music ensembles are found among the Chinese
communities of Malaysia. These ensembles may be grouped as follows:

1.   instrumental groups such as the Chinese orchestra and the
      harmonica ensembles;
2.   the music ensembles that accompany the Chinese opera, lion dance,
      weddings, funeral ceremonies and other celebrations;
3.   Western style orchestras that play classical Western music such as
      works by Beethoven, Mozart and so on;
4.   the brass ensemble; and
5.   the electric guitar band which plays popular music.

The Chinese opera (Plate 1.9) and the *po-te-hi* glove puppet show
(Plate 1.10) are very popular forms of theater among the Chinese people of
Malaysia.[9] Theatrical troupes from China entertained the great number of
Chinese immigrants to Malaysia in the 19th and early 20th centuries.
These troupes were professional, as the performers received income solely
from the opera. They were paid professional fees by the proprietor and
traveled together with the troupe. Many of the proprietors and performers
never went back to China and started their own theatrical groups in Malaya.
The professional troupes performed mainly at temple festivities,
amusement parks where other types of entertainment were also found and
at theatrical halls. Amateur associations that promoted Chinese opera were
also popular. In these associations, members learned to perform the opera

and to sing and play opera tunes from the professional opera actors and actresses.

In Malaysia today the Chinese opera is still performed by professional troupes in the Teochew, Cantonese and Hokkien dialects, while the po-te-hi uses only the Hokkien dialect. The Chinese opera is presented by human players, but the po-te-hi is presented by two puppeteers who wear glove puppets on both their right and left hands. The index finger of the hand moves the head while the thumb and middle fingers move the two hands of the wooden puppet. Although there are differences among the Teochew, Cantonese and Hokkien operas, there are some theatrical conventions, characters and musical instruments that are the same.

The function of the Chinese opera and the po-te-hi as religious ceremonies and social events is still found today. These forms of Chinese theater are performed to celebrate the birthdays of the Chinese deities, but these theatrical presentations also give the members of the Chinese community a chance to come together to interact and chat informally.

Prologue and story

A symbolic prologue is presented before the beginning of a story to express congratulations to the deities on their birthdays. Through the performance of this prologue the audience hopes that the gods will bestow happiness, wealth or long life upon them. (The Chinese words in this chapter follow the Hokkien terminology.)

Plate 1.9 A scene from the Chinese opera in Penang.

Plate 1.10 A scene from the *po-te-hi* [glove puppet theater] in Penang.

The prologue begins with the '*Pak Sian Ho Siew*' episode (A Birthday Greeting from the Eight Immortals). In this episode eight holy men or saints pay homage and convey a happy birthday to the god for long life.

The *Pak Sian Ho Siew* is followed by another episode called *Thio Kah Kuan*, a ritual performed as a sign of thanksgiving to the gods. This episode is performed by a non-speaking, white faced character who walks to the front of the stage. He holds a scroll with the Chinese characters welcoming the gods and the audience to the performance which immediately follows. The Chinese characters on the scroll also express hope that the members of the audience will have prosperity in the future.

After that, the episode known as *Tien Lu Sang Hai Tze* (The Goddess Presents Her Son to her Immortal Husband) is performed. In this episode, one of the seven daughters of the Jade King arrives from the heavens to marry a poor scholar. This young princess requests a cloth to help her husband pay back money which he borrowed for his mother's funeral. After one year, the Jade King's daughter is compelled to return to the heavens because her husband has become an important government official. After many months the young princess reappears to give a son to her husband. Growing to adulthood, this child becomes famous as a chief scholar in China. With the performance of this episode the opera performers express hope that the members of the audience will have clever sons.

The Teochew and Cantonese operas also present the episode *Luk Kok Hong Siong* (Six Countries Invest a Chancellor). In this presentation, the opera troupe exhibits its richness in actors, costumes and acrobats.

The characters in the episode *Tien Lu Sang Hai Tze* and other actors leave the stage and present the deity of the opera to the gods of the Chinese temple. The *ang-pow* (money in a red envelope) and biscuits are given to the actors so that they will have good luck.

In the po-te-hi glove puppet theater only the *Thio Kah Kuan* episode is performed. The puppets are not carried into the Chinese temple. In contrast, a stage worker carries the po-te-hi theater gods into the temple. He also gives the *ang-pow* and biscuits which are passed around to all the actors as a sign of good luck.

After this prologue, the story for the night is performed. There are four kinds of stories performed in the Chinese opera and the po-te-hi:

1.   stories about the life and good deeds of the kings, noblemen and generals of China;
2.   stories about love between a scholar and a pretty maiden, sorrow because of their parting and happiness upon their re-uniting;
3.   stories about the deities from the heavens; and
4.   stories based on battles and triumphs over uncivilized tribes.

Sometimes, two or three nights are needed to complete a single story.

Characters, facial characteristics, costumes and stage props

The characters in the Chinese opera and the po-te-hi are categorized according to four important role types:

1.   *seng* (male): usually in the role *lau seng* (an older man such as a king, father, or uncle), *sio seng* (a young man such as a scholar, handsome fellow) and *bu seng* (a military character such as a general or soldier);
2.   *toa* (female): usually in the role *hoa toa* (a good and well-mannered leading actress such as a queen or a princess) and *kho toa* (a distressed woman such as a duty-bound daughter, a widow or a village maiden);
3.   *thiu* (comic character) such as *tiam chu* (a worker in a shop or tea house). These characters use common or street language; and
4.   *hoa bin* (painted face) such as the character *hong te* (a male deity) and *hong te niao* (a female deity) from the heavens.

In the po-te-hi there are also animal puppets such as tigers and horses.

The features and facial colors differentiate the characters in the Chinese opera and the po-te-hi. Accordingly, a refined character such as a woman has small eyes while a coarse character has large eyes. A civilian clown wears a moustache, while a comic character playing the part of a petty court official has a pointed beard over the mouth and two wisps of hair protruding from either side of the face (Figures 1.15 and 1.16). A high-level, powerful character wears a long beard that covers his mouth (Figure 1.17). The color of the beard indicates the age of the character; a black beard for a character of middle age, grey for an old man, and white for a very old man.

The character *hoa bin* uses unusual and extraordinary makeup. The face and forehead colors are symbolic. The color red symbolizes allegiance and honesty, black and green colors show bravery, yellow depicts a character who is fair and just, while gold and silver colors are used by the gods. The comic characters are known by the white patches around their noses. In the po-te-hi the face of the *seng* and *toa* characters are painted white while the face of the *kang lang* (servant) character is painted light red.

In general, the color and ornaments on the costume illustrate the type, rank and status of a character. A red costume is worn by a good character of high rank; blue costume by a character of high rank who may be good or evil; yellow by a king. A courteous gentleman wears green, while an old man usually wears white. White is also a color for mourning. The color black is worn by a male character who is vicious and cruel or a good female character in trouble, and light red or blue is the usual color for a young character.

The decorations on a costume are based on symbolism found in Chinese fine arts. The phoenix bird and dragon which symbolize prosperity and fertility or abundance are used on the costume of a king. The crane symbolizing long life is embroidered on the costume of a court official, while the plum flower symbolizing long life and femininity decorates a female's costume.

Head-dresses, hats and caps also differentiate the various characters. For example, kings wear a high golden head-dress studded with pearls in the middle and decorated with two dragons at each side. This headpiece is also ornamented with colorful silk pom-poms and two silk tassels hanging from the sides (Figure 1.18). High ranking characters such as poets and scholars wear hats made of hard cloth, while attendants and servants of low status wear simple soft black hats (Figures 1.19 and 1.20).

In both the Chinese opera and the po-te-hi a table and two chairs are placed on the stage before the beginning of the performance. The chair may represent a bench, stone or the ground whenever a character sits on it. There is greater realism in the po-te-hi when compared to the Chinese opera. For example, the puppets sit astride a horse made of thick paper, but in the Chinese opera only a horse whip represents the horse.

The musical instruments

The Chinese opera and po-te-hi orchestras are divided into (a) the military ensemble consisting of percussion instruments; and (b) the civil ensemble made up of stringed instruments.

This discussion focuses on the musical instruments in the po-te-hi which are classified according to Hokkien terminology used by the local Chinese in Malaysia. The names of the musical instruments are noted in the local Hokkien dialect.

Membranophones and idiophones   The military ensemble consists of membranophones and idiophones. This ensemble plays an important role in the performance because it announces the beginning of the show, signals the entrance of characters onto the stage, accompanies the action of walking by specific characters, and gives a signal that a dangerous situation is about to occur. The musical instruments in this ensemble are:

1.   *toa ko* (large drum), a barrel drum with a drum head which is tacked to the wooden body at its edge (Figure 1.21);
2.   *tiong ko* (medium drum), a small, flat drum covered with skin at the top but left open at the bottom (Figure 1.22). Sometimes a wood block is used as the *tiong ko*;
3.   *sio ko* (small drum), a wood block, rectangular-shaped, which is hollow with two long slits on its side (Figure 1.23);
4.   *pan* (a pair of clappers) (Figure 1.24).

All of these musical instruments are played by the same player who holds a wooden beater in one hand and the *pan* in the other hand.

In addition to these instruments, there is also a pair of cymbals (*la poah*) and two gongs called *toa lo* (large size) and *sio lo* (small size). Both of these gongs are played by another player who beats them with a padded wooden beater.

Chordophones   The civil ensemble for the po-te-hi consists of chordohones or stringed instruments which accompany the singing and dancing and complete the scene with background music. The instruments usually used are:

1. *kak ngah hian* (two-stringed bowed lute with a coconut shell body, called *yehu* in Mandarin) (Figure 1.25). This is the most important melody instrument in the po-te-hi;
2. *kim ngah* (moon guitar; called the *yueqin* in Mandarin) (Figure 1.26); and
3. *ji hian* (two-stringed bowed lute which is larger than that noted above; called *erxian* in Mandarin). This instrument is not used if there are not enough players in the ensemble.

Aerophones   In addition, there are the aerophones or wind instruments that are called *chhe* (to blow) in the Hokkien dialect or *sona* in Mandarin. Although this instrument is usually played by the kok ngah hian player in the civil ensemble, it is probably more accurate to classify it as an instrument in the military ensemble because its function is the same as the percussion instruments.

The chhe is played to announce the appearance of the king or a god, to depict a dangerous situation and to imitate the sound of a horse. This instrument does not accompany singing because its sound is always loud and resonant. (See the Chinese orchestra in Chapter 5 for illustrations of these wind and stringed instruments.)

The musical instruments in the military and civil ensembles are somewhat different in the Teochiew, Hokkien and Cantonese operas. Essentially, in the Cantonese opera orchestra the military ensembleconsists of three wood blocks, a drum, three gongs, two cymbals and the sona. The civil ensemble consists of the *erhu* or *yehu*. In the Teochiew opera the *yangqin* stringed instrument is used in the civil ensemble.

The music for the Chinese opera and the po-te-hi glove puppet theater consists of different vocal melody and speech types as well as instrumental and percussion music.

**Figure 1.15 Moustache of a
common clown.**

**Figure 1.16 Beard of a comic
petty court official.**

**Figure 1.17 Beard of a powerful
character.**

**Figure 1.18 Head-dress for
a king.**

**Figure 1.19 Hard cloth hat
for scholars.**

**Figure 1.20 Soft cloth hat
for attendants
and servants.**

Figure 1.21 *Toa ko*

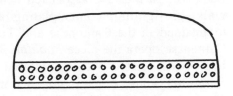

Figure 1.22 *Tiong ko*

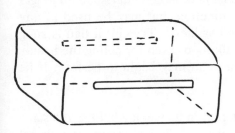

Figure 1.23 *Sio ko*

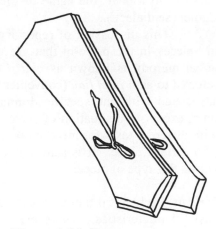

Figure 1.24 *Pan*

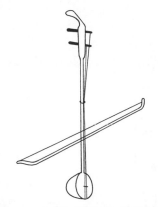

Figure 1.25 *Kak ngah hian*

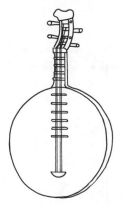

Figure 1.26 *Yueqin (Kim ngah)*

The repertory and musical features

Each type of music is associated with a special dramatic function such as walking, fighting, contemplating and so on. This tradition is still maintained in the Cantonese and Teochew operas. For example, in the Cantonese opera the piece *Faaidim Bongjia*, with a fast tempo and steady beat, is associated with an agitated or fretful situation, while the piece *Faansin Yiwong*, which is slow and melismatic, is associated with sadness. The piece *Bubujiao* is sung by young women while walking in a garden, and the piece *Dangzhou* is sung by the God of Law when he appears as an oarsman in a boat (the name of the Cantonese opera noted here is in the Cantonese dialect.).

This discussion of repertory and musical features concentrates on the pieces in the po-te-hi that are used today. The most commonly used vocal melody is known as *chit ji tiau* (seven syllable tune). It is also referred to as *li pian tiau* (convenient tunes) because the tunes are no longer associated with one specific dramatic function, but may be used at any time, except in a situation of sorrow and sadness. The chit ji tiau is sung with different texts for meditation or walking or even for noting the beauty of a certain place. It is said that a musician may begin to perform if he knows this type of piece.

Melody Each chit ji tiau is slightly different in its melody but has the same basic characteristics. There are a number of distinct layers of musical sound which are performed by the singer, the kak ngah hian, the *ji hian*, *pan* and the wood block (Example 1.20).

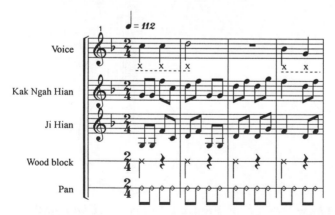

Example 1.20 *Chit Ji Tiau.*

Every chit ji tiau consists of singing seven or 11 bars that are separated by a musical interlude of four bars (Example 1.21). As indicated by the name 'chit ji tiau', the textual syllables in each vocal line occur in groups of seven syllables (three syllables + four syllables) as shown in Example 1.21.

Example 1.21 *Chit Ji Tiau* (vocal line). Key: x = textual syllable, ( ) = example of a vocal variation

The singer uses the basic melodic pattern for each vocal line. The first three syllables in each line are sung with a descending melodic contour:

or an ascending melodic contour (or a variation):

After these three syllables, there is usually one bar of instrumental music. The four syllables after the first three syllables are sung with a descending contour:

or its variation, such as:

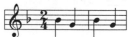

The sung section of 11 bars usually ends with a descending melodic contour:

Between all the sung sections, the same 4-bar musical interlude is played (see Example 1.21, final line).

In a sad scene, *kho chit ji tiau* (a piece of seven sad syllables) is used. Just as in the chit ji tiau, this piece has a steady beat played by the pan and the wood block. Each vocal line consists of seven syllables of text, sung using a slow tempo and, usually, with *rubato*. The kak ngah hian player improvises his part as he follows the singer. A 6-bar musical interlude is played after two phrases of seven syllables as illustrated in Example 1.22.

Example 1.22 *Kho Chit Ji Tiau* **(vocal line).**

Other than these two categories of pieces, the po-te-hi also uses the *sio tiau* (small tune) or the *kho sio tiau* (small tune). These are a repertory of pieces with specific names such as *Goa Me Li Sio Tiau* (small tune: 'I

Scold You') or *Geh Cheng Su Ai Kho Sio Tiau* (small tune: 'The Moon is Clear and One Thinks of Love'). The melodies of these pieces are adaptations of popular songs played on the radio or adaptations of folk songs. These pieces have beautiful melodies, and the themes and texts of the pieces express particular feelings by the singer. New texts are often composed for these pieces and the name of a piece changes according to its new text.

The piece *Bi Phang Sio Tiau* (small tune, 'The Fragrant Rice' – Example 1.23) is one example of a *sio tiau* that has a pretty and popular tune sung by a female who walks in the garden and sniffs the fragrance of the rice. Another important feature of this example is the imitation of the singer's cadential phrase by the kak ngah hian bowed lute and the toa ko drum (Example 1.23). The musicians say that this feature 'adds a flirting or joking ambience to the sio tiau pieces'.

Example 1.23 *Bi Phang Sio Tiau.*

In addition, speech types are often used in the po-te-hi such as when the Chinese monks pray. In Example 1.24, only three notes accompany the text *'o-mi-to-hoot'* (referring to 'Amitabha Buddha' – the ruler of the western paradise) which is sung by a monk. The wood block is played on every beat.

Example 1.24 The text '*o-mi-to-hoot*'.

Instrumental music is used to depict a dramatic situation. For example, the *chau kin tiau* ('run quick' tune) is played as a signal that a dangerous situation is coming up (Example 1.25). In this piece, four notes are repeated with a tempo that gradually accelerates.

Example 1.25 The instrumental music *Chau kin tiau*.

A repeated motif of two notes played by the chhe also tells of a dangerous situation (see Example 1.26).

Example 1.26   The music by the *chhe* that tells of a dangerous situation.

The chhe also accompanies a very dramatic scene such as when a person is killed by hanging (see Example 1.27).

Example 1.27   Instrumental music accompanying a very dramatic scene.

Scales Several types of scales are used in the pieces for the po-te-hi, but many of the pieces use a type of pentatonic scale (five tones) (Example 1.28).

1. the pentatonic scale in the *chit ji tiau* (Examples 1.21 and 1.22). The pitches G and D are stressed.

2. pentatonic scale in a hanging scene (Example 1.27). This scale is often used in Chinese folk music. The pitches G and C are stressed.

Example 1.28 Pentatonic scales.

Some pieces use heptatonic scales (seven tones) such as those scales shown in Example 1.29.

1. a heptatonic scale in the *kho jit tiau* (Example 1.22). The pitches D and A are stressed.

2. a heptatonic scale in the piece *Bi Phang Sio Tiau* (Example 1.23). The pitches G and D are stressed.

Example 1.29 Heptatonic scales.

In general, the intervals of the third, fourth and fifth are stressed in the melodies for the po-te-hi. (Examples 1.21-1.23)

Rhythm Finally, the percussion musical instruments announce the beginning of a performance, a change of scene, the entrance of a puppet on the stage and accompany the occurrence of dramatic movements and events (see Example 1.30).

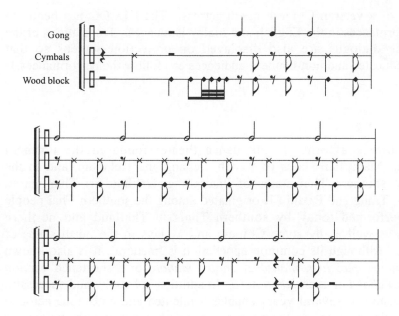

Example 1.30 Percussion music.

In conclusion, the Chinese opera and the po-te-hi glove puppet theater are still popular among the Chinese communities, especially in Penang, Kuala Lumpur, Ipoh and Johor Bahru. Performances by professional troupes are put on to praise the Chinese deities. In the month of *Phor Tor* (the 7th month in the Chinese calendar), the Teochew opera from southern Thailand and the famous opera singers from Singapore and Hong Kong are brought to Penang because of the great demand for performances and local performers are few in number.

To attract a younger audience, the opera groups, especially the Hokkien opera, have introduced several changes and adaptations. For example, popular Chinese and Western songs are sung for one or two hours before the beginning of the Hokkien opera story, using an electric guitar band which accompanies the pop singers. Because of this, the opera story is shortened to two hours (compared to four hours for a performance in former times). The local Hokkien dialect is used so that the young people who do not understand the classical Hokkien language can follow the story.

In addition, there has been a renewed interest in Chinese opera among a growing middle class of professionals, businessmen and housewives who are looking for their roots in response to modernity. They formed the Kuala Lumpur Chinese Opera Club (KLCOC) under the direction of a veteran Chinese opera actress. The KLCOC has begun to give performances in the English and Malay languages. Translations of the Cantonese dialogue are also displayed on projection screens so that English-educated and non-Chinese audiences can follow the performances.

Menora

The menora is a form of folk dance theater found in the northern Peninsular Malaysian states of Kedah, Penang and Kelantan, and in the bordering southern Thai states of Phattalung, Nakhon Sri Thammarat, Songkhla, Trang and Patani. It originated among the southern Thai people and is performed today by southern Thais in Thailand and northern Malaysia as well as by some Chinese and Malays in the north states of Malaysia. Although its common appellation is 'menora', it is also known by the names *manohra, manohra chatri, manora* or a shortened version *nora, nora chatri* or even *lakon nora.* In addition, a lengthy and successful apprenticeship of several years enables a talented and ambitious actor to earn the title 'menora' or 'nora' and to formally use this term before his name.

This theatrical form consists of stylized dance postures and movements, instrumental music, singing, story and improvised acting based on a given plot. The genre also includes a number of important rituals. The beliefs and rituals involve elements of the unseen or spiritual world as well as magical power. Usually a menora actor or even the entire troupe will express these beliefs through the ritual ceremonies in the performance for the purpose of praying for success in hunting, healing someone, fulfilling a vow and so on.

Performance practice

In former times, the menora was not performed on a specially built stage, but was presented on the ground in a courtyard or in a Buddhist temple yard. Today, however, a performance mainly for entertainment purposes takes place on a simple, roofed platform that is open on three sides, and behind it is a special room for costume changes. A backdrop or curtain separates the two spaces (B.S. Ang, 1997).

Both old and new stories are told in the menora tradition. It is believed that there were originally 12 stories obtained through the dreams of the original menora actor, Mesi Mala (*Nuen Thong Samli* in Thai). However, over the years new stories were created and are still being created today. Some tales are performed mainly for entertainment purposes, while other stories are more commonly connected to performances for high ritual occasions. In Kelantan, because many of the menora players are also makyung actors, the influence of the Malay theater on choice of story is very clear in terms of stories performed and music played.

It is believed that long ago, a menora performance used only three male actors. A female character would be played by a young boy with long hair. They acted the roles of the hero (a prince), heroine (a princess) and clown (a servant). Over time, women were allowed to perform, taking the female roles in a story, and today there are many more characters in a menora production. While the main character types use the southern Thai dialect in their improvised dialogue, the clowns play important roles in communicating intimately with the audience by using the predominant language of the given audience group. For example, in Kelantan the clowns speak Malay, while in Penang and Kedah they mix the Malay and Hokkien languages.

The elaborate costume for the main menora actor or the apprentice menora actor is thought to have originated from the attire of Thai royalty. Among the items of dress were the king's crown (*sert* in Thai, or *kecopong* in the Malay language), the shirt or vest of beads with criss-crossed panels and lapels (*sang wang*), arm bracelets (*kamlai khean*) and a locket at the waist band (*phan neng*). Over the years other items were added to the basic costume (see further B.S. Ang, 1997 and Plate 1.11). Today the characters also wear modern street attire including Western long-sleeved shirt and neck tie with trousers or the traditional Malay dress for men and women as appropriate for the story performed.

Dance is an important component in all menora performances. The mythology connected to the menora indicates that Mesi Mala (the original creator of the menora) witnessed a dance in the heavens consisting of 12 basic dance movement positions (that is, a particular dance step or movement ending in a given stance or position of the dancer). Over the years many other dance movement positions were created and today there is a standard repertory of these dance positions that must be learned by every menora actor.

The instruments and music

Instruments To accompany the dance movements and the singing, a repertory of music is played by a small percussion-dominated ensemble. This group consists of a short barrel drum called *klong* (like the Malay geduk --- Figure 1.6), a pair of goblet-shaped drums or *tab* (identical to the Malay gedumbak --- Figure 1.4), a pair of small knobbed gongs called *mong* (like the Malay canang --- Figure 1.2), a set of finger cymbals or *ching*, one Thai folk shawm called *pi*, and several pairs of concussion bamboo sticks called *krek* (Figure 1.10) (or sometimes called *trek* or *khrap phuang* (a hardwood clapper). Many of these instruments are shown in Plate 1.12.

Plate 1.11 A *menora* actor in traditional costume. (Photo by Ang, Bee-Saik)

Today other instruments are also added, including an electronic keyboard or sometimes the Thai fiddle called *saw uu* and the Chinese *erhu*, accordion, flute, bongo drums, tambourine and so on. The menora groups in Penang and Kedah mix modern and traditional instruments, using both the pi and the electronic keyboard to play melody. The entire ensemble is known as *khruang dontrii*, and the group of musicians is called the *luuk khuu* or *nak dontrii*.

Among these instruments, one of the most intriguing is the pi shawm, which may use a reed of four, six or eight layers of dried palm leaf. The tubular body of the instrument has a large bulge in the center with the finger holes placed along the front side of the tube. The reed is inserted into a holder at the top of the instrument and a long narrow cloth is wound round and round the reed and upper part of the body to serve as a support for the player's mouth. Like the Malay serunai player, the Thai pi player uses a continuous or circular breathing technique to produce long melodic lines, which often do not stop until a piece comes to an end.

Plate 1.12   The instruments of the *menora* ensemble: *klong* barrel drum, two *tab* goblet drums, and *mong* gong-chime. (Photo by Ang, Bee-Saik)

Types of musical pieces   Some five different types of music (or pieces, *pleeng*) are used in a menora performance. These types are:

1. the *pleeng khab naa man*, sung poetry by the menora actor as he sits behind the stage curtain (especially at the beginning of a performance), and accompanied by rhythmic patterns on the tab, mong and ching. Considered to be difficult poetry to sing, the themes of the verses focus on phenomena in the natural environment.

2. the *pleeng naa thread* (or *naa krek*), sung poetry accompanied by the krek concussion bamboo and the ching cymbals, but without dance. Each line of verse sung by the menora actor is answered in responsorial style by the musicians who also serve as the chorus.

The menora actor, in costume and sitting on a bench at center stage, sings this type of piece while donning the long upward-curved fingernails (*lap*) that are part of his costume.

3. the *pleeng rai thread* (or *rai krek*), sung poetry in which the lyrics adhere to certain strict poetic conventions, with dance. This piece is sung immediately following the naa thread above. The solo vocal part begins with the accompaniment of the ching and krek idiophones and is answered with a sung passage by the chorus. This vocal part is immediately followed up by instrumental music on the tab, klong, mong and ching to accompany the dance movements. There are about 50 different rai thread pieces from which the actor may choose in a given performance.

4. the *pleeng tab*, an accompanied song with dance. All the percussion instruments in the ensemble are active from start to finish in this type of piece as the solo menora actor and the chorus sing in responsorial style. The lyrics are more difficult and each line of text is longer than in other types of pieces.

5. the *pleeng tone*, a purely instrumental piece to accompany dance. This piece is played by all the musical instruments, including the melody instruments like the pi shawm, the electronic keyboard or the saw uu or erhu bowed lutes. The tunes played are both traditional and modern (or popular) Thai pieces. Those actually chosen in a performance depend upon the discretion of the pi or keyboard player.

During the many years spent as an apprentice, the menora actor devotes a good deal of the time learning all the different pieces and producing poetical verses spontaneously (a process called *muud toh kong sod*). The lyrics of pieces, based on particular themes, must be created and improvised quickly during a performance. This requires an actor who is highly talented and quick to think and create the appropriate lyrics on the spot. Among the themes used in these lyrics are the natural environment, social issues, religion, the economy and politics. The success of a good menora actor depends on his presentation of a good rendition of the songs and dances, and also on his ability to deliver spontaneous and interesting lyrics (the muud toh) to keep the attention of his audience.

Some actors who are less than expert in improvising the muud toh sing poetical lyrics composed beforehand by the head of the troupe. This type of memorized muud toh is called *klong* or *phuuk*, which is the main kind of muud toh heard among the menora troupes in Malaysia today.

Texture, Melody and Rhythm Like the folk music of many Malay genres, the polyphonic music of the Thai menora is linear in concept and texture. The melodic lines are played on the pi shawm or other melody instrument, while the rhythmic strata in the music is played on the tab and klong drums. The third layer of sound is the colotomic unit played on the time marking instruments, including the krek bamboo clappers, the ching finger cymbals and the mong gong-chime (see the score in Example 1.31).

In the sample of music shown in Example 1.31 the melodic lines are based on an anhemitonic 5-tone scale with two minor 3rd gaps. Other pentatonic scales are used in other types of pieces. The short melodic phrases are repeated throughout a piece as are the drum rhythmic patterns. Iterative structures are typical in the music.

The drum patterns are structured in repeated 8-beat units, with the tab goblet drum providing the specific pattern and the klong stick-hit barrel drum marking many of the main downbeats in an 8-beat phrase (see Example 1.31).

Example 1.31 The opening bars of *lagu cerita bermula* **[piece to begin the story].** (Transcribed by J. Yeoh)

The colotomic unit is typically 4-beats long and is repeated over and over, providing the time framework for the percussive patterns and melody. The mong follows the 2-beat stress pattern (weak stress/high pitch on beat 1 followed by strong stress/low pitch on beat 2) heard in some Malay music genres using the canang. This 2-level stress unit is further supported by the ching cymbals and the krek clappers, both of which stress the second of a 2-beat unit (see Example 1.31, the ching and krek parts on beats three and four of each bar). The overall effect is an end-accented 4-

beat pattern in the colotomic unit. This phenomenon is also typical of some traditional Malay music genres, and points to a borrowing of musical traits across cultural lines and national boundaries alike. In fact, several musical instruments and pieces from the Malay shadow play and Makyung theaters are commonly used in the menora as performed in Kelantan.

Notes

1   The Javanese gamelan for shadow play is tuned in the *slendro* system and features hanging knobbed gongs (the *gong ageng, gong suwukan* and the *kempul*) and other horizontal knobbed gongs (the *kenong, ketuk* and *bonang*). Nearly all the knobbed gongs function as time markers in the music, signifying the musical forms such as those called *sampak, srepegan* and *ayak-ayak*, the three main musical forms used in the Javanese shadow puppet play. In contrast, the metallophone instruments such as the *saron, demung, slentem* and the *gender*, as well as a xylophone called *gambang*, are used to produce main and ornamented melodies in the music. See further Hardjowirojo, *Sejarah Wayang Purwa* (Jakarta, Balai Pustaka, 1968), and Judith Becker, ed., *Karawitan Source Readings in Javanese Gamelan and Vocal Music*, 3 Vols., Michigan Papers on South and Southeast Asia. (Ann Arbor: University of Michigan Press, 1984-86).

2   The foods include parched rice, tumeric rice, eggs, bananas and betel nut, all of which are laid out on a tray and offered to placate the spirits who, in turn, will ensure a good performance.

3   The slightly cone-shaped body has a bell-shaped base end called the *kecopong*, a separate piece attached to the body. There are six or seven finger holes on the front and one thumb hole on the back side of the body. The quadruple reed is fitted onto a small metal tube at the top of the instrument with a small lip-disk located just below the reed. Further details on the construction of this instrument may be found in P. Matusky, *Malaysian Shadow Play and Music* (Kuala Lumpur and Penang: Oxford University Press and The Asian Centre, 1993 and 1997).

4   Ghulam-Sarwar Yousof, *The Kelantan Mak Yong Dance Theatre* (Ann Arbor: University Microfilms, 1976). Today the Pakyung role is also taken by male performers in makyung groups found in south Thailand (Patani region).

5   See Ghulam-Sarwar Yousof, *Panggung Semar* (Kuala Lumpur: Tempo, 1992).

6   For further details see Tan Sooi Beng, *Bangsawan, A Social and Stylistic History of Popular Malay Opera* (Singapore: Oxford University Press, 1993).

7   For further information on the origin of the boria see *Boria* (Kuala Lumpur: Kementerian Kebudayaan, Belia dan Sukan, 1980), pp. 8-12.

8   An analysis of the music and musical instruments of the boria may be found in Toh Lai Chee, *Boria: Perkembangan Mengikut Peralihan Masa* [The Boria: Development through Time], BA Thesis, Universiti Sains Malaysia, 1998.

9   There are two other types of Chinese puppet theater in Malaysia: the marionette puppets that are moved with strings, and the rod puppets moved using three rods.

Chapter 2

Music of the Major Dance Forms

The Malaysian musical traditions that accompany dance or dance drama without dialogue and singing exist as classical music or folk music. Two forms of music and dance considered to be strictly classical art traditions are the *tari asyik* from Kelantan and the *joget gamelan* from Pahang and Trengganu. In earlier times both of these forms developed in the sultan's palace and still retain highly refined characteristics to this day. Furthermore, these forms were performed by artists who were specifically trained to dance and play the musical instruments.

Aside from the two above noted traditions, other forms of dance and music existing in the palace, and also in the villages, are the Javanese *gamelan*, the *tarinai* and the *zapin*.

The classical Javanese dance is accompanied by the Javanese gamelan, which is performed by peoples of Indonesian ancestry in the state of Johore. This dance form and its music essentially retain the main characteristics of the Javanese tradition in Indonesia. The Javanese gamelan was brought to Peninsular Malaysia by peoples of Javanese descent during European colonial times and possibly earlier. Referred to as *karawitan*, this musical tradition is part of the complex of Javanese arts, which also includes dance (*tarian*), shadow puppet play (*pedalangan*) and vocal music (*sekar*) (Becker (ed), 1984-86). Several dance and theater forms, including the shadow puppet play, the dance drama, the *barongan* masked dance, the *kuda kepang* dance and other forms, which are accompanied by the music of the Javanese gamelan, were also brought to Peninsular Malaysia by the Javanese immigrants who came to settle and work in the south of the peninsula. In the southern states of Selangor and Johore (and also in Singapore) the various forms of Javanese dance and theater are still performed with the accompaniment of the gamelan.

In the northern state of Kedah the tarinai is accompanied by a small ensemble known as the *gendang keling* (or, today, the *gendang tarinai*). This dance and music was performed in the palace in former times but today exists only as a folk tradition in the villages and small towns. In the state of Kelantan a form of tarinai is performed that is different from the Kedah style. It is performed only in the villages as a folk art.   Another dance form that is found nurturing in both the folk and classical settings is the zapin dance and music.   Formerly found in the sultan's palace and in the small villages, the zapin today exists as a dance with accompanying music that is well known among nearly all communities throughout the country.

The *sumazau* dance from Sabah, and the *ngajat* and *datun julud* dances from Sarawak originated in the folk tradition and are still performed in the villages of those states.   Today, these dances and music are also performed in many different social contexts and for official state ceremonies in the urban centers.

The lion dance, a folk form, is very popular among the Chinese communities in both the villages and urban areas of Malaysia.   It is performed today for social gatherings and to celebrate the Chinese New Year.

Joget Gamelan

The music and dance that developed in the Malay palace setting as an art or classical tradition is called the *joget gamelan*.   The dance is accompanied by music played on the Malay gamelan [*gamelan Melayu*].

In the 18th century (and perhaps earlier) a dance tradition and its gamelan music was known to exist at the Riau-Lingga palace.   In 1811 the royal family of Riau-Lingga and the family of a high court official (*bendahara*) of Pahang celebrated a royal marriage.   In this celebration the instruments of the gamelan and the dancers moved from the Riau-Lingga palace to reside in the Pahang court.   By the middle of the 19th century the gamelan music and dance developed at the Pahang court and became known as the *gamelan Pahang* or the *joget Pahang*.   Several gamelan instruments still exist from this period and are exhibited in the Palace Museum in the town of Pekan in Pahang.

Early in the 20th century the Pahang gamelan and the group of dancers at the palace were moved to the Trengganu court to celebrate another royal marriage.   In 1913 the Sultan Sulaiman from Trengganu married Tengku Mariam, the daughter of the Sultan of Pahang.   The Tengku Ampuan Mariam was experienced as a dancer in the joget gamelan tradition and for her wedding the orchestra, musicians and dancers moved to the Maziah Palace in Kuala Trengganu.

From 1913 to 1942 both the king and queen of Trengganu were active in developing and patronizing the joget gamelan.   It was during this time that certain aspects of the music and dance differentiated the Malay style from the original Javanese model of the 19th century. These aspects included the dance movements, costume, the change in the tuning system for the musical instruments, the instrumentation of the orchestra, and also the use of melodies not originating from the Javanese tradition. As a result of these changes the musical tradition changed its name to 'gamelan Melayu' and 'joget gamelan'. These terms are used to this day to refer to a music and dance tradition that developed in the context of the Trengganu court. In former times, under the patronage of the king, the joget gamelan functioned as entertainment for the nobility during the crowning of a new sultan, for birthdays, engagements, marriages and to welcome and honor official state visitors.[1]

Although performances of this form stopped during World War II, it was revived in the 1960s and developed further, but outside of the palace and without the patronage of the sultan (Plate 2.1). Today the joget gamelan is performed for a number of purposes including entertainment for the general public, during official state celebrations, and for new dance dramas and compositions. The Malay gamelan along with new and old compositions may be heard today at most institutions of higher learning in the country including the National Arts Academy in Kuala Lumpur.

In earlier times the repertory of the joget gamelan consisted of about 50 musical pieces and dances, but today much of the old repertory has been lost and forgotten. All the dances are entirely interpretive in that the dance movements themselves explain the activity or intention in a given story. The stories, then, based on the Panji tales, epics and folk stories, are presented through dance with music.

Each dance has its own specifically named musical piece. For example, the dance called *Timang Burung* (which portrays a princess who catches a bird and her ladies-in-waiting who dance imitating the movements of the bird) is accompanied by the piece that is also called *Timang Burung*. A given dance drama may be created based on a certain story using several different dances and tunes from the repertory. In this tradition women are the dancers while men are the musicians in the orchestra. All performers are trained for many years before they are considered able to perform well. Today composers also compose tunes and new compositions for the Malay gamelan in the context of dance dramas, instrumental pieces and vocal pieces with instrumental accompaniment (see further Chapter 6 --- Contemporary Art and Popular Music).

Plate 2.1 *Joget gamelan* **dancers performing a traditional piece on a public stage.**

The musical instruments

The basic Malay gamelan consists of eight different instruments. From the idiophone classification we find the *saron barung* (medium size saron) and the *saron panerus* (small size, also called the *peking*), the *gambang kayu, kerumong, kenong, gong suwukan* and *gong   ageng*.   The only membranophone in this gamelan is the double-headed barrel drum called *gendang*.

Each of these instruments has a specific function in the music. For example, the medium-sized saron instrument plays the main, unornamented melody in the musical pieces. At the same time the small-sized saron, the gambang and the kerumong duplicate and enrich the main melodic part with ornamentation. The large gongs such as the kenong, gong suwukan and the gong ageng function as time-markers in the music system, and the gendang drum is used to play specific rhythmic patterns.

Gong   The gong ageng and the gong suwukan are a pair of large gongs made of bronze (Figure 2.1). These two gongs hang vertically from a wooden rack. Both are knobbed and measure about 70-80 centimeters in diameter (this size is rather small when compared to the gong ageng in the Javanese gamelan). They produce specific pitches when hit on the knob with a padded beater. The gong ageng (also called *gong agung*, [great gong]) has the lowest pitch in the orchestra while the gong suwukan produces a pitch about a semitone or a whole tone above that of the gong ageng. Both of these gongs play the colotomic unit, or gong unit, in the music and function as markers of time, signifying the musical forms of the various pieces.

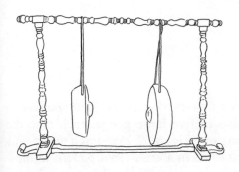

Figure 2.1 *Gong ageng,*
Gong suwukan

Figure 2.2 *Kenong*

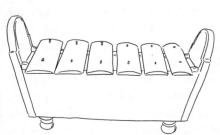

Figure 2.3 *Saron barung*

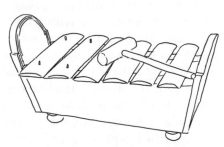

Figure 2.4 *Saron panerus*
(peking)

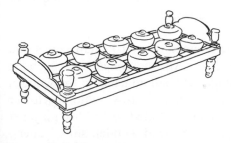

Figure 2.5 *Kerumong*

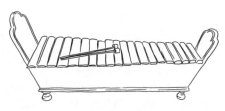

Figure 2.6 *Gambang kayu*

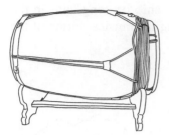

Figure 2.7 *Gendang*

Kenong The kenong also functions as a time-marker in the joget gamelan music system. This instrument consists of five large gongs, each placed horizontally in a wooden box resonator (Figure 2.2). Each gong is suspended from thick cord which is attached in a criss-cross pattern to the wooden box. Thus, the knob of the gong faces upward. When struck on the knob with a padded stick beater, each gong sounds out a specific pitch.

Saron The instrument that plays the melody in the joget gamelan pieces is the saron. In the Malay gamelan there are two sizes: the medium size instrument with a middle register is known as the saron barung (Figure 2.3), and the small size with a high register is called the saron panerus or the peking (Figure 2.4). The saron barung plays the main, unornamented melody in the musical pieces, while the saron panerus produces the same melody in an ornamented form (usually by playing double notes per beat).

All the above metallophones consist of six bronze keys that are tuned in the 5-tone pentatonic scale shown below. The keys are laid on top of a hollow, wooden box that serves as the resonator of sound. The bronze keys are struck with a beater in the shape of a hammer made either of wood or water buffalo horn. The playing technique for this instrument involves striking a given key, then hitting another key while simultaneously dampening the first key with the other hand (the two hand movements of damping and striking the keys occur simultaneously).

Kerumong The kerumong gong-chime is made up of 10 small gongs laid horizontally in a wooden rack (Figure 2.5). All the gongs are suspended on thick cords strung in a parallel arrangement and attached to the wooden rack. The small gongs are placed in two parallel rows with the lower octave of gongs closest to the player, and are tuned to the 5-tone joget gamelan scale. When struck with a pair of padded wooden stick beaters, each small gong produces a specific pitch, in low or high octaves.

Gambang The gambang is a xylophone made of a hard wood (Figure 2.6). About 28 wooden keys (made of woods such as jackfruit, *belian* and so on) are laid across the top of a hollow, wooden box that serves as the resonator of sound. The tonal range of this instrument is about three and one-half octaves, which reflects the low, middle and high registers found among all the instruments in the gamelan.

The wooden keys are struck with a pair of beaters in a special shape. The beaters consist of a long, thin straight handle made of water buffalo horn with a small wooden, padded disk at one end that is struck against the wooden keys. When hit with these beaters the wood keys sound out the specific pitches of the tuning system for the joget gamelan. The gambang plays an ornamented form of the main melody in the music.

Gendang The gendang is basically the same as the gendang found in the wayang kulit and makyung ensembles and was described earlier in Chapter 1. In the gamelan, however, the single gendang is often propped up on a stand while it is played (and see Figures 2.7 and 1.5).

Joget gamelan music

Tonal system Historically, it is possible that the tuning system for the Malay gamelan originated from the *slendro* (5-tone, equidistant) tuning system found in the Javanese gamelan. Hence, the notation system used to write down the joget gamelan tunes is based on the *kepatihan* notation system from Indonesia. In this system the successive pitches in the slendro scale (from the lowest to the highest tone) are numbered 1, 2, 3, 5 and 6. This numbering system is used today to notate joget gamelan pieces.

The tuning system for the Malay gamelan may be illustrated using the tones found on the oldest gamelan in Malaysia today (some of the instruments of this orchestra date from the Pahang period of the early 19th century). The instruments of this gamelan are still to be seen in the Palace Museum in Pekan, Pahang and exhibit a 5-tone tuning system, which has probably been adapted from the slendro parent tuning system from Indonesia.

The Malay gamelan has a pentatonic scale consisting of specific intervals.[2] As shown in Example 2.1, the nearly major 2nd intervals (200 Cents) are found between pitches 1 and 2, 2 and 3 and 5 and 6. Between pitches 3 and 5 there is a neutral 3rd (about 350 Cents, that is, a 3rd that is not major (400 Cents) and not minor (300 Cents). The special distinguishing characteristic found in the tuning system for the Malay gamelan is the use of the neutral 3rd interval between the pitches 3 and 5.

This interval is sometimes found in some slendro gamelan, and occurs in many kinds of folk music throughout the world.

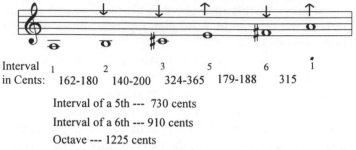

Interval   1   2   3   5   6   i
in Cents: 162-180   140-200   324-365 179-188   315

Interval of a 5th --- 730 cents

Interval of a 6th --- 910 cents

Octave --- 1225 cents

Example 2.1   The pentatonic scale of the Malay gamelan.[3]

The 5-tone scale found in the Malay gamelan serves as the tonal basis for all melodies in the repertory. Often the pitches 2, 3 and 5 of the scale are used as the pitch centers and as the ending tones for the various pieces. The particular pitch centers for given pieces is noted below in the discussion of the respective pieces.

Melody   In general the melodic motion is conjunct in joget gamelan tunes. To develop a melody, a melodic phrase in a piece is sometimes repeated several times with variation, or the melodic phrase may be repeated at a different pitch level from its original rendition. These two techniques to develop a melodic line are found in nearly all joget gamelan pieces. A clear example is the piece entitled *Timang Burung* (Example 2.2a) in which the first two   phrases (*a* and *b*) are immediately repeated (sometimes with slight variation) to comprise phrases 3 and 4 of the piece (Example 2.2a, staves 1 and 2). The pitch center for this piece is pitch 5 (that is, the pitch *e* in the transcription).

a) *Timang Burung*

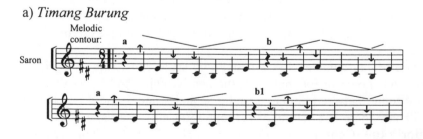

b) *Ayak-Ayak* (tune 1, transition, tune 2)

c) *Perang*

Example 2.2 Excerpts of melodies from *joget gamelan* pieces.

Balance and symmetry are important features found in almost all melodies in the joget gamelan repertory. Symmetrical phrases usually involve two parts (or motifs) of the same size which often exist in mirror imagery. The characteristic of balance also involves two parts (usually of the same size), but these two parts may stand in opposition or contrast to each other and, yet, may comprise one complete musical idea or statement.

Balance in the music may also involve two different phrases existing in an antecedent and consequent structure in which the answer (or consequent) explains and completes the antecedent part. For example, in the piece *Timang Burung* the melodic phase *a* is answered and balanced by the phrase *b*, while the melodic contour of phrase *a* is 'descending-ascending' and the contour of phrase *b* is the opposite (see Example 2.2a, melodic phrases *a* and *b*).

In the piece entitled *Ayak-Ayak* the melodic structure is balanced, with the first phrase *a* standing in contrast to the phrase *b* (see Example 2.2b). In this piece the phrase *a* begins with a rest and its contour is 'ascending-descending'. These features contrast with the melodic phrase *b* that begins with a pitch and not a rest and has a 'descending-ascending' contour (see Example 2.2b, melodic phrases *a* and *b*, and their variations *a1/b1* and *a2/b1*). The pitch center in this piece is pitch 5 (pitch *e*) of the pentatonic scale.

The melody in the piece *Perang* (see Example 2.2c) is symmetrical, with each melodic phrase, *a* and *b,* consisting of 4 beats with an 'ascending-descending' contour. In addition, balance in mirror imagery may also be seen here in the intervals used in the two phrases (phrase *a* has 3rds followed by 2nds, while phrase *b* has 2nds followed by 3rds).

Musical Form   In the joget gamelan repertory the different musical forms are based on a colotomic unit that is cyclical in nature, and structured by the subdivision of the unit in a binary way by the sounding of specific gong tones on specific beats. This time unit is repeated throughout a piece (see also wayang kulit Kelantan and makyung music in Chapter 1).   The instruments that signify the gong unit in this case are the gong ageng, gong suwukan and the kenong.   The length or number of beats of the gong units in traditional Malay gamelan music are always a multiple of two, and each unit is underpinned by a 2-beat stress unit (weak/strong stress).

The smallest colotomic unit in the music consists of 4 beats marked by the kenong and the gong suwukan.   Both of these instruments are played on beat 4, the final beat of the unit.   This gong unit and musical form is shown in Example 2.3 in an excerpt from the piece entitled *Perang*.

In this piece the gong ageng (lowest tone) is played only in the final gong unit when the music comes to an end.

Key to the symbols in Example 2.3:

1, 2, 3, 5, 6	= pitches in the Malay gamelan tuning system
∩	= one stroke on the gong suwukan
N	= one stroke on the kenong
O	= one stroke on the gong ageng
[ ]	= repeat sign
. 3	= a rest sign and pitch in quaver note values

Example 2.3 The musical form and excerpt of the melody from the piece *Perang*. (shown in cipher and standard notation)

Based on the repertory that is still known and played, other gong units consist of 8, 16, 32, 64 and 96 beats. For example, the piece *Ayak-Ayak* uses two different gong units in the entire dance piece: the first unit is 16 beats long while the second is eight beats.

As shown in Example 2.4a and b, the form in the 16-beat gong unit is marked by the kenong (sounding on beats 4, 8, 12 and 16), the gong suwukan (sounding on beat 8) and the gong ageng (on beat 16). In this dance piece the overall sequence of gong units and melodies follow the dance steps and sequences. Hence, the piece consists of several 'tunes' or melodies that are repeated a number of times, with a number of transitions in between each of the different 'tunes'. In the early part of the piece each tune and transition is based on a 16-beat gong unit (Example 2.4a-b), while in later 'tunes' the colotomic unit becomes 8 beats in length with a different internal structure (Example 2.4c).

a) The 16-beat gong unit and the musical form:

b) Excerpt of tune 1 in the piece *Ayak-Ayak* (16-beat gong unit):

<pre>
        N   N   N   N
                           ∩   O
[.   .5̄   3̄ 5̄   6   6   6   3   5   6 5 3 2   3 2 3 5]
</pre>

c) Excerpt of tune 4 in *Ayak-Ayak* (8-beat gong unit):

<pre>
                   N   N
                   ∩   O
      [3̄ 5̄   6   3   5   3   2   3   5]
</pre>

Example 2.4 Melody and form in the piece *Ayak-Ayak* (tunes 1 and
4). (Key to symbols: see Example 2.3 above)

In the joget gamelan repertory, other pieces are based on different gong units and forms, but a specific gong unit always functions as the framework or guide for the structure of the melody and the drum rhythmic patterns.

Rhythm When playing the drum rhythmic patterns in joget gamelan music, the drummer uses at least three different timbres. These sounds are vocalized by many drummers using the syllables 'bung', 'dung', and 'tak'. The timbre 'tak', a rather high and sharp sound, is produced on the small drum head when it is struck by the player's hand in the middle of the head. The two sounds 'bung' and 'dung' are played on the large drum head, which is hit with the right hand in the middle and the edge of the skin, respectively. The timbre 'dung' is heard as a damped, low- register sound (thud-like), while the timbre 'bung' is also of low register, but with a resonating quality.

Using these three timbres the gendang player performs specific rhythmic patterns for each of the pieces in the joget gamelan repertory that accompany the melody as well as the dance movements and steps. Generally, the rhythmic patterns are structured in 4- or 8-beat phrases following the section of the colotomic unit marked by the kenong or the large gong. The drum rhythmic pattern may be repeated several times to complete the length of the complete gong unit in the specific music.

An example of a 4-beat rhythmic pattern played in the time of a 4-beat gong unit is found in the piece *Perang*. The gendang is played at the quaver note level, while the melody and the time-marking instruments are played in crochet notes (see Example 2.5a). In this piece the length of the gendang rhythmic pattern follows the 4-beat gong unit and musical form (see Example 2.3a). This percussive pattern begins with a half-beat rest and alternates the two timbres 'dung' and 'tak'.

a) the 4-beat drum rhythmic pattern and colotomic unit in the piece *Perang.*

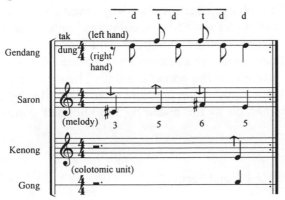

b) an 8-beat drum pattern used in the pieces *Ayak-Ayak* and *Timang Burung.*

Example 2.5 Drum rhythmic patterns in *joget gamelan* music.

There are also many different 8-beat rhythmic patterns in the Malay gamelan repertory, and these 8-beat patterns are usually structured in two short, contrasting 4-beat phrases (*a,b*). For example, the two 4-beat motifs in Example 2.5b use different note values (motif *a* features quavers while motif *b* consists only of crochet notes). These two motifs usually stand in contrast to each other in an 'antecedent and consequent' relationship.

Some 8-beat rhythmic patterns are used to emphasize the connection from one melodic line to another melodic line, while other 8-beat patterns serve as cadences to conclude a piece. In any case, the gendang rhythmic pattern follows the dance steps and phrases, the gong unit and the melody.

In general, the musical forms in the Malay gamelan repertory are based on the structure of the gong unit. There is a strong possibility that the forms in the gong units reflect the structure in the dances of the joget gamelan repertory, although no published documentation is available to support this observation. The polyphonic stratification in this music gives great importance to the melody, which is always symmetrical and balanced in structure, and always underpinned by a colotomic unit. The melody occurs in a basic, unornamented rendition simultaneously with an ornamented version, thus producing a heterophonic texture. The percussive rhythmic patterns are played on the gendang drum. These rhythms follow the structure of the dance steps, gong unit and melody, while the musical form or gong unit is marked in the music by the knobbed gongs in the ensemble.

Tarinai/Terinai (from Kedah and Perlis)

The tradition of music and dance known as *tarinai* or *terinai* exists in the folk and, formerly, in the classical traditions in the northwestern states of Kedah and Perlis in Malaysia. The dances are accompanied by a small orchestra called the *gendang tarinai* [tarinai drums], or, formerly, *gendang keling* [Indian drums]. It is believed that this orchestra and its music originated in the Middle East and was brought to Malaysia by musicians from India.

Today the tarinai repertory is known by musicians in the northwestern Peninsular states and is taught to young players using a rote teaching method. The musical pieces accompanying the dances are performed at wedding ceremonies (especially for the ceremony of staining the bride's hands and feet with henna [*inai*]). The pieces are also performed for processions and as entertainment at official ceremonies in the cities and villages. Sometimes the dancers carry small plates with lighted candles in their hands while dancing.

Musical instruments

The exact origin of this tradition and the original instrumentation are unclear, but today the tarinai ensemble consists of two gendang drums, one or two serunai shawms and a pair of knobbed gongs hung from a wooden rack (Plate 2.2).

Plate 2.2 A *gendang tarinai* ensemble, showing two *serunai* players and the hanging gongs (background). (Photo by Norlidah Mohd. Jalaludin)

Gendang The gendang in the tarinai ensemble exists in two sizes, each with a rather short, cylindrical-shaped body tapering very slightly at the ends to allow for two drum heads of different sizes. The drum heads are attached to the body with rattan laces (similar to the gendang in the music for the wayang kulit). The small head is usually hit with a rattan beater while the large head is struck with the player's hand (Figure 2.8).

Figure 2.8 *Gendang tarinai (gendang keling)*

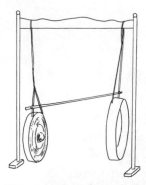

Figure 2.9 Shallow-rimmed gongs

The drum is held in a horizontal position on the player's lap so that the large head is on the player's right side while the small head (hit with the rattan beater) is at his left. The two drums, one slightly larger than the other, are always played by two different players in an interlocking style of drumming to produce resultant rhythmic patterns.

Serunai The serunai is a folk shawm. The body of the tarinai instrument is cone-shaped and is similar to the serunai found in the mekmulung ensemble (Chapter 1 and Figure 1.11). The serunai in both the mekmulung and tarinai has a short body and is smaller when compared to the serunai from Malaysia's east coast. However, the construction of the reed and the method of blowing the instrument are very similar in both the east and west coast types (see Chapter 1 --- wayang kulit and mekmulung).

Gong Compared to the tetawak, the gong in the tarinai ensemble is small (Figure 2.9), measuring about 50 to 60 centimeters in diameter, with a narrow rim and thin walls. Both gongs are struck on the knob with a padded beater, and two different pitches (about a Perfect 5th apart) are produced on these gongs.

The music

Like other genres of traditional music, the gendang tarinai music consists of melody played on the serunai, percussive rhythmic patterns played on the two gendang drums, and colotomic units played on the two gongs. However, in this music, the part that determines the musical structure is the gendang rhythmic patterns, and not the colotomic unit.

Colotomic unit Although the two gongs are used as time-markers in this music, in most pieces the gong tones follow and punctuate the ends of the drum rhythmic phrases and patterns. Hence, the length of the colotomic (or gong) unit is determined by the drum rhythmic pattern. In turn, the drummers follow the steps, movements and dance phrases of the tarinai dancer. In the colotomic unit itself, the high gong tone marks the ends of the short drum rhythmic phrases, while the low gong tone marks the end of the complete pattern. Example 2.6 outlines three typical colotomic units heard in tarinai pieces.

The examples show that the colotomic unit is continually repeated, that the low gong tone marks the final beat of a unit, and that the internal punctuation by the high gong tone does not necessarily take place in an even, regular, binary-oriented way (see Example 2.6b and c).

a) An 8-beat colotomic unit in the pieces *Permulaan* and *Senandong Sayang* (in these pieces the drum pattern consists of a 4-beat phrase followed by a contrasting 4-beat phrase).

```
[          g          G  ]   (high [g] and low [G] gong tones)
[    .  .  .  .  .  .  .  ]   (beats)
     1          4          8
```

b) A 32-beat colotomic unit from the piece *Selendang*

```
[                              g          g
[    .  .  .  .  .  .  .  .  .  .  .  .  .  .  .  .
     1          4          8          12         16
```

```
                              G          G  ]
     .  .  .  .  .  .  .  .  .  .  .  .  .  .  .  ]
                    24         28         32
```

c) A 28-beat colotomic unit from the piece *Bonda*

```
[                              g
[    .  .  .  .  .  .  .  .  .  .  .  .  .  .
     1          4          8          12
```

```
              g         g    g    G ]
. . . . . . . . . . . . . . ]
  16        20         24  26  28
```

Example 2.6   Colotomic units in *gendang tarinai* pieces. (Key: G-low gong tone, g-high gong tone, . -one beat in the colotomic unit, [ ] -repeated unit)

In some colotomic units, the high gong tone announces the approaching low gong tone that will occur on the final beat of the specific colotomic unit (see Example 2.6c, beats 24-26). It is interesting that frequently this high gong tone is played in a syncopated way, just before or after the downbeat on which it is expected to be heard.

In the colotomic units shown in Example 2.6, it is evident that the use of the gong tones is similar to their use in other traditional musical genres. However, the colotomic unit in tarinai music often is not structured in a binary way and does not obtain its specific form based on the regular, binary subdivision of the gong unit. Hence, the colotomic unit in tarinai music is used in a more general sense, that is, as the musical part that marks the end of a colotomic unit with a low gong tone and punctuates the drum rhythmic patterns usually with high gong tones.

Rhythm The rhythmic patterns played on the gendang drums are resultant patterns and are played in an interlocking style as described in the preceding chapter on wayang kulit and makyung music.

The large drum head on the small-sized gendang, is struck near the edge with the player's hand to produce a low yet resonant timbre. In contrast, the small drum head is hit with a light rattan beater producing a loud, sharp timbre.

The large gendang drum also produces specific timbres of sound. The large head on this drum is also hit with the player's hand near the center and the timbre is low and damped (similar to the timbre 'duh' in the wayang kulit and makyung drumming), while the small head is hit with a rattan beater.

Typically, the two gendang players beat out their own specific rhythms, and the timbres of the two patterns interlock to produce one complete rhythmic pattern, that is, a resultant pattern. In many pieces, the small gendang produces a 4-beat pattern in which the rattan beater begins on the upbeat and immediately stresses the following downbeat, while the drum strokes with the hand produce a rhythmic pattern consistently stressing the downbeat, such as:

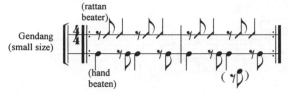

At the same time, the drum strokes with the rattan beater on the large gendang occur on nearly all the upbeats, while the hand beaten drum strokes produce a syncopated and highly ornamented pattern using the low timbre. The parts on these two gendang drums, played simultaneously, interlock to produce complete, resultant rhythmic patterns for all the pieces in the repertory.

Melody Many serunai melodies in the tarinai repertory are based on a heptatonic (7-tone) scale similar to the mixolydian mode. However, the pitch centers are usually found on the 4th or 5th scale degrees. As shown in Example 2.7, the pitch center for the piece *Bonda* is the 5th scale degree of the 7-tone scale.

Scale:

Example 2.7 Melody from the *tarinai* repertory.

The melodies basically consist of motifs that are repeated and chained together. In Example 2.7, a short excerpt from the piece entitled *Bonda*, the particular motifs are marked a, b, c, d and e. These motifs are repeated in various ways, including sequentially --- see motifs b and b1, in diminution --- motifs d/d1 and e/e1, or in augmentation --- motifs c/c1. These short melodic motifs feature conjunct melodic motion with a great tendency toward the most important pitches in the scale on which the tune is based. In Example 2.7, for instance, the motifs move mainly to the pitch *a* or to the pitch center *c*.

The melodies are also highly ornamented with trills (see Example 2.7, motif e), turns (motif b), appogiatura (motif e1), portamento (motif d/d1) and triplets (motif a/a1) which are fast moving in semiquaver or demisemiquaver note values. Although the melodies in the tarinai pieces use characteristic melodic ornaments similar to those in the wayang kulit or makyung repertories, in the tarinai music the use of a 7-tone scale and mainly non-microtonal intervals produce a nearly diatonic sound.

Tarinai of the east coast states

In several regions of the east coast of Peninsular Malaysia a dance called the tarinai is performed as entertainment at weddings and festivals in the villages. This form of the tarinai is danced by a solo dancer. To hold the attention of the audience the dancer incorporates movements and stunts similar to that of an acrobat. An appreciative audience will then contribute some coins or a paper bill of money to the dancer.

The tarinai ensemble accompanying this dance consists of two gendang drums (large and small sizes), two tetawak gongs, two small canang gongs, a pair of kesi cymbals and one serunai. This instrumentation and the music itself shows a mixture of elements from the wayang kulit, makyung and main puteri (healing ceremony) music ensembles from the local region.

The two gendang drums provide the particular rhythmic patterns, playing in an interlocking style just as in makyung music. The tetawak, canang and kesi serve as markers of time in the music, while the serunai provides the melodies in the various pieces. It is possible that the tarinai repertory to accompany the dances on the east coast is borrowed from the wayang kulit, makyung and Thai dance drama called *menora* (see Chapter 1).

Zapin

Zapin is a dance form introduced to Peninsular Malaysia by Arab communities that settled in the state of Johore before the 14th century C.E. For many years it was an exclusive tradition of the Arab-Malays (those of mixed Arab and Malay parentage) of Johore, but today it has spread throughout the Peninsula and is recognized as a national art form.

The two types of zapin dance and music recognized in Johore are referred to as the *Zapin Arab* [Arab zapin dance] and the *Zapin Melayu* [Malay zapin dance]. It is believed that both the Arab and the Malay zapin dances originated from the traditions of the Arabs from Hadhramaut on the Arabian peninsula located in the current day Republic of Yemen.[4]

The Zapin Arab is a robust and energetic dance and, today, is performed mainly by the Arab communities in Johore. Several elements in the performance of Zapin today echo the Hadhramic dance tradition. These include the linear formation of the performers who dance facing one another, the practice of rhythmically stamping the feet on the fourth beat of a 4-beat dance/music phrase, and a recurring forward and backward floor plan. In addition, there is the original solo vocal accompaniment in the form of a quatrain over a basic melody. Today the use of certain musical instruments such as the *ud* or *gambus* plucked lute, the *marwas* hand drums and the *dok* drum give the zapin a Middle Eastern flavor.

The Zapin Melayu originated as a result of cultural adaptation and assimilation from the Zapin Arab, and it is performed mainly by the Malays and Malays of Arab descent. The robust and energetic zapin of the Arabs with high skips, jumps and large stepping motions was changed to conform to the subtleties of controlled movements and the suppression of outward expression which is found in the Zapin Melayu. The lyrics of the songs may be in Malay or Arabic or both. The solo vocalist also plays the ud or gambus, and the musicians play interlocking rhythmic patterns on the marwas hand drums. The drummers also sing a refrain to indicate a change in the dance sequence and floor formation.

Two types of entertainment popular in Malaya in the 1930s and 40s, the *bangsawan* [Malay opera] and the *pentas joget* [public dance hall], were responsible for introducing the zapin to the general population, especially to the Malays all along the west coast of Peninsular Malaysia. The public dance halls were the main venues for such dances known as the *ronggeng, mak inang* and zapin along with Western cabaret dances and music. As noted earlier in Chapter 1, the bangsawan theatre, too, provided a stage for the development of the zapin dance and its music. By the 1950s the movie industry began to draw on the existing folk dance and music traditions, and the zapin dance and music in particular were taken out of the traditional village setting and served a new purpose, that is, as dance and music performed by movie stars and even chorus lines in the cinema. New dance motives introduced in the movies were imitated by zapin dance groups and this changed the course of zapin from a village tradition into a popular genre. The zapin in its new form became known nation-wide and today exhibits characteristics of its own which are quite different from the old village form.

The zapin dance serves both as secular entertainment and, to some extent, as religious celebration. The dance serves a secular purpose in that it is mainly folk entertainment traditionally found at wedding celebrations. In religious contexts, it was formerly associated with celebrations such as *Maulud Nabi* [birth of the Prophet Muhammad], *Hari Raya Puasa* [celebration at the conclusion of the Fasting Month], *Hari Raya Haji* [celebration for the return of those making the pilgrimage to Mecca] and *Maal Hijrah* [celebration of the Muslim new year]. It is notable that zapin was the only Malay dance tradition which was allowed to be performed in and near mosques and was performed only by men. Research into the history of zapin has shown that this dance and music was also found as entertainment for aristocrats in the sultanate of Riau-Lingga as early as the 16th century. The form developed under court patronage in Riau-Lingga and still, today, on the island of Penyengat the performers of the dance and music are descendants of the aristocratic class (Mohd. Anis Md. Nor, 1993).

The musical instruments

In its village or traditional setting, the melody of a zapin piece is carried by the vocalist, as well as the *gambus*, the violin, the harmonium or the accordion. The drum part is played on the *marwas* hand drums, often punctuated by an additional drum called the *dok*. In contrast to the village style, contemporary zapin orchestras found in the large urban areas use violin, accordion, gambus, and flute for the melody, while the dok, rebana frame drum and a tambourine are used to play the rhythmic patterns. The music of the contemporary zapin is also punctuated by a single knobbed gong. The violin and accordion used in the zapin ensemble are the Western forms of these instruments.

Gambus The gambus is derived from the Middle Eastern *ud*. Its short, fretless neck and wooden, pear-shaped body (rounded at the back) carry five to eight strings in double courses and a single high string. It is held horizontally in the player's lap and the strings are plucked with the fingers (Figure 2.10).

Harmonium The harmonium is borrowed from the Indian music tradition. It is an aerophone with free beating metal reeds, a keyboard and a pair of bellows operated by hand.

Marwas In a village orchestra the percussive rhythmic patterns in the music are played on the marwas hand drum, a double-headed, cylindrical drum with a very shallow body (Figure 2.11). The drumhead is about 16 centimeters in diameter while the body is about 12 centimeters in depth. The skins are attached to the body by laces of rope (nylon rope is frequently used today). The ropes are tied tightly to tighten the skin.

Figure 2.10 *Gambus*

Figure 2.11 *Marwas*

Figure 2.12 *Dok*

In performance the drum is held in one hand and only one head is struck using the fingers of the other hand. At least two different timbres are produced on this drum. These are obtained by striking the drumhead with the fingers in the middle of the drumhead or near its edge. In the Malay zapin the three or four marwas drummers play in an interlocking style in which each player contributes specific drum sounds on specific beats and in a given rhythm to produce a resultant rhythmic pattern.

Dok The second kind of drum in the Malay zapin ensemble is the dok (Figure 2.12). This drum has a cone-shaped body which is about 48 centimeters long. Only one drum head is attached to the body by rattan or rope laces. It is struck by the fingers of one hand while the other hand holds the body of the drum. The dok is used to punctuate only certain beats of a given marwas rhythmic pattern, often emphasizing upbeats (or offbeats). It provides greater dynamism to the already syncopated rhythmic patterns set up in the marwas section.

In contrast to the musical instruments in the village Malay zapin ensemble, the contemporary zapin orchestras found in the urban areas use additional instruments. In these urban orchestras the violin, accordion and gambus are retained, but often times the flute is added thereby enlarging the melody section of the orchestra. In the percussion section, the dok drum is usually retained, but the rebana drum, a tambourine and a single knobbed gong are added. The rebana is a single-headed frame drum in which the skin is attached to the body by rattan laces and made taut by wooden pegs inserted between the body and a cane ring located at the bottom end of the body. The drum is held upright in the player's lap and is struck with the hands. The gong used in the urban ensemble is usually the tetawak, a bronze, single-knobbed gong hung vertically and struck on the knob with a padded beater. The pitch of the gong is not necessarily related to the tuning of the other instruments in the ensemble or to the tonal center of a given piece. Its function is primarily that of a time marker in the music.

The music

The zapin dance is usually accompanied by vocal and instrumental music. Some contemporary zapin dance pieces use only instrumental music, and most of these pieces are available today on commercially produced audio cassettes and compact discs.

Melody and Scale The melodies of zapin pieces are sung by a soloist or played on the gambus, violin, accordion, flute or a combination of these, depending upon whether the style of the music and dance is village or urban (or contemporary). In the village style, the melody is usually produced by the same voice or instruments in every verse or strophe of a piece; however, in an urban zapin number the instruments may change from verse to verse.

The melodies generally are based on hexatonic or heptatonic scales which are either modal in nature or are diatonic major or minor scales. In Example 2.8a and b, the melodies of two different zapin pieces are shown, the pieces entitled *Gambus Palembang* and *Zapin Maulana*. As can be seen in the scales for each of the pieces, the melody for the *Zapin Maulana* uses a 7-tone scale similar to the hypodorian mode but based on the pitch *g*, the pitch center of the piece. In contrast, the piece *Gambus Palembang* uses a 6-tone scale with the interval of a minor 3rd at the beginning. In other respects this scale resembles a melodic minor scale on the pitch *c*.

a) *Gambus Palembang* (excerpt)
Scale:

b) *Zapin Maulana* (excerpt)

Scale:

Example 2.8 Melodies from *zapin* pieces.

Other modal scales as well as diatonic major and minor scales are found in other zapin pieces. The melodies are generally conjunct in motion, and some pieces encompass the melodic range of an octave or more. The melodic phrases are usually balanced in 2- or 4-bar units.

Rhythm and Form In most village style pieces the introduction section is an improvised melody in free rhythm called the *taksim*. This musical part accompanies the *sembah* or salutation dance phrase and is usually played on the gambus. The taksim is immediately followed by the traditional melody and zapin rhythm played by the gambus and the drum ensemble (see Example 2.8a, bar 9) In both the pieces, Gambus Palembang and Zapin Maulana, the familiar zapin rhythm in 4 beats is repeated within the various melodic phrases:

In the village style zapin the three marwas hand-held drums play a given rhythmic pattern, either in unison or in interlocking style. This is the main rhythmic pattern of the piece that accompanies the main dance motives. In the piece *Gambus Palembang*, for example, the three marwas drums play the main repeated 4-beat rhythmic pattern in unison. This pattern uses syncopation and is punctuated by the dok drum on the second half of beat 2 and on beat 4 as shown in Example 2.9a.

The piece *Zapin Maulana* also uses a 4-beat rhythmic pattern, part of which is played in an interlocking style (see Example 2.9b, marwas 2 and 3, beats 3-4). Other pieces in the repertory use a complex interlocking performance technique to produce resultant rhythms, which then comprise the main rhythmic patterns of given pieces.[5]

a) main rhythmic pattern of the piece *Gambus Palembang*

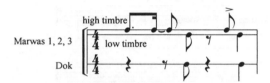

b) main rhythmic pattern of the piece *Zapin Maulana*

Example 2.9   Main rhythmic patterns for the pieces *Gambus Palembang* and *Zapin Maulana*.

Each piece ends with a coda or *tahtim* (also called the *wainab*) which utilizes an extension of the main melodic phrase and a new, loud drumming pattern called the *kopak*.

The kopak is played very loudly. The fingers and upper part of the palm are used to strike the center of the drum head to achieve a loud, sharp timbre. The kopak is usually played by the three marwas drummers in an interlocking style. It occurs at the end of each sung verse, and, as noted above, accompanies the final wainab section of the dance. This is a concluding section of a piece that features dance steps such as skips, turns, low *plie*, and standing and squatting positions.

The kopak drumming pattern can be 4 beats or longer. In the piece *Gambus Palembang* the entire kopak is only 6 beats in length (see Example

2.10a), while in the *Zapin Maulana* the 4-beat pattern is repeated three times to comprise the entire kopak of 12 beats (see Example 2.10b).

a) the *kopak* in the piece *Gambus Palembang*

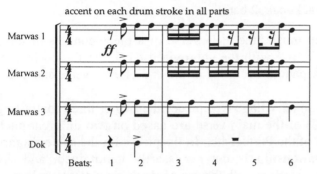

b) the *kopak* in the piece *Zapin Maulana*

Example 2.10 The *kopak* rhythmic patterns in *zapin* pieces.

The song texts or verses in all zapin pieces are sectional, found in either 2- or 3-part forms. As shown in the pieces *Gambus Palembang* and *Zapin Maulana* (Example 2.8a and b), the musical form consists of a *taksim* or other introduction, followed by two main contrasting parts, *AB*, which are further broken down into shorter musical phrases. These sections conclude with the wainab or tahtim coda. The overall form of the pieces given in the examples may be outlined as:

Gambus Palembang

(i)   Taksim, and introduction of the zapin rhythm
(ii) Part *A* (2 bars + 2 bars), pitch center *c*
      Part *B* (4 bar + 4 bars), pitch center *f*
(iii) Wainab/Tahtim (6-beat kopak) + melodic motif from *A* +
      Wainab.

Zapin Maulana

(i)   Introduction of zapin rhythm + kopak (2 bars)
(ii) Part *A* (4 bars + 4 bars), pitch center *d*
      Part *B* (2 bars + 2 bars), pitch center *g*
(iii) Wainab (4-beat kopak, 2 bars).

In some zapin music, the main verse of a piece consists of three contrasting sections (ABC) with the improvised taksim at the beginning, and the wainab kopak pattern occurring at the end of each verse and at the end of the piece.[6]

Furthermore, in all village-type pieces the two or three contrasting sections (AB or ABC) of the main verse are based on two different pitch centers at the interval of the Perfect 4th. In the pieces for the contemporary zapin this tonal relationship is not necessarily maintained, and the musicians take greater freedom with the use of rhythmic patterns, melodies and the tonal relationships within a given piece.

Ngajat and datun julud dances

Dance is an important means of expressing emotion and aesthetics in East Malaysian societies. Many different forms of dance abound among all the different ethnic groups in the East Malaysian states of Sarawak and Sabah. There are dances to act out specific activities or movements found in the natural environment as well as dances that are more abstract in nature.

In Sarawak the dance called *ngajat* [war dance], also referred to as the *ngajat lasan* among some groups, usually is danced by a solo male dancer among the Iban people, or by male or female dancers among the Kenyah, Kayan and Kajang communities. Today, a male dancer wears a loin cloth and decorated chest covering with an elaborate headpiece decorated with the feathers from the hornbill and other local birds. He also holds a traditional sword (*parang ilang*) and sometimes a shield (Plate 2.3). Female dancers wear an embroidered long skirt and top, a headpiece decorated with short bird feathers, and a cluster of long hornbill feathers attached to the top of their out-stretched hands. Among the Kajang, Kayan and Kenyah groups another dance is called the *ngajat asal* [lit., 'original war dance'], performed by two older women. While the ngajat dance usually involves a single dancer, the *datun julud* and line dances such as the *badek tiang* involve a group of dancers who step and move in unison.

The dances are accompanied by different ensembles. For example, the Iban ngajat dance is accompanied by the engkerumong ensemble, while the ngajat lasan and datun julud dances by the Kenyah and Kayan groups are accompanied by an ensemble of 2 *sape* lutes and one *jatung utang* xylophone. Sometimes the line dances performed by the groups who dwell in the interior of the state are accompanied only by singing or by the music of the *keluri* mouth organ.

The sape and jatung utang ensemble The sape (or, sapeh) is a plucked lute with a long body (about 1 meter or more) and a short neck (see Plate 2.4, and Chapter 4 for more details about this instrument). Usually three or four metal strings are attached from the end of the body to the tuning pegs (*otah*) at the end of the short neck. Several frets (*kiep*) are found beneath certain strings to tune the instrument for a particular piece.[7] The sape is held almost horizontally in the player's lap and the strings are plucked with the fingers. Some strings are used to play the ostinato or drone part in the music, while melody is played on a separate string. The sape is acknowledged among the Kayan and Kenyah peoples to be an instrument which is difficult to play well not only in terms of playing technique but also in the improvisation of a melody.

Plate 2.3 A *ngajat* dancer from the Upper Rejang River region, Sarawak.

When two sape are played as an ensemble, one instrument provides the melody and the other furnishes a drone or an ostinato (see Example 2.11b). If only one sape provides the music, then its player must provide both the drone and melody parts. In an ensemble of 2 sape and the jatung utang xylophone, usually one sape and the xylophone play the melody in unison (or nearly so), and the second sape provides the drone or ostinato (see Example 2.11a).

Jatung utang The jatung utang is a xylophone that may well be a recent addition to the ensemble of two sape to accompany dance, but the instrument itself is believed to have originated in Southeast Asia and dates from very ancient times.

Today, among the Kenyah and Kayan groups, the xylophone consists of 10 or more wooden keys (made of *keratong* or *jelutong* wood), which are tuned to specific scales. The wooden keys are strung together with thick string, which is then attached to a wooden box-like frame so that the keys hang over the box (see Plate 2.4). The keys may also be laid directly across the top of the 80 centimeter long box-frame which serves as a resonator. Two short wooden beaters are used to strike the keys. This instrument is usually tuned to a pentatonic scale without semitones, that is, an anhemitonic scale (see Example 2.11) (Matusky, 1986 and 1990).

Plate 2.4 Ensemble of *jatung utang* xylophone and two *sape*.

The music

The music for the ngajat lasan and datun julud dances consists of a melody played simultaneously with an ostinato or drone. In the above noted ensembles one sape plays the ostinato or drone part, while the other plays the melodic line.

Melody and Scale In the dance piece shown in Example 2.11a, the first sape and the jatung utang produce the 8-bar melodic line in unison (but an octave apart). In this melody, the first 4-bar phrase focuses on the low tetrachord (pitches *c-d-f*) of the pentatonic scale, while the second 4-bar melodic phrase is based on the upper tetrachord (pitches *f-g-a-c*) of the scale. Sometimes the sape provides a counter melody played simultaneously with the main melodic line by the jatung utang xylophone (see bars 17-20 in Example 2.11a), but the 4-bar + 4-bar structure is always maintained.

To support this 8-bar melody, the second sape in Example 2.11a plays an ostinato consisting of a repeated 2-bar phrase:

The ostinato pitch always gives a tonal referent and support to the 4-bar melody above it, moving to the base pitches of the upper or lower tetrachords, as needed.

Sometimes the ostinato at the upper tetrachord consists of the harmonic interval of a 3rd (the notes *f* and *a* played together, see bars 13-16 in Example 2.11a). The ostinato is repeated in a 4-bar unit (2 bars+2 bars as shown above), alternating pitches at the interval of a 4th throughout the music. The piece and ostinato finally end on the pitch center. The repeated 4-bar ostinato unit provides an 8-bar time phrase that is repeated throughout the piece and gives a time referent for the structure and organization of the melody (see Example 2.11a).

In the second ngajat piece, shown as Example 2.11b, the instrumentation is two sape lutes. The first sape provides the melody, while the second one plays the repeated ostinato figure. In this excerpt, two main melodic phrases (*a,b*) are presented, repeated and extended to develop the melodic line (Example 2.11b, bars 2-6 and 7-12). The pitch center of the piece serves as an anacrusis to begin the melodic line, which then proceeds to focus on a pitch level a Perfect 4th above it. In the end the melody returns to the pitch center.

The ostinato, a repeated 4-beat motif, stresses the final beat 4 with strong stress, and a harmonic interval (the pitch center and Perfect 4th above) on beat 4:

a) excerpt of a piece by two sape lutes and the jatung utang xylophone

b) excerpt from a piece by two sape lutes
Scale

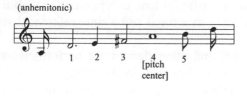

Example 2.11 Melodies from *ngajat* and *datun julud* dance pieces.

Generally, in dance music played on the sape and jatung utang, there is a focus on duple rhythm and end-accented rhythmic patterns. Melodies are based on pentatonic scales which occasionally are anhemitonic. In addition, melodies usually consist of different 4-beat motifs moving in terraced structures. These motifs are chained together and serve as the basis for improvisation in the melodic line. Melodies are usually accompanied by a drone or an ostinato that is repeated through a given piece. The ostinato serves mainly as a tonal and a time referent that is repeated over and over.

Today the ngajat, datun julud and other dances are performed as entertainment at weddings and other celebrations in the villages by the local performers, and in shows at hotels for tourists mainly in the urban areas.

The engkerumong ensemble The music to accompany the njagat war dance is played by the engkerumong ensemble among the Iban people of Sarawak. The engkerumong alone produces rhythm and melody, while the drum and large gongs reiterate and reinforce the rhythm.

Similar gong-chime ensembles in nearby Sabah and the southern Philippines are the kulintangan (in Sabah) and the kulintang (in the

Philippines). These two ensembles are used to play music for dance as well as to celebrate various occasions.

In the Sarawak longhouses, the engkerumong plays specific pieces for specific kinds of gatherings or events. For example, the high feast or festival (*gawai*) is accompanied by music known as the *'gendang gawai'* [lit., the drums for the high feast], and the ngajat dance is accompanied by *'gendang ngajat'* [lit., the drums for the war dance]. For celebrating the building of a new house the music repertory played is referred to as *'gendang berumah'* [lit., the drums for house building], and the music to accompany a wedding is referred to as *'gendang ngambi bini'* [lit., the drums for taking a wife]. Historically, female players are acknowledged as the especially skilled performers of engkerumong music, but today in the longhouses both men and women play the instrument.

Engkerumong The engkerumong is a gong-chime (Plate 2.5). It is an idiophone consisting of five to eight small, knobbed gongs[8] measuring 15-18 centimeters in diameter. They are placed horizontally in a single row in a wooden box resonator and are hit with a pair of wooden sticks (a soft wood is used).

Gong The two kinds of large, hanging, knobbed gongs in this ensemble are called the *tawak* and the *bandai* (Plate 2.5). Both types of gongs are hung vertically, each from its own rack, and are struck on the knob with a beater by two different players. The tawak is hit with a padded beater to obtain a resonant sound, while the bandai is usually hit with a wooden stick to produce a loud, sharp timbre. The tawak is a large, bronze gong with a wide rim and rather thick walls (see also tetawak in Chapter 1 --- Figure 1.1). The gong called bandai has a somewhat narrow rim and a medium-size diameter when compared with the tawak.

Ketebong The drum usually used in this ensemble is called *ketebong* (or *katebong*). It is a 'long drum' or 'waisted drum' with a body that tapers in the middle (Plate 2.6). The ketebong has one drum head attached to the body with rattan laces. Small wooden wedges are inserted between the body and the laces to tighten the drum head, which is struck with the player's hands as the instrument is held in a horizontal position in the player's lap.

Another kind of drum used in the engkerumong ensemble, especially among the Iban who live in the Saribas region, is called *dumbak*. This drum is cylindrical in shape with two drum heads attached to the body with rattan laces. Wooden wedges are used on this drum, too, to tighten the drum heads. It is held vertically or obliquely and hit with the player's hands.

Plate 2.5 The *engkerumong* ensemble of the Iban in Sarawak, showing the gong-chime (foreground, right), and *bandai* and *tawak* hanging gongs (background, left).

Plate 2.6   The Iban *ketebong* waisted drum (foreground) and the *bandai* hanging gong (background) in the *engkerumong* ensemble of Sarawak.

The music

The music by the engkerumong ensemble is polyphonic and consists of several independent musical parts that are arranged and heard in a linear way. Each instrument, the drum, engkerumong, tawak and bandai, provides a specific rhythmic pattern, all of which are related to one another in specific ways as noted below.

An important feature in this music involves the entrance of each instrument at a different time interval at the opening of the piece so that the specific entrances of the four instruments are staggered in time. As shown in Example 2.12, the drum begins the piece and the engkerumong enters at bar 2. Then the bandai gong starts at bar 3 and finally the tawak begins its part in bar 6.

Engkerumong music is based on rhythmic patterns. Although melody is produced because each gong is pitched, the tuning system for the large and small gongs is not standard and the pitches used are different from one ensemble to another. Also, the total number of gongs in the engkerumong may vary from five to eight which results in a variable number of pitches. Consequently, in this music the rhythm is very important, while the pitches and resulting melodies are less so.

In the music by the Philippine kulintang gong-chime ensemble, many rhythmic patterns known as 'rhythmic modes' have been identified and recorded. In Sabah and Sarawak, the music played by the gong-chime instrument also tends to focus on the performance of rhythmic patterns, although these patterns have not been systematically identified and documented as 'rhythmic modes'.

Example 2.12 *Gendang ngajat* [war dance music] by an *engkerumong* ensemble.

Rhythm and melody The rhythm generally is duple and the rhythmic patterns are played in an interlocking style by the drum, tawak and bandai. The basis of a piece is its rhythmic pattern that is usually introduced by the drum. In Example 2.12, the basic 4-beat drum rhythmic pattern is repeated with some variation such as:

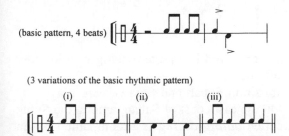

(basic pattern, 4 beats)

(3 variations of the basic rhythmic pattern)

(i)   (ii)   (iii)

The 4-beat rhythmic pattern is consistently end-accented by the timbre played, or the length of the note value, on beat 4.

The 4-beat drum pattern is taken up and played in the engkerumong part. Although the rhythmic pattern and the melodic motif by the engkerumong emphasize quaver notes on many beats, the 4-beat pattern and motif always stresses beat 4 with the repetition of the same pitch at the quaver note level on that beat (see Example 2.12, engkerumong part).

Many of the short melodic phrases in the engkerumong part are characterized by 'ascending-descending' contours as shown in Example 2.12, bars 4 and 6. These contours may be reversed and, even though the range of the melodic motif is somewhat narrow, a 'descending-ascending' pattern may be used as in bars 12-13.

Using the 4-beat melodic phrase structure, the given contours and the end-accent feature, the engkerumong player improvises rhythmic patterns and melodies starting in a low register on the instrument and then little by little rising to a higher register, and returning once again to the low register. The repetition of the rhythmic pattern and melodic motif and the time duration of the piece itself depends on the length of the dance it accompanies.

The rhythmic patterns that enrich and support the engkerumong part are played on the tawak and bandai gongs. Hit with a wooden stick, the bandai produces a sharp, loud timbre played on every other beat in the music. At the same time, the tawak produces a rhythmic pattern using a staccato style of playing. The tawak rhythmic pattern usually consists of a repeated 4-beat unit which imitates the pattern on the drum, but often with syncopation, such as:

Here the bandai and tawak parts are played in an interlocking way in order to produce resultant rhythmic patterns.

Other kinds of dance music in Sabah and Sarawak are played by different kinds of ensembles. On the east coast of Sabah, among the Suluk people, the music and dance called *daling-daling* is accompanied by an ensemble of a *gabbang* xylophone hit with a pair of padded beaters, and a pair of wooden sticks struck together (a concussion idiophone). In the interior regions of Sarawak among the Kenyah, Kayan and Kajang peoples, the group and line dances are performed to the accompaniment of songs sung by the dancers or with the music played on the *keluri* mouth organ (see Chapter 4 --- Mouth Organs). The ensemble of two sape alone or with the an added jatung utang xylophone is also used by the interior groups

Sumazau and magarang dance

The *sumazau* is a dance performed by the KadazanDusun people of the Penampang area and nearby plains on the west coast of Sabah. It is usually accompanied by a hanging gong ensemble, and is danced by pairs of men and women who wear the *sinambiaka* costume of black cloth decorated with locally made gold braid. The women wear *tangkong*, or three rows of small brass rings attached to rattan around their waists, with belts of 19th century Chinese dollars [*himpogot*]. The men wear colorful woven headcloths called *sig* or *sigar* that were originally made by the Iranun community and traded from the Bajau people on the coast further north.

The sumazau has two basic alternating body movements: at first the dancers shift their weight from one foot to the other, with knees bent and arms swinging by their sides in time to the music. With a cue from one of the men the dancers shift into the second posture, and dance on their toes with arms outstretched. The men move their arms with a gentle rolling motion, while the women move their arms, also outstretched but lower with bent elbows.

A similar dance type, the *magarang* (occasionally called *mongigol*) is found among the KadazanDusun of the Tambunan District in the interior. These people also perform another variant named *mangalai*. The term 'sumazau' is sometimes used for the dance *saazu* performed by the KadazanDusun of the Papar area on the west coast. This dance and its accompanying ensemble, however, vary somewhat from the typical sumazau performed in Penampang.

Like its counterparts in the interior, the sumazau has both a traditional ritual function and a celebratory role. In former times, the dance was performed at specific stages during certain ceremonies such as the *magang* performed following headhunting and for spirits inhabiting the *bangkavan* (skull collections). The dance also is a major component in the *kaamatan* or harvest festival in honor of the rice spirit, and is a feature of wedding celebrations and other important social gatherings.

The musical instruments

The sumazau dance from the Penampang area is usually accompanied by an ensemble named *sompogogunan*. This ensemble basically consists of six to seven hanging gongs of various sizes and names (Plate 2.7), and one double-headed drum called *gandang*. Very rarely, a *kulintangan* or gong-chime of eight or nine small knobbed gongs may also be in included in the ensemble (Figure 2.13). More frequently, however, a small metal nine-keyed metallophone is used (Figure 2.14). This metallophone is often named 'kulintangan' because its tuning and music follow that of the actual kulintangan.

Gandang The gandang drum is carved from a single piece of wood and has two heads of cowhide or goatskin that are bound to the body with cane hoops (Figure 2.15). Wooden tuning pegs are inserted into the cane at both ends. The gandang is usually placed more or less vertically and hit on one head with a stick covered with beeswax or with a hard piece of coconut frond stem.

Hanging gongs The hanging gongs are made from brass or sometimes bronze. Each has a name, which denotes the musical part that it plays. These names can vary from village to village, but for the purposes of this discussion, the sompogogunan of Kampung Guunsing, Penampang, will be considered. From the audience viewpoint, the instruments are arranged from right to left: *gandang*, then the hanging gongs *sasalakan*, *naanangong, hahambatan, hotungong, tontoongan* and *tatavag*. Each gong is struck with a stick covered with beeswax or rubber. The 'kulintangan' metallophone, if present, is placed in front of the hanging gongs, sometimes with the performer's back to the audience. This instrument is hit with two wooden beaters.

Of the hanging gongs, the first three noted above are of the type known in KadazanDusun as *sanang* (Malay, *canang*). These are relatively small gongs of thick brass with a single knob on the flat front surface, and a rim bent downward. The other three are heavy gongs of brass or bronze which are sometimes labeled 'tawag' in the interior KadazanDusun communities. They have a deep rim, and the front surface is raised near the center with a large single knob on the face of the gong.

Musical repertory

The music for the sumazau is often simply called 'sumazau'. Sometimes the verb *magagung* ('to hit a gong') or the phrase *magagung sumazau* is used, as is the noun *pogagungan*. This music consists of a rhythmic pattern of interlocking parts, beginning with the gandang and moving from the small sasalakan gong down to the tatavag. If present, the small kulintangan metallophone provides melodic ornamentation over the texture of the drum and gongs. There are no separate pieces for sumazau --- the same rhythmic pattern is repeated many times for as long as the dance sequence lasts (a music example may be seen in Chapter 3 --- Hanging Gong Ensembles).

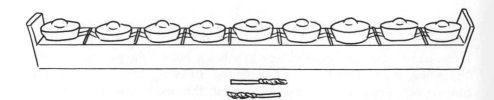

Figure 2.13 *Kulintangan* **(gong-chime)**

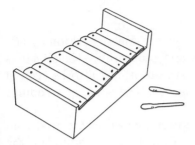

Figure 2.14 *Kulintangan* **(metallophone)**

Figure 2.15 *Gandang*

Plate 2.7 The *sompogogunan* hanging gong ensemble from the Penampang region in Sabah.

The Lion Dance

The lion dance is one of the most popular forms of Chinese performing arts in Malaysia, symbolizing harmony, peace and prosperity. Usually it is performed to celebrate the Chinese New Year, but it may also be seen at social gatherings such as the formal opening of a new shop, at weddings and at gatherings to welcome respected guests.[9]

The lion in this dance consists of a colorful paper mache head with moveable eyes and a body made of cloth. Two dancers manipulate the lion, the dancer at the front holds the lion's head and the dancer at the rear operates the body.

There are many legends about the origin of this lion. One popular theory says that the lion dance existed in the Tang Dynasty. At that time, the Chinese Emperor had opened China to foreign commerce, and traders from Persia brought two lions as a present to the Emperor because there were no lions in China. In earlier times the lions were purposely made extinct because they were wild and fierce. Eventually the two lions were tamed by a Buddhist monk at the command of the Chinese Emperor, and after they were tamed the two lions began to dance to entertain the Emperor.

The news of a lion which could dance spread throughout the land and everyone wanted to see it, but they were not given permission to do so by the Emperor. Consequently, the common people in the north and south of China created their own lion dance. Their dance was usually accompanied by a masked character playing the role of the monk who had tamed the two lions of the Emperor. Because the lions were a gift to the Chinese Emperor, the dance could only be performed at ceremonies expressing joy and thanks.

The lion dance was brought to Malaysia by Chinese immigrants in the 19th century. Today there are two kinds of lion dance in Malaysia: the south lion dance and the north lion dance.

The lion dance of the south is somewhat abstract and aggressive compared to the northern style. The body of the lion consists of a two and a half meter long piece of black, red, white, green and blue cloth and with many small bells attached to it. The colors of the southern style lion symbolize strength, agility and power or energy (Plate 2.8).

The head of the southern lion is associated with the four characters from the *Three Kingdoms* story. A head colored yellow and black with a white beard depicts Liu Bei who is remembered as a kind and generous person, while a head colored red and black with a black beard depicts Guan Ti who is known for his honesty. The black and white lion head with a black beard is associated with Zhang Fei, a general who is famous because of his braveness, and a multi-colored lion head with a white beard is associated with Zhao Zi Lung, famous for his cleverness and wisdom.

In former times, the southern lion dance performance went on for three or four hours. The dance experts of this tradition say that whenever the black bearded lion meets with a white bearded lion, the black bearded one must bow his head respectfully to the white bearded lion. But, if he meets with another black bearded lion then the two of them must fight.

In Malaysia today this story is shortened or ignored altogether. In fact, only one dance, the *Cai Qing* dance, is performed by the lion who goes from one house to another to perform during the Chinese New Year or for other celebrations. In the dance, the lion will wander here and there to look for food. The movements and positions of the body show many different emotions such as happiness, sadness or anger. The climax in the southern style lion dance is when 'the lion eats the green vegetables' (*qing*). This episode shows the skill of the dancer to get the vegetables and the *ang-pow* money put inside a small red envelope, which are tied to the end of a long pole that is secured or hung from a high place outside of the house.

When compared with the south lion dance, the northern style is more realistic physically. The north lion has a furry body, tail and feet. The fur is made from synthetic fiber and colored orange and yellow just as the real animal itself. The performance of the north lion dance consists of an acrobatic stage show and not a story. The north lion often jumps on a table or chair and walks on top of a large ball or see-saw.

Every lion dancer in both the south and north styles must train for at least six months before he has a chance to act the part of the lion. He must study the art of self defense and increase his stamina so that he can hold the lion's head which is about six to 10 pounds while balancing another dancer on his thighs when the lion stands on his back legs. The southern lion dancer must also train the position of his feet for stances known as The Horse Leg and Scissors. The north lion dancer must also be trained in acrobatic movements and the movements of a cat and dog so that he may imitate them in his performance. An apprentice also studies the music for the lion dance, for he may have to play the gong and cymbal parts in the music during a performance.

Plate 2.8 The southern style lion as found in Malaysia.

The lion dance group is operated like a martial arts or other sports club subsidized by donations and gifts that are collected during performances throughout the year.

The musical instruments

The *luo gu* percussion ensemble to accompany the lion dance implies the use of gong and drum. The musical instruments consist of the idiophones called *bo* (cymbals) and *luo* (gong) and the membranophone *gu* (large drum), which is called *che-ba-gu*. Sometimes two *luo* (*da luo* or large gong, and *xiao luo* or small gong) or two cymbals are played. Both the gong and the drum are struck with a wooden beater.

Luo The luo is a bronze gong with a thin rim (Figure 2.16). It is hung, and its flat, wide face is hit with a wooden beater. The player may place one hand inside the back of the gong to control the sound while it is played (see Figure 2.16 a-b).

Bo The bo is a set of cymbals made of bronze (Figure 2.17). The cymbals are held and struck together by the player (Figure 2.17 b). Two types of sound are produced --- a ringing sound and a dampened sound.

Gu The gu or che-ba-gu is a large barrel drum with one drum head at the upper end of the body. The body is made from wood about 60 centimeters in height and in diameter (at the widest part of the body). The drum head, made of cow hide with a diameter of about 58 centimeters, is nailed to the wood body with iron nails shaped like a triangle at the top end (see Figure 2.18a, Gu --- outside part). The bottom end of the body is left opened. Several metal springs are secured inside the drum as shown in the illustration (Figure 2.18b), and these springs give a special tone color to the sound of this instrument. The three basic kinds of timbres or sounds produced are: (i) a resonant and low sound when the drum head is hit in the middle, (ii) a sharp timbre when the drum is hit at the edge where the skin is nailed to the body; and (iii) a dampened timbre when the drum head is hit in the middle while applying additional tension with the other hand.

Lion dance music

In general, the lion dance music is percussion music in duple meter. The musical texture is polyphonic, with a drum part, a cymbal part and a gong part. The drum rhythmic patterns are closely tied to the movement of the lion. The piece entitled 'The Seven Star Rhythm' that accompanies the *Cai Qing* dance is a good example. The piece is divided into five parts following the movements of the lion (Example 2.13).

a) Playing method

b) The hand is placed behind the gong

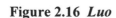

Figure 2.16 *Luo*

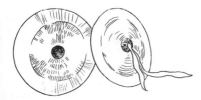

Figure 2.17a *Bo*

Figure 2.17b *Bo*, playing method

(outside view)

Figure 2.18a *Gu (Che-ba-gu)*

(note the metal wires)

Figure 2.18b *Gu*, inside view

Form and Rhythm The first part, A, begins with a percussion roll by the drum, cymbals and gong. The lion appears when the drum begins to play a rhythmic pattern in a specific tempo (Example 2.13, bars 5-17).

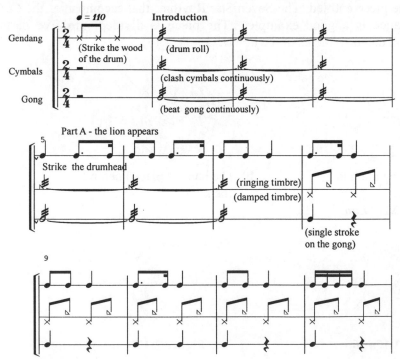

13

Part B - the lion bows 3 times

17

damped sound   (flexible meter)

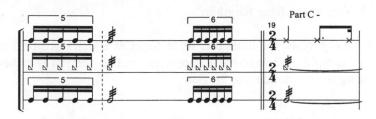

Part C -

19

- lion walks about looking for food

20

(strike wood of the drum

24

Example 2.13 The Seven Star Rhythm.

In the next part, B, the lion bows three times as a sign of respect to the audience (Example 2.13, bar 18). The meter in this section is rather flexible following the movements of the lion:

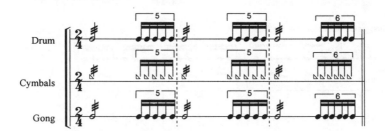

In part C the lion walks about and looks for food (see Example 2.13, bars 19-38). The rhythm played on the drum is based on a 4-beat pattern, which may be repeated in various combinations so that a long piece may be created (see Example 2.13). The rhythmic pattern from part A is also used here.

The 4-beat rhythmic patterns that are usually used to accompany the lion as he looks for food begin with a dotted rhythmic figure (see also parts A and C in Example 2.13). The possible rhythmic patterns, shown below in (a), (b) and (c), all begin with a dotted rhythm:

(a)

(b)

(c)

Other possible rhythmic patterns, noted here as (d), (e) and (f), begin with semiquaver notes :

(d)

(e)

(f)

Pattern (g) begins with syncopated rhythm:
 (g)

Throughout the piece the cymbals and gong play the patterns:

(a) cymbal rhythmic pattern:

(b) gong rhythmic pattern:

The percussion rolls by the drum, cymbals and gong are also played to arouse a feeling of restlessness, or when a difficult movement is executed by the lion.

In part D the lion finds his food (*qing*). The percussion roll by the drum, cymbals and gong happens again to set up a feeling of tension as the lion tries to climb or crawl up to eat the vegetables. The climax of the piece is when the lion snatches the vegetables and eats them. Then, the lion gives the food back to the head of the household.

Cai Qing, part D (flexible meter, the rhythmic pattern follows the movements of the lion):

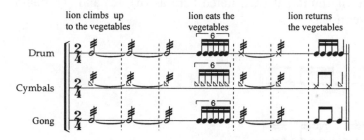

In part E the lion walks about again to the accompaniment of improvised 4-beat patterns such as in parts A and C. In part F the lion bows three times to the accompaniment of a percussion roll by the drum, cymbals and gong as in part B.

At the end of each part, the cymbals and drum are played in the same rhythmic pattern:

a) From Example 2.13, bars 15-17

b) After part D, *Cai Qing*

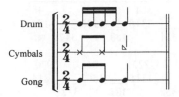

The drum player usually begins the piece with a sharp timbre played on the wooden rim of the drum (see Example 2.13, bar 1). The sound of the drum is also a cue to the cymbals and gong players that a new part or section will begin with a basic 4- or 8-beat pattern played softly or on the wood part of the drum (see Example 2.13, bars 5-7 and 19-20).

The lion dance is still performed in Malaysia, and today there are several hundred lion dance clubs throughout the country. These clubs have attracted the skill and interest of not only young Chinese men, but also the young Indian Malaysians. This is so because the lion dance develops the spirit of teamwork, cooperation, discipline and goodwill.

Notes

1   See also Marion F. D'Cruz, 'Joget Gamelan, A Study of Its Contemporary Practice', MA thesis, Universiti Sains Malaysia, 1982.

2   The pitch measurements are based on a report about the tuning system of the Malay gamelan exhibited in the Palace Museum in Pekan, Pahang (P. Matusky, 'Report on the Gamelan Research Project', Kuala Lumpur, April 1978, unpublished) which was submitted to the office of the Vice Chancellor for Research and Development, Universiti Sains Malaysia and the Culture Section of the Ministry of Culture, Youth and Sports in that year. All pitches on all instruments were recorded using the Uher 4000L tape recorder (open reel). Using the equipment in the Physics Laboratory at the Universiti Sains Malaysia, the recordings were played, pitch by pitch, and the sounds were channeled through an oscilloscope and oscillator, while a Counter recorded the specific measurements of the pitches in Hertz (Hz) (cps). Then each measurement in Hertz was changed to the Cents system, devised by Alexander J. Ellis. In the Cents system each semitone interval in the tempered tuning system of Western music has 100 Cents. One octave consists of 12 semitones (Western music) and, hence, one octave has 1200 Cents.

3   Pitch Measurements for the main instruments in the Malay Gamelan at the Palace Museum, Pekan, Peking.

<u>Pitch, Intervals and their measurements in Hertz and Cents</u>

Pitches:	1	2	3	5	6	1̇
Saron barung: Hz:	245	269	302	364	406	487
Cents:	632	794	994	1318	1506	1823
Interval in Cents		**162**	**200**	**324**	**188**	**317**
Saron peking: Hz:	490	541	598	727	811	970
Cents:	632	804	977	1315	1502	1814
Interval-Cents:		**172**	**173**	**338**	**181**	**312**
Kerumong: Hz:	489	272	294	363	403	963
(low octave) Cents:	629	809	948	1313	1494	1802
Interval-Cents:		**180**	**140**	**365**	**181**	**315**
Kerumong: Hz:	no gong	549	597	724	803	963
(high octave) Cents:		829	974	1308	1487	1802
Interval-Cents:			**145**	**334**	**179**	**315**
Kenong: Hz:	244			364	409	
Cents:	629			1318	1519	
Inteval-Cents:		**689**		**201**		

	Gong Suwukan	Gong Agung
Gong: Hz:	139	130
Cents:	851	735
Interval-Cents:	**116**	

4   Mohd. Anis Md. Nor, *Zapin, Folk Dance of the Malay World* (Singapore: Oxford University Press, 1993).

5   See also, the rhythmic pattern for the piece *Lancang Kuning* in Mohd. Anis Md. Nor, *Zapin*, pp. 64-7.

6   As in the piece *Lancang Kuning*, in Mohd. Anis Md. Nor, *Zapin*, pp. 63-9.

7   See also Virginia Gorlinski, 'Some Insights into the Art of Sape Playing', in *Sarawak Museum Journal*, XXXIX, No. 60 (New Series), Dec, 1988, pp. 77-104, and Peter Mulok Kedit, 'Sambe (Sape)' in Fumio Koizumi, ed. *Asian Musics in an Asian Perspective* (Tokyo: Heibonsha Ltd., 1977).

8   In *New Grove's Dictionary of Music and Musicians* (London: MacMillan, 1980) there are reports of the engkerumong gong-chime consisting of 8 gongs, but today the usual number is from 5 to 7 gongs.

9   The dance of the dragon is also performed in Malaysia. The dragon symbolizes good fortune and was a symbol of the Chinese Emperor. This dance is performed at celebrations to ensure prosperity and to welcome friends and guests.

Chapter 3

Music of the Percussion Ensembles

The types of percussion ensembles, their music and their uses are many and varied in Malaysia. As noted in the earlier chapters, almost all music ensembles are percussion-dominated, and many of those are associated with particular theatrical or dance forms.

Sometimes the music of certain gong-chime ensembles associated with dance, such as the caklempong and kulintangan (which actually accompanies both dance and the martial arts), also exists as music for general entertainment. In contrast, the music by the ensemble called the *gendang silat* [martial arts drums] in Kelantan accompanies only the martial arts. There are also percussion ensembles that exist independent of theater and dance, and these ensembles accompany work activities or special celebratory occasions and high rituals.

As noted in Chapter 2, the music of the Sabah hanging gong ensembles usually accompanies group dances such as the sumazau. Among some of the ethnic groups in Sarawak a similar kind of gong ensemble was formerly used to invoke spirits, but today it has lost that function. We now hear these ensembles accompanying processions, welcoming visitors to the longhouse, and providing music for entertainment at festivals and social gatherings. The hanging gong music for these occasions is discussed in the following pages.

Some percussion ensembles originated from agricultural activities, including the work of pounding rice. The implements for this kind of work eventually became the instruments of music making, and today this music is heard in the longhouses mainly for entertainment purposes, especially in the evenings when the inhabitants have returned to the longhouse from a day's work at the farm sites. The examples discussed here are the *kertuk kelapa* and *kertuk kayu*, the *antan* and *lesung*, the *tumbuk kalang*, and the *alu (alok)* and *tangbut*. In addition, various kinds of wood poles and bamboo tubes used as musical instruments are also discussed in the section on struck, stamped and stamping idiophones.

Among the drum ensembles, the music of the kompang groups is found in many contexts including processions for wedding celebrations and circumcisions, to accompany the singing of *zikir* and for processions at secular events such as greeting officials in state ceremonies and performing in competitions. A small ensemble of the very large *rebana besar* drums also accompanies the singing of *zikir* [texts in praise of Allah and the Prophet Muhammad] in Kelantan (see Chapter 4). In contrast, the *rebana ubi* drum ensembles are usually played in the villages of Kelantan as entertainment during the harvest season or at state festivals and other occasions.

A special ensemble associated with the sultan and played only for palace ceremonies is called the *nobat*. Made up of mainly percussion instruments, this ensemble and its music exist in the classical music tradition, making it unique in the realm of percussion music in Malaysia.

Gong ensembles

The knobbed gong is found in various sizes and forms throughout Southeast Asia. The gongs originating in the Archipelago are usually made of bronze and have thick walls, a deep rim and a knob on the center face of the gong. The gong is tuned and struck on the knob to produce a specific, focused pitch.

Archeologists have written that the earliest bronze gongs in Southeast Asia were made by inhabitants associated with DongSon and Hoabinhian cultures on the mainland. Factory sites have been identified where early bronze instruments and tools were made, and these bronze factories, associated with Hoabinhian culture, date from more than 3000 years before Christian times (Solheim, 1971). Although the so-called 'DongSon drum', the earliest bronze gong, was made on the mainland of Southeast Asia, the knowledge and technology of bronze and gong making eventually spread to the islands. By around 250 C.E. the bronze gong with a knob was made and used on the island of Java in the early gamelans.[1]

Centuries ago both Brunei and the island of Java were the centers of bronze knobbed gong manufacturing, but during the past several centuries the main gong factories have been located only in Indonesia on the island of Java. The gongsmiths and experts in gong making were located in the Central Javanese cities of Jogjakarta and Surakarta. The bronze knobbed gongs were never made in Malaysia, but it is believed that gongs were gotten from Brunei or Java in past times, while today Indonesia remains the main source for obtaining new knobbed gongs.

Caklempong

The musical tradition of the caklempong was brought to Malaysia by the Minangkabau people who settled in the southern state of Negeri Sembilan as early as the 14th century (Abd. Samad Idris, 1970, p. 15). Since those early times caklempong music has developed in Malaysia with continual influence from the Minangkabau tradition in Sumatra.

Formerly, it was played not only as general entertainment but also during the installation of the sultan. Today, caklempong music is played for many different events including official state ceremonies and various cultural events as well as for weddings. The music of the caklempong accompanies the *pencak silat* [martial arts], the *tarian lilin* [candle dance] and the *tarian piring* [dance with plates held in the hands]. It is also played for processions at weddings and for the *tarian inai* [dance for the ceremony of staining the bride's hands and feet with henna]. It is also found in the dance theater known as randai (see Chapter 1, and Mohd. Anis Md. Nor, 1986) during which the intermission time is usually filled with a comedy routine or by a performance of a full caklempong ensemble in order to keep the attention of the audience.

Caklempong enthusiasts have also taken this musical tradition into some of the teachers' training colleges where it is taught to the local student teachers with the aim of teaching the music in the government schools around the country. Its current teaching distribution, at the time of this writing, is primarily the schools in the southern part of Peninsular Malaysia where many people of Minangkabau descent live. Today there are also caklempong groups that rehearse and perform for payment, much in the manner of professional groups.

The musical instruments

The gong-chime is found throughout Southeast Asia where, on the mainland, the small knobbed gongs are placed in circular-shaped racks such as the *kyi-waing* of Myanmar and the *khong mong* of Thailand. In island Southeast Asia the racks appear in straight rows such as the *bonang* in Java, the *trompong* in Bali, the *kulintang* of the Philippines, the *canang* of peninsular Malaysia and the *kulintangan* and *engkerumong* of Sabah and Sarawak, respectively.

Among the Minangkabau of Sumatra (Indonesia) and Malaysia, the gong-chime ensemble is made up of at least three sets of small knobbed gongs, each set of gongs arranged in straight parallel rows on its own rack (or frame).

In the Minangkabau tradition the gong-chime is known as caklempong or *taklempong, celempong or telempong*. The various regional styles of instrumentation and repertory are also reflected in the variety of names used for this instrument. In general the knobbed gongs are about 16 centimeters in diameter at the top, 8-10 centimeters high with a knob about 2.5 centimeters in diameter. The gongs are struck on the knob with padded stick beaters.

Gereteh In the caklempong the main set of gongs is called *gereteh,* which consists of 15 gongs arranged in two parallel rows (seven gongs in one row and eight gongs in the other) (Figure 3.1). The gereteh carries the main melody in a piece of music. If a second gereteh is present in an ensemble it usually plays a counter melody [*melodi berbalas*].

Tingkah and *Saua* The other gong-chimes, tingkah and saua, each have eight knobbed gongs in single rows in their respective frames (Figure 3.2). The tingkah usually controls the tempo of the music, while the saua plays an ostinato-like rhythmic pattern throughout the piece.

In addition to the gong-chime, a traditional caklempong ensemble includes double-headed barrel drums called gendang and one *sarune* or *pupuik* reed pipe, or a *bangsi* flute.

Gendang The gendang barrel-shaped drums are very similar in construction to the gendang barrel drums in many other Malay music ensembles. In the caklempong ensemble they also appear in two sizes (one drum is about 2 centimeters larger than the other). The body has a slightly convex, barrel shape and the two drumheads, made of cow or goat hide, are attached to the body by means of ropes. The drumheads are struck with the hands by two different players who produce resultant rhythmic patterns in an interlocking style of playing.

Bangsi, Sarune, Pupuik The aerophones used in the traditional caklempong ensemble are either the bangsi flute (a recorder about 25 to 30 centimeters long) or the reed pipe called sarune or pupuik (see also Chapter 1 --- randai). The bangsi is made of bamboo with seven finger holes, and can produce a 7-tone scale that is compatible with the tuning of the caklempong gereteh.

The sarune consists of a small tube of bamboo, about 16 centimeters long, with another smaller pipe with a reed located at one end inserted into the larger pipe. This instrument has four finger holes and produces a pentatonic scale (usually the first five tones of the gereteh gong-chime). It is end-blown and provides a clear and loud sound to help carry the melody in a piece. To increase the volume of the sarune part, sometimes a second pipe and reed are attached to the original pipe (forming, in effect, a double sarune) and the two pipes are blown simultaneously by a single player.

The pupuik takes the form of a sarune with an added cone attached to the instrument at its lower end. The *pupuik gadang* uses a cone made from coconut leaf, while the *pupuik tanduk* has a cone made from the horn of the water buffalo. The added cone serves to amplify the sound and make it clearer than the regular sarune. These aerophones usually carry the same melody with the gereteh gong-chime in a given piece (Abdul Hamid Adnan, 1996-97).

Figure 3.1 *Caklempong Gereteh*

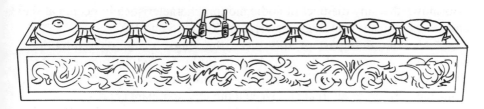

Figure 3.2 *Caklempong Tingkah* and *Saua*

In a modern caklempong ensemble the gereteh, tingkah and saua are retained, but the accompanying instruments may include the guitar and electric guitar, the western drums, the *rebano* or rebana frame drum, the accordion, the mandolin and other instruments. The music played on these instruments range from the traditional randai repertory to contemporary melodies.

The music

Melody and scale The pitches used in contemporary caklempong music are from Western diatonic scales, primarily the C major scale. The possible tuning of a full caklempong ensemble is as follows:

Gereteh:

Tingkah and Saua gongs:

The melodies are notated using a number notation system, but a variety of types of notation and styles of playing are found in Malaysia and in Sumatra, Indonesia.

The melodies in the gereteh part move mostly in conjunct motion, which is evident in the piece transcribed in Example 3.1. This example also shows that any disjunct melodic motion characteristically occurs at the ends of the phrases (see Example 3.1, bars 7, 11, 15 and 19).

In the first part of this piece the tingkah and saua provide a continuous ostinato, that is, a 4-beat rhythmic and harmonic pattern continuously repeated. This ostinato features the use of dotted rhythm, while the harmonies alternate between tonic and dominant chords.

The polyphonic texture of caklempong music usually offers the listener a rich diatonic harmony that emerges in the tingkah and saua parts. As shown in Example 3.1, the primary chords I, IV, and V are used throughout the piece, with an occasional secondary dominant enriching the harmonic base (see Example 3.1, bar 15). In this particular example there is also frequent use of the added, lowered 7th scale tone in the dominant chords (see bars 4, 6, 8, 10, 15 and 18).

Example 3.1   Excerpt from the piece *Ikan Kekek*. (Mohd. Anis Md. Nor, 1986)

The use of triads is borrowed from western music and added to the local melodies. Most, if not all, chordal structures are played in an inverted form so that the chords are rarely heard in root position. This compositional technique tends to give greater emphasis to the melodic line played by the gereteh. It also negates a strong sense of functional chordal movement as is normally heard in western classical music of the 17th-19th centuries as well as in pop music today.

Rhythm and Form   The rhythm of caklempong pieces is usually in duple meter. The rhythmic motion in the melodic line takes place at the crochet, quaver or semiquaver level, while the main downbeats in the accompaniment part are played at the crochet or quaver note level.

The internal form of a piece is usually sectional with repetition of the melodic phrases. As shown in Example 3.1, which represents only the first part of a long piece, the internal form is in two contrasting parts: *a*, *a1*, *b*, *b1*, with the entire passage repeated.

The melodic phrases in pieces tend to be regular, balanced and symmetrical. In the piece *Ikan Kekek* above, the *a* sections occur regularly in 4-bar phrases (see bars 4-7, 8-11, 12-15, and 16-19) with some variation and with a focus on the triads I and V7. We then hear melodic contrast in phrase *b* with a shift to the IV chord and briefly to its secondary dominant, V7/IV, as in bars 15-16.

In contemporary caklempong pieces the drum rhythmic pattern emphasizes the main downbeats along with the caklempong tingkah, while a guitar or bass instrument reinforces the harmonic background of the tingkah and saua parts. If present, a keyboard instrument would duplicate or ornament the main melodic line of the caklempong gereteh.

The caklempong tradition, as it has developed in Sumatra and Malaysia, reflects a local, syncretized tradition which has combined western tuning, the use of diatonic scales, local melodies, and instruments from both the western and Southeast Asian worlds. With its ties to the randai theatrical tradition (see Chapter 1), we find the caklempong providing music not only in the theatre, but also serving as the musical accompaniment to the arm, hand and foot movements of actual sparing competitors in at least one form of the martial arts known as *pencak silat* in the southern part of Peninsular Malaysia.

The use of the gong-chime in a martial arts context as well as for dance accompaniment is also found in parts of the East Malaysian state of Sabah where the instrument is called the kulintangan.

Kulintangan

In East Malaysia the gong-chime typically consists of five to nine small gongs laid horizontally in a single row in a wooden rack. The gongs are struck on the knob with a pair of wooden stick beaters, producing melody and rhythm. This small ensemble also has one or two double-headed drums struck with wooden beaters or with the players' hands, and two or more large, hanging knobbed gongs.

It has already been noted that in Sarawak the gong-chime, called engkerumong, is found exclusively among the Iban people of the state. This instrument accompanies dance, of which a famous example is the ngajat [war dance] discussed in Chapter 2. The engkerumong and its music to accompany the ngajat dance are described in the earlier chapter and are illustrated in Figures 2.15-2.18 and in Example 2.12, respectively.

In Sabah it appears that the gong-chime, called *kulintangan*, has been introduced only over the past two hundred years or so from the southern Philippines and Brunei. It is dispersed among the coastal communities but is not traditionally found in the interior regions unless there is accessible river access from the coast. Along the west coast of the state this instrument is used by the Bajau and Iranun peoples as well as by the LotudDusun, KadazanDusun from Papar, TatanaDusun and some BisayaDusun. It is also widely dispersed along the east coast, and can be found among some interior communities to the east, such as the Kadazan of the Labuk River and the Paitanic peoples of the Upper Kinabatangan River where there has been accessible riverine trade contact with the coast.

The kulintangan ensembles are played either to accompany dance or for entertainment at important social gatherings, and in some regions to accompany the martial arts. Each ensemble has a large repertory of pieces distinguished by names denoting the rhythm and pace of the piece.

The musical instruments and performance practice

The kulintangan of Sabah consists of small gongs placed horizontally in a single row on two chords stretched across partitions on a small wooden frame. On the west coast of Sabah the number of gongs is usually eight or nine, while on the east coast it is often seven, sometimes six or occasionally five.

Many of the brass kulintangan originating from the southern Philippines are yellow in color and often have a pattern stamped on the flat top surface around the knob of the gong. Some of the kulintangan from Brunei, particularly the older sets of gongs, appear to be made from bronze. Each small gong is molded into one piece and its top surface has a raised ridge around the knob.

The kulintangan is usually played by one skilled performer as the main melodic instrument in the gong ensembles along the coast of Sabah. In some communities such as among the LotudDusun, however, a second performer may sit beside the first and continuously strike the highest-pitched gong in time with the rhythm of the melody. The kulintangan ensembles usually include one or two drums and a number of large hanging gongs.

The *kuri-kurian* ensemble (sometimes also called *buni-bunian*) of the Bajau community of Kg. Menunggui in Kota Belud consists of a kulintangan of seven brass gongs, and four brass hanging gongs. The hanging gongs are two *babandil* or small, flat-surfaced knobbed gongs, and two *agong* or larger, deep-rimmed knobbed gongs. The ensemble also includes two double-headed, barrel-shaped *gandang* drums. Each gandang has rattan laces that can be adjusted to raise or lower the pitch of the goatskin drumheads.

The kulintangan is tuned to a pentatonic scale with the first gong tone serving as the pitch center. The fundamental pitch of one babandil is one octave below the pitch center of the kulintangan, while the other babandil sounds a semitone or full tone higher. Ideally, the two agong pitches lie an octave below the two babandil pitches.

During a performance the kulintangan is placed at the back of the performance space with the player seated on the floor. The two babandil are hung on either side of the kulintangan on long ropes so that the players can also be seated on the floor. The two gandang players sit in front of the kulintangan. The two agong gongs are hung on either side of the gandang and directly opposite the babandil. The large gongs are hung on shorter ropes so that the players stand while playing.

The agong are hit with wooden sticks padded with rubber, while the babandil and kulintangan are struck with plain wooden beaters (called *'titik'*, hence the music of this ensemble is sometimes referred to as *'bertitik'*). Each gandang player sits opposite the other and holds his drum horizontally. One drum head is hit with the hand while the other drum head is hit with a beater made of split bamboo. Sometimes the gandang are played vertically while the players stand and strike the top head with the two bamboo beaters, one in each hand.

Among the Bajau of Kampung Menunggui of Kota Belud the kulintangan and babandil are usually played by women, while the gandang and agong are nearly always played by men.

The music

The opening of the piece entitled *Andu-Andu* is shown in Example 3.2 as played by a kuri-kurian ensemble from Kota Belud. This piece begins with a short introduction by the two gandang drums. The kulintangan then enters in quadruple meter playing 2-bar melodic phrases, while the gandang supports the kulintangan part with an identical rhythmic pattern. The other gongs provide additional rhythmic support. By the 5th bar of the piece the babandil and the agong have established their respective rhythmic patterns. Each pair of gongs plays a separate rhythmic/melodic pattern, and this part along with the kulintangan and the gandang rhythmic pattern create a stratified texture in the music.

**Example 3.2   Excerpt from *Andu-Andu* by the *kuri-kurian* ensemble
from Kg. Menunggui, Kota Belud, Sabah.** (Transcribed
by J. Pugh-Kitingan)

In Kampung Semporna (Semporna District) on Sabah's east coast, the kulintangan ensemble is referred to as the *tagunggu* ensemble. It accompanies the *bola-bola* dance. This ensemble consists of a 6-gong kulintangan, two hanging agong gongs, and one military drum called the *tambor*.

The bola-bola dance is named after the wooden blocks that the dancers clap together in each hand as they dance. The use of these castanets and the military drum point to possible Spanish influence, which has come to Semporna through the Suluk/Tausug people who also perform a bola-bola dance. The costume of the dancers is also very similar to that of the Suluk/Tausug group of the southern Philippines.

The music to accompany the bola-bola dance is known as *'lilang'*. The example of lilang below, Example 3.3, begins with an introduction by the kulintangan and tambor. When the two agong gongs enter with the sound of the bola-bola, the music establishes a regular repeated phrase of four bars, each bar containing four main downbeats. The rhythmic parts for the kulintangan and the tambor actually take form in 2-bar phrases that are repeated to make up the 4-bar repeated pattern. In contrast, the agong maintains a pattern of alternating two pitches in quaver notes throughout the piece. Here, again, is a stratified music texture.

repeat 4 times
before playing
variations on the
kulintangan

Example 3.3   Excerpt of *'lilang'* music for the *bola-bola* dance, performed in Semporna, Semporna District, Sabah.
(Transcribed by J. Pugh-Kitingan)

The melody for the kulintangan in this piece occasionally uses chord-like structures including the intervals of thirds, fourths and fifths. The kulintangan tuning sounds diatonic with the pitches of the two agong gongs placed two octaves below the upper two pitches of the kulintangan as found in this example. The clear rhythmic and melodic patterns of 2- or 4-bar phrases used in this piece is quite different from the longer melodic phrases found in dance and other kulintangan music on the west coast of Sabah.

Other kulintangan ensembles in other parts of Sabah differ only slightly from those noted above. For example, the ensemble of the Bajau community of Kampung Putatan, located south of Kota Kinabalu, uses a 9-gong kulintangan along with the hanging gongs and a gandang drum. This ensemble accompanies the *limbai* dance. In the Iranun community the kulintangan ensemble is similar to the Bajau ensembles noted above but the ensemble is referred to as *'sakadaremetan a kulintangan'*. Like its Bajau counterpart, it consists of two hanging *babandir* gongs, two gandang drums, two agong gongs and a 7-gong kulintangan.

Hanging gong ensembles

The ensembles consisting mainly of large gongs hung vertically are found throughout the states of Sabah and Sarawak. The music of these ensembles is played for many purposes, including the accompaniment for dances, for funeral ceremonies or other activities associated with religion, for social gatherings especially when guests arrive at the longhouse, and for festivals (*gawai*).

The knobbed gong is also used for non-musical purposes. For example, in former times the beating of the large gongs was used to send news from one longhouse to another. In addition, the large gong is an item of hereditary property in a family and is considered to have a high monetary value in the community and culture. Nearly all ethnic groups in Sabah and Sarawak value the large, knobbed gongs as important instruments in terms of the economy, society, culture and religion.

In Sabah and Sarawak the tuning systems for the large gongs are not standard from one ensemble to another. However, these ensembles tend to focus on particular pitch intervals and on specific timbres of sound. A player usually strikes a gong with a padded beater or with a wooden stick on the knob, rim or other part of the instrument, depending upon the pitch or timbre desired in the music. Each player in an ensemble strikes his gong in a specific rhythmic pattern and, using an interlocking playing style, resultant rhythms, melodies and timbres are produced. In addition, usually one or two drums hit with sticks or with the player's hands are included in the ensemble. In each community there is a specific repertory of music to accompany various dances and activities or events in the village.

Although the large gong ensembles are ubiquitous in the states of Sabah and Sarawak, they usually have differing local features among the various ethnic groups. For example, the number of gongs in a given ensemble will differ from one community to another, as will the types and names of the different gongs.

Hanging gong ensembles in Sarawak

Among the Iban, Bidayuh, Kajang and Kayan peoples in Sarawak the large gong ensembles contain three to seven gongs of various types. The Kajang and Kayan groups who live along the Rejang River in the Belaga region, for example, use at least five different gongs. In a given ensemble the number of gongs may be doubled. In the Kajang communities the women usually play almost all the hanging gongs except the largest size, while in other communities both men and women equally play all the different types of gongs.

In Sarawak a typical ensemble of hanging gongs contains several bronze gongs in different sizes and also small gongs made of brass. These gongs are hung or held on the player's lap. The typical ensemble also contains one or two drums.

Tawak In general, the largest gong is called the *tawak* (or *tawag*) in most communities of Sarawak and Sabah. This large bronze gong has thick walls, a deep rim and a large knob on the center of its face (see Plate 3.1 and the tetawak gong in Chapter 1, Figure 1.1). In Sarawak the diameter of the tawak usually ranges between 40 to 60 centimeters and the rim is about 20 to 25 centimeters wide. The knob measures about 9 centimeters high. The tawak with a 40 centimeter diameter is usually called the 'small tawak' (*tawak kecil*) (Plate 3.1).

The tawak gongs are played with a padded beater or with a wooden stick. They are usually struck on the knob with a padded beater to produce a low and resonant pitch, but these gongs may also be struck on the knob with a padded beater in one hand while the other hand immediately dampens the sound to achieve a staccato effect. Some groups consider the tawak to have two knobs, that is, the main high knob on the center face and another 'knob', which is the slightly raised part of the face that immediately surrounds the high knob. This slightly raised portion of the gong surface is also struck with a padded beater to produce a specific timbre. The tawak is held in a vertical position or hung from the shoulder of a male player and struck on its knob or knobs. In Sabah, and also among the Bidayuh peoples of Sarawak, this large gong is usually hung from a wooden rack.

Agung In Sarawak another type of gong is called the *agung* or just 'gong'. The agung has a diameter of about 60 centimeters with a narrow rim about six to 10 centimeters wide, and a knob about one to five centimeters high (Plate 3.1). This gong also has a secondary knob, that is, the raised portion of the surface around the high knob. The Kajang and Kayan players support this large gong in a vertical position with one hand and hit the knob using a wooden stick with the other hand. Among the Bidayuh of Sarawak two agung are hung from a wooden rack and the knobs are struck with a pair of wooden sticks.

Bandil, Bandai, Selegai A knobbed gong smaller than the agung is called *selegai*, a local name given to this instrument by the Kajang people in

Sarawak (Plate 3.1, hanging gong). Other groups call the gong *bandai* or *bandil*. The selegai, bandai or bandil is medium in size with a diameter of about 40 to 50 centimeters, while the rim is around three centimeters deep. It has only one knob about three centimeters high (there is no secondary knob), and it is usually hung with thick rope from the roof beams of the longhouse. This gong is struck on the knob or rim with a wood stick.

Canang, (gan) In Sarawak the gongs called canang (or gan) are usually played in pairs, one gong of high pitch and the other low pitch. Its diameter measures about 25 to 30 centimeters with a rim about four or five centimeters deep and a knob about five centimeters high. Other than the main knob, the face of this gong is flat. Each gong of the pair is usually held vertically in the laps of two players and is struck on the knob with a wood stick. However, among the Bidayuh peoples the two gongs are hung from a wooden rack and played by only one person.

Katoa The drum in the hanging gong ensemble is known by many different names among the ethnic groups in the state. Many of the Kajang communities call the drum katoa. This is a large, single-headed drum with the skin laced to the body. The skin is tightened by large wood wedges inserted between the laces and the body of the drum (Figure 3.3).

The music

In the music of the hanging gong ensembles an interlocking playing style produces resultant melodies and rhythmic patterns. This phenomenon is found in the music making of many Southeast Asian music cultures, including the music of the Philippine gong ensembles, the angklung and gender wayang music of Indonesia, and in many forms of music in Malaysia. In addition, several different rhythmic lines are played simultaneously to produce a stratified, polyphonic texture in the music.

Rhythm and Form Resultant rhythmic patterns and melodies always involve two or more players, each player producing a specific rhythmic pattern. These separate patterns are played simultaneously and combine to result in one complete, resultant pattern. If the musical instruments involve pitch, then both rhythm and melody are produced.

Plate 3.1. The knobbed gongs in the hanging gong ensembles in Belaga District, Sarawak (from back to front: *selegai* hanging gong (similar to the *bandai* of the Iban), large *tawak*, two *canang* (left), *agong* (center), small *tawak*.

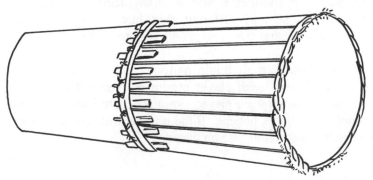

Figure 3.3 *Katoa*

Composers and researchers have written about the highly sophisticated resultant rhythms and melodies in the *angklung* and gamelan music of Bali in Indonesia (McPhee, 1966). In addition, the foregoing discussion of the many genres of traditional Malaysian music has also pointed out the interlocking performance technique producing resultant rhythms.

In the large gong ensembles, the interlocking performance style is predominant, and each type of gong in the ensemble has a special role in the music. In the Sarawak ensembles the smallest gongs, that is, the two canang (or gan), are usually played alternately to produce the running beat in the music, with one player striking his gong on the downbeat and the second player hitting his gong on the upbeat. In the music played by many groups in the interior regions of the state the two canang or gan are hit on the knob with a wooden stick to produce two pitches, high and low, on the upbeat and downbeat, respectively (see Example 3.4a --- Gan 1 and 2). The gan or canang part begins a given piece and sets the tempo in the music. The meter is usually duple.

In the gong music by the Kajang people in Sarawak (Example 3.4a) one selegai (or bandil) gong is hit on the knob and sometimes on the rim with a wooden stick. The selegai (or bandil) player begins a rhythmic pattern after the gan has set the tempo with the running beat pattern. This hanging gong produces a short rhythmic pattern or motif of four beats that is repeated throughout the piece as shown in Example 3.4a (see the selegai part in the score).

Soon after the selegai begins the two tawag gongs enter (see Example 3.4a, bar 3). Together these large gongs produce a resultant rhythmic pattern that is played simultaneously with the gan and selegai parts.

In contrast, the tawag pattern may be improvised, and the player may strike both the main and secondary knobs on this gong. As shown in Example 3.4a, the Tawag 1 player hits only the secondary knob to play an 8-beat pattern that is repeated throughout the piece. The Tawag 2 player uses both the main and secondary knobs to play a different 8-beat pattern. Both of these rhythms together produce the resultant rhythmic pattern (see Example 3.4b --- Layer 2). The resultant pattern of these two large gongs is played simultaneously with the other parts noted earlier. In this way, several lines or layers of rhythm are played simultaneously in this polyphonic music. Although there are several lines of mainly independent rhythmic patterns, all patterns are played in the same meter (see Examples 3.4a-b).

a) hanging gong ensemble rhythmic pattern (5-gong ensemble)

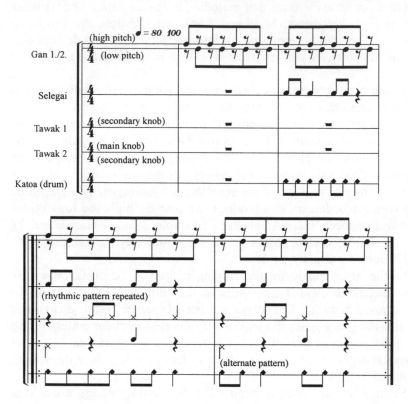

b) the stratified rhythmic patterns

Example 3.4   The rhythmic patterns by a hanging gong ensemble, played by the Kajang-Sekapan group of Belaga District, Sarawak.

In general, the hanging gong music features pitches and timbres. Whenever the main knob of a gong is struck, a focused pitch is produced, but when the secondary knob is hit a particular timbre results instead of a pitch. The large tawak gong provides a low pitch while the medium or small tawak produces a higher pitch. If the gong is struck on its rim with a wooden stick a different timbre is produced. The difference in the size of the gong, the place the gong is struck and the type of beater used (whether padded beater or a wooden stick) determine the resulting pitch or timbres. The different pitches and timbres enables the listener to hear the complex rhythmic lines that interlock with each other. It is the different pitches and timbres played in several strata of rhythmic lines by several different performers that achieve the sound ideal of this orchestra of gongs (the production of a particular melody is less important).

Sometimes a drum is added to the hanging gong ensemble. In Example 3.4, a piece by the Kajang people of Belaga District in Sarawak, a single-headed drum called katoa is hit with the hands or with a pair of wooden sticks. The rhythmic pattern by this drum is similar to the pattern of the selegai gong and is played simultaneously with it.

A somewhat larger hanging gong ensemble of seven gongs and two drums is used by the Bidayuh people in Sarawak. A piece by this ensemble is called *gondang sinoian.* It is played for entertainment at the end of the fruit harvest season in the village (see Example 3.5). Just as in the music played by other hanging gong ensembles, the resultant rhythmic patterns, stratified texture and duple meter are featured in the music. Another common feature is that the musical instruments begin a piece in staggered entrances, each instrument entering at a different time interval.

In the piece *gondang sinoian* the canang, played by a single player, begins the music and sounds out the running beat at the quaver note value. The two large agung gongs, also played by one player, provide a 4-beat rhythmic pattern with a high pitch on beat 1 and a low pitch on beat 3. These two gongs are struck with a padded beater to obtain a deep and resonant sound. The two sets of gongs, canang and agung, then, play the running beat in the music and set the tempo of the given piece. The meter is duple.

A single small gong, called the engkerumong, is held in the player's lap and is struck with a wooden stick. To achieve a staccato affect, the knob is hit with the stick beater and immediately dampened with the player's fingers. This engkerumong gong plays a 4-beat syncopated pattern that is repeated throughout the given piece of music (see Example 3.5, Engkerumong, Player 4).

Other gongs that contribute to the music texture are the large tawak producing a low pitch and the medium-sized or small tawak producing a high tone. These two gongs are played by a single player who hits the knobs with a pair of padded beaters. Once the knob is struck the player immediately dampens the knob with the beater to achieve a staccato affect. In the piece *gondang sinoian* the tawak player beats out a specific rhythmic pattern of three bars (or 12 beats) that is repeated throughout the piece. This rhythmic pattern may be improvised, but the technique of staccato playing and the alternation of the high and low pitches is always maintained (see bars 1-2 in Example 3.5, Tawak, Player 3).

gondang sinoian (7-gong ensemble)

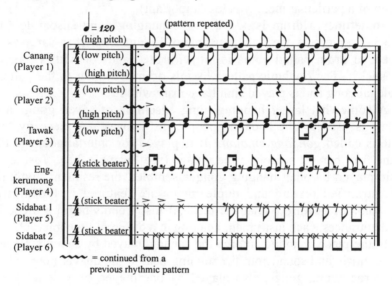

Example 3.5   Rhythmic pattern by a hanging gong ensemble, played by the Bidayuh in Sarawak.

Finally, the double-headed drums in this Bidayuh gong ensemble are called *sidabat*. They are hit with pairs of light sticks or with the players' hands. In Example 3.5, Drum Player 1 plays a 3-bar (or 12-beat) pattern with stress on beats 1-3, while syncopation and improvisation may occur on beats 5 through 12. The Drum Player 2 in this example plays and reinforces the running beat in the music played on the canang.

A stratified, polyphonic texture is obtained in this music in which the main rhythmic pattern is played by the two tawak gongs and, at the same time, interlocks with the short rhythmic pattern of the engkerumong gong. The running beat of the canang, agung and Drum 2 forms another layer in the music, while Drum 1 produces the final layer of sound.

Hanging gong ensembles in Sabah

In the state of Sabah many large gong ensembles are found that are known by various names among the different ethnic groups who play them. For example, an ensemble of several large gongs, a hanging canang gong and a drum accompanies the *sumazau* dance as well as certain ceremonies of the Kadazan community of the Penampang area (see sumazau dance in Chapter 2). The ceremonies using gong music include welcoming the new rice crop at harvest time as well as the festival honoring the rice spirit itself. In addition, the hanging gongs are played for large gatherings of people for various purposes in the village (Hajah Zaiton Ajmain and Hamdan Yahya, 1987, p. 17).

Among the Dusun people who live in the Tambunan region, the hanging gong ensemble is called the *sopogandangan* and consists of a total of eight gongs. There are seven hanging gongs of various sizes, one small gong held by a player and one singe-headed drum (Pugh-Kitingan, 1987, pp. 27-72). The sopogandangan performs music to accompany the magarang dance, and it plays a repertory of other music for funerals and other ceremonies.

The musical instruments

The sopogandangan normally has seven knobbed, hanging gongs (see sumazau and magarang dance and Plate 2.7 in Chapter 2), including: three small- to medium-sized gongs called *sanang sumaring* (or *koritikon*), *sanang lapis*, and *sanang tinukul*, and two each of the large gongs called *tagung*, and *tawag* (*tawak*) (see the score in Example 3.6) (Pugh-Kitingan, 1987, p. 29). The eighth gong is known as the *koritikan* (Figure 3.4) or the *sanang sumaring*. It is held by the player and hit on the knob with a wooden stick. Only the tawak is made of bronze, all others are made of brass.

The sanang gongs are found in various sizes, from medium to large, and all have a rather narrow rim when compared to the tawak. The tagung type is large in diameter with a narrow to medium rim, and the tawak is the largest gong with a very deep rim. These two types of gongs, the tagung and tawak, are usually found in pairs; the medium size is referred to as *laid* and the larger size is called the *buah*.

Karatung The karatung is the only drum in the ensemble. It is a single-headed, barrel-shaped drum. The skin is laced to the body and it is hit with a wooden stick (Figure 3.5).

Figure 3.4 *Koritikon*

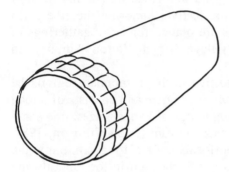

Figure 3.5 *Karatung*

All the hanging gongs are struck with a padded beater, while the koritikon gong is hit with a wood stick. Although the pitches are specified in the transcription in Example 3.6, the tuning system of the gongs in these ensembles is not standard and the actual pitches used vary from one ensemble to another.

Sopogandangan music

Like the music of the Sarawak hanging gong ensembles, sopogandangan music is composed of several resultant rhythmic patterns played simultaneously with a running beat pattern and also a syncopated rhythmic pattern. All the musical instruments begin a piece in staggered entrances at specific time intervals.

Rhythm and Form In the magarang dance music played by the sopogandangan, one koritikon gong starts the music with its rhythmic pattern in a particular tempo (see Example 3.6, bar 1). The meter in this dance music is compound with 12 beats in each bar. The koritikon gong immediately begins its short syncopated rhythmic pattern and repeats it throughout the piece. The drum called the *karatung* is used to play a rhythmic pattern identical to the koritikon gong, but begins only in bar 3 of the piece.

and so on …

Example 3.6 *Magarang* **dance music by the** *sopogandangan* **ensemble (8-gong ensemble).** (J. Pugh-Kitingan, 1987, pp. 53-55)

The two tagung gongs are played in interlocking style and alternate a high pitch and a low pitch to produce the running beat in the music at the dotted crochet note level (see Example 3.6 and Example 3.7, Layer 1). At the same time, two sanang gongs and the two tawak gongs are played in interlocking style to produce another resultant rhythmic pattern. These two resultant rhythmic patterns are superimposed upon each other so that the density of the texture becomes greater (see Example 3.7, Layers 3 and 5).

In addition, the sanang sandangau gong is used to play a 5-bar rhythmic pattern that is repeated over and over. This sanang part along with the koritikon syncopated rhythm provide counter rhythmic lines to the two former patterns by the tagung and tawag gongs (see Example 3.7, Layers 2 and 4).

Although a melody may be played by this ensemble, the gong tones are not standard from one ensemble to another, and the melody will change whenever the same rhythmic patterns are played by a different sopogandangan ensemble. The melody is of secondary importance in this music, while the rhythmic patterns and the stratified texture are clearly the featured elements.

We find, then, particular kinds of gongs and drums performing rhythmic patterns of pitches and timbres in linear textures. This is the predominant musical style that accompanies dances, ceremonies and important gatherings in the longhouses and villages in both Sabah and Sarawak.

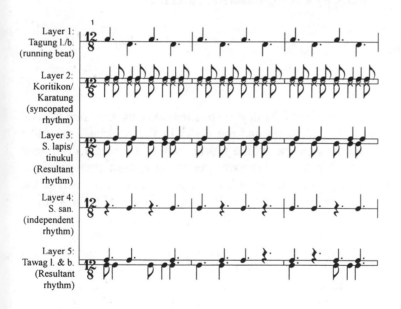

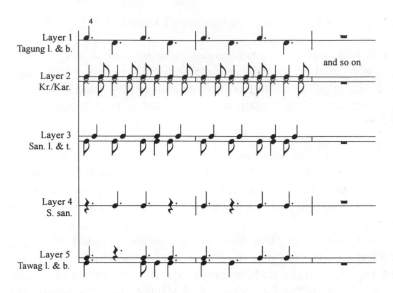

Example 3.7   The stratified rhythmic patterns in *magarang* dance music by a *sopogandangan* ensemble.

Drum ensembles

Kompang

The *kompang* is a traditional Malay instrument having the same basic shape as the rebana in Indonesia and the *dufuf* in the Middle East. The instrument is a membranophone with a frame body and a single drumhead made of skin. Drumming on the kompang results in instrumental music to accompany the reading and singing of Islamic poetry in genres such as the *zikir* [verses in praise of Allah and The Prophet Muhammad], the *selawat* [verses to The Prophet Muhammad] and sometimes the *marhaban* [verses praising The Prophet Muhammad (sometimes sung unaccompanied).[2]

The art of playing the kompang among the Malays originated from the Arabic tradition that was brought to the Indonesian islands around the 13th century C.E., and since that time it has influenced the Malay arts. In the beginning, the singing of Arabic songs was accompanied by the kompang drum (*dufuf*) played by Arab traders who used it to attract crowds of people to buy their goods. The Arab missionaries also used kompang drumming to accompany the singing of Islamic poetry and to attract the local Malays. Indeed, the Malays imitated the drumming on this instrument.

In early times in Malay society, groups of kompang drummers were invited to celebrate and enliven wedding ceremonies or Islamic celebrations in the villages. Today kompang playing has extended to urban and suburban areas with performances for official and social ceremonies such as welcoming the arrival of local and foreign leaders. Kompang groups may consist of young men, women, or mixed groups, and in a given performance an appropriate uniform or costume is usually worn. Certain manners in performance are followed, such as not placing the kompang upside down (on the skin-side) and, in fact, when it is stored the kompang is placed with the head (the skin side) facing upward.

At wedding celebrations the kompang is played when the bride and groom walk in procession and sit on the dais before the wedding guests (the *bersanding* ceremony). Sometimes the kompang is also played after the ceremony of staining the bride's hands and feet with henna [*upacara berinai*]. Many Islamic celebrations such as the *Maulud-an Nabi* (the birthday of the Holy Prophet), the *Maulidur Rasul* (welcoming the Prophet Muhammad) and the *Id* festivals such as *Hari Raya Puasa* (celebration at the end of the Ramadhan fasting month) and *Hari Raya Haji* (celebration upon returning from the pilgrimage to Mecca) are also celebrated with kompang drumming by large and small groups.

In the 20th century the role, function and distribution of kompang music broadened considerably. Today, thundering kompang drumming can be heard at state ceremonies welcoming local and foreign officials, in the National Day parades, and at sports programs such as football competitions to arouse team spirit among the players. In addition to the traditional rhythmic patterns that are still played, patterns from the traditional dances called *joget, zapin, kuda kepang* and others are also played as suitable for the celebration taking place.

The musical instrument

The main parts of the kompang are the body [*baluh* or *balong*], the skin or drum head [*belulang* or *kulit*], the metal tacks and a strip of red cloth around the circumference of the body where the skin is attached to it. Other important parts are the rattan brace to tighten the drum head [*sedak*], and the tool to insert the rattan brace into the space between the skin and wooden body inside the drum [*penyedak*].

The body of the kompang is made from a hard wood (*cengal, pulai* or *leban* wood) that is carved and shaped like a basin, about 6.5 to 13 centimeters deep and open at the bottom. This part is the frame of the drum to which a goat skin head is attached (Figure 3.6).

The drumhead is made of skin from the female goat. This type of skin is chosen because it is thin and emits a clear and resonant sound when stretched and hit. The skin is scraped and cleaned, soaked in lime water for several days (to rid the odor from the skin), and stretched and dried in the sun. Then it is attached to the body of the drum using nails. A strip of copper attached with brass nails covers the nailed skin, and a strip of red cloth secured with brass tacks covers the nails.

Figure 3.6 *Kompang*

The *sedak* is the rattan brace used to tighten the skin in order to obtain a clear and resonant sound. To tighten the drumhead, the rattan brace is inserted inside the kompang, between the edge of the skin and the body of the drum, using a stick-shaped wooden tool (called *penyedak*).

The size of the drumhead varies from 20 to about 38 centimeters in diameter. Usually a drum of 33 to 35 centimeters is used for an adult-sized instrument, while an instrument with a diameter of 30 centimeters or less is used for a child.

Method of Playing Kompang playing can take place while sitting, standing or walking. For example, the players may be seated on the floor or on chairs when playing at a house during the henna staining ceremony at a wedding celebration, and at these times long songs such as religious texts (zikir or other vocal genres) are performed. Whenever the kompang players stand while playing to entertain the bride, groom and other important persons in the wedding, they arrange themselves in neat and orderly rows. In the context of a procession, kompang drumming may occur when the groom and his entourage go to the house of the bride on the wedding day, or when the performers walk from place to place to accompany other important persons in the ceremony. In this case the kompang players walk closely together in orderly rows as they play.

The kompang pieces (*lagu*) consist of resultant rhythmic patterns, and different types of drum strokes are required to produce the different timbres for the percussive patterns. To begin, the wooden frame is placed in the palm of the left hand (for those who are not left-handed) with the thumb gripping the wood of the body inside the kompang just at the base of the drumhead. The fingers of the left hand are placed outside the drumhead without pressing on the skin so that the drum sounds are not distorted or muffled. The drumhead is then hit with the palm and fingers of the right hand to produce two main timbres called 'dum' and 'tak' (these timbres are also known as 'prang' and 'ding' among some kompang groups).

To obtain the low timbre 'dum' the thumb, first, and second fingers and the palm of the right hand are slightly bent. With the palm in a convex-like position the drumhead is hit as the hand waves or whirls like a whip at the center of the drumhead. In contrast, the sharp timbre 'tak' is played with all fingers of the right hand close together (excluding the thumb), and the edge of the drumhead is hit with the end of the fingers near the rim. A sound of high quality is produced with a hand movement similar to a whipping or slashing [*sembat*] motion (also likened to an elastic motion) so that the right hand is immediately lifted off the skin after the initial impact.

The music

In a kompang piece usually three groups of players perform three different drum patterns that combine to produce a resultant rhythmic pattern. These three groups are called: (i) the *Melalu*, (ii) the *Menyelang*, and (iii) the *Menganak*. Sometimes a fourth group, the *Mengocok* is present to add some variation to the Menganak part and to enrich the overall sound. The specific function of each part is as follows:

(i) The group called the *Melalu* (or *Menalu* or *Pembolong*) is a group that plays the main drum strokes in unison (see Example 3.8). These drum strokes result in a basic rhythmic pattern (called *dasar*), played in unison and sometimes repeated throughout a piece.

(ii) The part called *Menyelang* (or *Menyilang*, or *Peningkah*) usually follows or anticipates the drum strokes of the Melalu part. The Menyelang part is also played by the person who leads the kompang group and is responsible for starting and stopping a given piece. Unless the lead Menyelang player (the *kalifah*, or leader of the group) gives the signal to end, the kompang piece will not stop (see the ending signal in phrase b2, beats 5 and 9, in Example 3.8). The *kalifah* [leader] also beats out the basic, repeated Menyelang part following or anticipating the beats of the Melalu part and interlocking with that part to complete the resultant rhythmic pattern.

(iii) The part called *Menganak* (or *Melanak* or *Penyelang*) is played by drummers who function as intermediaries between the *Melalu* and the *Menyelang* with drum strokes that further interlock with the first two parts. With the addition of this rhythmic pattern the sound of the overall kompang drumming is fast and lively (see the Menganak part in Example 3.8).

(iv) Whenever a group comprises less than 10 players and the rhythmic patterns need to be more dense, the part called *Mengocok* comes into play with *ad lib* drum strokes, but following the main rhythmic pattern of the piece played.

As a general rule, the drummers of the ensemble arrange themselves in a set pattern at their performance venue. The 1st and 2nd (if present) Melalu groups stand on one side (right or left) of the stage or other venue, and the Menyelang players on the other side, just opposite the Melalu group. The Menganak players stand in front of the Menyelang players. The leader (the kalifah) places himself at or near the middle of the group so that his signals and tempo may be heard by all.

To obtain a surging and resonant sound in the drumming of a large kompang ensemble, the number of players in the Menganak and Menyelang sections can be increased, but the total number of players should not be greater than the Melalu group. Also, a player from the Menyelang group must function as the head or the khalifah to ensure that the ensemble plays together whenever starting, stopping or maintaining the tempo of a piece.[3]

The division of the different groups playing the rhythmic patterns need to be appropriately balanced to obtain the typically thundering but clear sound of the rhythmic patterns. For example, for each of 20 players there should be eight Melalu and eight Menyelang players. These two basic parts would then be supplemented by two Menganak drummers and two added Melalu players. The supplemental parts provide additional off-beat patterns to interlock with the main Melalu and Menyelang parts. In this way the musical texture becomes quite dense. Some pieces in some kompang groups actually use a specified number of players on the specific parts. For example, in one ensemble from an urban region of the country, certain pieces in their repertory use, specifically, two drummers on the Menganak part, nine players beating the Menyelang part and nine on the Melalu part.

The music

Tempo and rhythmic patterns As noted above, the kompang pieces are essentially resultant rhythmic patterns. Typically, among the currently existing kompang groups in the country each maintains a repertory of original or basic rhythmic patterns, each with its own special identity. For example, the Ezhar Kompang Group uses six rhythmic patterns (or *lagu* [pieces]) which must be known by all the players, that is, the pieces called *Pukulan Bertih, Pukulan Baru, Pukulan Silat, Pukulan Hadrah Pendek, Pukulan Hadrah Kepang* and *Pukulan Rancak*.

These pieces usually begin with an introduction, referred to as the '*kepala pukulan*' (see Example 3.8, the piece *Pukulan Baru*). As the introduction to a piece, the *kepala pukulan* is very important because it sets the tempo, thus influencing the entire rhythmic character of the piece.

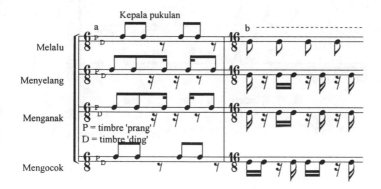

Example 3.8 *Kompang* **piece** *Pukulan Baru.*

The piece entitled *Pukulan Baru* contains four different parts, although only three of the parts are usually active in a performance. The fourth part, the Mengocok, can be added if a kompang ensemble has less than 10 drummers. The four rhythmic parts, then, are played by the Melalu, Menyelang, Menganak and Mengocok groups (see Example 3.8).

The musical structure in this piece is clearly sectional. In the introduction (referred to as phrase *a* in Example 3.8), the Melalu and Mengocok play the rhythmic pattern in unison in six quaver beats. The Menyelang and Menganak parts also begin in unison with the first two parts, but then break away to anticipate the Melalu and Mengocok by using semiquaver drum strokes on the off-beat.

The sections that follow are delineated by phrases in the score of Example 3.8. The first section (phrase *b*) is called the 'beginning piece' [*permulaan lagu*] in which the Melalu produces the basic rhythmic pattern [*dasar*] of 16 beats. The Menyelang and Menganak begin on the downbeat of the pattern, then anticipate the Melalu part by playing mainly on the upbeat throughout the remainder of the 16 beats. The Mengocok part in this section is a contrasting rhythmic pattern that interlocks with the other parts.

In the next section of the composition (phrase *b1*), the 'continuation' [*sambungan lagu*], the Melalu plays a varied version of the basic rhythmic pattern. Here the Menyelang interlocks each quaver note of the Melalu with a semiquaver beat. The Menganak and Mengocok, again, play a contrasting rhythmic pattern that makes the musical texture more dense. This section (or phrase) is repeated.

In the section 'ornamented piece' [*bunga lagu*] (phrase *c*), the Melalu produces a new rhythmic pattern of nine quaver note beats, each of which interlocks with a drum stroke by the Menyelang, Menganak and Mengocok groups who play in unison. Played only one time, this phrase *c* may be seen as a bridge passage to the next section of the composition.

The *Pukulan Baru* continues with several sections of 'continuation of the ornamented piece' [*sambungan bunga lagu*], consisting of phrases *d* (repeated three times), *e* and *f*. In all these phrases, the Melalu group plays the basic rhythmic pattern while the other three parts provide separate patterns to interlock with it.

The 'closing' [*penutup lagu*] is indicated as phrase *b2* in Example 3.8. This closing section ends with a pattern based on the earlier phrase *b1*. The basic pattern interlocks with the Menyelang. A drummer from the Menyelang section, serving as the kalifah, ends the *Pukulan Baru* by accenting two semiquavers on beat 5, and one quaver on the final beat 9. All parts or groups end the piece in unison on beat 9.

With the forms in kompang pieces typically sectional in nature, we see repeated sections with some development of early material occurring later in a piece (see, for example, phrases *b*, *b1* and *b2* in Example 3.8). In the composition of a kompang piece by individuals or by groups, there is an attempt to maintain a sense of balance among the sections, if not in the overall structure of the piece. In the *Pukulan Baru*, for example, a short introduction (six beats) is followed by two major sections of considerable length (phrase *b* of 16 beats and phrase *b1* of 32 beats). After a short bridging passage (phrase *c*), another two sections of considerable length (phrase *d* (24 beats), and *e* and *f* for 15 beats) find their closing in a relatively short concluding cadential pattern (nine beats).

Sometimes the rhythmic patterns of the kompang are accompanied by song. At first, lyrics in the Arabic language were taken from the *kitab berzanji* (collection of religious verses) or other collections of verses that contain Islamic messages about godliness and other religious themes. Slowly the lyrics changed to the Malay language so that it would be easier for all to understand. Eventually these themes broadened to current issues such as social and economic development, and new song lyrics were composed and sung for specific functions. Today one finds kompang groups performing songs in Malay, and in Arabic if there is an Islamic message. The performances usually start with the prayers to the Prophet Muhammad (see also Chapter 4 --- Zikir).

In summary, the kompang pieces involve at least four parts or groups, that is, the Melalu/Pembolong, the Menyelang, the Menganak and the Mengocok. These groups play different rhythmic patterns in an interlocking style. The basic pattern in a piece (the *dasar*) is always played by the Melalu group, with the other groups providing rhythms that interlock with the dasar pattern. Thus, resultant rhythmic patterns are highly important and characteristic in kompang music.

Form in this music is sectional. A given piece usually starts with an introduction (*kepala pukulan*) that sets the tempo, which is usually moderate or fast. After the introduction, the piece continues with several sections featuring different rhythmic patterns. Usually some musical material from the early sections returns at the end of the piece, pointing towards the importance of reverting musical forms in this drumming tradition.

Rebana Ubi

In the northeastern state of Kelantan many different kinds of entertainment are presented at weddings and social gatherings in the villages, and at the various competitions among the villages after the harvest season. One of those types of entertainment and competition is known as *rebana ubi*, a name that refers to the musical instrument and to the repertory of music it plays.

The instrument

The body of the rebana ubi is cone-shaped and the single drum head is attached to it with rattan laces, and with a cane brace (at the base end of the body). The drumhead is made taut by the use of long wooden wedges that are inserted at the base of the drum, between the body and the cane brace. Another drum called the *rebana besar* [large rebana] (see Chapter 4 --- Zikir) is nearly identical to the rebana ubi, but it is slightly larger in all dimensions.

The body of the rebana ubi is about 55 centimeters high with a diameter of some 68 centimeters. The long wooden wedges are over 40 centimeters long. This drum is painted in bright colors and decorated with painted spiral designs, flower motifs and geometric forms. It is found in ensembles of six or more drums that are always played outdoors. Each drum is hung from the roof beams of a gazebo-like structure (Plate 3.2), or may alternately be placed vertically on the ground, resting on the wooden wedges and a small wooden stand placed beneath the rim of the drumhead. The rebana ubi is struck with a padded beater or with the player's hands.

The music

A given rebana ubi ensemble consists of six to eight drums, which are played by 12 to 16 players (each drum is played by two drummers). The drummers stand opposite one another on either side of the rebana ubi so that the drumhead is easily accessible.

The drumhead is struck with the player's hands or with a stick beater padded with rubber at one end. If the drumhead is hit with the hands, the players strike it in the center to obtain a low timbre or at the edge to play a high timbre. Both of these timbres are similar to the sounds vocalized as 'dung' and 'tak' on the small-sized rebana that is hand-held or placed on the drummer's lap (see Chapter 1 --- mekmulung). If struck with a padded beater, the drumhead is usually hit in the center and only one timbre is produced.

Rhythm   Like kompang music, particular rhythmic patterns comprise the pieces in the rebana ubi repertory. In a typical piece, several drummers play the running beat in the music. Using an interlocking performance style, one player on one of the drums provides strokes on the downbeats, while the other player on the same drum plays on the upbeats. Usually several pairs of players produce the running beat on their respective drums. At the same time, only one player beats out a specific rhythmic pattern different and independent from the running beat pattern (see Example 3.9a). That specific rhythmic pattern interlocks with the running beat to produce a resultant rhythmic pattern.

Plate 3.2 A *rebana ubi* ensemble in a Kelantan village.

When the rebana ubi is played with the hands, the resultant rhythmic pattern is usually made up of two or three parts that are also played in an interlocking style. As shown in Example 3.9b, a piece begins with a specific rhythmic pattern played in unison by the entire ensemble, including the solo player. Both of the timbres 'tak' and 'dung' are used in the rhythmic pattern. The entire ensemble continues to play in unison until the tempo increases. At that point the solo player begins to beat on the upbeats of the pattern so that, in effect, he anticipates each drum stroke played by the remainder of the ensemble (see Example 3.9b, second system in which the tempo is about 144 beats per minute). In this type of drumming, the solo drummer plays an 8-beat pattern, which interlocks with that of the ensemble. It is repeated several times at the fast tempo.

When the tempo increases even more, both the ensemble and the solo player change their respective rhythmic patterns. Each part (the solo and the ensemble) play two different patterns that interlock to produce a resultant rhythmic pattern. The resultant pattern is repeated a number of times until the solo player gives a cue to play a new pattern or to beat out a closing cadence to end the piece (see Example 3.9c, the tempo is about 192 beats per minute).

a) rhythmic pattern --- running beat and soloist's pattern (played with a padded beater)

b) 8-beat pattern --- the solo player at first plays in unison and later anticipates the drum strokes played by the ensemble (played with hands to produce the timbres 'tak' and 'dung')

c) 8-beat pattern --- the solo player and the ensemble each play a different rhythmic pattern (played with the hands)

OR

d) cadence pattern to close a piece

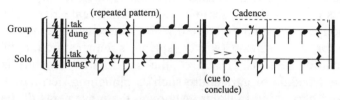

Example 3.9 *Rebana ubi* **rhythmic patterns.**

   To conclude a piece, the solo player usually signals a closing cadence with two accented drum strokes (2 beats) at the beginning of the repeated 8-beat pattern being played at the given time. With this signal the ensemble players immediately play the cadence pattern that closes the piece (see Example 3.9d).

   In the rebana ubi repertory some music is based on shadow play pieces. The basic shadow play rhythms are adapted so that the patterns may be played using only the two timbres 'tak' and 'dung' on the rebana drum. Two of the favorite shadow play pieces adapted for this purpose are entitled *Perang* and *Hulubalang* (See Chapter 1 --- wayang kulit Kelantan).

   In general, the rhythmic patterns played on the rebana ubi exhibit the typical features of percussion music found along the east coast of Peninsular Malaysia. These features include the use of 8-beat rhythmic patterns, an interlocking performance style, use of a gradually increasing tempo throughout a piece, repetition of rhythmic patterns, sectional formal structure within a piece and the use of a reverting type of formal scheme. However, the end-accented pattern often found in other traditional music is not necessarily found in rebana ubi pieces.

24 Season Drums (Er Shi Si Jie Ling Gu)

A final type of ensemble made up exclusively of drums is found in the Chinese Malaysian community (see Plate 3.3). The '24 Season Drums' were first performed by Chinese associations in Johor Bharu in 1988. Nine big Chinese drums were performed at the opening ceremony of the Ninth National Dance Competition.

Following this performance, which drew enormous crowds, the Chinese associations in Johor Bharu decided to pool their resources to buy 24 drums and to set up a permanent group. They secured the services of drummer/percussionist Chen Wei Chong of the Foon Yew Chinese Secondary School in Johor Bharu to train the musicians.

As implied in the name, this ensemble consists of 24 drums, each of which represents an agricultural season in the Chinese calendar. The name of each season is written on each drum with Chinese calligraphy. In the Chinese calendar, each season (winter, spring, summer, autumn) is divided into 6 smaller seasons. Each of the six smaller seasons is associated with the schedule of agriculture such as ploughing, fertilizing, sowing, planting and harvesting in China. Although the movements of the musicians and rhythmic patterns generally vary from troupe to troupe, they reflect the movements of the farmer and the atmosphere on the farm.

Since the 1990s, the 24 Season Drums have become popular in Chinese schools and associations throughout the country. They can be performed in an enclosed hall or in an open space. Props such as masks, colorful flags and banners are also used to enhance the performance. Very often more than 24 drums are played in performances, held in conjunction with festivities organized by Chinese political parties, so that a grand sound is produced. In recent times, the 24 Season Drums have been combined with the rebana ubi, tabla and other drums of Malaysia to form spectacular drum ensembles as icons of modernity. These drum ensembles are performed at National Day celebrations and for tourists to show unity in a culturally diverse country.

The musical instrument

The drum (*shigu*) resembles the lion dance drum (see Chapter 2 and Plate 3.3 below). The body of the drum is barrel-shaped and the single drumhead, made of cow-hide, is nailed to the wooden body. The drum is about 60 cm high with a diameter also around 60 cm. Metal springs are attached inside the drum that give it its characteristic reverberating sound. The drum is put on top of a rack and struck with two wooden sticks.

Playing Techniques Each player is able to produce sounds with different tone qualities and timbres by using different techniques of playing. As shown in Examples 3.10 and 3.11 below, a low resonant sound 'dung' is produced when the drummer hits the center of the drum with the stick. The sound 'tik' that is high and short is produced when the player hits the two sticks together. The sharp and short sound 'tak' is produced when the player hits the side of the drum with the stick where the skin is nailed to the body. Other timbres are produced by hitting or touching different parts of the drum surface with the stick or with the palm of the hand.[4]

Plate 3.3   The 24 Seasons Drums at a primary school (Sin Min National (Chinese) School in Semenyir, Selangor). (Photo by Soon, Y.-W.)

The music

Each performance begins with two sounds, 'tak' 'tak', by the leader of the group who hits the side of the drum with his stick. In the music of the 24 Season Drums, an interlocking playing style produces resultant rhythmic patterns, which are repeated. The group is usually divided into two to four groups, each group playing a specific rhythmic pattern.

Although individual groups constantly create new patterns, several basic rhythmic patterns are known by all troupes in Malaysia. These basic patterns were first created by Chen Wei Chong and reflect the movements of the farmer or the atmosphere on the farm.

Rhythm and Texture The piece *Da Gu* (Example 3.10) is about threshing paddy [*padi*]. The musicians are divided into two groups. They each play a 6-beat pattern that is repeated.

The Group A plays the timbre 'tik', while Groups B and C play 'dung'. The drummers in Group A jump from the right and then to the left every two bars hitting their sticks as if they are threshing paddy.

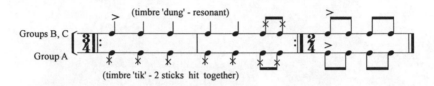

Example. 3.10 *Da Gu.* (Transcribed by Soon, Y.-W.)

To show rain falling on the roof tops, the performers play drum rolls alternating between the timbres 'dung' and 'tak' in the piece *Yu Shui* (Example 3.11). The drum rolls become gradually louder and then softer throughout the piece.

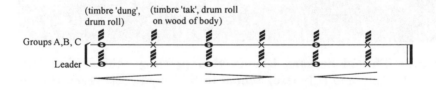

Example 3.11 *Yu Shui.* (Transcribed by Soon, Y.-W.)

Struck and stamping bamboo and wood ensembles

The ensembles consisting of idiophones made of wood or bamboo are found in folk cultures and traditions throughout the world. Some of these idiophones are concussion instruments consisting of two similar or identical parts, that is, they exist as a pair and the two parts are struck together. Other idiophones consist of two or more parts, existing as a set, which are struck with a beater or stamped upon an object or other surface. Yet others may be shaken, plucked, rubbed or scraped. All of these types of instruments are found in Malaysian folk music.

Instruments such as these are some of the earliest musical instruments in the history of mankind. In ancient times some idiophones developed as a result of motor impulses that were associated with work activities. In Southeast Asia the work implements or tools used by farmers in activities related to the cultivation of hill rice and wet rice eventually became musical instruments. Some idiophones are also used to chase away mice and other pests from the longhouse or from the rice plants still growing on the hilly fields. In earlier times these musical instruments were also used in ceremonies to heal sick people. As entertainment, instrumental ensembles such as the *togunggak* in Sabah, or the *peruncung* and *kesut* in Sarawak, produce rhythmic patterns to enliven processions and for welcoming guests. Some of these ensembles also imitate dance music that is usually played by the large, hanging gong ensembles.

Alu (alok) and Tangbut

The Dayak and other peoples who live in the mountainous regions of Sarawak plant hill rice using swidden agricultural techniques. In Sarawak women traditionally take a dominant role in planting, storing and processing rice, and they also have important roles in the rituals connected to rice cultivation.

Nevertheless, both men and women take the responsibility for specific tasks related to the rice growing process. For example, Kayan men determine the specific time to prepare the land and sow the rice seeds, chase away pests such as insects, mice and so on from destroying the hill rice, and harvest and carry the paddy to the rice-barns at the longhouse location. The women choose and save the rice seeds that will be planted in the next season. The Kayan women also sow the paddy seeds, cut the hill rice plants, and harvest the early (or young) rice grains in any given harvest season. In addition they also pound and winnow the rice grains and cook it to eat. It is also the women who learn and pass on the knowledge and folklore of rice cultivation to their daughters.

As activities connected to the cultivation of rice, the women play several types of music such as the *'alu (alok) and tangbut'* [the pestle and bamboo tubes] and the *'antan and lesung'* [the pestle and mortar]. Among the Kayan people the alu and tangbut music is played immediately before the paddy harvest begins, and the performance of it is carried out to welcome the new rice grains which will shortly be harvested. This music is played by a small ensemble consisting of several pestles (the alu or alok) and two short bamboo tubes (the tangbut). The pestles used as musical instruments are the actual pestles used to pound the paddy before it is cooked.

The musical instruments

In this ensemble six women play six pestles, each about 1.5 to 2 meters in length. All the pestles are placed cross-wise on top of two parallel wooden beams set on the floor about 1.5 meters apart (see Figure 3.7). A total of six pestles are arranged in three pairs on top of the parallel wooden beams, and each pair is played by two players who sit on the floor at either end of the pestle facing each other. All pairs of pestles are struck together or are struck on the wooden beams beneath them. Each of two pairs of the pestles are struck together or hit against the lower beams in unison to play the running beat in the music (see Example 3.12, Players 1-2 and 3-4). The third pair of pestles is held stationary by one player at one end and struck together by another player at the opposite end (see Example 3.12, Players 5-6). This third pair of pestles plays a specific rhythmic pattern.

The tangbut used in this ensemble are bamboo tubes of two different lengths. The tubes are closed at one end and left open at the opposite end. Each of two players holds his tube and strikes it with a thin stick made of wood or bamboo. The short tube, producing a high timbre, measures about 29 centimeters long and 4 centimeters in diameter, while the long tube produces a low timbre and is about 85 centimeters long with the same diameter as the short tube.

Figure 3.7 *Alu* and *tangbut* ensemble from Sarawak.

The music

The music played by the alu and tangbut ensemble consists of rhythmic patterns. Although various rhythmic patterns may be performed by this ensemble, only one example is given here to illustrate the typical formal and stylistic features of this music (see Example 3.12).

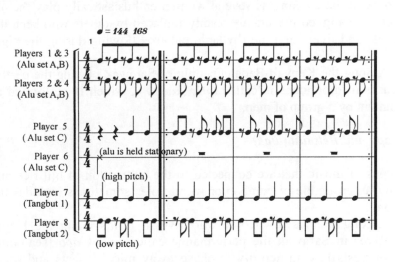

Example 3.12 Rhythmic patterns by the *alu* and *tangbut* ensemble.

Rhythm and Form This polyphonic music is played in an interlocking style to produce resultant rhythmic patterns, which are the specific 'tunes' or pieces [*lagu*] in the repertory. In order to play the running beat in the music two pairs of alu, Pairs A and B in Example 3.12, play in unison on the downbeat and upbeat. The third set, Pair C is held stationary at one end by Player 6 while Player 5 at the opposite end of the two pestles beats out a specific rhythmic pattern. The rhythmic pattern of Player 5 interlocks with the running beat established by the other wood pole players in the ensemble.

The rhythmic pattern by Player 5 (the 'soloist') in Example 3.12 may be seen as a 2- or 4-beat motif which is repeated and syncopated with strong stress on the upbeat. The player improvises short rhythmic motifs giving importance to beats at the quaver note value.

The pattern of the high-timbre tangbut reinforces the running beat with a stroke on each downbeat (see Example 3.12, Player 7). Like the 'solo' pestle player in this ensemble, the low-timbre tangbut plays a 2- or

4-beat pattern that is improvised, but maintains stress on the upbeat. Usually the low-pitched tangbut part and the Set C pestles interlock to produce a resultant rhythmic pattern as shown in Example 3.12. At the beginning of the piece the tempo is moderate but gradually it becomes quite fast.

These concussion pole players entertain the longhouse dwellers for many hours in the evening as several women enthusiastically play the alu and tangbut. Fatigued players are readily replaced by others who keep the tempos fast and lively and the rhythmic patterns flowing during the night hours.

Among the Kenyah-Badang people of Sarawak playing the pestles as concussion idiophones is called *tatip kamang*, which is performed as entertainment by a group of men.

Huduk apa and Beh alu (alok)

Other types of music that are connected to the cultivation of hill rice and played by an ensemble of bamboo or wood poles sometimes includes the tawak gong.

Among the Kayan people who live in farms along the Upper Rejang River in Sarawak the performance called *huduk apa* [searching about (for pests)] is an activity to chase away mice, insects and other harmful pests which could ruin the growing hill rice plants. This activity includes rhythmic patterns played on stamping wooden poles and struck gongs. While several wooden poles are stamped on the floor or ground in a running beat pattern, several large gongs (the *tawak*) provide a repeated, resultant rhythmic pattern that accompanies the yelling, hissing and rustling about by several players.

Likewise, before the paddy is harvested and carried to the longhouse, the men perform the *beh alu*. In this activity several men bear the weight of the wooden pestle (the antan or alu) on their backs as they crawl along the floor to the accompaniment of specific tangbut rhythmic patterns as if they were carrying the newly harvested rice on their backs in baskets of about 60 kilograms each. Through the *beh alu* performance the players exhibit the hard work required to bring the harvested rice to the longhouse, and at the same time they request, to the rice spirit, that the harvest be abundant for all the inhabitants of the longhouse. This performance is accompanied by the resultant rhythmic patterns played on two tangbut bamboo tubes of two different pitches.

Kesut

While stamping wooden poles are used in the Huduk Apa activity to chase away pests, in some communities the stamping bamboo poles were formerly used in much the same way, but today they mainly accompany processions.

The musical performance and also the ensemble referred to as *kesut* is found in select regions of Sarawak including the Upper Rejang River area. The musical ensemble consists of several bamboo poles struck on the floor by the players who walk in a single-line procession (Plate 3.4).

The motion of the stamping instruments such as the bamboo poles is believed to originate in the movements of walking, stamping the feet and moving the arms. In ancient ceremonies among the Kajang peoples of Sarawak several stamping bamboo poles about 1.5 to 2 meters long are used. The kesut is decorated with shavings from the surface of the bamboo pole itself (Figure 3.8). A bamboo pole is held vertically by a player and stamped on the floor while the player walks in a group procession. Usually women play this instrument in an ensemble of five or more bamboo poles.

Figure 3.8 *Kesut*

Plate 3.4 *Kesut* **stamping bamboo poles at a Kajang longhouse.**

The music

All the players taking part in the kesut ensemble walk in a procession along the veranda of the longhouse. The lead player of this procession may use two bamboo poles to play a specific rhythmic pattern throughout the procession. The other players each hold one bamboo pole. Several of the players stamp the bamboo on the downbeat while others stamp the bamboo on the upbeat, thus establishing the running beat in the music (see Example 3.13).

a) kesut stamping at a Kajang-Lahanan longhouse in Sarawak

b) kesut stamping by Kajang-Sekapan people in Sarawak

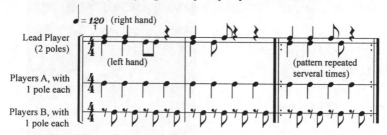

c) kesut stamping by Kajang-Kejaman Lasah people in Sarawak.

Example 3.13 *Kesut* rhythmic patterns.

Most players in the group play the running beat, while the lead player stamps out a specific rhythmic pattern. The two parts in the music, that is, the running beat and the independent rhythmic pattern interlock to produce a resultant rhythmic pattern. As shown in Example 3.13, the resultant rhythm may be isometric with an unchanging meter as in Examples 3.13a and b, or heterometric as in Example 3.13c. In this music there is no end-accented pattern, as is often found in other folk and classical music genres in Malaysia. The short resultant rhythmic pattern is repeated throughout the procession and, thus, the form is iterative in this music.

Ding Galung and Goh

While the kesut music is played with long stamping bamboo poles, several other genres of percussion music are played with short stamping bamboos. The short bamboo idiophones called *ding galung, goh* and other local names are bamboo tubes stamped on wood or other material (Figure 3.9).

Among the aborigines of Peninsular Malaysia these stamping bamboo tubes are used to play music to accompany various ceremonies and rituals, including ceremonies to heal sick people. The bamboo musical instrument is called *ding galung* among the Jah Hut aborigines, while the name *goh* is used by the Temiars.[5]

The Jah Hut people perform rituals to exorcise bad or evil elements through singing accompanied by stamping bamboo tubes as a shaman (*poyang*) searches for the wandering spirit or soul of the sick person. The music functions as a guide for the soul of the shaman while he travels far and wide to find the lost soul of the afflicted one. The chorus sings a song in unison while all the singers and other players stamp several bamboo tubes in a specific rhythmic pattern.

Among the Temiar of Kelantan dream songs[6] are sung to the accompaniment of stamping bamboo tubes. The dream songs are performed for a number of purposes including the healing of sick people, to celebrate the harvest, to welcome guests and to enliven official meetings in the village. These songs are performed by a male soloist in responsorial style with a female chorus. The members of the chorus also stamp the bamboo tubes in a specific rhythmic pattern.

The bamboo tubes (*ding*) stamped by the Jah Hut aborigines measure about 90 to 120 centimeters long with a diameter of 5 centimeters, while the bamboos stamped by the Temiars (the *goh*) are about 77 to 92 centimeters in length with a diameter of some 7 centimeters (Couillard, 1979; Roseman, 1991). Each tube is closed at one end and left open at the opposite end. These bamboos are played in pairs so that the long tube produces a low timbre, and a short tube plays a high timbre. Among the Temiar the long tube is called the 'male' while the short tube is the 'female'. Two bamboo tubes are held by one player and stamped against a piece of wood called the *galung* by the Jah Hut, and against a wooden beam by the Temiar.

The music

The bamboo tubes of each set, that is, two tubes of different size, are stamped in alternation so that two different timbres are produced in a particular rhythmic pattern. For example, in the Jah Hut ceremony to heal a sick person, the rhythmic pattern played on the tubes consists of a 2- or 3-beat unit with strong stress on the final beat of each unit (see Example 3.14a).

Figure 3.9 *Ding Galung* and *Goh* of the aborigines of Peninsular Malaysia.

Among the Temiar group, the bamboo tubes are also played in alternation so that the high and low timbres comprise a specific rhythmic pattern. For example, to accompany a dream song for celebrating a specific calendric day, such as the celebration for harvesting certain fruits, the bamboos are stamped in duple rhythm. The rhythmic pattern in the dream song for this event features high and low timbres in 2-beat patterns that are repeated throughout the music (see Examples 3.14b and c). In this music the strong stress is played on the final beat of the 2-beat pattern.

Simultaneously with the stamping bamboos, a male vocalist sings a particular lyric and melodic line, which is repeated by the female chorus in responsorial style. The chorus of women sing in unison. Sometimes the rebana drum is played in unison with the bamboo tubes and the knobbed gong is added to increase the resonance of the musical sound.[7]

a) *Ding galung*

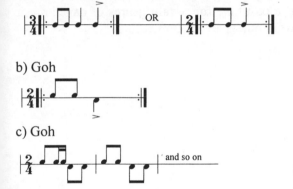

b) Goh

c) Goh

Example 3.14 The rhythmic patterns of the *ding* and *goh* stamping tubes (from Couillard et al., 1979, and Roseman, 1991).

With the singing of the dream songs and the stamping of rhythmic patterns by the bamboo tubes, the Temiar people celebrate a gathering of many people in the village, they carry out a ceremony to heal a sick person, or they engage in some other important event in their community.

Other forms of traditional music using bamboo or wood instruments that are struck or stamped are found in East Malaysia. These include the *togunggu* or *togunggak* and the *lantai lansaran*, which are played by the Kadazan, Murut and other peoples in Sabah.

Togunggak and Togunggu

If there is no gong ensemble in a given community, the bamboo tubes of different sizes are played instead. These bamboo tubes are called *tagunggak* among the interior Murut peoples in Sabah (Figure 3.10). The *Dusun groups from the interior regions of this state call it togunggak,* while the name *togunggu* is used by the KadazanDusun people from Penampang.

Each player holds a bamboo tube and strikes it with a beater made of coconut leaf stem that has been stiffened with bee's wax. The names of these instruments and the musical parts they play are parallel to the gongs of the specific gong ensemble in the community in question.

The bamboo ensembles may be used to accompany dance or even to accompany the dancers walking in a procession. It is possible that this type of ensemble was used at a past time for certain genres of dance music before gongs were imported from other parts of Borneo.

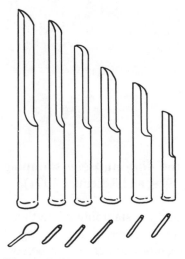

Figure 3.10 *Togunggak/togunggu*

Peruncung

In the state of Sarawak a set of several bamboo tubes that are struck with a stick in imitation of music by the hanging gong ensembles is called *peruncung* or *keruncung*. The Bidayuh people, for example, play the peruncung during their journey on foot from the hill rice fields back to their villages. In this ensemble a bamboo tube with the highest pitch is used to play an ostinato, while the other tubes emitting other pitches produce rhythmic patterns that imitate music usually played by the hanging gong ensemble of the community (see above --- Hanging gong ensembles and Example 3.5).

Lantai Lansaran

Struck beams and slabs of wood used in the performance of music are called *lantai lansaran* by the Murut people of Sabah. The lantai lansaran refers to the instrument (a special kind of floor), the musical genre and the dance that is performed upon the special floor. This floor is usually located in the community house of a Murut village in the interior regions of Sabah. The lantai lansaran is about three meters square and is built about one meter lower than the normal floor in the community house. The special floor is made from flexible wooden boards and is supported below with large wood planks and beams that are placed horizontally so that when a number of people step or dance on the floor, the floor boards knock against the wood beams beneath it (Frame, 1976, pp. 161-3).

Many players stand on the special floor and move their feet in specific steps as they shift their weight so that the floor bounces off the large wood beams located beneath it. In this way the lantai lansaran becomes a percussion instrument that produces loud, running beats to accompany the singing. While they dance, the performers also sing pantuns (4-line verses) and other songs monophonically and with a shouting voice quality. A group of male singers/dancers sing in antiphonal style with a group of female singers/dancers. Although in former times the lantai lansaran performance was connected to head hunting ceremonies, this dance and song is now used for celebrations in the village or to welcome visitors. Today several gongs may also be played to accompany the singing.

While the lantai lansaran constitutes a unique musical instrument made up of concussion wood beams, we find the use of struck wood in yet other forms, shapes and soundscapes in Malaysian traditional music. One of the popular instruments utilizing struck wood is the mortar and pestle, known by various local names among the different communities in Malaysia. The musical traditions involving this kind of instrument arise from the work activity originally associated with it, that is, the pounding of rice.

Antan and Lesung

Before the process of cooking rice takes place, the rice grains must be pounded and winnowed. Women usually carry out this work, and in Sarawak it is often accompanied by singing folk songs commonly known in the community. The rice is pounded with the wooden pestle (*antan* or *alu*) and a mortar (*lesung*). The heavy pestle is raised high and stamped quickly upon the unprocessed rice grains in the well of the mortar. Steady, repeated rhythmic patterns are created from this work. The Kenyah-Badang women in Sarawak pound rice in groups of two, three or four people, alternately pounding into the well of a single mortar. Several rhythmic patterns are usually generated as shown in Example 3.15.

The rhythmic patterns are usually in duple meter and the order of pounding is fixed as shown in Example 3.15. Originally not intended as a musical activity, these rhythms, resulting from the rice pounding, form the basis for the creation of musical sound.

a) two people pounding rice --- arrangement of the   A
                                       players (A & B):   mortar
                                                                                 B

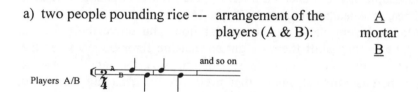

b) three people pounding rice --- arrangement of the   A
                                       players (A, B, C):   B mortar
                                                                            C

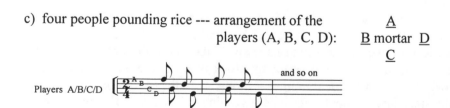

c) four people pounding rice --- arrangement of the   A
                                         players (A, B, C, D):   B mortar D
                                                                                  C

Example 3.15 Rhythmic patterns as a result of pounding rice.

In the villages of Sabah and Sarawak the instrument used to pound rice, the pestle and mortar, is used as a musical instrument. Among the Kayan people of the Upper Rejang region of Sarawak, the women play the pestle and mortar as entertainment, especially in the evenings. The surface of the mortar is stamped upon using several pestles, usually three players stamp one mortar (Plate 3.5). In this context the mortar, originally an implement for work, becomes a stamped idiophone.

In performance, the mortar is stamped upon in specific places on its surface to produce different timbres of sound. According to the Kayan women, usually each of two players holds a pestle and stamps the mortar near, but not in, the well at the center of the surface. This stamping location produces a rather low timbre or thud-like sound. These two players stamp out the running beat in the music, the first player stamps the pestle on the downbeat while the second player stamps her pestle on each upbeat as shown in Example 3.16.

At the same time a third player stamps the surface of the mortar near its edge, thus achieving a high timbre different from those of the running beat. The third player stamps out a specific, independent rhythmic pattern.

Sometimes two additional players play the tangbut bamboo tubes simultaneously with the stamping pestles. The two tangbut are struck with a light wooden stick to produce two different sounds, a high and a low timbre. These two timbres on the tangbut reinforce the running beat in the music, with a high timbre played on every upbeat and a low timbre played on each downbeat in unison with the two pestle players.

The music of the antan and lesung features an interlocking playing style that may be seen in Example 3.16. The running beat pattern at the quaver note level is played by the two pestle players who stamp near the center of the mortar and the two tangbut players who strike their bamboo tubes. The third pestle player stamps near the edge of the mortar's surface in a rhythmic pattern four beats long. The 4-beat pattern is repeated several times and then alternates with a 2-beat syncopated pattern. The 2-beat pattern stresses the upbeat. The tempo of this music usually starts at a moderate pace and little by little becomes extremely fast.

Usually several groups of players alternate, playing this music on the veranda of the longhouse in the evening hours. Generally the task of pounding rice with the antan and lesung is women's work, but playing the antan and lesung is everyone's entertainment.

Example 3.16 *Antan* and *lesung* ensemble rhythmic patterns.

Plate 3.5 *Antan* and *lesung* in a longhouse in Belaga District, Sarawak.

Tumbuk Kalang

Another type of music using the pestle and mortar is known as the *tumbuk kalang* among the rice farmers in the state of Negeri Sembilan in Peninsular Malaysia. Although this music originated from the work of pounding rice, as in Sarawak, today it is performed as entertainment (Abdul Razak Hassan, 1985-86).

Originally the tumbuk kalang was played during the harvest season. A performance would usually start after the evening prayers [*sembahyang Isyak*] and continue throughout the night. Sometimes the tumbuk kalang would be performed several nights in a row, and each night the performance venue would change from house to house in a given farming community. Today it may be performed for any event such as a cultural show, a ceremony to welcome a visitor, a school event or a formal gathering in the village.

A tumbuk kalang performance may take place in the traditional way, that is, as an ensemble of the mortar and pestles along with a flute. The flute provides the melody while the mortar and pestle players produce resultant rhythmic patterns. In addition, several vocalists join in the performance to sing pantun (4-line verses) in responsorial style. A traditional performance may last a few hours or the entire night.

In recent years though, the tumbuk kalang ensemble and music has also been used in the performance of a dance drama [*taridra*], which includes instrumental music, singing and dancing. For a dance drama, the musical instruments added to the original ensemble are a gong, a rebana drum and a caklempong gong-chime. A narrator introduces the story for the dance drama while the flute provides the background melodies. After the introductory comments, the tumbuk kalang plays a piece (that is, a rhythmic pattern) in unison with the rebana and the caklempong. During the piece, a man and a woman alternately sing verses of pantun or other poetry accompanied by the tumbuk kalang, and sometimes a chorus is also used. As the poetry is sung, a number of male and female dancers perform steps and movements which reflect the theme of the pantun or other verses.

The musical instruments

Originally the tumbuk kalang ensemble consisted of a mortar and three pestles of various sizes, including a long and a short pestle, and a third one small in diameter. A flute was also part of the early ensemble. As this ensemble developed, however, other instruments were added, including a gong, rebana and caklempong gong-chime.

Lesung The lesung or mortar used in this ensemble is known as the *emping lesung* or *tumbuk kalang lesung* [mortar for pounding young rice], which measures some 100 centimeters long. Its surface is flat and rectangular in shape and has a depression or well about 9 to 10 centimeters in diameter in the center. In former times, the well would be filled with rice grains that would be pounded to make *emping* [newly pounded young rice]. The mortar is made from a hard wood.

Antan The antan or pestles are of specific types and sizes. The 'long pestle' is about 112 centimeters long and shaped somewhat like a cone about 3 centimeters in diameter at its playing end and only slightly larger at the opposite end. This pestle is the original type used to pound the newly harvested young rice. The second type of pestle, called the 'short pestle', measures about 60 centimeters long and is also cone shaped with a diameter of about 3 centimeters at its playing end. The third type, known as the 'small pestle', is about 90 centimeters long with a cylindrical shape about 2 centimeters in diameter.[8]

Long ago the short and small pestles were added to the tumbuk kalang ensemble in the musicians' search for new timbres and sound qualities. Usually the small pestle plays the *melalu* part that is stamped on the right side of the top of the mortar. The long pestle plays the interlocking or *meningkah* part stamped on the left side of the top of the mortar, and the short pestle plays the *membapak* part which is stamped on the left or right lateral surfaces of the mortar (Abdul Razak Hassan, pp. 63-4).

The frame support for the mortar is a wooden rack used to hold the mortar in place on the floor or the ground. The mortar itself is suspended on thick string or ropes attached to the rack. In this way, the mortar is able to produce loud and resonant sounds when it is stamped upon using the pestles.

Seruling The seruling is a flute made of bamboo measuring about 25 centimeters long. This is a recorder and has seven finger holes at the front and a thumb hole at the back side. The holes are equidistant.

Gong The gong used in the tumbuk kalang ensemble is similar to the tetawak (see Chapter 1 --- Figure 1.1), and the caklempong gong-chime consists of five to eight small knobbed gongs. The gongs are placed horizontally on their own wooden rack (see Figures 3.1-3.2). The rebana is a frame drum, and its single drum head is struck with the player's hands (see Chapter 1 --- Figures 1.12-1.13).

The music

Today the tumbuk kalang repertory includes about 30 tunes (Abdul Razak Hassan, pp. 79, 122). The song lyrics describe daily activities in the villages in past and current times, including the social and economic aspects of village life. Certain tunes are commonly heard in given regions, while different tunes are performed in other districts of the countryside.

Rhythm, Form and Melody The number of pestles used in a particular performance depends upon the piece played. Some pieces use only three pestles while other pieces require four or more additional pestles. As noted above, tumbuk kalang music features an interlocking performance style that produces resultant rhythmic patterns. Usually the meter is duple and most rhythmic patterns are 4 beats long. A specific rhythmic pattern is repeated throughout a tune such as shown in Example 3.17a (see bar 5 onward), the piece *Tiga Beranak*.

a) *Tiga Beranak*

Scale

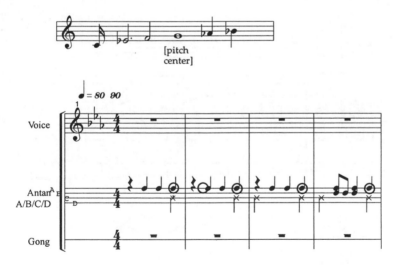

b) *Timang Kak Janda* (excerpt)

Scale

x = the pestle is pounded on the right side (C) or left side (D)
   of the mortar.

Example 3.17 **Excerpts from *tumbuk kalang* pieces.** (Abdul Razak Hassan 1985-86, pp. 134-6 and 138-40, transcribed by P. Matusky)

Example 3.17a illustrates that typically all the pestles begin stamping at a different time interval (see bars 1-5). The resultant rhythmic pattern is shown in the score of the piece *Tiga Beranak*, but this pattern actually consists of four separate 4-beat patterns as follows:

Pestle A   (stamped on the surface of the mortar
(*melalu*)   to the right of the well; beat 4 in the well):

Antan B   (stamped on the surface of the mortar
(*meningkah*)   to the left of the well):

Antan C   (struck on the left side of the body
(*membapak*)   of the mortar):

Antan D   (struck on the right side of the body
(*membapak*)   of the mortar):

The four separate rhythmic patterns combine to form the resultant rhythmic pattern. Another feature that is clear in the pieces given in Example 3.17 involves the use of an end-accented rhythmic pattern. In these examples, and in other pieces as well, a rhythmic pattern usually has the strongest stress on its final beat. This characteristic is also found in other folk and classical music in Malaysia and in Southeast Asia in general (Becker, 1968, pp. 173-91).

While the specific rhythmic patterns are played on the tumbuk kalang, the poetry is sung by a soloist and a chorus, if present. As shown in Example 3.17a, a melody may be structured in short repeated phrases, *a*, *b*, *a*, *b*, *c*, *d*, and these are sung by the soloist. The verse is completed by the chorus that sings two phrases, *d1* and *e*, always with the same text. The form, then, is strophic incorporating a short refrain sung by a chorus.

The lyrics of other pieces in the tumbuk kalang repertory are pantun (traditional verse in four lines). In the sung pantun the same melodic line may be repeated for each phrase of text. This kind of piece is iterative in form as shown in Example 3.17b, the piece entitled *Timang Kak Janda*.

The pitches in the melodic repertory of the tumbuk kalang tradition are similar to those of the Western tuning system. But the melodies themselves are based on 4- , 5- , or 6-tone scales. The piece *Tiga Beranak*, for example, uses a hexatonic scale containing a minor third interval, while the pitch center is the 4th scale degree. In contrast, the melody for the piece *Timang Kak Janda* is based on a 4-tone scale containing the interval of a Perfect 4th and a minor 3rd, each found on opposite ends of the scale. In this piece the pitch center is the 2nd scale degree. These scales reflect the folk tradition in which the tumbuk kalang song repertory is rooted.

Kertuk kayu and kertuk kelapa

Our discussion of music produced on musical instruments using struck or stamped wood concludes with two genres of music found in the northeast state of Kelantan in Peninsular Malaysia. These genres are called the *kertuk kayu* [lit., struck wood] and *kertuk kelapa* [lit., struck coconut].

In former times, in the state of Kelantan, the instrument called *kertuk kayu* was played for entertainment purposes. This instrument consisted of several cylindrical-shaped beams of wood or tubes of bamboo about 60 centimeters long (Sheppard, 1972, pp. 54-5). All the pieces were hung horizontally in a rack and struck with a wooden stick to play rhythmic patterns (Figure 3.11).

Today the more popular instrument that is still played in the villages is the *kertuk kelapa*. This instrument resembles a one-keyed xylophone (Figure 3.12). Usually four to eight or more instruments form a set, with each instrument played by a single player. The kertuk kelapa ensembles are usually heard after the rice harvest when the farmers in a region have time to participate in this as well as rebana ubi performances and other kinds of entertainment and competitions.

The kertuk kelapa is usually heard, too, during special celebrations and festivals in the towns. A likely time to hear this ensemble is during the annual celebration of the sultan's birthday in the town of Kota Bharu, Kelantan. At a festival, teams of players usually compete for a prize based on the originality, uniqueness and liveliness of the rhythmic patterns they beat out on the kertuk kelapa.

Figure 3.11 *Kertuk kayu*

The instrument

To make the ketuk kelapa a young coconut is cut open at the top, cleaned and set in the sun for several weeks until it is completely dried. Then it is attached to a wooden frame about 18 centimeters high that holds it upright and stable (Figure 3.12). A thin slab of *nibong* wood (a hard wood), about 46 centimeters long and 9 centimeters wide, is placed over the hole at the top of the coconut shell. The wood slab is secured using three wooden pegs like the keys on a xylophone. The wood slabs may or may not be tuned to specific pitches, but usually highness and lowness of pitch is discernible when several instruments are struck in an ensemble.

Each wood slab is struck by one player using a padded beater or using the wooden tip of the beater that is not padded.

The music

Rhythm and Form   The musical pieces played by the kertuk kelapa ensemble consist of rhythmic patterns. These patterns are played in an interlocking style by an ensemble of four to 10 or more players. Each player strikes one kertuk kelapa with a beater. Each beater is made so that the player may strike the wood key with the padded part of the beater or with the bare wood of the beater at its tip. In this way, a single player may obtain at least two different timbres from his instrument.

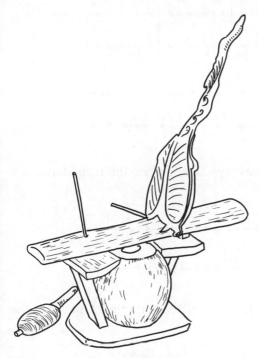

Figure 3.12 *Kertuk kelapa*

In the rhythmic pattern transcribed in Example 3.18, the timbre produced using the padded part of the beater is notated with the symbol of a normal crochet or quaver musical note, while the timbre played using the wooden part of the beater is notated with a percussion symbol (x).

The kertuk kelapa rhythmic patterns are usually in duple meter. These patterns are of the resultant type and consist of two or three different parts played by two or three different sections in the ensemble. If two different parts are featured in the music, then several players in the ensemble play the running beat with some of those playing the downbeats and others playing the upbeats (3.18a, Groups A & B). At the same time, one player beats out a specific rhythmic pattern that interlocks with the running beat as shown in Example 3.18a (Lead player). The independent pattern is often syncopated by stressing certain upbeats at the quaver note level. This pattern interlocks with the running beats to produce the resultant rhythmic pattern.

a) two sections play (1) the independent rhythmic pattern, and (2) the running beat

b) two sections in the ensemble play separate rhythmic patterns that interlock

c) three sections in the ensemble play different rhythmic patterns that interlock

Key: a note head designated by 'x' indicates that the key is hit with the wood part of the beater; all other notes are played with the padded part of the beater.

Example 3.18   Excerpt from rhythmic patterns played by a *kertuk kelapa* ensemble in Kelantan.

In other rhythmic patterns, two groups of players in the ensemble may play two separate patterns that interlock, using the different timbres possible on the instrument.   The use of different timbres is shown in Example 3.18b and c.

If three parts occur in the music, such as two small groups and a solo player, then three different rhythmic patterns interlock to produce the complex resultant pattern such as that shown in Example 3.18c. In this example the two different timbres, produced by the padded and unpadded part of the beater, are also used.

The musical structure in a kertuk kelapa piece is usually sectional with sections repeated in various ways. The rhythmic patterns are usually 4 or 8 beats in length, and these may be repeated to comprise a larger section of music. In a typical piece, we would hear the statement of the initial rhythmic pattern, then a different 4- or 8-beat pattern would follow, and eventually the original pattern would return later in the piece. This is especially so in longer pieces where the reverting type of form is commonly found. Sometimes the reverting scheme is quite regular in the return of the original material, but in a varied version. A scheme of this kind might be outlined as *A, A1, B, A2, C, A3, D, A4* and so on. Other pieces are structured using other schemes within the reverting type of form.

Percussion and wind ensembles

Gendang Silat

As its name implies, the *gendang silat* [lit., martial arts drums] is an ensemble and form of music that accompanies the Malay *silat* or art of self-defense.   The gendang silat also accompanies stylized martial arts movements performed as dance for certain ceremonies. Just as the opening episode involving a battle scene is played each time the shadow play is performed (see Chapter 1--- wayang kulit Kelantan), many types of theatrical performances also open with a short silat dance to ensure a successful performance.

There are several types of local silat music in Malaysia such as that played by the caklempong and the kulintangan ensembles. The music is generally fast-paced with a strong rhythmic drive to accompany the quick, strong movements by the silat competitors.   Another example of a highly dynamic and aggressive music to accompany the action of the martial arts is performed by the gendang silat from the east coast states of Peninsular Malaysia, especially from Kelantan. This small ensemble features two drums and a gong along with one serunai that is used to play the melody. The ensemble and its music are referred to simply as 'gendang silat'.

The musical instruments

Gendang   The Malay gendang drum is used in the silat ensemble of Kelantan.   It is an elongated barrel drum, slightly convex, with two drumheads of different sizes.   As described in Chapter 1 (wayang kulit Kelantan and makyung music), the drumheads are attached to the body with rattan laces or thick nylon rope.   Just as found in the shadow play and makyung ensembles, two drums are used, one large in size (the *'gendang ibu'* [mother drum]) and the other slightly smaller (called the *'gendang anak'* [child drum]) (See Figure 1.5).

The two gendang are played by two drummers who sit on the floor facing each other.   The drums are placed horizontally on the floor, but the large drum head is slightly propped up and supported by the players foot to stabilize the drum for ease in playing it.   Sometimes a wooden stand may be used to further stabilize the drum as shown in Plate 3.6.   The large drumhead is hit with a wooden beater, while the small drumhead is hit with the player's hand.   When the gendang is struck with the hands the sounds produced are vocalized as 'pak', 'cak', 'ting', and 'duh', just as in other genres of traditional music using this drum (see also Chapter 1 --- wayang kulit Kelantan).

Gong   One large knobbed gong is used in the gendang silat ensemble.   It is usually made from a metal barrel with a diameter ranging from 40 to 60 centimeters.   The walls are somewhat thin and when hit with a padded beater one pitch is emitted.   It is usually hung from the roof beams or from a wooden rack.   Sometimes the face of the gong is painted in bright colors with geometric designs.   A tetawak gong may be used in place of the gong made from a metal barrel (Figure 1.1).

Serunai   The large-size serunai is used to play the melody.   The instrument is identical to that used in the shadow play orchestra in Kelantan.   It is blown using a circular or continuous breathing technique so that, once begun, the melody does not stop until the piece and the silat action comes to an end (See Figure 1.7 and Chapter 1 --- wayang kulit Kelantan for details on the construction and playing of the serunai).   A given piece may last as long as 10 minutes or more.

The music

Silat music is polyphonic and features a melodic line, percussive rhythmic patterns and a colotomic unit played on the gong.

Melody The melody in a silat piece is played by the serunai player. The continuous or circular breathing technique allows for long melodic lines that are played for several minutes with no break, usually lasting throughout an entire silat bout. The improvised melodic line consists of short melodic motifs that are strung together. The short motifs usually consist of fast-moving notes of short time values (such as semiquavers and demisemiquavers). The motifs also contain many melodic ornaments such as the acciacatura, double acciacatura, cambiata, appogiatura and portamento or sliding from one pitch to another. The use of semitone and microtonal intervals and the technique of the portamento all help to create a feeling of extreme tension in this music (some of the melodic ornaments are indicated by a horizontal bracket beneath the notes in Example 3.19).

Just as in the music for the Kelantan shadow play, a given melodic line in a silat piece features the contrast between long sustained notes with no vibrato or tremolo ('dead tones') and other passages of fast-moving notes. The sustained, static passages clearly contrast with other motifs of fast moving notes in which the various melodic ornaments are imbedded. When the tempo is slow the melodic line is heavily ornamented (Example 3.19, bars 1-17). However, when the tempo becomes fast, the melodic ornamentation decreases and sustained notes and dotted rhythm are characteristically used in the melodic line (Example 3.19, bars 38-40, and 46-53).

The tempo, at the beginning of a silat competition, is extremely slow, but gradually increases to a very fast speed in synchronization with the quick and aggressive movements of the silat competitors (see the wide range of tempo markings throughout Example 3.19).

It is interesting to note that when the tempo becomes fast, the tonal focus changes and rises to a higher pitch than the original (see Example 3.19, the focus of the serunai melody shifts from *e-flat* upwards to *g-flat*). A fast tempo, then, usually implies a slightly rising tonal level in the melody that helps to project a sense of tension in the music.

Rhythm In gendang silat pieces the rhythm is usually in duple meter. As noted above, the tempo starts very slowly, and gradually becomes very fast. In addition to rising pitch levels in the melody, the fast tempo along with syncopated rhythmic patterns also instill a feeling of tension and aggressiveness in the spirit of the participants who are fighting in the silat competition.

Plate 3.6 *Gendang silat* **drummers and** *serunai* **player (foreground) at a competition in Kota Bharu, Kelantan.**

Key: c = timbre 'cak', t = timbre 'ting', p = timbre 'pak', d = timbre
    'duh', x = use wood beater, ∿ = continued from preceding music.

Example 3.19 Excerpt of *gendang silat* music from Kelantan.

Two gendang players perform the rhythmic patterns in an interlocking style. Each of the two drummers simultaneously plays a separate rhythm, which produces a resultant rhythmic pattern. To accompany a given silat competition various resultant patterns are used, but most are four beats long. In a typical pattern, the large gendang is oriented toward beats 1 and 3, while the drum strokes on the small gendang tend to focus on beats 2 and 4. This orientation of strokes on the two drums is similar to many percussive patterns in the shadow play and makyung music, and may be seen early in the transcribed silat piece when the tempo is slow (Example 3.19, bar 12 onwards).

The rhythmic patterns in silat drumming are improvisatory in nature. The short 4-beat patterns are repeated and played in various ways as the music progresses, and at times drum rolls are featured (as in Example 3.19, bars 24-6). With a fast tempo, dotted rhythm is found in the drum parts, as shown in bars 39 and 44 of Example 3.19. The strong accent of the stick-hit beats and the dotted rhythm enhances the overall dynamism of the music.

Form   The rhythmic patterns and melodies of the silat pieces are supported by a colotomic unit played on the single gong in the ensemble. When the tempo is slow the 4-beat colotomic unit is marked by a stroke of the gong on beat 4, but when the tempo becomes fast the colotomic unit changes to 2 beats and the gong is hit on every other downbeat. The 2- or 4-beat colotomic units are repeated throughout given sections of a piece. These time units support the duple meter in the rhythm of the music

The form of silat pieces is determined by the rhythmic patterns played by the two gendang players. The overall form of a silat piece is sectional, and the musical structure tends to be progressive. The changes in the drum patterns occur throughout the several musical sections of a piece and coincide with the tempo changes (see Example 3.19, a short excerpt from a silat piece lasting some 10 minutes or more.

In general, the music played by the gendang silat ensemble offers strong contrasts. A very slow tempo, eventually giving way to an extremely fast tempo (see Example 3.19, tempi ranging from 30 to 216 beats per minute), along with variations and differences in the rhythmic patterns, generates a music that enhances the drama of the competition between two fighters. The sharp timbres produced with the stick-hit drum strokes bring attention to the more subtle sounds of the hand-hit drum strokes. The contrast of the low, thud-like timbres with the high 'tak' timbres and loud, sharp stick-hit sounds gives a dramatic and unique quality to the music.

In the melodic lines, specific pitches in long sustained note values are contrasted against passages using many fast-moving notes. The ornamented melodic motifs also contrast strongly with the long, sustained, vibrato-less pitches. The use of the specific melodic ornaments, the microtonal intervals, fast tempo, syncopated rhythm and the unique percussive timbres produce a type of music highly suited to accompany the sudden, quick and strongly aggressive movements of the silat competitors.

Nobat

Among the Malays of Peninsular Malaysia, nobat, an instrumental musical genre of the court tradition, has long been accepted as a symbol that helped to signify status and power in society. The nobat is part of the royal regalia used in all royal ceremonies to uphold the sovereignty of the king as embodied in the socio-political world view of the Malays, particularly in earlier times.

In the history of this ensemble, the nobat, as part of the royal regalia became a political symbol that expressed the meaning of *daulat* [divine essence] to the Malays and linked them to a wider political and social structure. As music in the service of the king, accompanying all royal rituals and ceremonies, it is believed to be endowed with the divine essence or *daulat* that is communicated to it through the king's body.

Nobat was an Arabic musical genre that was introduced into the courts of the Malay rulers in the 13th century. Even up to the present, the Malay Sultanates still retain the nobat in all their functions. Its instruments are part of the royal regalia put on display and carried in procession during state ceremonies. The solemn music gives an aura of sacredness to all royal occasions reminding the royal subjects of the divine power of their kings and the absolute respect due to him. Although not all rulers of the states in Malaysia possess a set of nobat instruments, those who have, such as Kedah, Perak and Kelantan, always lend their nobat to other rulers who are being installed. According to the *Hikayat Raja-Raja Pasai*, when a saint introduced Islam to Pasai (Sumatra) and installed the king who was converted to Islam, he brought along the nobat tradition which since then became a permanent feature in the Malay courts (Ku Zam Zam Ku Idris, 1993).

The nobat has always been a court music even in its place of origin, the palaces of the Middle Eastern rulers. This music genre, known as *naubah* or *naubat* in the Middle East, became popular in Arabia during the reign of the Abassid Caliphate in the 9th century (847-945 C.E.). During this period, the term naubah or naubat referred to a company of musicians who took turns performing at certain periods of the day. In the course of time naubat came to refer to the periodic playing of the caliph's military band at the time of the five Muslim daily prayers.

The military band of *naubah* became one of the most important emblems of sovereignty for the caliph. In the beginning, the ensemble was made up of a square tambourine (*duff*) and a reed pipe (*mizmar*). Later when the Muslims of Al-Hijaz came in contact with the Arabs of Al-Hira and Ghassan, other instruments such as a second reed pipe (*surnay*), the spirit-stirring drum (*tabl*), a large metal trumpet (*bud-al-nafir*), a kettle drum (*dabdab*), a shallow kettle drum (*qasa*), and cymbals (*sunuj*) were added to the ensemble.

In the 13th century *naubah* became one of the most important types of composition in Arabian music. It assumed a new character as suite or cassation, that is, a number of movements played in succession. The cassation was different from the music of the military band of the earlier period. There were five movements in it, namely the *qual*, *ghasal*, *tarana*, *frudasht* and *mustazad*. Naubah also took the form of a type of vocal and instrumental music known as cantata, which was performed when entertaining and honoring guests of the king.

As Islam spread so did nobat. From Arabia it was introduced to the courts of other Muslim rulers in Iran, Iraq, Syria, Turkey, India and also the Malay Archipelago. In all these places it continued to be the music in service of the king, used to enhance his status and power.

In the Malay Archipelago, it is believed that nobat was first introduced to the courts of Bentan and Pasai in Sumatra in about the 13th century. The introduction of the nobat to the Malay Peninsula was made by the son-in-law of the Queen of Bentan, Sri Tri Buana, who established the first kingdom at Tumasik (Singapore). According to legend, the king lost his crown when his ship was hit by a storm while sailing to the island of Tumasik and, therefore, he had himself installed to the beat of the nobat. From that time onward it was believed that all Malay kings of the Peninsula were installed to the drums of the nobat. The term for enthronement was changed from 'crowning' or *mahkotakan* to 'drumming' or *tabalkan*. The term *tabal*, which means enthronement of the king, might have been derived from the Arabic word *tabl* that referred to the spirit-stirring drum in the earlier ensemble. When the kingdom of Melaka was founded in the 15th century, its first Muslim ruler, Mohammad Shah, instituted certain court ceremonies and nobat became a royal institution.

Although the nobat retained its tradition as music in the service of the king, it took on a different cultural significance in the Malay courts. It became a sacred music, a receptacle of the divine essence of *daulat*, which not only enhanced the status of the kings but also legitimized their right to rule. Filled with this divine essence, nobat helped to consecrate the king as the epitome of power and status in Malay society. The music itself could only be played by a select group of musicians who were believed to be mystically related to the king himself. These musicians were referred to as *Orang Kalau* or *Orang Kalur*. Today the nobat ensemble can be found in the sultan's palace in the states of Kedah, Perak, Selangor, Trengganu and Kelantan.

The musical instruments

The basic nobat ensemble used in each Malay court is basically the same, although each ensemble differs in size from one state to another and from time to time.

Each ensemble normally consists of a *serunai* (reed pipe), *nafiri* (long silver trumpet), two *gendang* (double-headed drums) and a *nehara* (kettledrum; also called *nengkara*). Sometimes one hanging knobbed gong is used also. Because of their special quality and function, when played the instruments are placed in a special building called *Balai Nobat* [nobat hall] (as in the states of Kedah and Perak), or in a special room in the palace referred to as the nobat room. The instruments are encased with yellow cloth, the royal color of the king, which signifies light and the power of gold and the sun (Plate 3.7).

The serunai used in the nobat is made of a hardwood with the bell-shaped lower end made of silver (see Figure 1.7 and description in Chapter 1).

The nafiri is a straight, valveless trumpet usually made of silver about 70 centimeters long. The tube of the trumpet is cone-shaped and has decorative bands encircling it (Plate 3.8).

The nehara or nengkara drum in the ensemble is a single-headed kettle-shaped drum about 40 centimeters in diameter (Figure 3.13). The drumhead is made of deer or goat skin and is attached to the wooden body with rattan laces. It is struck using two thin wooden beaters.

The gendang or gendang nobat consists of two double-headed barrel drums (in large and small sizes, see Figure 1.5 in Chapter 1 and Plate 3.7 below). Like the nehara, the body of these drums is made of a special hard wood (*kayu teras jerun*). The skins are attached with rattan laces, and the drumheads are struck with the hand or with a slightly outward-curved wooden stick.

Plate 3.7 The *gendang nobat* (wrapped in yellow cloth designating royalty), one drumhead is hand-hit and the other is stick-hit. (Photo by Kweh, S.-B.)

The music

Whenever a ruler holds a royal audience or whenever there is a royal function in the palace, the nobat music must be played. These royal functions include all rites of passage such as coronations, weddings, circumcisions and burials as well as ceremonies honoring guests and dignitaries.

The nobat orchestra plays instrumental music that is referred to as *'man'* (Ku Zam Zam, 1996, pp. 244-51). It is believed the term 'man' is a shortened form of the Sanskrit word 'mantra'. The nobat pieces are considered to be like mantra, which when sounded are connected to magical power to give sovereignty to the king. The number of pieces in the nobat repertory vary from state to state. In Kedah, for example, there are 19 pieces or 'man', 16 of which use a mnemonic notation system called *'dai'*.

Plate 3.8 The *nafiri* trumpet of the *nobat*. (Photo by Kweh, S.-B.)

Figure 3.13 *Nehara (nengkara)*

The *dai* use Jawi letters (an Arabic derived script) as symbols or notation that represent specific sounds or timbres for the gendang drums and the gong. The Jawi letters are used in the *dai* system to signify the gendang timbres called 'tang', 'tik', 'dam' and 'kap'. The basic units in the dai system are nine Jawi letters, which represent the different timbres as in the several examples shown below:

Letter	Meaning (for gendang and gong parts)
ر	timbre 'tang' --- drum stroke with the left hand in the middle of the small drum head of the gendang Nobat.
س	timbre 'dam' --- drum stroke repeated like a thundering sound (drum roll) in unmetered rhythm. The gendang nobat is struck with the wooden beater on the large drumhead (right).
ا	timbre 'dam' --- struck on the large drum head with the wooden beater (right), one drum stroke only.
أ	timbre 'dam' --- one stroke on the large drum head of the gendang nobat in unison with a stroke on the gong.
•	one stroke on the gong which signifies movement from one section of a piece to a different section of the piece.
ب	timbre 'dam' --- a stroke on the large drum head (right) of the gendang nobat with the wooden beater left on the drumhead for a duration of 30 seconds.
و	timbre 'dam' --- a stroke with the hand on the edge of the small drumhead (left side) of the gendang. The timbre is resonant.
ه	timbre 'tik'.
م	timbres follow in succession 'tak-tik-tang-tang', rhythm and meter are not specified.

As additional notation, the symbols o or x signify the sound of the nafiri trumpet. An example of the use of the dai system is shown in an excerpt from a piece entitled *Belayar* in Example 3.20a and b below. Because Jawi letters are written from right to left, the standard music notation in Example 3.20b is also written from right to left to show the musical events and the corresponding dai letters.

a) the *dai* system used to notate the *gendang* and gong parts for the *nobat* piece *Belayar*

اا أصᵒ ر . رصᵒ ر×اا أر أ اⅠⅠ ×ر ⅠⅠ أر أ ᵓ ر ᵓ رᵓوᵓ×

اⅠر أ و ᵓ رᵓ×

سأر ب ب رⅠⅠ×أ ᵓ رᵓ ×Ⅰ رⅠⅠ×أ Ⅰ ᵓ ررⅠ

ⅠⅠ . Ⅰ . Ⅰ رⅠⅠ أᵓ رᵓ .

b) the *gendang* timbres, gong stroke and corresponding *dai* symbals in the piece *Belayar*

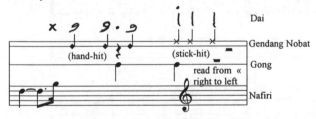

c) excerpt of the piece Belayar in standard music notation

Example 3.20 Excerpt of the piece *Belayar* from the repertory of the Kedah nobat. (Recorded by Ku Zam Zam, 1991 in Alor Setar, transcribed by P. Matusky)

In the transcription of the piece *Belayar* in Examples 3.20b and c, it is clear that only a part of the complete rhythmic pattern is written using the dai system. Therefore, this notation functions mainly as a mnemonic system to help the musicians remember the specific piece.

The music of the nobat tends to be medium to slow in tempo and is very stately and majestic. A piece especially important for the installation of the king is transcribed in Example 3.20c. As shown in this excerpt, the polyphonic music of the nobat consists of a melodic line played on the serunai, a rhythmic part played by two types of drums, that is, the gendang nobat and the nengkara, and a third strata of sound played on the nafiri. In the Kedah nobat tradition there is also a gong part that usually marks the ends of the drum rhythmic patterns.

Scale and Melody   The melody of the nobat piece in Example 3.20c is based on a heptatonic scale with the natural and sharp forms of the second scale tone (pitch *g*) and the fifth scale tone (pitch *b*). The pitch center is on tone 3 (pitch *a*) in this scale (see Example 3.21).

Scale

Pentachord on pitch *g#*

Pentachord on pitch *f#*

Example 3.21 The scale and pentachords for the *nobat* piece *Belayar*.

Early in the piece *Belayar* the melody focuses on a pentachord that is based on the pitch *g#* (Example 3.20c, bars 2-6), then the melody shifts its focus to another pentachord based on the pitch *f#* (Example 3.20c, bars 7-12). In this musical tradition, the serunai melody is highly ornamented with trills (Example 3.20, bars 2-3), triplet figures (bars 4-5), acciacatura (bars 5-6), portamento (bar 4), appogiatura (bars 11-12) and turns (bars 16 and 19-20).

In contrast to the serunai melody, the melodic line of the nafiri is rather static with a focus on the interval of a Perfect 4th, minor 3rd, or a single sustained pitch. The dotted rhythm and the appogiatura are featured in this nafiri melodic line using sustained pitches that are clear and loud (Example 3.20c, bars 3-4).

Rhythm   The rhythmic pattern played by the drummers of the two gendang nobat is not only the basic rhythm of a piece but it also identifies a given, named piece. Although several timbres are used, the two drummers play mainly in unison. The timbres of the gendang are differentiated by the use of the wooden stick beater or the hand to strike the drumhead. There is a tendency to use rhythmic patterns of 16 beats, but segmented into smaller units or phrases. For example, in Example 3.20c, sections A, C and C2, the

16-beat rhythmic pattern is structured in a 4-beat phrase followed by a 12 beat phrase. Sometimes 10-beat rhythmic patterns, or patterns of other lengths, are featured.

The nengkara drum usually plays the running beat in the music in order to control the tempo in the pieces. This instrument also indicates the ending cadence by using a triplet figure at the end of specific rhythmic patterns (Example 3.20c, bars 2 and 16).

Form   The musical form in nobat pieces is usually sectional with variation and repetition. The piece *Belayar* (Example 3.20c), for example, may be divided into sections noted as Introduction, A, B, C, B2, D, D2, E and so on. Specific rhythmic patterns and tonal material identify these sections. Section A is based on a 16-beat rhythmic pattern and the pentachord $g\#$ to d^l (bars 3-6), while Sections C and C2 use the 4-beat + 12-beat rhythmic pattern with the pentachord $f\#$ to c^l (bars 9-18). Section D uses a 10-beat rhythmic pattern with a mixture of pitches from the two pentachords. The form of this piece is progressive with new melodic lines and rhythmic patterns successively added as the piece progresses. In the analysis of other nobat pieces the reverting form is also found.

Originating from a secular Middle Eastern musical tradition, nobat music developed in Malaysia as a tradition that is special for the Malay kings. Featuring slow tempos, highly ornamented melodic lines, loud and precise rhythmic patterns, and the fanfare-like motifs on the nafiri to announce new musical sections, this music tradition projects power, majesty and appropriateness for the institution of Malay kingship. With its special acoustic characteristics and aesthetics, nobat music has supported the power and legitimacy of the Malay kings since the 15th century.

Notes

1   See also Mantle Hood, 'South-East Asia: The gong-chime ensemble' in *New Grove's Dictionary of Music and Musicians*, Vol. 17 (London: Macmillan, 1980), pp. 763-4.

2   In the *Hadith*, as related by Ibn Majah and Tarmizi from Aisyah binti Abu Bakar, the Prophet said, 'You must announce your marriage ceremony and solemnize your wedding in the mosque, and beat the kompang'.

3   A basic element in performing a piece is to control the tempo. In order to ascertain a tempo and stable timing, a general rule of thumb for the leader of the ensemble is that the placement of the hand hitting the drumhead and the hand holding the kompang should have a distance of at least 0.25 to 0.5 meters. This distance of hand to drumhead is important since the motion of striking the drumhead follows the specific tempo.

4   See Chan, Suet-Ching, '24 *Jie Ling Gu* (Gendang 24 Musim): Perhubungan Muzik dan Koreografi dengan 24 *Jie Qi* Dalam Kalendar Pertanian Cina', MA Thesis (Music), Universiti Sains Malaysia, 2001, for an in-depth analysis of the playing techniques and choreography.

5   See also M. Couillard et al. 'Jah Hut Musical Culture', in *Contributions to Southeast Asian Ethnography*, I (1982), pp. 35-55, and M. Roseman, *Healing Sounds from the Malaysian Rainforest* (Berkeley: University of California Press, 1991)

6   So named because the songs come to a singer in his dreams. See further M. Roseman, 1991.

7   See M. Roseman, *Dream Songs and Healing Sounds in the Rainforest of Malaysia* (Washington D.C.: Smithsonian Folkways) Compact Disc No. 40417. Booklet, p. 2.

8   Abdul Razak Hassan, *Persembahan Tumbuk Kalang* [The Tumbuk Kalang Performance] (Honors paper, Malay Studies Dept., University of Malaya, 1985-86), pp. 20-31; and Ku Zam Zam Ku Idris *'Tumbuk Kalang, Satu Genera Muzik Kerja Pertanian Padi'* [Tumbuk Kalang: A Work Music Genre of the Paddy Farmers] in Nik Safiah Karim, ed., *Segamal Padi Sekunca Budi* (Kuala Lumpur: Akademi Pengajian Melayu, Universiti Malaya, 1993), pp. 210-13.

Chapter 4

Vocal and Solo Instrumental Music

Vocal Music

Vocal music in the folk and classical traditions involves many aspects of life from the birth of a child, to the processes of human socialization, to death and burial. In addition, the oral literature of a society is often disseminated through singing, and the genealogy of an ethnic group may be known primarily through chants and song. Various aspects of religious practices may also involve singing. In this chapter several genres of vocal music are discussed which reflect the way of life, creative expression and musical skill of the many ethnic groups in Peninsular Malaysia, Sabah and Sarawak.

On the Peninsula many kinds of vocal music are, also, used in performances of theatricals such as the shadow puppet play, makyung, mekmulung and Chinese opera. These kinds of vocal music are discussed in Chapter 1, which concerns music for the main types of theatre found in the country. The vocal music sung by soloists or small groups of people in non-theater contexts are discussed here.

Zikir

People everywhere try to achieve contentment and peace of mind in many different ways. Among these are expressing ill feelings and troubles to those willing to listen, or by participating in various forms of meditation.

The Islamic religion encourages and inculcates the practice of *zikir* with the intention of obtaining peace, tranquility and happiness. As recorded in the *Qur'an* [Holy Book of Islam] and *Hadith* [Sayings and Deeds of the Prophet], the practice of zikir embodies focusing the mind in order to overcome problems of spiritual stress, to obtain peace, happiness and gifts from Allah. The word 'zikir' originates from the Arabic word *zikr* [lit., to say, to utter, to remember, to guard, to mean, good deeds]. The word zikir also means oral expression or gesture that is known by the names *tahlil, tahmid, tasbih* and *takbir,* and any kind of practice that is done to obey Allah and bring oneself closer to Him.

The Characteristics of zikir   The zikir can be practiced orally, through gesture (bodily movement) and by emotional inspiration as taught by Islam to become closer to Allah. The performance of zikir expresses the wonder and joy of Allah that is bestowed upon man, such as seen in the zikir of *al-Ma'thurah* [the practices of the Prophet Muhammad and his followers].

Practicing zikir makes a person contrite and guards against the temptation of Satan. It is a form of worship, prayer, pardon (requesting forgiveness from Allah), blessing and greeting. It is also a kind of formal prayer [*solat*], and a form of obedience, all focused on Allah. Furthermore, reading lines of the Qur'an during a performance of zikir is highly encouraged.

According to Ibnu Ata', a Sufi scholar who wrote *al-Hikam* (the *words of Hikmah*), zikir is divided into three parts or kinds:

1.   *Jali* (zikir that is clear, evident)
        The *Jali* zikir is also called *Az-Zikr bil Lisan* (spoken zikir), which features a clear voice so that feeling accompanies the oral expression, such as in performing the *Tasbih, Tahmid, Tahlil, Takbir, Solawat,* and in reading the Qur'an. The *Jali* zikir has two characteristics:
        (a)   *Muqayyad* (bound to specific time, place or practice). Examples are reading the Qur'an, sayings in the *solat* formal prayer, when fulfilling the *haj*, and prayers before eating, after eating, for sleeping, awakening, leaving the house, beginning work or studying, seeing a companion's new suit of clothes, entering and leaving the toilet and so on.
        (b)   *Mutlak* (not bound to specific time or place). Examples are reading the *tahlil* (uttering *La ila ha ill Allah* [There is only one God]); *tasbih* (uttering *Subhana Allah* [God of the Greatest Purity]); *takbir* (uttering *Allahu Akbar* [God is Great]).
2.   *Khafi* (zikir that is done with full devotion and remembrance). The *Khafi* zikir is also called *Az-Zikr bil Qolb* [zikir of the heart or feelings]. This type of zikir is done with deep thought and recollection (with or without oral zikir) about the greatness and power of Allah, such as His creation of the sky and earth.

Ultimately, this type of zikir brings one to an intense awareness of the Creator of the universe.

3.   *Haqiqi* (zikir that is done with the entire body and soul, with external and internal feelings, and at any time or place).

Th e *Haqiqi* zikir is also called *Az-Zikr bil Jawarah* [protect and guard the body and soul from all prohibitions as set down by Allah]. It accomplishes and satisfies all forms of obedience such as striving to fulfill the prayers, fasting, performing the *haj*, traveling from place to place to fulfill religious orders and scholarly functions. This type of zikir reminds us not to be negligent or careless and keeps us close to Allah.

Examples of zikir The type of zikir that is exemplified by the Prophet is easy to do by anyone. In the Hadith, a passage by Aisyah binti Abu Bakar describing the nature or character of a Muslim, says that the Prophet remembers Allah every second of the day. From this Hadith it says:

1.   'If I utter *Subhana Allah, al-hamdu lil Allah, la ilaha ill Allah* and *Allahu Akbar* [God of the Greatest Purity, Praise be to God, there is only one God, and God is Great], then my utterance is more beneficial than obtaining all the riches under the sun.' (see Example 4.1a)

2.   'Whoever praises Allah, completing the *solat* 33 times, the *tahmid* 33 times, the *takbir* 33 times, then rounds up with 100 times *La ilaha ill Allah wahdahu la syarikalah, lahu al-mulk wa lahu al-hamd wa huwa 'ala kulli syai'in qadir* [There is only one God, He has no partners, His Kingdom is steadfastly praised, He is the most powerful] is surely forgiven his sins even though his sins are as many as the waves on the ocean.'

3.   'Who ever utters *Astaghfirullah* 70 times each day, Allah will surely forgive 700 of his sins. Pity be to those who sin more than 700 times a day.' (see Example 4.1d)

4.   'Whoever utters a *selawat* on my name will surely be rewarded with 20 selawat, his position shall be raised 10 fold, his record shall be given 10 virtues, and his misgivings shall be reduced by 10.'

The zikir can be performed by one person or by a group of people who sing out or who express the zikir silently without raising their voices. If the zikir is vocalized out loud it should be accompanied by sincerity and with one's thoughts and feelings focused on Allah, without merriment and without disturbing nearby people who may be praying or reading the Qur'an. A clear and honest expression and a moderate voice should be used.

The performance of zikir should be organized and disciplined, beginning with the *Jali* zikir, then proceeding to the *Khafi* zikir and finally to the *Haqiqi* zikir. All thoughts and feelings should be focused on Allah with full confidence and hope so that He receives the zikir and, in turn, the singers' expectations are fulfilled. In contrast to other acts of devotion such as praying, fasting and reading the Qur'an, the zikir is usually easy to do and can be performed immediately regardless of time or place, and with very strong feelings.

Usually the zikir is vocalized without the accompaniment of musical instruments. It can also be done while meditating alone or in a group such as at a meeting of Muslims to praise Allah. The Sufi followers, also, perform the zikir in a group with voices that are clear and loud while expressing praise to Allah and the Prophet Muhammad.

The music

The zikir may be sung by a soloist or a chorus, but the texture is usually monophonic. It may or may not be accompanied by musical instruments.

The singing style is predominantly syllabic, but often short melodic ornaments occur near the ends of phrases and, in fact, melismas often elongate a final phrase in a piece, as shown in the *Allah* zikir in Example 4.1c. The typical melodic ornaments heard in zikir pieces are grace notes and a slight wavering of pitches (see Example 4.1a), short trills, turns, triplet figures and the use of portamento (Example 4.1b). These ornaments are often imbedded in the melismas.

Form is usually strophic in zikir pieces with the same or very similar melodic lines repeated for several successive verses of text. The internal melodic phrases in a given zikir, however, may exhibit 2-part form (*AB*), progressive patterns (*ABC* etc.), or reverting forms (*ABA*). These possible formal patterns may be seen in Examples 4.1a, b, and c, respectively.

The rhythm used is sometimes unmetered, but more usually a metered rhythm in duple or quadruple patterns is more commonly heard. Sometimes the zikir resembles the style of reading the Qur'an, which is not metered, but instead uses various rhythmic patterns, as shown in Example 4.1d.

a) the *tahlil, tahmid* and *takbir* zikir

b) the *Syahadah* zikir

c) the *Allah* zikir

d) the *Astaghfirullah* zikir in unmetered rhythm

Example 4.1 Types of *zikir*.

Forms related to the zikir

In Kelantan a particular tradition of vocalizing zikir is performed by a group of men who sing in unison. While singing they hit the *rebana besar* [large rebana] drum, which hangs vertically with the drum head facing the singer.

The rebana besar is about 1.2 meters high, about 1 meter in diameter, and weighs about 100 kg. The body is shaped like a cone and the

one drumhead is attached to the body with rattan straps and a large cane
brace at the base end of the body. The thick drumhead of water buffalo
hide is tightened with large wood wedges that are inserted between the
brace and the bottom edge of the drum. A small metal ring is attached at
the center of the body so that the drum can be hung with the drumhead
positioned vertically. The drumhead of the rebana besar is always hit at the
center or at the edge with the player's hands.

Even though this instrument accompanies the performance of zikir,
it can also be drummed, in pairs, as entertainment in the villages.
Sometimes it is known by nicknames that sound like the low and resonant
sound it makes (Sheppard, 1972, p. 54).

Two or three rebana besar drums (Fig. 4.1) are played in unison
with the appropriate rhythmic patterns to accompany the singing of the
zikir. Specific rhythmic patterns are usually in duple meter and use at least
two different mnemonic sounds or drum timbres, that is, the timbres called
'tak' and 'dung'. As in the playing of other rebana drums (see, for
example, Chapter 1 --- mekmulung and Chapter 3 --- kompang), the rebana
besar produces the timbre 'tak' when it is hit with the hand at the edge of
the drum head, while the timbre 'dung' is produced when the drumhead is
hit near the middle.

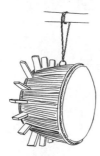

Figure 4.1 *Rebana besar*

In the sample of zikir with rebana besar accompaniment in Example
4.2, the rhythmic pattern in the accompaniment is characterized by quaver
note motion and dotted rhythm. The 4-beat rhythmic pattern is repeated
continuously throughout the piece, and both the timbres 'tak' and 'dung'
alternate every two or three beats (see Example 4.2, bars 3-4 and 6-7).

Even though the drum that accompanies zikir is usually called
'rebana', there are many kinds of rebana drums found in various regions of
the country, just as there are various regional styles of singing zikir. In the
states of the southern part of the Peninsula, for example, this vocal music is

accompanied by beating the frame drum called *kompang* (see Chapter 3). Kompang music is played by a group of players hitting the drum in different rhythmic patterns while singing. Sometimes this frame drum is made with small metal disks (or jingles) inserted into the frame, in which case the drum is called *hadrah*. In contrast, the type of vocalization called *marbahan* (sung verses in praise of Allah and the Holy Prophet) usually does not use musical accompaniment at all.

Example 4.2 The opening line of a *zikir* with accompaniment on the *rebana besar* drum.

The genre called *zikir rebana* is performed in the state of Negeri Sembilan. It is performed to praise the Prophet and messengers of Allah, to accompany a wedding procession and the *bersanding* ceremony, and to celebrate a circumcision. The zikir is sung in the Arabic language and is accompanied by rhythmic patterns played on the rebana and gong. Many zikir rebana ensembles use from 12 to as many as 20 rebana drums and a single knobbed gong.

Another type of vocal music found in Kelantan that is related to the vocalization of zikir is known as *rebana kercing*. In the rebana kercing, a group of men vocalize zikir while playing rhythmic patterns using a drum called rebana kercing. The rebana kercing is a single-headed frame drum with small metal disks inserted into the frame. The metal disks jingle when the drum is hit. At a specific time in the performance a group of young boys joins in the performance by singing songs and dancing, while a group of older men plays the rhythmic patterns in a fast tempo to accompany the dancing by the boys. The dances usually consist of simple steps and hand movements.   The rebana kercing performance may take place to accompany the groom in a procession to the bride's house during a wedding ceremony, or to celebrate a festival in connection with a birthday celebration of the king or other royalty.

Finally, in Kelantan the *dikir laba* is sung by a group of men who hold small fans or other props and wave them rhythmically while singing the zikir in responsorial style.

Rodat and Hadrah

The two forms of theater called *rodat* and *hadrah* were possibly connected to the tradition of singing zikir, or at least influenced by it. The hadrah theater is found in Perlis and Kedah, while the traditional theater called rodat is performed in Trengganu. Both of these kinds of theater possibly originated in the Middle East but were brought to Malaysia following different paths and by different peoples. They are found in the folk theater traditions of Malaysia today, and like other forms of music and theater, they both feature small percussion-dominated ensembles.

Rodat   Although the rodat is found in the states of Selangor, Perak, Johor and Pahang, the type of rodat which is better known in the country is the style found in Trengganu on the east coast. This theater features singing and dancing to the accompaniment of drumming.   According to the musicians, the rodat was introduced to people on the Malay Peninsula by traders from Sumatra and Kalimantan in the 19th century.

In the history of this theatrical, several rodat groups existed in Kuala Trengganu in the early 20th century and they performed a basic style that consisted of singing zikir without dance. Later the dance was added to the performance and the groups expanded to some 20 or 30 players, including women. By the 1930s the rodat was performed at weddings, circumcisions, after the harvest season and for ceremonies and state celebrations.

Even though a rodat performance has local and regional characteristics, some features important to this theater form and its music performed in Trengganu are briefly summarized here. A given rodat performance may occur in any setting. The players (called *pengadi*) who play the drums known as the *tar* sit on the floor (or ground, if outdoors), and the male dancers called the *pelenggok* sit in front of the pengadi group. The male dancers sing while swaying their bodies, hands and arms back and forth in time to the singing. Another group of dancers, the female dancers called the *inang*, dance between the pengadi and pelenggok groups. This group of women dancers are guided by a lead dancer, the Mak Inang, and they also sway their arms and hands back and forth and perform simple steps while singing (Harun Mat Piah et al., 1983, pp. 28-31).

Figure 4.2 *Tar (rebana kercing)* **used in the *rodat* theater.**

The membranophone known as the *tar* (or the *rebana kercing*) is the only type of musical instrument used in the performance. The size of this drum is about 20 to 25 centimeters in diameter, and the single drum head of cow hide is attached to the body with small metal tacks. Several small brass disks (called *caping*) are inserted into the drum frame, and these disks jingle whenever the drumhead is struck (Figure 4.2). There are usually about eight tar players in an ensemble.

A performance of rodat involves singing 8 to 12 verses from the *Kitab Zikir* [book of verses praising Allah and the Prophet Muhammad] in responsorial style between the two groups of chorus members (the male and female groups). The singing is accompanied by rhythmic patterns played on the tar (or rebana kercing). Today the signing of the third and subsequent verses are interspersed with popular Malay and Hindustani tunes that are sung by the female singers/dancers.

Hadrah According to the musicians of traditional music, the hadrah and rodat theaters are different forms and came from two very different sources.   The hadrah, they say, was brought to the states of Kedah and Perlis by Indian peoples from Bengal and Nagore.

The original form of the hadrah consisted of singing zikir accompanied by drumming, similar to the rodat.   But slowly dances and popular Malay and Hindustani songs were incorporated into the performance.   The song texts may be in Malay, Urdu or Arabic.

From early times until today only men perform the hadrah.   The female roles in the performance are also played by men who wear colorful women's blouses (*baju kebaya*) and skirts (*sarong*) along with women's makup.   Today historical dramas are enacted as a main part of the hadrah, and popular Malay and Hindustani tunes sung by the female impersonators are interspersed between the acts of the story.

The hadrah ensemble today uses up to eight or 10 rebana frame drums called *gendang hadrah* [lit., hadrah drums], along with a smaller size rebana-type drum called the *gendang anak* or *peningkah*.   While the gendang hadrah provides the main rhythmic pattern in a piece, the peningkah drum plays an interlocking pattern with it.   The two types of drums, thus, produce resultant rhythmic patterns.   Some hadrah troupes sometimes add the *biola* [Western violin] to accompany the songs that are sung by a soloist, and when needed the drummers function as the chorus. In a given piece the solo and chorus parts alternate, followed by drumming on the frame drums.   In addition, there is usually one hanging knobbed gong that serves as a time marker in the music (see further, Mohd. Ghouse, 1976).

Today, both the rodat and hadrah theaters are no longer connected to religion in any way.   In today's society these are secular forms put on for entertainment at weddings, circumcisions, local festivals and other state or national celebrations.

Nasyid

Nasyid songs comprise sung poetry using Middle Eastern rhythms with Islamic themes for the purpose of spreading Islamic values.   It is believed that nasyid originated in Middle Eastern folk songs. The earliest nasyid in the history of Islam was recorded during the Prophet Muhammad's journey from Mecca to Medina, when he was welcomed by the people of Medina as they sang the nasyid piece *Tola'al Badru*.

These songs remind us of our human nature (especially for Muslims who read and study the Qur'an and the Hadith [Practices and Sayings of the Prophet Muhammad]).   They also serve to inculcate good values, morals and habits, and stress the importance of religion and allegiance to nation.

The word 'nasyid' or *'insyad'*, is derived from the word *'nasyada'* meaning 'to look for' or 'to search'. Adding the letter a̲ to the beginning of nasyada results in *'ansyada'* meaning to recite poetry or verses with high and low vocal inflections as if singing zikir (see above). Hence, nasyid is generally connected with song (or music) resulting from singing serious (or classical) poetry, and with the expression of patriotic sentiment.

Nasyid is characterized by singing with a loud, strong voice, and it exists in many different musical forms and styles. In Malaysia the performance of nasyid has been enthusiastically developed by both male and female readers of the Qur'an, especially in Kedah and Penang where the Islamic Holy Book was taught directly or indirectly from Middle Eastern sources before World War II.

Performance practice Originally nasyid was performed informally at home while seated on the floor in a circle formation after studying the Qur'an. The teachers taught while the students sang nasyid. The process of teaching and learning took place by rote method and in call and response style without using any musical instruments. The voices alone carried the song texts and their messages, as the lessons took place from day to day.

Plate 4.1 A women's *nasyid* group in performance. (Photo by Fakhariah Lokman)

Nasyid began to be used as entertainment for the masses in the 1950s. It functioned as interludes at state and national Qur'an reading competitions. In the 1960s the celebration and atmosphere of the fasting month [*Ramadhan*] was enhanced by the birth of the International Qur'an Reading Competition, and with it the singing of nasyid. During these early days the nasyid songs were performed on a stage, with the performers (a group of men, women, or mixed group) standing in a row. The singers stood upright with both hands at their sides or with the right hand crossed over the left. Their facial expression was serious or sad and no hand movements of any kind were used to express their feelings. The women participating in nasyid were required to dress modestly in accordance with Islamic custom, and likewise for the young female singers (Plate 4.1). The men, also, needed to dress modestly, including covering the head with a Malay hat (*songkok*) or a turban, which reflected Islamic culture.

The musical instruments

Originally, musical instruments were not used because both the male and female Qur'an readers (that is, the potential nasyid singers) had good, capable voices as a result of their training in reading the Qur'an. However, whenever nasyid was performed as a social activity, the drums were used to accompany the singing, especially the rebana and the kompang (frame drums, see Figures 1.12. and 3.6). These instruments were played to control the tempo and the rhythm of a song.

The changes in the nasyid performances over time generally followed the developments in music throughout the years and decades. For example, in the 1940s there was no accompaniment except for the use of the drums, but in the 1950s nasyid was accompanied by an *asli* or *ghazal* ensemble (see Chapter 5), and in the 1960s by a pop music ensemble [*kugiran*]. In the 1970s nasyid songs were often accompanied by an orchestra, a synthesizer or an acoustic instrument, but they could also be heard without accompaniment, like an *a cappella* performance in Western music.

Nasyid music

Melody, texture and form Over the years nasyid performers, that is, the readers of the Qur'an and their Islamic religious teachers, were exposed to songs of Middle Eastern character. Hence, the melodies of nasyid pieces were cast in Middle Eastern rhythms and in the *maqam* system of Arabic art music (a system of scale-like patterns to compose melody). The same maqam were used in nasyid songs as were found in chanting or reading the Qur'an, maqam such as *Bayyati, Rast, Nahawand, Hijaz, Soba, Kurd, Sikah* and *'Ajm* (see Example 4.3a). In addition to the Arabic maqam, nasyid pieces also used tonalities akin to Western minor scales, such as those tonalities often found in old Malay songs.

Today, melodies are not limited to the maqam of Arabic music, but they are also built on the major and minor scales of Western music and the scales of Chinese and Indian classical music.

a) two *maqam* used in *nasyid* pieces

b) poetic lyrics (*syair*) and melody

c) rhythmic pattern for *Surah al-Iklas*

Example 4.3 *Maqam*, melody and rhythm in *nasyid* songs.
(Transcriptions by Fakhariah Lokman)

Nasyid songs are usually monophonic and may be sung by a soloist, or even by a chorus in which case they usually feature call and response style. The singing may be syllabic or melismatic with the use of many melodic ornaments, a characteristic influence from Qur'anic sound art with which nasyid has a significant connection. The form of a nasyid piece is subject to the lyrics that usually consist of four lines in a verse. The usual forms may be outlined as AAAA, AAAB, AABA or even ABCD (see Example 4.3b).

Lyrics and rhythm Originally, the nasyid songs in Malaysia had lyrics in the language of the Qur'an, that is, classical Arabic, because the pioneers in developing the nasyid were those who read or chanted the Qur'an and also Islamic religious teachers who were influenced by Middle Eastern culture. This language, classical Arabic, cannot be separated from Islam because the Muslim Holy Book is the main base, which the entire Muslim community, made up of many different nationalities and races, is required to read. Because of the strict rules of Qur'anic recitation and pronunciation, the use of classical Arabic opened the possibility to produce many different rhythmic patterns (Example 4.3c).

Today nasyid is found in many different languages with the purpose of spreading the message of Islam. The lyrics in the different languages are accompanied by melodies in various Middle Eastern rhythms. The masri rhythmic pattern is usually used for nasyid in Malaysia.

In the 1990s, international, state and local school competitions of nasyid began to take place, and with these competitions there were new developments and changes in nasyid. Malaysia has led the way for what some have called the 'New Era of Nasyid' [*Nasyid Era Baru*]. Today, Muslim artists in Malaysia are encouraged to be creative in composing nasyid to launch a new phenomenon, that is a nasyid POP music industry. The Muslim artists who are active today, and who have ignited interest and success in nasyid pop include nasyid groups and individual singers such as Raihan, Brothers, Rabbani, Hijjaz, Huda, An-Nur, Imad, Khairil Johari Johar, Sharifah Aini and so on. Raihan, Brothers and Rabbani are marketing their songs in Singapore, Indonesia, and Islamic countries of the Middle East (see further, Chapter 6).

Welcoming Songs

Vocal music is found in abundance throughout the states of Sabah and Sarawak. Pieces are sung for many different purposes including entertainment at festivals, to welcome visitors, for funeral ceremonies, to prepare for travels to given places, and to heal the sick.

Specific song repertories exist, too, for wedding ceremonies, for the birth of a child, lullabies, and for accepting a person as an adult member of society. There are also songs for building a new house, hunting animals, and for ceremonies connected to the cultivation of rice.

Several ethnic groups in Sarawak sing a vocal repertory to welcome visitors to the longhouse. The welcoming songs are performed in a public place, usually on the veranda. The longhouse dwellers sit around the newly arrived visitors and a small group of women singers gathers close by. The singers perform the welcoming songs while offering drinks to the visitors. These songs may be performed for an hour or more by a small chorus of women along with a soloist from the group. This type of song may be heard throughout the Upper Rejang River region of Sarawak.

In the welcoming song a soloist sings the main text of the song in a syllabic singing style and with a rather narrow melodic range as shown in Example 4.4. The chorus sings a refrain that consists of the lyrics 'jon ta-na-ne' using a single pitch functioning as a drone in the music. The refrain part follows after each main textual phrase by the soloist, and sometimes the solo and chorus parts overlap for a few beats (see for example, Example 4.4, bars 4-5, 10-11, 17-18). The conclusion of the song is signaled by a melodic line that rises to a high, indeterminate pitch and the song abruptly ends.

Using the song in Example 4.4 as a typical example, several important musical characteristics may be pointed out. These include the use of short melodic lines repeated over and over, a syllabic singing style, a rather narrow melodic range, the use of a sung drone or ostinato, dotted rhythm at the quaver note value, and responsorial style singing between a soloist and a chorus.

In addition, the melody is based on a pentatonic scale with a gap of a minor third at the beginning of the scale. Another important tonal feature is the interval of a Perfect 4th (pitches *A* to *d* in the score) that is stressed at the end of each main melodic phrase (see Example 4.3, bars 4, 10, 17). The meter is duple and the form is iterative. In this type of form the main melodic phrase in the piece (Example 4.4 phrase *a*) is repeated over and over with some variation in the rhythm.

Pentatonic scale

Example 4.4 Welcoming song by Kayan singers of the Upper Rejang River in Sarawak.

Pantun

Pantun in Sarawak The singing of verses, normally called pantun, is enjoyed by many different ethnic groups throughout the states of Sabah and Sarawak. The pantun may be sung by a soloist or a small group of singers in performances that can take several hours to complete.

Among the Iban in Sarawak the pantun is sung by a man or a woman without any accompaniment. It is usually vocalized in free rhythm using melodic lines that follow the length and flow of the textual phrases. The melodic lines are repeated with variation. The singing style is mainly syllabic, but sometimes a melisma or portamento embellishes a given melodic line (see Example 4.5).

The pantun transcribed in Example 4.5 is sung by an Iban singer using a soft, gentle voice with only slight nasal resonance. The soft voice is typical of the intimate singing tradition of these people. The listeners gather closely around the singer while he or she sings the pantun and its message to entertain the longhouse dwellers during evening hours or for special events in the community.

In the excerpt shown in Example 4.5, the melodic lines are clearly shaped in predominantly descending contours. This particular piece is based on a hexatonic scale with emphasis in the melody on a Perfect 4th (pitches $g\#$ to $c^1\#$, and $c^1\#$ to $f^1\#$).

The Kenyah people in the interior regions of Sarawak also sing verses that are sometimes called pantun. Among these people the pantun are sung by a group of men who comprise a soloist and a small chorus. The chorus sings a moveable drone that occurs periodically throughout the song. Just as in the Iban pantun, the melodies of the Kenyah-Badang pantun also stress the Perfect 4th interval in the melodic lines sung by the soloist and the chorus. Among the Kenyah-Badang who live in the Upper Rejang River region of Sarawak, a male soloist sings the pantun with a voice that is nasalized but clear, while the chorus sings the drone loudly and resonantly.

Scale

et   na   eh——

Example 4.5 Excerpt from a *pantun* sung by an Iban singer.

Pantun in Sabah In the west coast regions of Sabah, members of the Bajau and Iranun communities sing pantun as entertainment. Among the Iranun peoples, the performance is responsorial between a man and a woman, and is accompanied by rhythmic patterns beaten on an over-turned brass bowl. The Bajau people of Sabah also perform the pantun by male and female singers in responsorial style. However, among the Bajau the *biola* (violin) is used to accompany the pantuns (see also Instrumental Music in this chapter and Figure 4.11).

In the interior regions of Sabah the Murut peoples sing pantun using a large chorus. While singing, the chorus members dance on a special floor called the lantai lansaran, described in Chapter 3. The singers rhythmically step and execute a slight hop in unison so that the flexible floor (*lantai*) will strike the wooden boards placed below it. Whenever the floor strikes the wooden boards beneath, a steady, percussive rhythmic pattern is set up to accompany their pantun singing.

Wa

In Sarawak a type of sung narrative or song in the form of a story is known as *wa* among the Kajang peoples who live along the Upper Rejang River in the interior region of the state. This narrative is usually sung by a group of women comprising a soloist and a small chorus. The soloist sings the main text of the story. The melodic phrases are determined by the structure of the text in which a specific number of words and syllables constitutes a given textual line or phrase (Strickland, 1988, pp. 67-75). The soloist's part is answered by a refrain sung by the chorus.

The wa vocal narrative can focus on various topics and themes including expressions of greeting and welcome, genealogical stories (called *lagu tusut* or *lagu asal-usul*). The text may also present a suitable closing for a specific gathering or meeting, in which case the sung narrative is called *lagu parap* [closing piece]. Thus, the specific lyrics depend upon the event that is taking place and its purpose.

Plate 4.2   Singers performing the *wa* narrative in the Upper Rejang River region of Sarawak.

Even though the lyrics change from one performance to another, for the purpose of the closing [*parap*] of a specific event, several basic elements must be present in the text. These elements include an opening section that greets the visitors and offers thanks to them for their presence at the event. The song continues with the statement of a specific problem followed by an expression of hope that the problem will be resolved (and sometimes a resolution is stated). Finally, the wa ends by offering thanks once again as well as an invitation to the participants to return to the longhouse in the future.

The chorus usually begins the piece as illustrated in Example 4.6, an excerpt of a wa to close an event, sung by a Kajang-Sekapan group in Sarawak. The chorus sings a passage in unison using only the syllable 'ei', that sets the tessitura for the piece and signals the starting pitch to the soloist who sings the main text (see the first melodic phrase in Example 4.6).

The singers use a clear but nasalized voice with a great deal of tension in the vocal production. Sometimes the voice of the solo singer is not very loud and the listeners must sit close by in order to hear the lyrics. In addition, a soloist usually covers her mouth with one hand when singing (considered to be a gesture of modesty and politeness) (Plate 4.2). In contrast, the chorus members sing out loudly and strongly as if they were shouting.

Example 4.6 Melodic lines in the *wa* by a Kajang-Sekapan soloist and chorus in Sarawak.

In Example 4.6, the melody is based on a hexatonic scale with a minor 3rd gap in the middle. The main melodic line (by the soloist) focuses on either the lower (pitches A to d) or upper (d to g) tetrachords of this scale.

A unique feature of the refrain on the syllable 'ei', by the chorus, is the use of heterophonic texture in which each singer simultaneously performs the same basic melody but uses his or her own variations in pitch and rhythm. The melodic line of this part of the wa always has a 'descending' contour, starting with the pitch center of the piece and descending to the same pitch one octave lower (see Example 4.6, chorus part). The refrain is melismatic with the acciacatura and many portamentos used as melodic ornaments.

The Kajang-Punan Bah and other neighboring peoples of the Upper Rejang River also sing the wa narrative in a similar style, but with the use of much dotted rhythm in the soloist's part.

Kui (Kue)

In Sabah and Sarawak some genres of vocal music are associated with the cultivation of rice. Among the Kenyah-Badang of Sarawak a genre of vocal music called *kui* (or *kue*) is performed just before the rice seeds are sown. The kui is sung by a male soloist and a large chorus made up of all the people who will participate in the rice-planting activity. With this song, which also includes prayers, all people of the longhouse give honor and praise to God before the rice planting commences. In the lyrics a request is made for strong and healthy rice plants to ensure that the resulting harvest of this staple food will be abundant.

In the performance, all singers stand in a line on the veranda of the longhouse while holding onto a long thin bamboo placed horizontally. Several long pieces of bamboo overlap at the ends to make a continuous, long piece. If enough bamboo is not available the singers simply hold hands from one person to the next to make an unbroken chain that reflects the unity of the people in the task of rice planting that will follow.

The kui is polyphonic music. A male soloist begins the song and sets the pitch level for the chorus. He sings the main song text while the chorus sings a moveable drone throughout the piece. The resulting harmony stresses the Perfect 4th, 5th, the unison and the octave. The rhythm is not metered and the singing style is mainly syllabic with some short melismatic passages. The melodic lines of a kui, performed by a Kenyah singer in Sarawak, are based on a heptatonic scale with focus on the lower or upper tetrachords of the scale (Matusky, 1990, p. 145). The musical style of the kui is similar to other vocal music found in the interior regions of Sarawak and in the central regions of Kalimantan.

Timang (Pengap)

In Sarawak another genre of vocal music is known as *timang* or *pengap* among the Iban. The timang (pengap), or chant, is sung by a singer called the *lemambang* (a bard) in the Iban community. These chants use lyrics or texts that are performed at specific ceremonies to invite spirits to a *gawai* or feast, or the texts may be sung for healing and other purposes. In the case of the gawai, it can be held for planting or harvesting rice, to honor the *kenyalang* [horn bill] bird, or for other important rituals. In Iban culture there are many types of timang, of which some of the more significant are the *timang tuah* (chant for the earthenware jar festival], *timang benih* [chant for blessings on the paddy seeds or other crops in the field], the *timang batu* [chant for the whetstone used when clearing a swidden] and *timang gawai amat* [chant for the most elaborate and prestigious ritual occasion].[1]

In one style of timang, at least four people sing the chant, which usually lasts for many hours. The lemambang sings the first two lines of text, a couplet that is called the *genteran*. A chorus of several men sings the refrain, the part that is repeated throughout the chant. Then, in response to the lemambang, the assistant lemambang sings the second two lines of text that are called the *timbal*, and this couplet is also followed with the refrain by the chorus. The lemambang strikes a walking stick (a stamping pole) on the floor in a steady rhythm to keep time while singing (Masing, J., 1997).

In other local styles of timang, a single lemembang sings the entire chant. He strikes the stamping pole on the floor in a steady rhythm to stress the downbeat in his sung melodic lines. In timang from the Rejang region, some lemambang sing each verse or section of their text using characteristic melodic motifs to begin a given textual line, and then establish two main chanting tones in each verse or section. Invariably the chanting tones are a Perfect 4th apart, with the lower of the two tones serving as a closing tone to each verse or section. The singing style is mainly syllabic as the lemambang concentrates on his communication, often with other-worldly elements, in the timang (see also Sather, C., 2001 on Iban shamanism and chant).

There are many other genres of vocal music in Sabah and Sarawak including the those known as *ensera* (legends), *renong* (story), *sabak* (funeral dirges) and other songs for healing, battle, love and entertainment. Through the pantun, timang and nearly all genres of vocal music, the oral folk literature is kept alive and disseminated in these two states.

Music and Storytelling

A final note on genres that are sung or chanted concerns the age-old tradition of storytelling. The art of storytelling through song or chant in Malay culture has existed since ancient times in an oral tradition, but today most professional storytellers have passed away without passing down their tradition to younger performers.

In former times on the Peninsula, this art was found in the states of Kelantan, Trengganu, Pahang, Kedah, Perlis, Langkawi Island, and Selangor. Some of the main elements of storytelling in the Malay tradition included the use of a special form of the language, singing, chanting, musical accompaniment, drama and the stories themselves. It was performed by professional storytellers who told folk tales (referred to as *penglipur lara*) (see also Chapter 1 --- Randai).

In former times there were several kinds of storytelling that were known by specific, localized names. The names of the different types were usually associated with the title of the main tale or the principal hero in the main story.

The *Tarik Selampit* from Kelantan, for example, was performed by a storyteller called *Tok Selampit* who accompanied himself on the Malay rebab (see further, A. Sweeney, 1995). Another type of *Selampit* was found in the state of Perlis, but the storyteller from this northwestern state usually did not use a musical instrument.

In contrast, the *Awang Batil* or *Awang Belanga* storyteller from Perlis accompanied his monologue and singing with rhythm beaten out on a *batil* or overturned brass bowl (Mustafa Mohd. Isa, 1987). In earlier times the tradition known as *jubang linggang* was performed in Kedah, in which the storyteller sung his tale without the accompaniment of any kind of instrumental music.

Another type, the *kaba*, is performed by the Minangkabau peoples of Selangor and Negeri Sembilan, and long ago this storytelling was accompanied by music played on the rebab. Nowadays the violin has replaced the rebab.

In addition to these forms, in the states of Trengganu and Pahang folk tales were performed by storytellers with musical accompaniment. Sometimes the professional tellers of tales simply sung their stories unaccompanied, and sometimes they used the rebana drum to play rhythms to accompany their sung narration and monologue.

Music functions in various ways in the various storytelling traditions. In general, certain melodies or rhythms serve as a stimulant in the process of telling a tale. A melody sung or played on a rebab, or even a rhythmic pattern beaten out on a brass bowl or rebana drum, helps to hasten a reaction or thought in the mind of the storyteller; it is even said that musical elements inspire and encourage the storyteller to continue to creatively develop his story.

In addition, a melody played on the rebab may serve as a cue for a given pitch or pitch level needed to sing particular lyrics in the telling of a tale. Furthermore, the rhythm played by beating the brass bowl or rebana drum can support and control the tempo in the process of storytelling. Musical elements can also enhance the beauty and charm in a story, thus making it more enjoyable and attractive to the audience. In the Awang Batil of Perlis the element of drama comes into play when the storyteller dons a mask or different masks to depict certain characters in his story. By using the masks the storyteller not only vividly illustrates characters in his story, but he also makes sure he does not lose the attention of his listeners.

In the past, especially when radio and television were not available in the villages and small towns, the tradition of storytelling was valued and storytellers were held in high esteem for their ability to entertain an audience with well-known tales. However, as the 20th century drew to a close, modern media (particularly television) invaded homes even in the smallest villages of Peninsular Malaysia. The cinema and other entertainment became enormously popular, and the traditional storyteller found himself lacking an audience as well as students to whom he could pass down his art. Today storytelling is rarely heard on the Peninsula, but it is still found among the various longhouse-dwelling groups in Sarawak and in Sabah, too.

Instrumental Music

In Malaysia various types of aerophones, chordophones and idiophonic instruments made of bamboo or wood are used to play melodies and pieces for individual pleasure or for entertainment in small, intimate groups. In Sabah and Sarawak, too, there are many musical instruments which may be used to play music for personal entertainment in solitary or quiet settings.

Mouth organs

In the category of aerophones, one of the common types found in both Sabah and Sarawak is the mouth organ. This instrument is locally called *sompoton* in Sabah and *keluri*, *keledi* and *engkerurai* in Sarawak (Plate 4.3).

There are several basic parts in the mouth organ, including a gourd that functions as the wind chest, several small bamboo tubes (pipes) of different lengths that specify pitch, and a reed in each tube that vibrates whenever the instrument is blown.

It is generally thought that the mouth organ originated in Southeast Asia, and that it is possibly the earliest musical instrument to produce harmony. Today various forms of mouth organs can be found in Southeast Asia, China and Japan. For example, in mainland Southeast Asia (notably in Thailand and Laos) the bamboo tubes are arranged either in a circle or in two parallel rows, and the wind chest (the gourd) is often located at the middle section of the tubes. In contrast, the East Malaysian mouth organ has a wind chest located at the base end of the tubes (see Plate 4.3).

In ancient times the mouth organ was carried from East Asia to West Asia and Europe. In Europe the acoustic principle of using a free beating reed in an instrument has been used since the 19th century in musical instruments such as the harmonica, reed organ, accordion and, in India, the harmonium.

Sompoton   The sompoton mouth organ originates in Sabah from Kampung Tikolog, Tambunan District. In former times it was traded from there throughout the other Dusun communities.

Traditionally in Tambunan, the sompoton was a solo instrument played for personal entertainment by both men and women. It could be played whenever the performer had free time. Sometimes, in the case of an arranged marriage, a new husband might play the sompoton to help his bride feel more at ease so that she would freely follow him back to stay in his village after the wedding ceremonies. Sometimes the sompoton is played for public entertainment at festivals where it may also be used as solo accompaniment for magarang dancing if no sompogogunan gong ensemble is present (see Chapter 2 --- Sumazau and magarang dances, and Figures 2.19-2.22).

The sompoton consists of a double-layered raft of eight *sumbiling* [a type of bamboo] bamboo pipes inserted into a gourd (called *korobu*) and affixed with beeswax (called *sopinit, sopihut* or *sopilut*). Seven of the pipes each has a small *sodi* or reed made of *polod* palm wood inserted into its side near the base. The eighth pipe (one of the two longest pipes) is soundless and merely balances the bundle. The pipes are arranged in the typical double-layered raft formation, bound with thin cane strips and stopped at their base ends with beeswax (see Plate 4.3). Then the raft of pipes, at its base end, is sealed into a dried and prepared gourd.

Plate 4.3   Mouth organs: the Iban *engkerurai* (left) of Sarawak, and the KadazanDusun *sompoton* of Sabah (right).

Two of the intermediate- and one of the shortest-sized pipes have finger holes cut low in the side of the pipes, which are covered by the player's thumb and finger to allow these pipes to sound during performance. The remaining pipes (excluding the soundless pipe) need to be closed at the top by the player's fingers to prevent them from sounding when air is blown into the instrument via the mouth hole (gourd stem). Sometimes the group of four shorter pipes are loosely named *kombitan*, a term which strictly refers to the plucking of a stringed instrument, because the finger actions for the opening and closing of these pipes resembles a plucking movement.   A detailed nomenclature for the parts of this instrument evolved in Kg. Tikolog, Tambunan District, acknowledged to be the birthplace of the instrument (see further Pugh-Kitingan, 1987).

The sompoton can be held in three basic positions. If the performer is standing, it is held with the pipes upright or tilting towards the player's right side (Plate 4.4). If seated, some players hold the instrument with the four longest pipes against the left shoulder. This may involve crossing the hands in front of the chest, and allows for a slightly different fingering. This arrangement may also be used if the performer is lying down; sometimes a performer keeps the sompoton close at hand while sleeping during the night. Early in the morning before rising he then plays the instrument to wake up the rest of the household. Music played in both of these positions features the *lombohon* pipe [longest sounding pipe] as a drone. A third playing position involves sitting with the sompoton inverted. This allows the longest pipe to be stopped on the thigh when required, giving the lombohon a melodic role in the music.

Plate 4.4 A *sompoton* player in Sabah, showing the typical playing method.

Sompoton music Sompoton music can imitate magarang dance music and songs [*sinding*], or it can merely be a performer's own creation. The instrument is played in many contexts.

A solo sompoton performance imitating magarang dance music is shown in Example 4.7. This piece is played while the performer holds the sompoton upright, and thus the lombohon or deep-sounding pipe functions as a drone throughout the piece and not as a melody pipe.

In the excerpt of magarang music on the solo sompoton in Example 4.7a, the basic beat and syncopated magarang rhythm are clearly apparent. The pentatonic melodies among the shorter pipes resemble the melodic patterns of the gong ensemble that usually accompanies the magarang dance. In this piece two basic melodic phrases are used, each one bar in length. The two basic phrases are repeated in the sequence *a*, *a1*, *b*, *b1*. This sequence of the two phrases is repeated throughout the dance piece.

a) excerpt of *magarang* dance music played on the solo *sompoton*

b) excerpt of *magarang* music by three *sompoton* and one *koritikon* gong, from Kg. Tokolog, Tambunan, Sabah

Example 4.7 Examples of *sompoton* music from Sabah. (Transcribed by J. Pugh-Kitingan)

A group of three to six or more sompoton accompanied by a koritikon gong (Figure 3.4) can also be used for magarang dance music. If no koritikon is available, a karatung drum (Figure 3.5) may be used. The

Example 4.7b above illustrates a magarang performance by three sompoton and one koritikon in Kg. Tikolod. The koritikon has the same repeated rhythm as in the sompogogunan hanging gong performance, but starts on beat 6 of the rhythmic pattern (compare with Example 3.6 --- Hanging Gong Ensembles). The three sompoton play the same melodic material in unison, and in the same rhythm shown in Example 4.7a.

Although it is only a small village, Kampung Tikolog is famous throughout Sabah for sompoton manufacture. Today, as in the past, instruments are traded from this village to many Dusun groups in Sabah.

Keluri/keledi/engkerurai   The mouth organ played by the Kajang, Kayan and Kenyah people of the Upper Rejang River region of Sarawak is called *keluri* or *keledi* (see Plate 4.5), while this same basic instrument among the Iban is known as the *engkerurai* (Plate 4.3).

Although the method of making this instrument may differ somewhat from place to place, the same acoustic principle of a single, free beating reed is used, and the form or shape of the instrument is nearly the same from one group to another. On the engkerurai, made by the Iban, a short cone is placed at the top of the drone tube (usually the longest and low octave bamboo pipe called the *indu* or *apai*). This cone is called the *terumbong* and serves to make the sound of the drone more resonant. It is sometimes decorated with bird feathers and other material.

The keluri and engkerurai have six or seven bamboo tubes that are bound together in a circle as shown in Plate 4.3. The ends of these tubes including the reed are enclosed in the gourd wind chest. In one example of a mouth organ from the Upper Rejang River region the gourd is about eight centimeters in diameter, while the bamboo tubes range from 30 to 60 centimeters long. The six bamboo tubes in this particular instrument produce five different pitches, one of which is doubled at the octave. If seven tubes are used then one of the tubes does not sound.

Keluri music   The keluri tune in Example 4.8 accompanies a line dance with the keluri player leading the line of men and women dancers (Plate 4.5). The keluri player performs the melody while he dances. In this melody, the end of each phrase is stressed by agogic accent that coincides with the particular dance steps and foot stamping on the same beats.

There are specific repertories for both the keluri and engkerurai which not only accompany dances but also provide music for general entertainment in the longhouse.[2] This instrument is usually played by men, since great stamina is needed to blow and finger the instrument while simultaneously dancing.

Plate 4.5 A *keluri* player leading a line dance at a Kajang longhouse in Belaga District, Sarawak.

Pentatonic scale

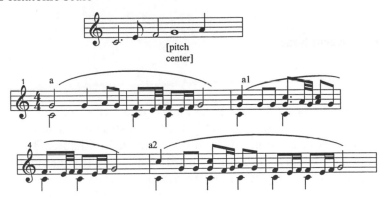

Example 4.8 Excerpt of a *keluri* melody to accompany a line dance by Kajang performers in Sarawak.

In this keluri piece the melody is based on a pentatonic scale with a major 3rd at the beginning of the scale (see Example 4.8). The 2-bar phrases of the melody are repeated with some variation and, hence, the form is iterative (outlined as *a, a1, a2, a3* and so on)

A typical keluri melody, then, is structured in 4- or 8-beat phrases that are repeated with variation (see phrases outlined in Example 4.8). The drone is produced at the low and high octaves and can be heard both above and below the main melodic line. The harmonic intervals that are important in this polyphonic music include the minor 3rd as well as the Perfect 4th and 5th. The rhythm is quadruple with the strong stress on beats 1 and 3 of each bar in the music.

Whether played to accompany dance or for general entertainment, the mouth organ is popular among many different ethnic groups in both Sabah and Sarawak.

Flutes and Free Aerophones

Kidiu

An aerophone not having a tube or pipe is known as a free aerophone, and a typical example is the bull-roarer. This type of instrument is found in Sarawak and, like several kinds of music discussed in Chapter 3 (see Struck and stamping bamboo and wood instruments), this free aerophone and its music, called *kidiu*, originate from the motions of work.

The kidiu consists of an oval-shaped, flat disk of wood or other material. The disk is attached to a string (about 70 centimeters long) and the string is attached to an equally long stick that serves as a handle (see Figure 4.3). The stick is held by the player, and the string along with the wooden disk are quickly swung through the air, sometimes in a circular motion, until the wooden disk begins to vibrate. As the disk vibrates, the air around it also vibrates and a pitch is produced. A small wooden disk swung very quickly produces a high pitch, while the use of a larger disk results in a low tone.

Figure 4.3 *Kidiu*

This free aerophone and its musical sound is found among the Kenyah-Badang who live in the Upper Rejang River area of Sarawak. The kidiu is associated with hill rice cultivation. At least two instruments are played in the rice fields when the plants are ripening, and their actual purpose is to prevent pests such as mice, birds and insects from destroying the rice plants. The player holds the wooden stick of the kidiu and swings it through the air to chase away pests. At the same time, two or more players produce resultant melodic patterns (Matusky, 1990, pp. 133-4).

The instruments are played in an interlocking style with each kidiu producing two different pitches. As shown in Example 4.9, the two players alternate swinging their respective instruments through the air and a short rhythm and melody results. Using the kidiu the farmers are able to chase away the pests from the maturing hill rice in a very musical way.

Seruling/suling

The flutes found in Malaysia are end- or side-blown with breath from the mouth or the nose.

x - approximate pitch

Example 4.9 *Kidiu* **music played by the Kenyah-Badang of Sarawak.**

The flute and its music, as found in folk societies around the world, is often associated with love, affection, life and death. The breath from the nose is very important in some societies because of the belief that nose breath contains the soul or spirit of a man. Hence, the music of the nose flute becomes important in mourning for the deceased. Although in some communities in Malaysia the sound of the flute is still associated with affection, love and dying, today the instrument is also played for entertainment.

Figure 4.4 *Seruling/suling* **end-blown flutes from Sabah (left) and Sarawak (right).**

The end-blown flutes called seruling and suling (Figure 4.4) are played by many ethnic groups throughout the country. In Sarawak, the seruling is made from bamboo about 65 centimeters long and 2 centimeters in diameter. The usual four finger holes are sometimes equidistant, but not always so. There is also a thumbhole at the back of the pipe. The Sarawak seruling is usually held in an oblique position to the player's lips at an appropriate angle so that air can be blown across the mouth hole (see Plate

4.6). Other seruling are held vertically and blown from the end of the instrument.

Typical seruling melodies in Sarawak are based on tetratonic scales. The melodic lines use conjunct melodic motion, some ornamentation and free rhythm (see Example 4.10). Although the melodies are improvisatory, certain features remain constant from one player to the next. The scales usually have fewer than 5 pitches with a gap of a third at the upper end of the scale. A phrase may begin or end with a sustained note, but contrast lies in the ornamental notes within the phrase. The ornaments used are mainly the grace and double grace notes and dotted rhythmic motifs. A piece is normally in free rhythm and the predominant melodic contour is descending as shown in Example 4.10.

Plate 4.6 A *seruling* player from Belaga District in Sarawak, showing one of the playing methods on the instrument.

Tetratonic scale

Example 4.10 A s*eruling* melody by a Kayan flute player in Sarawak.

Nabat/Seruling

In contrast to the seruling found in East Malaysia, many of the flutes in Peninsular Malaysia called seruling or suling are actually recorders (fipple flutes).

The nabat recorder used by the Jah Hut community has seven finger holes and a thumb hole at the back of the tube (M. Couillard, 1982, p. 45). All finger holes are equidistant. The pitch range covers one octave and long melodic lines are featured in nabat pieces. There is a specific repertory of nabat flute music which is associated with certain Jah Hut folk tales.

Siloy/Begut

Among the Jah Hut aborigines the flutes called *siloy* and *begut* are side-blown. The siloy is made from a short piece of bamboo, about 14 centimeters long. One end of the tube is closed with the natural bamboo node, while the other end is opened. A small hole is cut at the closed end to control the pitch. The siloy is held horizontally and side blown with air from the mouth.

There are no finger holes on the siloy flute, but various pitches are produced when the small hole at the end of the tube is slightly opened or closed by the hand of the player. This flute is used to play tunes that imitate bird calls, and it is also associated with particular spirits in the belief system of the Jah Hut peoples (M. Couillard, p. 47).

The flute known as the begut is also played by the Jah Hut who live in Pahang. This instrument is made from a tube of bamboo that is closed by the natural nodes of the bamboo. Three equidistant finger holes are used, and the melodies played on this flute consist of short phrases that are repeated over and over within a narrow melodic range (M. Couillard, pp. 47-8).

Selengut

The flute called *selengut* is played by many Kajang groups who live in the Upper Rejang River region in Sarawak. The flute is made from bamboo and usually measures around 50 centimeters long. It is end-blown with air from the nose (Plate 4.7).

Plate 4.7 *Selengut* nose flute from Sarawak.

One end of the instrument is closed with the natural bamboo node and a small hole is cut in the surface of the node in order to blow air into the tube. This flute is held horizontally and placed beneath the player's nose so that one nostril is closed and the other blows air across the small hole at the end of the tube. There may be three or four non-equidistant finger holes and a thumb hole at the back of the pipe.

A selengut piece consists of short, repeated melodic phrases as can be seen in Example 4.11 below.

Scale

[pitch center]

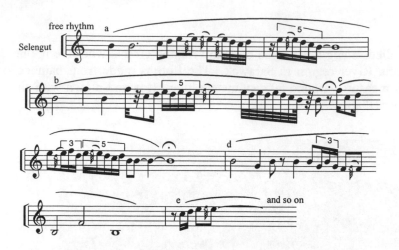

Example 4.11 Excerpt of a *selengut* melody by a Kajang flute player in Sarawak.

The melodies played on the selengut are usually in free rhythm. A specific tune consists of melodic phrases ornamented with grace notes and passages of fast-moving, running notes (see Example 4.11). The melodies are based on 6-tone scales usually with a gap at the middle of the scale.

The melodic phrases are usually shaped by 'ascending-descending' and simply 'descending' contours. Like the seruling music in Sarawak, the selengut melodies move mainly stepwise. But at the beginning or the end of a specific phrase the melody may move in leaps (see, for example, Example 4.11, phrases *b* and *c*). Often times a cadence is signified by disjunct melodic motion in intervals of perfect 4ths or 5ths (see phrase *d*).

The melodies played on the selengut are only moderately ornamented with fast moving semiquaver and demisemiquaver notes. Sometimes the acciacatura is used depending upon the skill and taste of the player.

Suling/Pensol

The aborigines of Peninsular Malaysia also play the nose flute. This flute is called 'suling' by the Jah Hut who live in Pahang, and *pensol* by the Temiar people of Kelantan. The Temiar believe the nose flute came from the Semai peoples who live in the neighboring state of Perak.[3] Both of these nose flutes are made of bamboo and have 4 finger holes. Men and women may play the instrument, which is especially used to express love and sadness.

The pensol melody in Example 4.12 is based on a tetratonic scale consisting of a major 2nd and one minor 3rd. In the melody, the Perfect 4th and 5th intervals are stressed, but the minor 3rd (pitch *B* to *d* in phrases *a*, *b* and *c*) is also used.

The 'ascending-descending' melodic contour is important in this music (see Example 4.12, phrases *b* and *c*) and the melody moves mainly in conjunct motion, but concludes in leaps at the cadence.

Example 4.12 Excerpt of a *pensol* melody by a Temiar flute player of Kelantan. (M. Roseman, 1995; transcribed by P. Matusky)

Just as in other nose flute music, improvisation is important in Temiar pensol tunes. In the above example the melodic motifs are varied in a number of ways, including a change in rhythm, by augmentation of the motif, fragmentation and so on (compare motifs a1, a2 and a3 in Example 4.12).

Among the Temiar, music played on the pensol signifies feelings of sadness and love. Usually this music is played in the afternoons and can be played by one or two players resulting in monophonic or heterophonic texture.[4]

Turali

In Sabah the *turali* (also called *turahi* by the KadazanDusun from Tambunan, and *tuahi* in the Penampang region) is a nose flute widely distributed throughout the Dusun areas of the state. It is a solo instrument played as a form of personal expression by both men and women in various contexts, according to the culture in question.

The traditional turali is cut from a length of *sumbiling* bamboo (called *humbising* in Penampang) that is open at one end. A small nose hole is made in the node at the top of the tube. There are three equidistant finger holes and a thumb hole at the backside of the pipe (Figure 4.5).

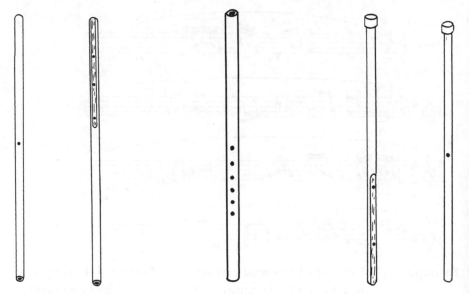

Figure 4.5 *Turali*

The length of this instrument varies. For example, the turali of the RugusDusun of Kudat is comparatively short and ranges between 30 to 38 centimeters in length, while among the KadazanDusun it can vary from 38 to about 90 centimeters long. The LotodDusun of Tuaran distinguish between the shorter *turali toniba* of around 38 centimeters and the longer *turali do anaru* of up to nearly a meter long.

The turali is often held toward the right while the left nostril blows the nose hole. Blowing the turali with the nose involves inhaling through the mouth and exhaling through the open nostril.

Nowadays, the turali from Tambunan is often adapted as a mouth flute. It has the same basic structure as the traditional nose flute, except that it is shorter and has a mouth hole cut in the side of the upper end that is partially covered by a bamboo mouthpiece (see Figure 4.5).

Turali music

The turali flute is played as a form of personal expression, and its music varies according to the skill and creativity of the performer. Turali music from most areas can imitate the melodies of various songs and ritual chants, or it can be the free composition of the player. In the central portion of the Tambunan district and in Penampang, however, the sound of the turali evokes sadness. It is usually played to express grief when recalling the recent death of a relative or friend. In Tambunan, such music imitates the melodic patterns of the *pogigiad* or crying by female mourners beside the body of the deceased.

The turahi performance in Example 4.13 is typical of music for mourning the deceased. The melodic patterns in the piece represent the sound of a person crying and mourning for the death of a loved one. The trills played on the pitch center serve not only as an ornament but also to suggest sobbing at the end of each melodic phrase.

Pentatonic scale

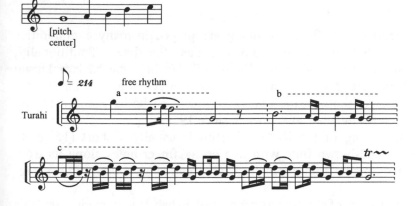

+ = quarter tone sharp

Example 4.13   Excerpt from a *turahi* melody from Kg. Timbou, Tambunan. (Transcribed by J. Pugh-Kitingan)

The melody is based on a gapped pentatonic scale (see Example 4.13). The contour of most melodic phrases is 'ascending-descending'. In fact, most of this flute music is an alternation between a descending melodic line to the pitch center (as in phrase *b*) and the ascending and then descending melodic contour in the upper octave (as in phrase *c*). After alternating these patterns in the upper octave, the performer repeats them in the lower octave as shown in Example 4.13.

Suling

Short bamboo mouth flutes or suling are played in many communities throughout Sabah as solo diversions to pass the time. Traditionally, Sabahan suling were end-blown flutes. Today in some KadazanDusun communities there is a trend among the younger performers to make side-blown flutes like those of the Lun Dayeh people who have migrated into the state from Kalimantan and Sarawak since 1956.

The suling of the KadazanDusun is usually a short (15 to 20 centimeters) end-blown flute with five or six finger holes along its front surface. It is made from *sumbiling* (also called *sumbihing, humbising*) bamboo.

The suling of the Iranun peoples of Sabah is also made from this bamboo (named *bakayawa* in Iranun), but it has four holes and its construction is more complex. During its manufacture, the bamboo is cut lengthwise and Qur'anic verses are inscribed on the inside. Brightly colored thread is used to re-seal the bamboo. This flute has an air hole near the back top part of the tube, beneath the mouthpiece.

As with other solo instruments in Sabah, each suling player has his own repertory. Suling music may imitate the tunes of various songs, or be a newly composed tune by the performer. The Iranun suling is sometimes played during courtship when its music may imitate the rhythm of the name of the beloved. It is also claimed that some performers use this instrument as a charm to attract a girl (J. Pugh-Kitingan, 1987).

Rurum Lun Suling ensemble The Lun Dayeh pipe band or Rurum Lun Suling is mentioned here as a final type of music which involves flutes found in Sabah. This band comprises about fourteen female flute players, accompanied by nine or more bamboo horns or bas blown by men.

The Lun Dayeh who play this ensemble have come into Sabah from Kalimantan and Sarawak (where they are named Lun Bawang) to settle in Kg. Barujumpa, Tenom, since 1956. Their lun suling and bas instruments are said to have been developed by Indonesian school teachers (especially Minahasan from Sulawesi), and acculturated into Lun Dayeh music through the school system in Kalimantan.

Although played by women in the ensemble, the lun suling can be performed as a solo instrument by either women or men. It is a side-blown flute with six finger holes. Measuring around 35 centimeters long, the pipe is made from *bulu' sabiling*, a bamboo which resembles the KadazanDusun sumbiling type.

The bas is made from large *bulu' talang* bamboo, which is open at the top and closed at the lower end. A long mouthpiece of sabiling bamboo enters the body of the instrument at right angles near the top and extends into a rectangular handle on the other side. A large hole is cut in the side of the instrument near its lower end, with a smaller hole on the opposite side near the top. The bas is held at an angle, with its lower end pointing down to the right. It is blown with buzzed lips and, hence, is classified as a horn.

There are five sizes of bas, ranging from the small 20 centimeters long *doo dita*, to the large *bas sol banah* of around 80 centimeters. Most of the instruments have undecorated surfaces, but the longest ones may be carved and are painted red and black.

In the Rurum Lun Suling there are fourteen bas; the numbers of instruments of each size, from shortest to longest, are: two *doo dita*, two *bas baidita*, three *bas mii*, three *doo arang* and four *bas sol banah*. The fundamental pitches of the five sizes from the shortest to longest resembles a descending diatonic major scale from tonic to subdominant.

When played as a solo flute, the lun suling may imitate the tunes of various traditional and modern songs or the tunes of gong music to accompany dancing.

The repertory of the Rurum Lun Suling ensemble is mainly Christian songs and hymns which are normally sung by the Sidang Inyil Borneo Church, of which most Lun Dayeh are members.   During performance the lun suling flutes play the melodies of the songs, while several bas provide a diatonic bass below.

Tube Zithers

The tube zither in Malaysia is usually made from a piece of large bamboo with a diameter of 10 centimeters or more.   The bamboo tube is often closed at both ends with a slit about 1 centimeter wide running almost the full length of the tube.   Both heterochordic (separate strings attached to the body) and idiochordic (strings cut from the cortex) types are found in Malaysia.   Usually several strings are located to the left and right side of the long slit.   The bamboo tube is held in the player's hands and the strings are plucked with the fingers.

The tube zither has existed since ancient times and is found throughout island Southeast Asia.   There are zithers made from a full or half tube of bamboo.   Although most of the zithers found in Malaysia are full tube zithers (with one exception in Sabah), the half-tube zither is the first model or prototype for the many board zithers found throughout East Asia (C. Sachs, 1940, p. 186).

Kecapi

The music usually played by gongs and drums in the shadow puppet play in Kelantan is sometimes played by one person using the tube zither called the *kecapi*. This music is played for individual enjoyment as the kecapi player imitates the various musical pieces of shadow play or other music.

The kecapi, found in some Kelantanese villages, is an idiochordic tube zither made of bamboo and played by the rural Malays (Plate 4.8).   It is about 45 centimeters long and around 12 to 14 centimeters in diameter. Both ends of the tube are closed by the natural nodes of the bamboo.   Two pairs of strings are cut from the cortex of the instrument, a pair on either side of the tube.   The strings are stretched and tuned using small bridges placed beneath the ends of each string. Each pair of strings, at its mid point, is attached to a thin square piece of bamboo which, in turn, is placed just above a square hole cut into the side of the instrument that serves as a sound hole (see Plate 4.8). The two pair of strings are tuned to imitate the pitches of the two hanging tetawak gongs in the shadow play ensemble, while two more strings are cut from the cortex and tuned to approximate the pitches of the canang gong-chime in the shadow play orchestra.

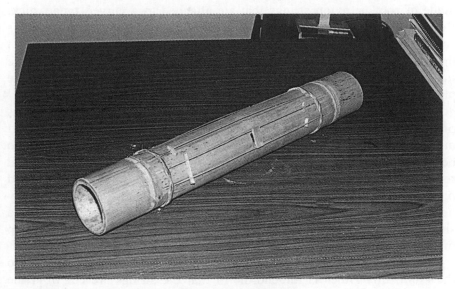

Plate 4.8 The *kecapi* tube zither from Kelantan.

This zither is held almost vertically and the lower end of the bamboo is supported against the player's thigh or lap. The player can pluck the strings with both hands, or he can use only one hand to pluck while holding onto the instrument at its upper end with the other hand. Sometimes the upper hand strikes the end of the tube in rhythmic patterns. These rhythmic patterns usually imitate the rhythms found in the music of the shadow play pieces heard in Kelantan (see, for instance, Example 1.5 in Chapter 1).

Krem/Pergam

Tube zithers are also played by the aborigines of Peninsular Malaysia. The Jah Hut people of the state of Pahang play two types of tube zithers, one is idiochordic and the other is heterochordic (M. Couillard, 1982, pp. 50-1).

The instrument called *'krem'* is a heterochordic tube zither. The body of the krem is made from a bamboo tube with one opened end. There are several short slits cut into the side of the bamboo to serve as sound holes. In former times, the strings were made from certain roots, but today nylon strings are used. Usually two strings of different lengths are attached to the body and small bridges are inserted under the strings at the open end of the tube.

The strings may be plucked or bowed on the krem. The bow is made of root or nylon strings that are attached to a curved rattan stick. Resin is applied to the root or nylon strings so that a loud, firm sound is easy to produce. When bowed, the instrument is placed horizontally with the open end of the tube against the chest of the player. When plucked, the instrument is placed nearly vertically with the closed end against the player's chest. The strings are plucked with the fingers of both hands.

Based on studies of Jah Hut culture, we learn that the krem is played mainly by women (M. Couillard, p. 51). A tune consists of short melodic lines that are repeated with variation. The pieces are intended to be peaceful and tranquil, to be enjoyed by a small group of friends and relatives on a leisure afternoon or evening. However, when fast-paced pieces are played to accompany walking in the forest to look for daily necessities, the strings are plucked. In general, the krem is played by a single player for individual enjoyment or for the pleasure of a small group of people in an intimate setting.

The Jah Hut people also play the pergam tube zither. In contrast to the krem, this zither is idiochordic in that the strings are cut from the surface of the bamboo tube. The bamboo is closed by the natural nodes, but a small hole is cut in the node of one end to serve as a sound hole.

Usually four strings are cut from the bamboo surface, and they are arranged in pairs (Couillard, pp. 48-9). A pair of strings is separated by a small rectangular hole that is cut in the side of the bamboo. A separate, thin, flat piece of bamboo is placed above the hole and two of the strings on either side of the hole are attached to this flat piece of bamboo (much like the kecapi of the Malays). Small bridges are placed under the ends of each string to tighten and tune them.

When played, this instrument is held oblique to the performer's body with one end of the tube against the player's chest. The strings are plucked with the fingers, while one hand supports the instrument and also hits the upper part of the bamboo, as if playing the kecapi described earlier. The strings are tuned in minor 3rd intervals, and the short melodic motifs and percussive rhythmic patterns are repeated over and over (M. Couillard, p. 50). The Jah Hut people usually play the pergam for ceremonies to heal the sick. In these ceremonies the instrument is mainly used to play the rhythmic patterns that are repeated in the music.

Kereb

The instrument known as the *kereb* is played by the Temiar people of Kelantan. This heterochordic tube zither is made from bamboo and has two strings.[5] The strings consists of roots of different size and thickness that are attached to the bamboo tube and plucked with the fingers.

Just as in the Temiar stamped bamboo tubes called goh (see Chapter 3, Struck and Stamping Bamboo and Wood Instruments), on the kereb the long string is referred to as 'male' and the short one is considered to be 'female'.

This instrument is usually played by women for entertainment and individual enjoyment. It is played in the afternoons and its music produces a soothing and tranquil atmosphere, or it imitates the sounds of the natural environment depicting the sounds and movements involved in work activities. For example, the piece in Example 4.14 depicts the motions of cutting small trees and clearing brush in the fields before planting seeds. Just as the motions of cutting twigs and brush are repetitive, the melodic motifs played on the kereb are also repeated throughout the piece (see Example 4.14).

x - approximate pitch

Example 4.14 *Kereb* music of the Temiar people of Kelantan. (M. Roseman, 1995; transcribed by P. Matusky)

A tritonic scale is used in this kereb music, and the melodic line is developed using different melodic motifs (see Example 4.14, motifs *a, b* and *c*). Although the motifs *a* and *b* may be repeated, motif *c* usually is used as a cadence. The individual motifs are shaped in 'descending-ascending' or simply 'descending' contours. Because the melodic motifs are repeated with some variation throughout the piece, the form in this music is iterative.

Satong

The tube zither is named *satong* or *lutong* by different ethnic groups in Sarawak. This idiochordic zither is made from bamboo about 50 centimeters long with a diameter of 9 to 11 centimeters. The bamboo is closed by the natural node at each end of the instrument and a slit about one centimeter wide is cut into one side of the tube for sound resonance (see Plate 4.9). Geometric patterns are usually carved on the surface of the bamboo tube.

Four strings are cut from the cortex of the satong and small bridges are inserted beneath each end of each string. Although the tuning of the strings is not standard, the satong is tuned to obtain various 4-tone scales among the Kajang groups in the Upper Rejang River area of Sarawak. These scales are different in pitch from one instrument to another, but the intervals between the pitches are similar (see Example 4.15a-b: the intervals here include a neutral 3rd (354 and 329 cents), a near major 2nd (196 and 211 cents), a neutral 2nd (163 cents), and a quarter tone (41 cents).

a) Kajang-Sekapan *satong*: tetratonic scale and tuning of the strings

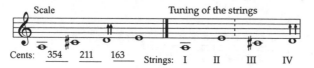

b) Kajang-Kejaman Lasah *satong* tetratonic scale and tuning of the strings

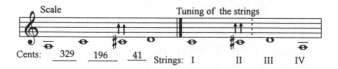

c) *satong* melody by a Kajang-Sekapan performer in Sarawak

d) *satong* melody by another Kajang-Sekapan performer

Example 4.15 *Satong* **tunings and melodies among the Kajang groups in Sarawak.**

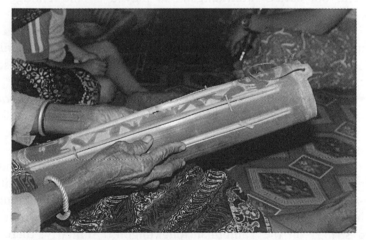

Plate 4.9 The *satong*, made and played by a Kejaman-Lasah woman from Sarawak.

A melodic line played on the satong consists of one or two short, repeated motifs. Duple or triple meter may be used as shown in Examples 4.15c and d.

Heterometer is sometimes found in the melody, as in Example 4.15d when the meter changes from a 4-beat bar to a 5-beat bar and then back to a 4-beat bar once again. Typically, triplet figures and syncopated rhythm are also found in the melodic lines of music played on the satong.

Satong music is improvisatory in nature. A given tune consists of different melodic motifs that may be repeated many times with variation (see Example 4.15d, bars 1-3). The melody usually moves stepwise, while one pitch functions as a drone. The use of the drone results in rudimentary harmony that focuses on the intervals of the Perfect 5th and the neutral 3rd in the music (see Example 4.15c and d). The form in this music is usually iterative.

The skill in making and decorating one's own satong is paralleled by the player's creativity to compose and improvise a melody. The diversity of melodic motifs and rhythmic patterns is considerable in this music, which is used to entertain dwellers in the longhouse in the quiet afternoons or evenings.

Tongkungon

The *tongkungon* is a bamboo tube zither that is plucked and played by many Dusun groups in Sabah (Figure 4.6). An identical musical instrument, but called 'kulintangan', is played by the Timugon Murut peoples of Tenom in Sabah.

Usually the tongkungon (or kulintangan) is played as a solo instrument to provide entertainment during leisure time. This instrument is also used to accompany dance in small groups for non-ritual purposes if the gong ensemble is not present in the community.

The tongkungon is made from the type of bamboo called *poring* (or 'tongkungon' in Tenom). It is about 70 centimeters long, and its thin, fine strings are cut from the surface of the bamboo tube. The strings are slightly raised using wood or rattan bridges at either end of each string.

The number, tuning and names of the strings correspond to the hanging gongs in the gong ensemble found in the given community. The *sopogandangan* gong ensemble of the KadazanDusun in Tambunan has seven hanging gongs and one hand-held gong, just as there are seven plucked strings on the Tambunan tongkungon. Similarly, there are six hanging gongs in the *sompogogunan* ensemble of the KadazanDusun in Penampang just as there are only six plucked strings in the tongkungon

found in Penampang. The LotodDusun peoples use three hanging gongs
and a single drum in their ritual music. Hence, their tongkungon has four
plucked strings. Also in Tenom, the kulintangan of the Timugon Muruts
has nine plucked strings that are named and tuned according to the nine
hanging gongs in their *sampangigalan* gong ensemble.

A long slit for resonance is cut in the body of the instrument,
usually on the portion facing the performer (see Figure 4.6). The
tongkungon of the LotudDusun, however, is made from two node lengths
of bamboo and has its extended top carved in the shape of a crocodile's
jaw, with a circular sound hole in the 'mouth' of the reptile-form and
another hole in the base.

The tongkungon may be held vertically or leaned against a wall
and strummed with the player's fingers.

Although it is a solo instrument, it may sometimes be played as
part of a duet. In Tambunan, a single tongkungon may occasionally be
accompanied by the small hand-held koritikon gong (Figure 3.4).
Sometimes two tongkungon may perform a duet, one will play the music of
the seven hanging gongs of the sompogogunan from Tambunan, while the
highest-pitched string of the second will be struck with a thin bamboo stick
in the rhythm of the koritikon. In Kg. Tikolod, Tambunan, a tongkungon
may be accompanied by a rare struck zither named *takobung*.

The music   The music of the tongkungon (and the 'kulintangan' of the
Timugon group) usually imitates that of the gong ensemble of the
community in question, with the strings tuned to pitches approximating
those of the gongs. As shown in the excerpt of music notated in Example
4.16, the rhythm and melodic structure of the magarang music is clear
(compare with Examples 3.6 and 4.7). The continuously repeated melodic
and rhythmic motifs indicate that an iterative formal structure is typical in
this music.

Example 4.16 Excerpt of *magarang* music played on the *tongkungon*.

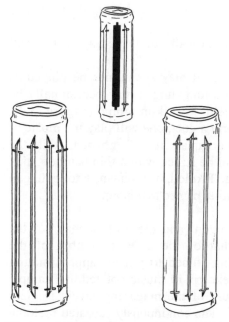

Figure 4.6 *Tongkungon* tube zither from Sabah. (Slit in the tube faces the player; strings are cut and supported with bridges to the left and right of the slit)

Takobung/Tongkibong

The *takobung* (also pronounced *'tokubung'* and *'takabung'*) and the *tongkibong* are rare types of zithers occasionally found among the KadazanDusun people today. These instruments are similarly shaped and may be considered variant forms of each other. Both were frequently played in former times, but after World War II they became less popular than other instruments, and it is only in recent years that one or two players have attempted a revival. However, these instruments are little known among the general public, and they are simply played as if they were a tongkungon. Apparently, today the takobung is somewhat more widespread than the tongkibong which is only found in the village of Sunsuron in Tambunan District.

Like the tongkungon, these solo instruments may be played by men or women. Today a few performers still play the takobung or tongkibong for personal entertainment, but they are also used to accompany non-ritual dances in small groups if there is no gong ensemble present in the community.

The takobung and tongkibong are made of a large piece of poring bamboo. On the takobung, one side of a piece of bamboo is cut off to obtain a flat surface from which three strings are cut, two strings from one edge and a third string from the opposite edge. The strings are slightly raised with small wooden bridges (called *tukod*) that can easily slide along the entire length of the strings. At the mid point of the third string a small, thin tongue-shaped piece of bamboo (called the *tampudila*) closes a hole in the surface beneath the string every time the string is plucked. Another hole in one end of the bamboo also serves as a sound hole.

The takobung is placed horizontally on the floor with the set of two strings closest to the player. The player imitates music for the hanging gong ensembles as he plucks the strings in different places, including the string with the tampudila, and at the same time his left hand hits the left end of the bamboo in drum rhythmic patterns.

The tongkibong from Sunsuron village in Tambunan is similar to the takobung, but it only uses two strings. The tampudila on this instrument is located on the outside string as the instrument sits on the floor before the player. The tongkibong also has a place for the player's foot to support the instrument at one end of the bamboo. A sound hole is cut into both ends of the tube.

The player sits on the floor while plucking the strings of the takobung or tongkibong. It is held in the lap on the left knee while the other end is cradled by the player's foot. The music usually imitates gong music to accompany dance (the magarang dance in Tambunan, and the sumazau dance in Penampang).

Lutes

Sape

The sape plucked lute (also written and pronounced as s*ampeq, sambe* or *sapeh*) is usually played as a solo instrument or in a small ensemble of two to four sape, or sometimes two sape with the jatung utang xylophone (see Ngajat and datun julud dance music in Chapter 2). This instrument is played by men among the Kenyah, Kayan, Kelabit and other interior peoples of Sarawak.

The body of the sape is shaped roughly like a rectangular box about 1 to 1.5 meters long (Figure 4.7). Because of its shape, it is often called a 'boat lute'. The neck is short, measuring only about 20 centimeters. The homogeneous body and neck are carved from one piece of tree trunk (the local *aro* tree is used) and the back side of the body is left open. Other Southeast Asian instruments similar to the sape include the *chapey* from Cambodia, the *kacapi* or *kucapi* of Indonesia, the *kudyapi* from Mindanao and the *kusyapig* from Palawan in The Philippines.[6]

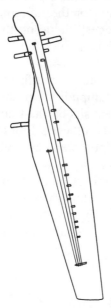

Figure 4.7 The *sape* plucked lute from Sarawak. (see also Plate 2.4)

In former times, only two strings of fine rattan were used on the sape, but today three to four metal strings are usually found, and sometimes an electric device is attached to the instrument to amplify the sound. The strings run atop a bridge located at the end of the body and over several moveable frets (called *kiep*). They are tightened with lateral tuning pegs (*otah*) located at the end of the neck. Although the sape strings are tuned in specific intervals, the pitches of the strings is not standard and depends on the size of the instrument and the type of strings used. As a typical tuning for many of the pieces in the repertory, the first and second strings are tuned an octave apart and the other strings are tuned to produce a Perfect 5th with the main string. After the strings are tuned, several frets are placed beneath the strings to produce a specific scale, depending upon the piece to be played.

The two or three strings are plucked with the thumb to produce a drone or ostinato, while only one string is plucked with the other fingers to play the melody.

In the past, the sape was used to accompany special rituals and for courting, but today in Sarawak it is played for general entertainment or to provide music to accompany dance. A repertory of dance music is known, as well as pieces to express particular emotions or feelings. Other pieces imitate sounds from the natural environment such as birds, fowls and so on.

Sape Music As noted earlier, the sape is played as a solo instrument or in small ensembles of two to four instruments, and its music consists of a drone or ostinato that is played simultaneously with a melody. If only one sape is played, then both the drone and melody are played on the same instrument. But whenever two sapes are played as an ensemble, one provides the drone or ostinato and the second one plays the melody.

Sape melodies are usually based on pentatonic scales (see the Examples 2.11a and b, music for dance in Chapter 2). The melodic lines typically consist of 2- or 4-beat motifs that are repeated with variation in pitch and rhythm. The melodic motifs are the basis for improvisation on the sape, incorporating melodic ornaments such as the acciacatura, double or triple acciacatura, dotted rhythm, neighboring notes and so on (see several transcribed examples in V. Gorlinski, 1988). The melodic lines may be played alternately in high and low registers on the instrument.

Rhythm in sape music is usually in duple or quadruple meter. A continuous drone part carries a particular rhythmic pattern to stress the downbeat in the music and to give tonal support to the melody above it. Alternately, an ostinato may accompany a melody in which case a rhythmic pattern and a short melodic line will be heard against the melody. Like the drone, the ostinato reinforces and supports the rhythm and important pitches in the melodic lines (see Examples 2.11a and b in Chapter 2).

Sundatang and Gagayan

Several traditional plucked lutes and one bowed lute are found in the state of Sabah. The *sundatang* is a long-necked plucked lute played in many Dusunic communities. It is normally a solo instrument, often played only by men, but among the KadazanDusun from Tambunan women also play the sundatang (Figure 4.8). The *gagayan* is played by men of the LotudDusun community of Tuaran (Figure 4.9). It resembles a larger version of the sundatang.

Sundatang The sundatang is made from a soft wood such as jackfruit (KadazanDusun *nangko*) and has two brass strings. Formerly, roots (particularly *gimam* roots) were used for strings. The higher-pitched string is fixed to the neck with beeswax, and has five or six cane frets below it. In contrast, the frets on the sundatang from Tambunan, and the gagayan lute of the LotudDusun people lie horizontally along the neck of the instrument. The two strings run atop a small bridge in the middle area of the body. They are plucked with the fingers of the right hand near the bridge as the left hand stops the strings on the frets to obtain specific pitches.

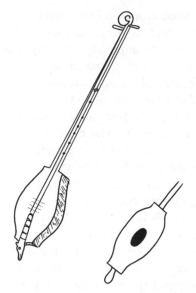

Figure 4.8 The *sundatang* plucked lute from Sabah

The sundatang may have a rather small body and short neck (about 50 centimeters among the RungusDusun of Kudat in the north), or the neck may be quite long (the entire instrument measuring about 1 meter among the KadazanDusun from the Tambunan area). Usually the overall length of this instrument is slightly less than 1 meter.

The use of the sundatang is rare nowadays among the Kadazans of Tambunan, Penampang and Papar regions of Sabah, but it is still widely played among the RugusDusun.

The sundatang is nearly always a solo instrument. Sometimes in Tambunan, however, it may be accompanied by the small hand-held koritikon gong (see Figure 3.4 in Chapter 3 --- Hanging Gong Ensembles) if its music accompanies the slow, sedate magarang sundatang dance. In Konarut, in the coastal area between Penampang and Papar, the sundatang may sometimes be played with the tongkongon and the takobung tube zithers.

Gagayan The gagayan of the LotudDusun from Tuaran has a large somewhat rectangular shaped body, with a very long neck, and its total length is well over 1.5 meters. This instrument is still widely played by the Lotud men.

Figure 4.9 The *gagayan* plucked lute from Sabah

Like the sundatang, the gagayan is held in a guitar-like position, with the left hand stopping the higher pitched string and the right hand strumming both strings. The performer either sits on a seat or cross-legged on the floor.

Among the LotudDusun people, the gagayan may be played either as a solo instrument or as a duet (called *batangkung*) with another gagayan.

The music The repertory for these instruments varies widely according to the community and individual performer. The music may imitate the melodies of various songs and chants, or copy the rhythms and tunes of dance music.

The music of the Rungus sundatang usually imitates songs and chants, as does that from many of the KadazanDusun areas of Sabah. In Tambunan in former times, it accompanied the sedate magarang sundatang dance that was similar to the common magarang of today. The magarang sundatang was suitable for a handful of people dancing in a confined space, probably in non-ritual contexts.

.An example of sundatang music is given in Example 4.17 below. The *kawat* string sounds a repetitive support, that is, a drone below the melody played on the *tansi* string. As shown in the example, the melodic structure features long, unmetered phrases. The triplet rhythmic figure is dominant in the melodic line with an occasional grace note used as a melodic ornament. Each melodic phrase ends with a rising minor 3rd interval. The rhythm of the magarang dance is suggested in the syncopated rhythmic patterns of the drone string.

Scale

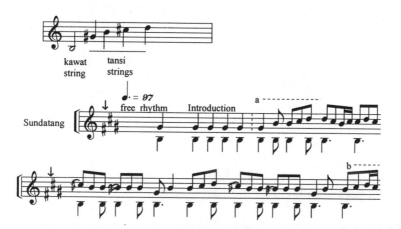

Example 4.17   Excerpt of a *sundatang* melody from Kg. Timbou, Tambunan. (Transcribed by J. Pugh-Kitingan)

Gambus and Biola

Gambus   The gambus (Figure 4.10) is a plucked lute of Arabic origin, which is sometimes found among East Malaysian coastal Muslim communities, particularly the Brunei and some Bajau groups (see also the zapin dance in Chapter 2). It is played at night, mainly by men, as a form of relaxation and entertainment after work. Sometimes it may be used to accompany certain Malay dances.

It has possibly been introduced into Sabah only in more recent times, and is not found in the remote interior. Along the east coast, however, it is beginning to become acculturated into some older indigenous cultures. A long gambus (over 1 meter long) is now made and played among some eastern Kadazan communities near the mouth of the Labuk River in similar contexts to the sundatang.

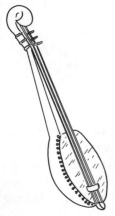

Figure 4.10 *Gambus* plucked lute from Sabah.

The gambus has a hollowed-out body of jackfruit wood that is made in one piece with the neck, totaling around 70 centimeters in length. A membrane of the monitor lizard skin covers the front of the body and is affixed to the wood with metal studs. This lute uses three pairs of nylon and metal strings which are plucked with a plectrum made from the scale of a pangolin (Malay: *tenggiling*, KadazanDusun: *bolukun*). The gambus is played in a guitar-like fashion, with the left hand stopping the strings while the right hand plucks the strings with the plectrum.

The music for the gambus often imitates dance music such as the Malay *zapin* and *joget* (see also Chapter 5 --- *Ronggeng*).

Biola Bowed lutes are not traditionally found among the older indigenous communities of the interior of Sabah. The *biola* (among the Iranun peoples known as *biula*) is a three-stringed bowed lute possibly of Arabic origin, which is played among coastal Muslim communities (Figure 4.11). It may be played by men or women in various contexts, and can be used as a form of personal recreation or public entertainment at weddings and other social gatherings during the night.

Figure 4.11 *Biola* bowed lute from Sabah.

The biola or biula and its bow are carved from soft wood such as jackfruit. The instrument has the same structure as the western violin, but uses only three metal strings. Traditionally brass was used, but nowadays the strings are made of steel. The bow strings, which were formerly made from the hairs of a cow's tail, are now made of nylon strings.   During performance, the instrument is held vertically on its base end in front of the player who sits cross-legged on the floor.

The biola has a wide repertory depending on the community and context. A particular genre is the *pamiula* of the Iranun community of Kota Belud (in Bajau this genre is called *isun-isun*), which involves singing accompanied by biula playing. This usually consists of call and response patterns (in the *sembaga a pantun* verse structure) sung between a man and a woman. In this context the woman usually plays the biula, but men also play this instrument as a solo music. If only one singer is present, the verses form a soliloquy.

Jew's Harp

One type of plucked idiophone, known as a linguaphone or jew's harp, has a tongue or lamella that is attached to the frame or body of the instrument. If the tongue or lamella is carved or cut from the body of the instrument itself, then the instrument is idioglottal, but if the tongue is separate and attached to the body, the instrument is described as heteroglottal. A heteroglottal jew's harp is often made from metal and only one of these is found in Malaysia. It is played among the Bidayuh of Sarawak and is called the *jungon*. All other jew's harps are idioglottal types.

Tong/Ruding/Jongon The jew's harp in Malaysia consists of a body that is made from bamboo, wood, metal or plant stem. The jew's harp found in Sarawak is usually made of bamboo or metal, and the local names for this instrument include *tong* among the Kajang people, *ruding* among the Iban, and *jungon* among the Bidayuh as mentioned above.

In Sarawak the body of the wood or bamboo jew's harp is about 15 to 17 centimeters long and rectangular in shape (similar to the Sabahan *bungkau*, see Figure 4.12 below). The player plucks one end of the body with his finger, while the opposite end forms the handle. A tongue, about 5-6 centimeters long, is cut in the middle of the body.

The jew's harp is held horizontally between the player's lips so that the tongue or lamella vibrates whenever the end of the instrument is plucked (Plate 4.10). In this context the mouth cavity of the player is the resonator that amplifies the fundamental pitch and also specifies the overtones. The size of the mouth cavity and the placement of the tongue and teeth determine the overtones that are heard.

The Bidayuh people in Sarawak make the jungon jew's harp from metal. This instrument plays music known as *totog*, and in former times it was used in ceremonies to heal a sick person. Today, however, it is played only for entertainment. Sometimes the jungon music accompanies the rhythmic patterns of drums and gongs in the music of the Bidayuh community.

Plate 4.10   The *tong* jew's harp, played by a Kajang woman from Belaga District in Sarawak.

The *tong* jew's harp, found in the interior regions along the Rejang River in Sarawak, is also used to play music for entertainment. This instrument may be played without accompaniment, or it may be played simultaneously with the satong tube zither as a small ensemble. As an ensemble, the satong produces a melodic line while the tong plays an accompanying rhythmic pattern (see Example 4.18).

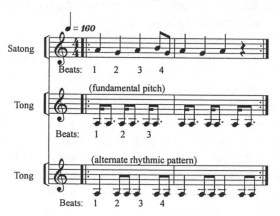

Example 4.18 *Satong* and *tong* music by the Kajang from Sarawak.

In this music, the 2-bar melody is repeated throughout the piece and the form is iterative.

The tong is played simultaneously with the satong, but with a different meter and rhythm. The tong part consists of dotted rhythm in triple meter giving a 3-beat bar as the main repeated unit. The repeated 3-beat bar of the tong is played against the 4-beat bar of the satong part, thus producing hemiola in the rhythm of the music (see Example 4.18). However, in the same piece, the tong player may change the rhythm as shown in Example 4.18, 3rd line in the score. The tong player improvises the rhythmic patterns switching back and forth between triple and duple meters.

The tong is also used to play short melodies and rhythms that imitate specific speech patterns or sounds of the natural environment such as bird calls, insect sounds and so on.

Ginggong/Genggong/Ranggong   The Jah Hut aborigines of the Malay Peninsula play a jew's harp called ginggong (M. Couillard, 1982), while the Temiars play the genggong and the ranggong (see further M. Roseman, 1991).

The ginggong is made from wood, while the Temiar genggong is made from metal, and their ronggong is fashioned from parts of a palm leaf. These three jew's harps are idioglottal. The ginggong is plucked using a string attached to the end of the body of the instrument that is pulled rhythmically to activate the sound, while the genggong and ranggong are directly plucked with the player's finger. All these instruments are used to play tunes that imitate the sounds from the natural environment including the chirps of beetles, crickets, certain birds and so on. The music produced by these instruments features many overtones that sound simultaneously with the fundamental pitch.

Among the Jah Hut aborigines this instrument may be played by anyone, but in the Temiar community the genggong and ranggong are played only by men. The Temiar jew's harp music tells of sadness and love, but may also be used simply to entertain the village dwellers. The music consists of short melodic motifs that are repeated, sometimes with the incorporation of sounds imitating those of animals and fowls from the surrounding rain forest, a constant influencing factor on the lives of the aboriginal inhabitants and their music.

Bungkau The *bungkau* is a small jew's harp played throughout Sabah, but especially among the Dusunic peoples. It is known by various names in the different communities. Among the KadazanDusun, the RungusDusun, the

Eastern Kadazan and most other Dusunic areas it is named bungkau. The LotudDusun of Tuaran call it *uriding*, while the TindalDusun (the Kadazan Dusun from the Kota Belud area) refer to it as *turiding*. These two terms are akin to the *kuriding* of the Bajau from Kota Belud, and the *kubing* of the Iranun people (see Figure 4.12).

This instrument is nearly always made from the stem of the *polod* palm (known as *tapikan* in the Iranun language), like the sodi (reed) of the sompoton mouth organ. The bungkau measures between 10 and 15 centimeters long. It is cut from a strip of polod with a sharp knife to produce a thin sodi or tongue (lamella) that vibrates freely within the body of the instrument. Pieces of *sopinit* or beeswax may be added to the back of the tongue to lower its pitch if required.

When not in use, the bungkau is stored in a small case made of sumbiling bamboo that is joined to the basal end opposite the tongue by a length of twine, as shown in Figure 4.12. The basal end of the instrument is a plain handle or *tiigitan* on the KadazanDusun bungkau, but is carved into a pattern on the Iranun kubing.

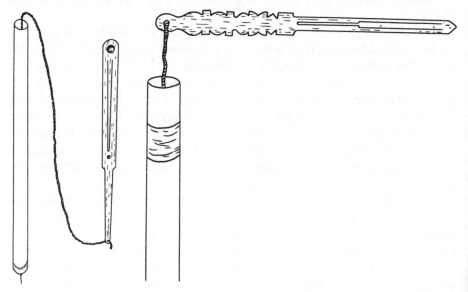

Figure 4.12 The *bungkau* (left) and *kubing* (right) from Sabah.

The tongue of the instrument vibrates as the performer strikes the basal end while holding the instrument between the lips. The resulting sound energy is reshaped by the performer's oral cavity to produce music among the upper partials (overtones).

Bungkau music In the Tambunan region of Sabah there are five traditional styles of bungkau performance. These are:

a) bungkau *ponininong do tugarang*, played in the early morning to attract small lizards from bamboo to cook and eat. This style is based on the repetitive rhythmic pattern:

b) bungkau *sinkokolu*, to express sadness when a close friend or brother is going away. It may be played as a form of remembrance, and is based on the pattern:

c) bungkau *kaamatan*, played after the harvest. The rhythm is:

d) bungkau *tintod susumangod*, is played as a send-off for warriors heading towards a distant battle, and as a salute when they return. The basic repeated pattern is:

e) bungkau *sumagarang gulugulu*, imitating magarang gong patterns (see Example 3.6. in Chapter 3). A brief fragment of a performance is shown in Example 4.19. Because the common staff music notation is not suitable for transcribing jew's harp music, a system of notation previously developed for research in Papua New Guinea has been used here.[7] Each horizontal line represents an outstanding pitch frequency, while the note head size indicates the relative intensity of the pitch. Since the instrumental spectrum has not been measured in the example below, the most audible frequencies are labeled according to cipher notation with the pitch *F* as the fundamental. The characteristic magarang rhythm is clearly seen, along with its changing melodic shape over the four phrases. The form is iterative and may be outlined as phrases *a, a1, a2, a3, a4* and so on.

Bungkau sound spectrum (measured by ear)

Example 4.19 An excerpt of *bungkau* music (*sumagarang gulugulu*). (Transcribed by J. Pugh-Kitingan, 1987)

While the bungkau may imitate the magarang dance music, it is more generally played for personal entertainment by both men and women. Among the Iranun people, a young man may also play the jew's harp, called *kubing* (Figure 4.12), to attract a girl during courtship.

Notes

1   Benedict Sandin 'The Iban Music', in Mohd. Taib Osman (ed.), *Traditional Music and Drama of Southeast Asia* (Kuala Lumpur: Dewan Bahasa dan Pustaka, 1974), pp. 320-6.

2   For a list of engkerurai pieces see Alexander Anak Wong and Soraya Mansor, *Engkerurai: Alat Muzik Masyarakat Iban, Sarawak* (Kuala Lumpur: Kementerian Kebudayaan, Kesenian dan Pelancongan, 1996).

3 *Dream Songs and Healing Sounds in the Rainforest of Malaysia* (Smithsonian Folkways compact disc no. 40417, 1995), recording and booklet by Marina Roseman.

4 *Ibid.*

5 *Ibid.*

6 See also Jose Maceda, *A Manual of Field Music Research with Special Reference to Southeast Asia* (Quezon City: College of Music, University of the Philippines, 1981); and Margaret Kartomi, 'Kucapi' and 'Hasapi' in *The New Grove's Dictionary of Musical Instruments* (London: MacMillan, 1980)

7 Jacqueline Pugh-Kitingan, 'Huli Language and Instrumental Performance', *Ethnomusicology*, 21 (2), 1988, pp. 205-32, and 'Language Articulation using Musical Instruments in the Southern Highlands of Papua New Guinea', *Tenth International Congress on Acoustics*, Sydney, 3 Vols., pp. 1-151, and other works by this author.

Chapter 5

Social Popular Music and Ensembles

Many different kinds of music ensembles are played for entertainment during celebrations such as weddings, and for formal and informal social gatherings among all ethnic groups in both the rural and urban areas of Malaysia. Some ensembles, such as the *ronggeng*, accompany social dances as well as singing *pantun* (Malay verses), like the genres *dondang sayang* and *dikir barat*. They also accompany *keroncong* and *ghazal* singing. Instrumental music may also be performed by the Chinese orchestra for entertainment.

Most of these ensembles play syncretic or acculturated types of music, music that mixes local musical elements with foreign elements such as Chinese, Indian, Western and Arabic music. Musical instruments, melodies, scales, textures and themes of song lyrics are derived from many different sources. Over the years and still today these syncretic genres are widely broadcast and disseminated by radio, television, audio cassettes and compact discs. They are sung by popular musicians, too.

This chapter describes the music of the dikir barat, the Chinese orchestra and the ensembles that play the syncretic tunes of the asli, inang, joget, dondang sayang, ghazal, keroncong, and Portuguese musical genres. Other syncretic forms, such as the music of the bangsawan and the zapin, were discussed in Chapters 1 and 2.

Ronggeng

The *ronggeng* is a type of social dance involving sung pantun (traditional Malay 4-line verses) in repartee with the accompaniment of the violin, accordion, rebana and gong. In former times, the ronggeng was very popular as entertainment at special gatherings such as weddings in the villages and even in the cities. The term ronggeng also refers to the joget dance that forms one of the main components of the ronggeng repertory.

It is not known when the ronggeng was first developed, but there are references to a similar genre in ancient Malay texts such as the *Hikayat Hang Tuah* and *Tuhfat al-Nafis*. For example, the *Hikayat Hang Tuah* from the 17th and 18th centuries, tells of singing pantun with the accompaniment of the rebana, gong and the *kecapi* (a type of plucked chordophone). Although the kecapi rather than the violin was used, it is possible that the ronggeng ensemble was already present on the Malay Peninsula in the 17th and 18th centuries.

In the 1930s and 40s, ronggeng groups were widely found in the entertainment parks of the urban areas of Malaya and Singapore. Ronggeng music performed at amusement parks were known as *pentas joget* [joget stage]. The male patrons bought tickets to dance with the female ronggeng dancers.[1] As noted in the discussion of the bangsawan (Chapter 1), the ronggeng tunes were also performed in the stories and the extra turns of the bangsawan in the 1930s and 40s. Through the bangsawan, the ronggeng incorporated many Western elements such as harmony, a Western singing style and musical instruments such as the flute, trumpet, trombone, bass, piano, guitar, Western drums, maracas and tambourine.

Today the ronggeng groups still entertain visitors at weddings and other feasts particularly in Penang and Malacca. At these gatherings the ronggeng female entertainers dance with the male guests and the music is provided by the ronggeng ensemble. Singing is done by special singers and not by the dancers themselves. Today, the ronggeng tunes such as the asli, inang and joget are also performed by pop bands, the orchestra of Radio and Television Malaysia (RTM) and by symphony orchestras.

Several types of pieces are played in a given traditional ronggeng performance today, namely: (i) the asli pieces such as *Bunga Tanjung, Tudung Periok, Mas Merah* and *Seri Mersing*; (ii) the inang pieces such as *Mak Inang, Inang Cina* and *Inang Kelantan*; and (iii) the joget pieces such as *Hitam Manis* and *Tanjung Katong*. Depending upon the dance to be accompanied, each piece evokes a different feeling and ambience. For example, the asli pieces are slow and sad, the inang tunes are lively and melodious and the joget pieces are fast-paced and happy.

The zapin (also referred to as *gambos*), *masri*, dondang sayang and keroncong pieces also are performed by many groups with or without additional musical instruments such as the gambus (for the zapin) or the guitar and ukelele (for the keroncong). (See also the discussion of the bangsawan in Chapter 1, the zapin dance in Chapter 2 and the keroncong in this chapter.)

The musical instruments

The original ronggeng ensemble consisted of the violin, accordion, rebana and knobbed gong. The violin, accordion and rebana drum were brought to the Malay Peninsula by the Portuguese in the 16th century. It is believed the rebana or frame drum was imported to Portugal during the time of Moorish colonization and is still used in Portugal today (Plate 5.1).

Plate 5.1 A *ronggeng* ensemble, showing (from left to right) the knobbed gong, two *rebana* drums, violin and accordion.

In these recent times other instruments such as the flute, *oud* (or gambus) and guitar are often added to the traditional ronggeng ensemble. The ensemble is also known as the '*asli* ensemble' [lit., native or original ensemble] today. Ronggeng tunes are performed by pop bands consisting of electric guitars, synthesizers and Western drums (see Chapter 6). The studio orchestra of Radio and Television Malaysia and the symphony orchestras also play the ronggeng repertory using various other instruments such as strings, brass, winds and percussion.

The music

Basically, ronggeng music combines Malay and Western characteristics, but aspects of music from China, the Middle East, India and other countries have also been assimilated. Just as in bangsawan music, the traditional ronggeng tunes are also syncretic.

Tonal system In general, the ronggeng pieces are based on diatonic major and minor scales with added chromatic tones such as the flat 7 (Example 5.1, bars 4 and 8), flat 3 (bars 9-12, 15-16) and the sharp 4 (bars 3 and 7).

Example 5.1 *Mak Inang (inang).*[2]

The augmented 2nd interval (see Example 5.2, bars 6 and 11) found in Middle Eastern, Indian and Spanish gypsy music is also popularly used in ronggeng tunes. It is highly possible that the scales with the augmented interval were brought to Malaysia by the Portuguese settlers because these scales are still used in Portuguese folk music today.

Example 5.2 *Seri Mersing (asli).*[3]

Other than added chromatic tones, the melodic phrases or cadences found in Chinese and Middle Eastern folk music are also found in many traditional ronggeng tunes. The piece *Mas Merah* (an asli piece) contains melodic phrases identical to those found in some Chinese folk music. These phrases stress the minor 3rd interval found in the Chinese pentatonic scale. As examples, the pitches 6 and 5 are played with the pitches 6 and

1, as shown in Example 5.3a; and the pitches 3 and 2 are played with pitches 3 and 5 as shown in Example 5.3b.

a) *Mas Merah*, biola part (use of pitches 6, 5 and 1)

b) *Mas Merah*, biola part (use of pitches 3, 2 and 5)

Example 5.3 *Mas Merah*.

Also, in the piece *Seri Mersing* (an asli piece) the intervallic structure of the scale is almost the same as the mode *Hicaz* found in Middle Eastern music (see Examples 5.4a and 5.4b).

a) the melody from the piece *Seri Mersing*

b) the mode *Hicaz*

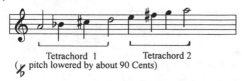

Example 5.4 *Seri Mersing* melody and mode.

Texture   Ronggeng music uses a linear texture.   In the piece *Bunga Tanjung* (an asli piece shown in Example 5.5) there are many melodic lines and rhythmic patterns which are independent.   First, the voice sings a melody with semitones and ornaments such as the tremolo (bars 3-7) and the portamento (bars 4 and 7).

Secondly, the violin and accordion play heterophonically with the voice. The violin and accordion play a variation of the vocal melody using ornaments such as the trill (Example 5.5, bars 3 and 5) and turn (bar 7). The two musical instruments coincide at the end of the phrases (bars 4 and 8).

Third, the rebana drum provides the asli rhythmic pattern (Example 5.5, bars 2-3) and the gong marks the end and beginning of the rhythmic cycle (bar 4).

Melody At first the Malay singing style was used to vocalize the ronggeng pieces, a style featuring a narrow range with a vocal quality that was tense, hoarse and nasal. However, in the 1940s and 50s, as a result of Western influence, an open and wide vocal range and style called crooning replaced the earlier style.

Key: ∿ Tremolo, ⁄ Portamento, 'dung' - mnemonic for rebana;
hand strikes middle of drumhead to produce a low, resonant timbre,
'tak' mnemonic for rebana, hit edge of drumhead for a ringing timbre.

Example 5.5 *Bunga Tanjung.*

Unique melodic patterns appear in the ronggeng tunes. For example, in the piece *Sambut Kekasih* (an inang piece) (see Example 5.6), the singer embellishes the melody with ornaments such as the tremolo and the portamento (bars 2 and 4 in Example 5.6). The singer does not enter on the first beat of each sung phrase, but rather always uses *rubato* (holding the notes or prolonging the main beat played by the rebana drum).

Example 5.6 Excerpt from *Sambut Kekasih* (*inang*).

In the asli tunes the melodic pattern or cadence called the *patahan lagu* is used. This melodic pattern immediately identifies the piece as an asli tune. Each ronggeng musician improvises the patahan lagu with different ornaments and cadences. Several of these patahan lagu patterns are shown in Example 5.7.

Example 5.7 The *patahan lagu* played on a violin.

Rhythm and tempo The asli, inang and joget pieces each use a particular rhythmic pattern. The rebana part in each type of piece is based on a cyclical, repeated rhythmic pattern of four or eight beats.

Asli is the name of a sad, slow dance and musical piece in quadruple meter. The asli pieces use an 8-beat rhythmic pattern played on the rebana drum (see Example 5.8a). In this pattern only the first beat of the first bar, and the first, second and third beats of the second bar are definite. The other beats may be improvised such as in Example 5.8b.

a) the *asli* pattern

b) the asli pattern --- improvised beats (two possible patterns)

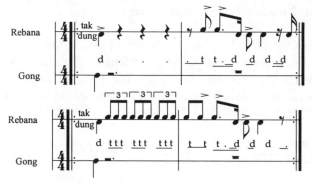

Example 5.8 The *asli* rhythmic pattern. (key: see Example 5.5)

The asli rhythmic pattern is played with the right hand. The left hand improvises, using the timbre 'tak' between the beats played with the right hand (see Example 5.9).

Example 5.9 The *asli* rhythmic pattern --- improvisation with the left hand.

The inang is a fast dance and tune in quadruple meter. The 4-beat inang rhythmic pattern is shown in Examples 5.10a and b.

a) the *inang* pattern

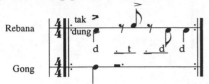

b) the *inang* pattern --- improvisation with the left hand

Example 5.10 The *inang* rhythmic pattern.

The inang pieces also accompany other dances such as the *tari piring* [dance with plates held in the dancers' hands], *tari lilin* [dance with candles held in the hands] and the *tari payung* [dance with umbrellas held by the dancers].

The joget (or ronggeng) is a very fast dance and tune in a 4-beat rhythmic pattern. The gong is played on every two beats (see Example 5.11).

a) the *joget* pattern

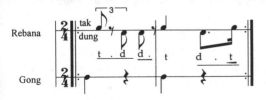

b) the *joget* pattern --- improvisation with the left hand

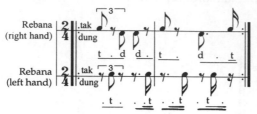

Example 5.11 The *joget* rhythmic pattern.

A unique feature in this rhythmic pattern is the use of units of two notes and three notes played in succession (see Example 5.12).

Example 5.12 *Serampang Laut* (a *joget* piece).

As shown in Example 5.12, the melody of the joget piece usually alternates between 2/4 and 6/8 meters. This feature is also found in Spanish and Portuguese music showing a strong influence of these musics on the joget.

Form The ronggeng pieces are in strophic form. All pieces begin with a short introduction, and then each stanza of a piece is sung with basically the same melody, although the singer is given the freedom to improvise on the melody.

The text of each stanza consists of one verse of a *pantun*, a 4-line verse with a 2-part semantic scheme known as the *pembayang* [lit., shadow or imagery] and the *maksud* [intent or meaning], or one verse of a *seloka* (a 4-line verse based on the same theme). The rhyme scheme *a,a,a,a* or *a,b,a,b* is used. Several lines of text are always repeated in a ronggeng piece.

The asli, inang and joget pieces are divided into two parts. As shown in Examples 5.1 and 5.2 above (the pieces *Mak Inang* and *Seri Mersing*), part A of the piece is the *pembayang* section of the pantun and part B is the *maksud*. In the joget pieces there is usually a part C or long instrumental coda to accompany the dance.

In conclusion, the traditional ronggeng music is syncretic. The features of Malay music found in the ronggeng pieces include a cyclical, repeated rhythmic pattern, a text in the form of a pantun, the use of the patahan lagu melodic pattern and a linear texture with rather independent musical lines played simultaneously. The features of Western music found in ronggeng pieces include the use of Western musical instruments, triple meter and diatonic scales. Just as in the bangsawan pieces, other elements such as scales and rhythmic patterns from other countries are also combined in the ronggeng pieces.

Today the ronggeng tunes played by the pop bands, studio orchestras or symphonic orchestras feature mainly Western elements in the use of musical instruments, vocal style and homophonic texture with functional harmony.

Dondang Sayang

The phrase *dondang sayang* means 'love song'. It originated from the words *dendang* [singing] and *sayang* [love]. In a dondang sayang performance a singer sings a pantun of four lines and another singer answers the first singer with an appropriate pantun. They are accompanied by a violin, two rebana drums and a knobbed gong. An amiable and enjoyable atmosphere emerges when two or more performers sing pantun verses back and forth [*jual beli pantun*] while teasing each other.

The verses are created spontaneously and are based on themes of love, wisdom, the natural surroundings, comedy, luck or fate and so on. Formerly there was no time limit on the performance of this genre, and the singer who could not think of an appropriate response in the pantun format was forced to withdraw himself from the performance.

A dondang sayang performance can take place anywhere, including the living room or the verandah of a house, in a park or other public place. It is sung at weddings, other celebrations and at the Malacca *Pesta Mandi Safar* [an annual festival celebrated in the second Muslim calendar month]. In a performance of dondang sayang usually the inang, joget and asli tunes are used as interludes. A tradition existing in Penang long before the second World War, the dondang sayang is sung during the *Chap Goh Meh* celebrations (the 15th day of the Chinese New Year). On the evening of *Chap Goh Meh* the Straits Chinese girls (*nyonya*) of Penang would get on horse-drawn carriages heading for the seaside to throw oranges into the sea, believing that this would earn them a wise and rich husband. To attract the attention of the women in the carriages the Straits Chinese men would sing the dondang sayang, travelling about the town in bullock carts.

There are two theories concerning the origin of the dondang sayang. The first theory is that it originated in Penyengat (Riau), while the second train of thought is that it started in Malacca at the height of the Malay kingdom of Malacca in the 15th century. Just as in dating the ronggeng genre, the old Malay texts such as the *Hikayat Hang Tuah* and the *Tuhfat al-Nafis* indicate that the dondang sayang already existed in the 17th and 18th centuries. Since that time, this musical form has not only attracted the Malays and Straits Chinese, but also the Indian and Portuguese communities of Malacca.

The musical instruments

The dondang sayang ensemble consists of one violin, two rebana drums (see Plate 5.1) and a knobbed gong (Figure 1.1). Today the harmonium or accordion, guitar and tambourine are also used. This is essentially the same instrumentation as the ronggeng ensemble, and hence the asli, inang and joget tunes are performed as interludes by the dondang sayang groups. Sometimes the rebana players also sing.

The music

The tonal system   All dondang sayang pieces are based on only one melody. The *D* major scale is usually used in the dondang sayang, but sometimes the piece is based on *C* major. Just as in the asli tunes, the sharp 4th and flatted 7th chromatic pitches are added to the scale tones used (see Example 5.13a). In the second part of the dondang sayang piece (Part B (bar 16) in Example 5.13b) the melody changes key from *D* major to *G* major (the subdominant). Hence, in the new key the pitch *C* replaces the *C-sharp*. In the dondang sayang scale the pitches *D* and *A* are stressed.

a) Scale

b) the *dondang sayang* piece

Example 5.13 The *dondang sayang* piece.

Texture, melody and rhythm In the music for the dondang sayang there are four lines of melodic/rhythmic patterns that are rather independent (see Example 5.13b). Hence, a linear texture is typical of this music.

In a dondang sayang performance, the voice sings the melody with repeated notes (Example 5.13b, bars 10, 18, 21) or with whole tones (bars 6, 14, 22). The ornaments such as the portamento (bars 6, 7, 10, 18, 19), the tremolo (bars 6, 7, 10, 11) and the appogiatura (bars 6, 11, 18) are used. The melody that is sung by each singer is a little different in terms of vocal timbre, melodic contour and ornaments.

The violin plays an independent melody. The dondang sayang piece is introduced with a 5-bar opening melodic phrase played on the violin. The first two bars of this phrase are known as the 'dondang sayang tune':

The violin player improvises, based on the melody vocalized by the singer, but he plays a fixed melodic pattern at the cadence as a signal to the singer:

1. fixed melodic pattern at bar 4 (Example 5.13b)

2. fixed melodic pattern after the key change to the subdominant at bar 17 (Example 5.13b):

The patahan lagu used in asli tunes (see ronggeng in the previous section) is also used in the dondang sayang:

1. Patahan lagu at bars 10 and 21 (Example 5.13b)

In general, the violin melody is embellished with ornaments such as the acciacatura (Example 5.13b, bar 5), the trill (bars 5, 11, 14, 19), the mordent (bars 5, 13) and the portamento or slide (bars 11-12). Even so, sometimes the violin player just plays long held notes when the singer is singing (bar 6).

One rebana drum in the ensemble plays the basic asli rhythmic pattern and the second rebana plays in between the strokes of the basic pattern:

The final layer of sound in a dondang sayang piece, the gong part, marks the end and the beginning of the 8-beat repeated, cyclical pattern.

Form   The dondang sayang piece is in strophic form. Each stanza consists of seven sung lines. The musical form is based on the structure of the 4-line pantun with the repetition of some of the pantun lines such as:

lines 1 and 2 --- *pembayang* [suggestion/imagery of the pantun]

line 3 --- repetition of line 1

lines 4 and 5 --- *maksud* [intent/meaning of the pantun]

line 6 --- repetition of line 4
line 7 --- repetition of line 5

The phrases of affection such as *'dondang sayang'* [love song], *'ala dendang'* [ala singing], *'ala kawan'* [ala friend], and *'cik adik'* [younger sister] are often inserted between lines 4 and 5, and lines 6 and 7 of the verse.

The dondang sayang piece may be divided into two parts: Part A (see Example 5.13b) is associated with the suggestion or imagery in the pantun text (lines 1-3) and Part B is associated with the actual intent or meaning of the pantun text (lines 4-7). In Part B the tune changes key to the subdominant.

Themes of the poetry

The poems are usually sung in the form of a pantun and focus on the theme of love. A typical example, from *Pantun Asmara* [Love Poems] (Gustam Nagara, 1954, pp. 4-5), follows:

English translation

Question:
Burung putih burung dara,   White bird virgin bird
Bersama dengan burung kedidi,   Together with the sandpiper
Dari mana datang asmara   Where does love come from
Menjadi idaman pemuda pemudi?   [It] has become the desire for
                                        the young.

Answer:
Pancing ikan pakai perahu   Use a boat to go fishing
Bawa sebilah pisau belati   Bring a long knife
Kalau tuan hendak tahu   If sir would like to know
Dari mata turun ke hati.   [Love] descends from the eye
                                        to the heart.

Question:
Banyak bunga tepi istana,   There are] many flowers
                                        near the palace
Bunga melor bertandan-tandan,   Bunches of jasmine flowers
Cinta asmara kalau terkena,   If one falls passionately in
                                        love
Apa jadi nasib badan?   What is the destiny of the
                                        body?

Answer:
Melaka tuan berpagar kota,   Malacca sir is a fenced city
Hujungnya sampai ke tepi laut,   Its tip stretches to the sea
Kalau terkena asmara cinta,   If one falls passionately in
                                        love
Akhirnya boleh membawa maut   At the end it can bring death.

Other popular themes include wisdom, advice, the natural surroundings, fruits, comedy and so on. An example of a pantun that gives advice is as follows (from *Pantun Amaran* [Poetry of warning] (Gustam Nagara, 1954, pp 19-21):

	English translation
Question:	
Kereta kerbau ditarik sapi,	The bullock cart is pulled by a cow
Di atas kereta dibentang tikar,	On top of the cart is spread a mat
Tidakkah takut bermain api,	Aren't [you] afraid of playing with fire
Nanti tangan habis terbakar?	In case you burn your hand?
Answer:	
Kalau memerah susu sapi,	If [you] press milk from the cow
Hendaklah taruh dalam bijana,	Put it in the ground
Orang berani bermain api,	A brave person plays with fire
Lambat laun dapat bencana.	Gradually [he will] encounter disaster.
Question:	
Kalau pakai kalung mutiara	If you wear a necklace of pearls
Yang kilat hendaklah cari,	Look for shining ones
Kalau suka bermain asmara,	If you like to play with love
Apa faedahnya kemudian hari?	What is the use in the future?
Answer:	
Kalau kiri dikata kanan,	If it is left, [you] say right
Itu tanda jalan pesona,	That is a sign that you walk spell bound
Cinta asmara bukan permainan,	Falling in love is not a game
Itu penyakit jiwa merana.	It is a sickness that will make you suffer.

Today the dondang sayang has undergone many changes. In Malacca it is often performed at formal gatherings, festivals and singing competitions but rarely at someone's home. In Penang the dondang sayang singers still go around the town for *Chap Goh Meh* but they sing in a bus and not in bullock carts (Plate 5.2). The performance by the babas is for general entertainment and no longer to attract the attention of the ladies, as in the past.

New themes are created but still utilizing the pantun form of poetry. The popular poetic verses focus on themes of unity, allegiance to country, or they touch on politics and culture of the country. Finally, during formal gatherings the time for the performance is limited, and sometimes only a single singer performs the dondang sayang, in which case the repartee singing is excluded.

Plate 5.2 Buses carrying the *dondang sayang* performers in Penang.

Keroncong

The *keroncong* originated in Betawi (Jakarta) in the 16th and 17th centuries. At first, Portuguese melodies were sung with the accompaniment of several guitars by the black Portuguese known as the *Mardijker*s. Slowly by the end of the 19th century the keroncong was performed by the lower class of people of mixed Dutch and Indonesian descent (*orang Serani*) in Jakarta. It was sung by the young men of mixed parentage who were called the *Buaya Keroncong* [Kerconcong crocodiles]. They traveled around the city of Jakarta in the evenings while singing *pantun*s (verses) focusing on love and passion in an attempt to charm the women, if not cast a spell on them. They were accompanied by the ukelele or a small guitar. It is believed that the name 'keroncong' originated from the sound 'krong, krong' emitted by the ukelele. Other musical instruments such as the violin, guitar and tambourine could be added to the ensemble (Harmunah, 1987, pp. 7-9).

The keroncong melodies were sung in the *komedi stambul* theater which appeared in Surabaya in 1891 (O. Knaap, 1971). At first, the melodies were accompanied by chords played on the guitar, piano or other instruments present in the theater orchestra. These melodies became known as Stambul I and Stambul II keroncong pieces.

In the 1920s keroncong music was broadcast widely in Jakarta and other cities in Java through the popular komedi stambul theater and the *tonil* [Dutch term for theatrical play] as well as by the sale of 78 RPM records put out by the recording companies.

It is not really known when the keroncong was first brought to Malaysia, but the catalogues and recordings of 78 RPM records show that in the 1920s keroncong and stambul pieces were used in the extra turns in the bangsawan, mainly in the classical (Western) and Javanese stories. The tonil theater groups from Indonesia, visiting the Malay Peninsula, announced their keroncong pieces in the newspaper advertisements at that time.

According to the music performers, the keroncong and stambul pieces were very popular among the *babas* (Straits Chinese male singers) in Penang and Malacca in the 1920s. They set up their own keroncong music groups. A book on keroncong music was printed by H.S.L. in 1924 in Penang, which contains 16 pieces with notation for the melodies and chords for the guitar. The published pieces include *Stambul Satoe*, *Stambul Dua*, *Keroncong Meritzkey*, *Keroncong Pulau Jawa*, *Keroncong Pandan* and so on (Tan, 1993, pp. 157-8). The examples of music in this book and the 78 RPM recordings of that time show that keroncong melodies were accompanied with chords played on the guitar or the piano.

In the 1930s keroncong music became one of the most popular kinds of music on the Malay Peninsula. Keroncong pieces by local singers were recorded by the 78 RPM recording companies. In addition, keroncong competitions took place in the entertainment parks in the cities of the Malay Peninsula.

Since the 1930s, the formation of a new style and instrumentation was established in Indonesia and on the Malay Peninsula. The formation of this new style defined a special keroncong idiom which is still used by keroncong groups to this day. It is this new style of the 1930s that is illustrated in the sections on musical instruments and texture below.

The musical instruments

Since the 1930s and onward, the typical keroncong ensemble consists of one or two singers, musical instruments carrying the melody and other instruments that play the rhythm parts (Plate 5.3).
The melody instruments include:

1.   the Western violin with metal strings that are bowed (the tuning is g - d' - a' - e''); and
2.   a flute made of wood, bamboo or metal.

The instruments that play the rhythm parts consist of:

1.   the guitar with plucked metal strings (the tuning is E - A - d - g - b - e');
2.   the ukelele (also called the *cuk*) with plucked nylon strings. The cuk may have 3 strings (the tuning is a'' - b - e'') or 4 strings (with the tuning g'' - c'' - e'' - a'');
3.   the banjo (also called the *cak*) with plucked metal strings. The three strings may be tuned g'' - b' - e'' or g' - b' - e'';
4.   the cello with 3 plucked strings made of nylon or gut (with the tuning C - G - d); and
5.   a double bass with 4 strings (with the tuning E - A - D - G) or 3 strings (with the tuning A - D - G).

Although a standard instrumentation may be documented, exceptions were made and other instruments could be used. At times the mandolin or a second ukelele would replace the banjo. Other instruments such as the accordion might be added to play the melody. In the 1940s and 50s, the big bands of jazz and swing that consisted of trumpet, trombone, clarinet, piano and double bass were used to play sub-styles known as the 'rumba keroncong', and the 'slowfox' and 'tango keroncong'. The Hawaiian guitar was used in the 'Hawaiian keroncong'. Today the synthesizer often replaces instruments such as the violin, cello, double bass, cak and cuk.

The music

In the 1990s and the first decade of the 21st century, the keroncong is still played at celebrations, and at all kinds of concerts and shows in hotels. It is also performed by the ronggeng and dondang sayang groups.

Plate 5.3 A *keroncong asli* ensemble in Malaysia.

There are a number of different kinds of keroncong music, all of which are played in a typical idiom and with the instrumentation explained here. The types of keroncong pieces are:

1.   The *keroncong asli*, a piece in the original Javanese keroncong style using the same chord sequences each time it is played (see the section below on texture). Some examples include the pieces entitled *Keroncong Moritsko* and *Keroncong Sapu Lidi*.

2.   The *keroncong stambul*, a tune that was played in the komedi stambul theater and in the bangsawan in former times. Usually, these pieces were named Stambul I and Stambul II, for example, *Stambul I Jampang* and *Stambul II Baju Biru.*

3.   The *keroncong langgam*, a piece not originally in the keroncong asli or stambul categories, which is played in the idiom and with the instrumentation of the keroncong. The piece entitled *Bengawan Solo* is famous in the keroncong langgam style.

In Indonesia there is also keroncong music that originated from areas outside of Jakarta using lyrics in the local dialects and local musical elements. An example, the *langgam Jawa* originating in Central Java, is sung in the Javanese language and uses the pelog scale. Its instrumental style imitates gamelan music. The guitar is used in place of the sitar or celempung, the body of the cello is struck to imitate the accompaniment of the ciblon drum, and the double bass replaces the gong. An example of a piece in the langgam Jawa style is entitled *Putri Gunung.*

The *keroncong Malaysia* [Malaysian keroncong] is a type of keroncong langgam music that originated in Malaysia. The melody and song texts are sung with an accompaniment and instrumentation in the keroncong style. The piece *Tanjong Bidara*, by A. Rahman Ghani, is an example of a Malaysian keroncong.

Texture   The texture of keroncong pieces is similar to the textures of other ensemble music in Indonesia and Malaysia, that is, it is linear in nature (like gamelan music). Several lines of melody and rhythm, played simultaneously, are somewhat independent.

Melody   The singer must perform variations on the existing melody in a piece. As shown below, in the excerpt from the piece *Keroncong Moritsko* (Example 5.14), the singer's melody is embellished with ornaments such as the trill (bars 2 and 4) and the appogiatura (bars 2 and 3).

Music as written out:

Music as sung:

Example 5.14   Excerpt from the piece *Keroncong Moritsko.* (Harmunah, 1994, p. 29)

The portamento from one pitch to another is often used (Example 5.15, bar 3). The singer also uses rubato, and is rather flexible with the rhythm and the actual pitches of the notes (see Example 5.15).

Example as written out:

Example as sung:

Example 5.15 Excerpt from the piece *Keroncong Moritsko*. (Harmunah, 1994, p. 30)

The violin and flute players improvise heterophonically with the singer and fill in the passages between the singer's phrases. These two instruments imitate the portamento sung by the singer by producing notes that run in half-steps (see Example 5.16, bars 8-9 and bars 14-15).

Bars 7-9

Bars 13-15

Example 5.16   Excerpts from *Sapu Lidi* (a *keroncong asli* piece). (The complete score for this piece, arranged by Wawang Wijaya, may be found in the Appendix.)

Rhythm The rhythm part in keroncong music is played by plucked string instruments and consists of:

1.   the cak and cuk, which alternate with each other like the saron or bonang that play in interlocking style in the gamelan;
2.   a guitar fills in the rhythmic movement;
3.   the cello is played pizzicato to imitate the gendang drum that plays in interlocking style in the gamelan;
4.   the double bass plays the bass notes of the chords.

The piece *Sapu Lidi,* Example 5.16 bars 7-9 above, illustrates how the parts played by all the rhythm instruments combine as a single unit to provide a solid rhythmic base for a piece.

Harmony At the same time, the fundamental harmony based on the I, IV and V chords is used. It must be remembered that the chord sequence for all keroncong asli pieces is the same (see also, the score in the Appendix):

Introduction

```
I  I  V  V      II  II   V  V
V  V  IV IV      IV IV-V  I  I
V  V  I  IV-V  I  IV-V  I  I
V  V  I  I      Coda.
```

As far as can be ascertained today, there is only one exception to the above chord sequence, that is the piece *Keroncong Kemayoran,* which uses a different chord sequence.

An overall texture that combines linear features (each musical instrument plays a melody and rhythm that is rather independent) and a homophonic texture (using fundamental harmony) produces a special characteristic and unique style in the keroncong idiom, which has existed since the 1930s. The Malaysian keroncong is also performed in this idiom, but the melody and song texts concern Malaysian themes. In addition, the ronggeng and dondang sayang groups performing the keroncong in Malaysia have replaced the cak and cuk with two rebana drums (played in interlocking style), the double bass with the gong and the flute with the accordion.

The tonal system In general, the diatonic major and minor scales with added chromatic tones are used in keroncong pieces (see Example 5.16 and the complete score of the piece *Sapu Lidi* in the Appendix). Nevertheless, exceptions exist in the regional Indonesian langgam keroncong such as in the langgam Jawa pieces.

Form All types of keroncong pieces are in strophic form. Usually each stanza is repeated two times with different text. In the keroncong asli, each stanza consists of six vocal lines. The keroncong asli form is based on the structure of the 4-line pantun (see dondang sayang in this Chapter) with the repetition of some of the pantun lines. The text for the piece *Sapu Lidi* is one example of the keroncong asli form (see full score in the Appendix):

Part A   Vocal melodic phrase

Introduction
line 1   *pembayang* /imagery   a
line 2   (repetition of line 1)   b
         'a-hai, ya tuan'
line 3   *pembayang*/imagery   c
line 4   (repetition of line 3)   d

Part A1

line 5   *maksud*/meaning   a1
line 6   *maksud*/meaning   d
Coda

The words such as *'ya tuan'* [yes, sir], *'a-hai'* [a-hai], *'ya nona'* [yes, miss], *'jiwa manis'* [sweetheart] are inserted to complete the singer's phrase. Today, many new keroncong asli and keroncong langgam pieces do not use the pantun form.

In general, each stanza of the keroncong asli pieces may be divided into two parts with a melody that is nearly identical (see the score in the Appendix). Part *A* is associated with the *pembayang* or 'imagery' stated in the text of the pantun (Lines 1-4). It is sung with the melodic phrases *a*, *b*, *c*, and *d*. The next part of the piece, *A1*, is connected to the *maksud* or 'meaning' part of the pantun (Lines 5-6). This part is sung with the melodic phrases *a1* and *d*. A keroncong asli piece starts with an introduction and ends with a short coda.

The keroncong stambul piece is usually composed with a stanza of 16 bars in the form *AB*. However, various other forms may also be used in this style of keroncong, including the popular form *AABA* (32 bars) in the langgam pieces influenced by the Western popular songs. A good example is the keroncong piece entitled *Bengawan Solo*.

Textual themes

Today, most Indonesian keroncong song texts are about love and the beauty of the natural environment of a given place. However, in the 1940s and 50s, because of the Indonesian revolution, songs of patriotism and love of country such as *Pahlawan Merdeka* and *Indonesia Tanah Pusaka* were frequently sung.

The Malaysian keroncong, composed by local keroncong musicians in this day and age, reflect the feelings of love of country, landscape scenes and history of Malaysia. The piece *Permata Ku* is a good example:

Permata Ku (Lyrics by Ariff Ahmad, from the album *Keroncong Malaysia* (1992), EMI TC-FM 30093)

	(English translation)
Permataku indah permai	My jewel that is beautiful
Negara yang damai	My country that is peaceful
Tanah tumpah darah suci	Birthplace that is pure

Ibu pertiwi.	Motherland.
Tanah subur yang menghijau	Fertile land that is green
Sawah ladang tasik danau	The paddy fields, lakes and streams
Kampung halaman terbilang	Famous village courtyards
Alam permata, tersayang.	World of jewels, most beloved.

At this time, the keroncong has experienced many changes. Various types of keroncong styles such as pop keroncong (based on pop music), classical keroncong (based on classical Western music), *dangkron keroncong* (mixing the *dangdut* rhythm and keroncong) and the rock keroncong (influenced by rock music) are some examples. Still, the basic playing style and the function and use of the musical instruments as discussed above can still be seen in all the new keroncong styles that exist.

Ghazal

Another form of social popular music is the *ghazal*, a form of syncretized music in Malaysia. It is still performed at weddings and other celebrations in several states, but is mainly heard in Johore in the south of the Peninsula.

The word *ghazal* is an Arabic word meaning 'love poem'. Ghazal poetry is believed to have originated in the urban centers of Mecca and Medina and in the cities of Iraq in the 8th century C.E. By the 13th century, the ghazal was already known as a musical form in India, and the singing of this love poetry became famous in the 18th and 19th centuries in the Indian palaces at Delhi, Lucknow and Rampur (S. Sadie, ed., 1980, Vol. 9, p. 142).

When did the ghazal come to the Malay Peninsula? There are two different theories about the origin of the ghazal in Malaysia. First, according to Dato Abdullah bin Mohamed, a ghazal authority before World War II, the ghazal was possibly brought to the Malay archipelago by Indian traders in the 19th century and developed in the Riau-Lingga Sultanate by the Malay nobility who lived there (Abdullah bin Mohamed, 1974, pp. 28-9). After the government of the Malay ruler Temenggung Abu Bakar moved from Telok Belanga in Singapore to Johor Baru on the Malay Peninsula, the ghazal also moved with him. In Johore the *Dato Bentara Luar* (Mohamed Salleh bin Perang) has played an important role in further developing and spreading ghazal music when he was ordered by the Sultan of Johore to open new cities such as Muar, Batu Pahat and Endau.

In the second theory, the development of the ghazal in Malaysia is associated with the coming of the Parsi theater [*wayang Parsi*] from India to Johore in the early 20th century (Abidah Amin, 1979, p. 59). Several military officers such as Colonel Musa, Colonel Yahya and Major Lomak, who were taken with ghazal music, studied the Indian harmonium pumped organ and tabla drums from the Persian theater groups. They sang ghazal melodies to lyrics from traditional pantun verses, and musical instruments such as the gambus and the violin were added to the ensemble. Adibah Amin also has found that the ghazal was very popular among the Malay nobility and others of high status on the Malay Peninsula, especially in the 1930s.

Although the date and arrival of the ghazal in Malaysia is uncertain, what can be ascertained is that the ghazal was brought to the Malay Peninsula from India. In the early 20th century, the ghazal players often entertained the upper classes and nobility of the state of Johor. Slowly ghazal music became widespread in Johor, and was also sung by the extra-turn singers in the bangsawan theater. Their renditions of ghazal pieces were also recorded by the 78 RPM record companies, pieces such as *Gazal* by Simun (HMV NS 586, 1939) and *Gunong Ledang* by D. Hamzah with S. Hiboran Ghazal Party (Pathe PTH 118, 1950s). The ghazal was so popular in Johore that a wedding was not considered complete without it. Today, the ghazal groups also perform asli, joget, keroncong and pop pieces.

The musical instruments

As a syncretic music genre, the ghazal combines musical instruments and features from Indian, Arabic, Malay and Western music. The music instruments comprise:

1.   the Indian harmonium, and tabla and baya;
2.   the Western violin, guitar, maracas and tambourine; and
3.   the gambus, a type of lute originating from the Middle Eastern *ud* (see zapin dance music in Chapter 2 and Figure 2.10).

On the gambus, the first four nylon strings are paired to facilitate plucking as this instrument plays fast repeated notes in ghazal. The fifth and sixth strings are made of metal, are not paired and are used to play the lower bass notes.

The music

Texture, rhythm and scale In terms of musical texture, both Malay linear musical texture and Western harmony are used (see Example 5.17). The melody instruments such as the harmonium, gambus and violin play a variation of the singer's melody using characteristic phrases and melodic ornaments. The guitar and gambus players control the tempo. The guitar plays bass notes that make up part of the Western triads formed by additional notes on the gambus and harmonium.

The rhythmic patterns of Indian popular music and the Malay asli and joget rhythmic patterns (see ronggeng in this Chapter) are employed in ghazal music. In addition, Western major and minor diatonic scales are commonly used.

Form and texts Ghazal songs are in strophic form. The texts, based on pantun, *syair* and *seloka* Malay verses, are usually about love, fate, advice and so on. The piece *Gunung Pulai* (Example 5.18) instills the patriotic spirit in listeners.

Example 5.17 **Excerpt from the *ghazal* piece *Pak Ngah Balik*.**
(Arranged by Major Lomak, sung by Fadzil Ahmad,
with the accompaniment of Sri Maharani Ghazal group
of Muar on the album *Nasib Panjang*, (1982), WEA)

Each stanza is divided into two parts that are repeated. As shown
in Example 5.18, Part A of the piece entitled *Gunung Pulai* is the
pembayang section of the pantun and Part B is the *maksud* (pembayang and
maksud are explained in the discussion of dondang sayang above).

di ba_____ dan_____   Ha - - - jat

di ha - ti_____   Ha-jat di - ha - ti ti-dak kan

le - pas_____   (Key: ∿ a vocal vibrato)

Example 5.18 The *ghazal* piece *Gunung Pulai*. (Transcribed by Johar Hj. Jonid)

Dikir Barat

The *dikir barat* is a very popular form of entertainment in the villages and towns of Kelantan. The musicians tell us the name of this genre is derived from its place of origin, namely the Malay villages in the southern Thai states. In Kelantan the westerly direction (or '*barat*') refers to the country of Thailand. In southern Thailand this genre is known as *dikir karut* because of the presence of the main solo singer called the *tukang karut*. Also, in southern Thailand the term *zikir* (or *zikr*) is pronounced '*dikir*'.

It is highly possible that in former times this popular form developed from the chanting and singing of zikir as practiced by the followers of Islam. However, the dikir barat has developed as secular entertainment among the village Malays and features the singing of the 4-line pantun, sometimes in responsorial style between a solo singer and a chorus.

In early times, the themes of a dikir barat performance told of the happenings in local daily life with considerable stress on comic elements. Today, new thematic subjects involve the economic policy, political messages, social development, education, social unity and so on. Whenever the dikir barat is performed on television, the themes dwell on propaganda by government agencies to educate the people about health and social issues, such as the danger of the aedes mosquito and dengue fever, or even about HIV and AIDS. In 1998, the dikir barat was temporarily banned because of sexual connotations in some lyrics, but today it is performed all around the state.

Usually the dikir barat is performed as entertainment or as a competition between groups from different towns and villages. As entertainment it may be heard during the harvest season in the rural areas, or at weddings, circumcisions and festive gatherings. Usually a simple roofed, open-wall structure is built and a dikir barat group performs on a slightly raised platform under the roofed area so that all viewers can see the performance as if it were theater-in-the-round. In the context of a competition, the two dikir barat teams both sit on the platform. The two groups or teams perform the songs and pantun verses, and compete in terms of the subject matter and lyrics, the use of appropriate melodies, hand movements and the general style of the presentation. In urban settings it is often performed on a stage in a community hall or other venue.

In the villages, a dikir barat team usually consists of only men, especially in former times. But, performances in the urban areas and on television take place by mixed gender groups. For performances on television and in competitions the members of the team or group usually wear colorful uniforms.

Performance practice

Awok-awok A dikir barat group usually has from 10 to 15 participants who comprise the chorus called the *awok-awok*. This chorus is trained by one of the main singers called the *Tok Juara*. The pantuns are performed by the chorus in unison singing and in responsorial style with the solo singer. Although a specific melodic line is sung by the chorus, it is often less than clear because of the shouting quality of the voices. During a performance the members sit on the floor in a circular formation facing one another.

While singing they rhythmically move their arms, hands and upper torso of the body as if they were dancing in time to the music. Hand clapping and loud, sharp shouting (usually on the syllable '*hei*') is important in the performance. Usually the movements, along with the clapping and shouting, stress specific beats in the music, such as shown in the transcription of a dikir barat piece in Example 5.19 and in the score in the Appendix.

Juara The singer who begins the vocal part in a performance is known as the juara [trainer]. The *Tok Juara* (the specific person is referred to as the Tok Juara) trains the dikir barat group and introduces the poetic theme at the beginning of the performance. He usually sits near the instrumental ensemble, and to open the piece he sings the song lyrics in unmetered rhythm and slow tempo and with a moderately ornamented melodic line. The singing style is similar to that of unmetered zikir (see Chapter 4).

It is believed that the Tok Juara's strong, melodious voice can instill the spirit of competition and team work in the dikir barat group. The themes or poetic topics that are introduced by this singer may also serve as a guide to the second solo singer, the *tukang karut* who will compose other lyrics and pantun later in the performance.

Tukang karut The tukang karut is the second solo singer in the dikir barat and is highly important in the second main part of the dikir barat piece. The tukang karut usually moves about the stage while singing. He is clever in spontaneously composing lyrics in the form of the pantun, and must have the natural talent to compose lyrics that are interesting, clever and funny. These lyrics are often based on the theme introduced earlier by the Tok Juara. The tukang karut sings a couplet using a particular melodic line, and the chorus immediately repeats the lyrics and the melodic line. A responsorial style of singing takes place between the tukang karut and the chorus.

A dikir barat performance opens with a short, fast rhythmic pattern played by the instrumental ensemble with hand clapping by the chorus. The Tok Juara then begins to sing the lyrics of a pantun (4-line verse) without accompaniment and in a very slow tempo. At the end of his sung pantun the chorus takes up the text of the pantun, singing it with instrumental accompaniment. At this point, the tempo is moderate and the rhythmic patterns by the ensemble are exact and decisive. The chorus and the Tok Juara alternate several times with the chorus usually repeating the lyrics of the solo singer.

After the pantun is sung for the last time by the chorus, the tukang karut comes to the front of the stage and begins to improvise his lyrics, also in the form and style of the pantun. Each couplet of the sung pantun by the tukang karut is repeated by the chorus in responsorial style, and at this time the tempo becomes very fast. The tukang karut also sings tunes which he might compose himself.[4]

The musical instruments

In published sources on the dikir barat, the smallest ensemble described consists of two rebana drums and a tetawak gong.[5] These sources also write about instrumental ensembles consisting of a gedumbak drum (Figure

1.4), two gongs, a serunai (Figure 1.7) and two rebana drums (Figure 1.12). However, according to research in the 1980s and 90s the typical dikir barat ensemble has only two rebana (large and small sizes), one hanging gong, a pair of maracas, and a pair of canang gongs (high and low pitches, Figure 1.2).

Rebana The hand-hit rebana drum in the dikir barat ensemble appears in two sizes. The large rebana (called *ibu* [mother]) is about 50 centimeters in diameter with a wooden frame body about 12 to 15 centimeters deep. Two basic timbres or sounds are produced with this drum, the timbre called 'tak' (high, sharp quality) and another called 'dung' (low, resonant sound). The small rebana (called *anak* [child]) is also a frame drum about 20 to 25 centimeters in diameter with a rather deep body about 15 to 18 centimeters wide. This drum mainly produces the timbre 'tak' in the rhythmic patterns of the dikir barat tunes. It is held horizontally and hit with the player's hands.

Tetawak, Canang, Maracas The three idiophones in the dikir barat ensemble include the tetawak, canang and maracas. The tetawak is a large, hanging knobbed gong hit with a padded beater (Figure 1.1). The canang is a gong-chime consisting of two small gongs struck with padded beaters producing a high pitch and a low pitch (Figure 1.2). The maracas are a pair of shaken idiophones borrowed from popular Western music. A dried gourd with a handle is filled with seeds and shaken to produce sound. Today the dikir barat ensemble usually includes two maracas shaken by one player.

The music

The texture of dikir barat music is polyphonic and consists of one or more vocal parts and several percussive rhythmic patterns (see the full score of a dikir barat tune in the Appendix, and excerpts of the piece in Example 5.19). The rebana, canang, maracas and tetawak produce the rhythmic patterns and a colotomic unit, while the vocal part consists of one melodic line sung by the soloist or by the chorus (in unison).

Melody and Scale As a typical dikir barat tune from the repertory, Example 5.19 and the full score in the Appendix, shows a melodic line based on a heptatonic scale. The intervallic structure in this scale is similar to the mixolydian mode. However, the pitch center of the tune in this example is the 5th tone of the scale (in contrast, the *finalis* of the Western modes is the 1st pitch of the scale).

The melodic line and lyrics by the Tok Juara begin the piece and set the atmosphere for the entire performance. The melodic lines in this piece are only moderately embellished using the acciacatura and melisma (see Example 5.19a, phrases *a*, *b*, and *d*). The singing style is mainly syllabic and the melody moves by whole or half steps. An 'ascending-descending' melodic contour is featured in this song.

In contrast, the sung melodic line by the tukang karut and the chorus are not complex (see Example 5.19c, bars 79-81). In this part of the performance by the tukang karut there is a focus on clarity of the lyrics, and simplicity of the melodic lines. These features are characteristic of a vocal music that is easy to understand and attracts the interest and attention of the audience.

a) Heptatonic scale

b) The Tok Juara sings the first rendition of the pantun without accompaniment

c) the Tukang karut improvises lyrics in responsorial style with the chorus

Example 5.19 Excerpt of a *dikir barat* piece. (Recorded in Kelantan in 1994; a full transcription may be found in the Appendix)

The typical patterning of the sections in a dikir barat performance, written in score in the Appendix, are as follows:

1.   Introduction: Short passage of steady, rhythmical hand clapping and drumming in a fast tempo (not transcribed in the score)
2.   Intro. Pantun A: By the Tok Juara; *a capella* and free rhythm
3.   First set of pantun (A, B, C etc): The Chorus and Tok Juara alternate several times in metered rhythm (a pantun is sung in 24 bars of music in 4/4 time)
4.   [Bridge passage by percussion (1 bar)]
5.   Second set of pantun: The Tukang karut and Chorus in responsorial style, alternating every two or four bars; lyrics are improvised.

Rhythm Both metered and unmetered rhythm are found in the music. The lyrics and the melodic lines in the introductory part (sung by the Tok Juara) use unmetered rhythm. The tempo is very slow and in a style similar to the singing of unmetered zikir. In contrast, the musical part sung by the chorus is in duple or quadruple meter in a moderate tempo. The tukang karut part is also in duple meter, and usually in a fast and lively tempo.

      The instrumental accompaniment features a specific colotomic unit and resultant rhythmic patterns. The resultant rhythmic patterns are produced by the large and small rebana drums that play in an interlocking style. The large rebana plays a given rhythm, usually 4 beats long. Although each dikir barat group may play different rhythmic patterns, a typical rhythmic pattern is shown in the score of a dikir barat piece in the Appendix and in Example 5.19. If the tempo is moderate, the large rebana is played at the crochet note level, stressing beats 3 and 4 in the rhythmic pattern with the low timbre vocalized as 'dung' (see dikir barat, Appendix, bars 24-29):

Rebana ibu (moderate tempo)

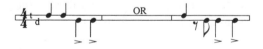

When the tempo becomes fast, the large rebana pattern features quaver notes, but still has the strongest accent on the last beat (beat 4), of the pattern (see dikir barat, Appendix, bar 49):

Rebana ibu (fast tempo)

Whether the tempo is fast or slow, the small rebana drum usually stresses the upbeats (or offbeats) in the 4-beat pattern (see dikir barat, Appendix, bars 23-40) using both the 'tak' and 'dung' drum timbres:

Rebana anak (fast tempo)

The large rebana is played simultaneously with the small rebana in an interlocking style to produce resultant rhythmic patterns. To obtain contrasting rhythms in the piece sometimes the two rebana drums play patterns featuring hemiola against the rhythm in the melodic line and colotomic unit. To produce the hemiola, the two rebana drums play three or six main downbeats against four or eight main downbeats in the other parts of the music (see dikir barat, Appendix, bars 41-42).

All the other instruments in the dikir barat ensemble function as time markers in the music. These instruments mark the 4-beat colotomic unit that underlies the melody and the drum patterns. The canang and the maracas mark each down beat and upbeat at the quaver note level in the colotomic unit. The gong is played on beat 4 of each bar, thus marking the end of each 4-beat colotomic unit (see the dikir barat, Appendix, bars 23-77). In addition, one loud hand clap by all the members of the chorus supports and stresses the final beat of each colotomic unit.

Depending on the tune sung by the tukang karut, sometimes the colotomic unit changes to two beats, as transcribed in bars 86-87 of the dikir barat piece in the Appendix. Although the tempo is moderate, the repeated colotomic unit marked by the gong is only two beats long.

Form In general, the structure of the tune sung by the Tok Juara and the chorus is based on the 4-line pantun poetic form in which the first two lines are the *pembayang* or imagery aspect of the poem, and the second two lines are the *maksud* or actual meaning of the poem. However, each line of the lyrics is sung using two musical phrases. This structure is clearly seen in both the Tok Juara's rendition and the chorus' rendition of the pantun (see bars 23-77 in the dikir barat piece in the Appendix, and the outline below).

As shown below, the first couplet consists of four melodic phrases, *a, b, a1, b* in a reverting type of structure with contrast as well as repetition of the phrases.

The second couplet in the pantun also consists of four melodic phrases *c, d, e, f*, but all phrases here are different. Thus, a progressive type of structure exists in the second couplet where new melodic material is constantly added.

The pattern of melodic phrases in the chorus part is shown in the outline below (the terms 'pembayang' and 'maksud' are explained in the earlier discussion of form in ronggeng and dondang sayang pieces):

Pantun (4 lines of text)	Melodic phrases	
line 1 ---	**a**	**b**
(*pembayang*)	chorus: 3 bars	chorus: 3 bars
line 2 ---	**a1**	**b**
	chorus: 3 bars	chorus: 3 bars
line 3 ---	**c**	**d**
(*maksud*)	solo: 4 bars	chorus: 3 bars
line 4 ---	**e**	**f**
	chorus: 3 bars	chorus: 2 bars

Musically, the complete pantun is 24 bars divided into eight melodic phrases. In the first couplet of the pantun all melodic phrases are symmetrical and the same in length. However, in the second couplet of the poem the four phrases are not symmetrical in length (phrase *c*=4 bars, *d*=3 bars, *e*=3 bars, *f*=2 bars), yet the four melodic phrases are maintained. A symmetrical musical structure in the first part of the pantun is balanced and contrasted with a non-symmetrical musical structure in the second part of the pantun.

In addition, contrast and balance are also found in the musical piece with the reverting type of form used in the first couplet and a progressive form in the second couplet. The duality of symmetry contrasted with non-symmetry, and reverting contrasted with progressive, reflects the contrast of *pembayang*/imagery and the *maksud*/meaning in the poem itself.

In the tune sung by the Tukang karut, the musical form is not complex and is usually iterative in nature (see the excerpt of the Tukang karut section in the dikir barat piece in the Appendix). The focus of the Tukang karut is to improvise witty lyrics spontaneously in the form of the pantun, and in the dikir barat this is the most creative part of the performance. The creative ability of the Tukang karut is at stake here to compose lyrics that are clever, funny and amusing in order to hold the attention of the audience to the end of the performance.

Huayue Tuan [the Chinese orchestra]

The *Huayue tuan*, or Chinese orchestra, is one type of ensemble that is popular among the Chinese in Malaysia. This ensemble developed in China in the early 20th century at which time China was strongly influenced by Western ideas. Many students including music students furthered their studies in Europe, imitating the life style and values of Westerners. There were those students who felt that the regional music of China was out of date. Thus, it is not surprising when this group returned to China in the 1930s, they began to form a unique orchestra that had never been seen in China. The results of their creation is a synthesis of Chinese and Western music. The decade of the 1930s marks the beginning of the Chinese orchestra.

This orchestra was larger than the regional ensembles, and followed the seating arrangement of the western orchestra and the use of a conductor and musical score. As in the Western orchestra, the treble strings in the huayue tuan are located to the left of the conductor while the bass strings are at his right. The winds are in front of the conductor and the percussion is at the rear of the stage (Plate 5.4).

Although the Chinese orchestra was highly influenced by Western ideas, several Chinese elements were still retained. Notably, the traditional musical instruments existing in China were still used, but in a new and 'improved' form following the western principles of equal temperament so that a louder sound and a wider range could be obtained and modulations from one key to another could be executed with ease. In addition, like the first and second violins and violas in a western orchestra, the strings in the Chinese orchestra were divided into first and second *erhu* and *zhong hu* sections. In terms of the music itself, composers combined the Chinese melodies, scales and textures with western harmony.

The Chinese orchestra appeared in Malaysian Chinese society in the 1960s as a result of several local musicians furthering their studies in Hong Kong, and also because of the popularization of the modern orchestra through recordings sold in Malaysia. Traditional Chinese musical instruments were brought to Malaysia at the end of the 19th and beginning of the 20th centuries when Chinese people immigrated to Malaysia. But, in the 1960s, the new instruments, which had already been adapted were imported from China for use in the huayue tuan. Today, this orchestra is found all around Malaysia, mainly in the urban areas where large numbers of Chinese live such as Penang, Kuala Lumpur, Ipoh, Alor Star, Malacca, Johor Bahru, Kuantan and Kuching.

Plate 5.4 The Chinese orchestra in Penang.

Generally, the huayue tuan is supported by Chinese associations, religious societies and schools. The size varies from 12 to 50 or more members, and most players are between 14-35 years of age. In one year a huayue tuan is able to present at least one performance. Other than entertaining the audience, the performance is also used to collect money and donations for the individual societies or for the general welfare of the community.

The musical instruments

According to Chinese musicians, the musical instruments of the huayue tuan are divided into four sections: the bowed strings, the plucked and struck strings, the winds and the percussion. The names of the musical instruments noted here are in Mandarin:

The bowed string instruments   The bowed string instruments (chordophones) are the largest section in the Chinese orchestra, because these instruments are the softest in sound. In addition, the huayue tuan is influenced by the classical western orchestra in which the bowed strings constitute the largest section.

The general name for the bowed lutes is *huqin*. The word *huqin* means 'violin from non-Chinese' or 'barbarians' because the instrument originated in Central Asia and was brought to China by foreigners. The huqin has a cylindrical or hexagonal body made of bamboo, wood or coconut shell. The backside is left open while the front face is covered with snakeskin. A long neck transverses the body and rests on a piece of wood at the base end of the body (see Figure 5.1). The small wooden bridge, which the strings pass over, is located on the center face of the instrument. Two metal strings tuned in a Perfect fifth are stretched from the lower end of the body to the tuning pegs located at the back of the tuning peg box. This instrument is played with a small bow made of rattan and horsehair that permanently attached between the two metal strings (see Figure 5.2). The huqin stands vertically on the player's lap when it is bowed. A similar instrument is called the *sa dueng* in Thailand and the *kei kin* in Japan.

The bowed string instruments may be divided into three sections:

1.   The treble section consisting of the e*rhu, panhu* and *gaohu,*
2.   The tenor section consisting of the *zhonghu*, and
3.   The bass section that consists of the *gehu* and the *beida gehu.*

(Bowed strings --- treble section)
Erhu (*er*: two, *hu*: foreigner)   Sometimes this instrument is called the Chinese violin because its function is the same as the violin in the classical Western orchestra. Its very expressive tone is well known. The term *er* indicates that this instrument has two strings (see Figure 5.1), and although the strings are tuned to the pitches *D* and *A*, this tuning may be changed according to the requirements of the music whenever the instrument is used in a solo situation.

The erhu has a range of three octaves, and in the huayue tuan this section is divided into the erhu I and erhu II, just like the violin I and II in the Western orchestra.

Panhu (*pan*: wood, *hu*: foreigner) As indicated by its name, the body and face of this instrument is made of wood. Its body is smaller than the erhu, and its sound is sharper and louder. The shape of the face is round (see Figure 5.2), and its range is one octave higher than the erhu. In general, only one panhu is used in the orchestra and it is always played by the leader of the erhu I section. The leader of the erhu section places his panhu and the gaohu on the floor when he plays the erhu.

Gaohu (*gao*: high, *hu*: foreigner) The *gaohu* is identical to the erhu. Its sound is louder than the erhu but softer than the panhu. This instrument is appropriate for playing beautiful melodies and long, sustained notes. Generally the gaohu has a tuning a 4th higher than the tuning of the erhu, therefore it is named gaohu or 'high' hu.

(Bowed strings --- tenor section)
Zhonghu (*zhong*: middle, *hu*: foreigner) The *zhonghu* was created in 1937 in China and is so named because the range of its sound is between the treble and bass bowed string instruments. This instrument is similar to the erhu but it is larger and has a sound that is lower and mellower than the erhu. Like the viola in the classical Western orchestra, the zhonghu section is divided into zhonghu I and zhonghu II. The zhonghu is made in three sizes and the tuning of the two strings is *G* and *D*, *A* and *E* or *D* and *A*, depending on its size.

(Bowed strings --- bass section)
Gehu (*ge*: alter, *hu*: foreigner) This instrument is so named because its shape is somewhat different from the huqin, combining the shape of the cello and the huqin (Figure 5.3). Like the cello, it has four strings tuned to *C*, *G*, *D*, and *A*. It may be bowed or plucked and its tone is low and rich. In many huayue tuan in Malaysia the cello is also used in the orchestra and sometimes replaces the gehu.

Beida gehu (*bei*: many times; *da*: large; *ge*: alter; *hu*: foreigner) This is a new instrument and is shaped along the principles of the Western double bass and the Chinese huqin (Figure 5.4). It is several times larger than the gehu, and like the double bass, its strings are tuned to *E*, *A*, *D*, and *G*. It plays one octave lower than the gehu. In many huayue tuan in Malaysia both the double bass and the beida gehu are used, and sometime the double bass replaces the beida gehu.

Plucked or struck string instruments The chordophones in this section are divided into:

1.   String instruments that are plucked with the fingers, fingernails or a plectrum, consisting of the *pipa, liuyueqin, yueqin, ruan, sanxian, guzheng*; and

2.   The *yangqin* whose strings are struck with a bamboo beater.

The plucked string instruments are included in the huayue tuan because of the abundance and variety of such instruments in China. In contrast, there is no brass section in this orchestra because in China there are very few brass instruments.

(Plucked string instruments)
Pipa (*pi*: forward movement of the finger when the string is plucked; *pa*: backward movement of the finger when the string is plucked). In former times, the word *pipa* was associated with all plucked instruments. Nevertheless, today the pipa is used for the short-necked lute from China (Figure 5.5). It originated in the region of Central Asia and was brought to China by foreign delegates during the Tang Dynasty.

The pipa has a shallow, pear-shaped body, and the sound board is made of wood. The four strings, representing the four seasons, are tuned to *A, D, E* and *A*. These strings are tied to a string holder at the lower end of the body and to four lateral tuning pegs located at the sides of the tuning peg box. In 1937 the pipa was given 27 wooden frets --- six upper and 21 lower frets. It has a range of 4.5 octaves and chromatic tones may be played on it. The pipa is identical to the *biwa* from Japan.

Liuyueqin (*liu*: willow tree; *yue*: moon/leaf; *qin*: string instrument) This instrument is sometimes known as the 'willow leaf stringed instrument' because of its shape which is nearly identical to the leaf of the willow tree. It is also called the younger brother to the pipa because its shape is identical to the pipa but smaller in size. Its tuning is *G, D, G* and *D*. The four strings are tied to four lateral tuning pegs at the side of the tuning peg box and to the lower end of the body, and they transverse a wooden bridge.

Yueqin (*yue*: moon; *qin*: string instrument) The *Yueqin* is also called the 'moon guitar' because of the round shape of its body, like the full moon (Figure 5.6). The body is made of wood with a short neck, and it has 9-10 frets and four metal strings. The strings, which are plucked with a plectrum, are attached to a string holder at the end of the body and to the tuning pegs at the sides of the tuning peg box. A pair of strings tuned to *A* and another pair tuned to *D* are used so that the sound will be loud. This instrument is identical to the *gekkin* in Japan, the *wol kum* in Korea, the *cai nguyet* in Vietnam, and the *cha pei toch* in Cambodia.

Ruan (the name of the creator of the instrument) The *ruan* was constructed in China in the 3rd century by a person named Ruan. Like the yueqin, its body is made of wood and its shape is round like the full moon (Figure 5.7). Its body has two sound holes decorated with carved plastic. Usually two ruan in different sizes (the *zhongruan* and the *daruan*) are used. The four strings on the instrument are tied to a string holder at the lower end of the body and to four tuning pegs located at the sides of the tuning peg box. The zhongruan strings are tuned to *G*, *D*, *A* and *E*, while the strings of the daruan are tuned to the pitches *C*, *G*, *D* and *A*. The neck is longer than that of the yueqin. It is used as a bass plucked string instrument.

Sanxian (*san*: 3; *xian*: strings) This instrument is so named because it has three strings which are plucked with a plectrum (Figure 5.8). It was imported from Western Asia. The body is made from wood and is slightly rectangular in shape. The two faces are covered with snake skin. A long flat neck, attached to the body, has no frets and is about four feet long. The strings are tied to the lower part of the body at one end and to tuning pegs at the sides of the tuning box at the other end. This instrument is similar to the *shamisen* in Japan.

Guzheng (*gu*: old; *zheng*: zither) The guzheng is a type of zither and has 12, 13, 15 or 16 strings, which are supported by moveable wooden bridges. At first silk strings were used but now metal strings are also used. The player plucks the strings with hand movements in right and left directions to produce sound. The gu zheng is the same as the *koto* in Japan. It is often played as a solo instrument and sometimes is used in the modern Chinese orchestra.

(Struck string instruments)
Yangqin (*yang*: foreign, *qin*: string instrument) This instrument is called a 'foreign' *qin* because it originated outside of China and was brought from Turkey or Europe in the 16th century.

The yangqin is a dulcimer, a trapezoid-shaped box about 10 cm high, 58 cm long, and 29 cm wide. It has fine metal strings in sets of two, three, or four for each note. All of these strings are stretched over wooden bridges and tied to tuning pegs at the left and right sides of the body. The yangqin is placed on a table or other flat surface and the strings are struck with a pair of bamboo beaters. This instrument is similar to the *san gen da kin* from Japan.

The wind instruments The wind section in the modern Chinese orchestra is smaller than in the Western orchestra and consists of the following aerophones:

1.   The *dizi*, *xiao*, and *sheng*, each of which produces sound the same as its counterpart in the Western orchestra,
2.   The *suona*, whose sound is similar to the sound of the brass in the Western orchestra.

Dizi (*di*: transverse flute; *zi*: suffix added to the name of a thing) This instrument is a side-blown flute made of bamboo, and was brought to China from Tibet during the Han Dynasty. It has eight holes, actually six finger holes, a mouth hole (the blowing hole) and a membrane-covered hole (Figure 5.9). Its sound is more sparkling and shrill than the Western flute because of the vibration of a thin bamboo membrane covering one of the holes when it is blown.

Today there are many different kinds of dizi including bamboo, wood and metal types. Generally, 12 different types and sizes of dizi are used in the huayue tuan (Figure 5.10). This instrument is very prominent in the orchestra because of its loud and shrill timbre and, therefore, usually only one or two dizi are played at the same time.

Xiao (vertical flute) The *xiao* is a flute blown from the end of a tube made from bamboo, and its sound is gentle and mellow. It has six finger holes (five in front and one at the back; see Fig. 5.11). At the top end there is a small notch that serves to channel the air into the pipe when it is blown (Figure 5.11). The range of this instrument is two octaves.

Sheng (mouth organ) The *sheng* consists of an air chamber made of metal with short reeds and 17 pipes or bamboo tubes inserted and secured into the air chamber in a circular formation. Each bamboo tube is encased in a brass tube to enhance the sound and make it resonant (see Figs. 5.12 and 5.13). A free beating reed is attached to each tube and a finger hole is placed in the tube above the reed. This finger hole must be closed for the reed to vibrate and the tube to sound out when blown (see also Mouth organs in Chapter 4).

The Chinese believe that the sheng was invented by a mythical female godess-queen called Nu Wo some 3000 years ago. This instrument symbolizes the phoenix bird *fenghuang*, and the pipes or tubes are arranged symmetrically with the longer pipes in the middle to depict the body of the bird.

Sound is produced when the player closes the finger holes and blows or sucks air through the reeds. The sound is like that of an organ. With the same pitch issuing from a pipe no matter whether the air is blown out or sucked in, this instrument is able to play long melodies or chords.

Suona (from the word *surnai*) The *suona* (or *sona)* originated in the Arab world and was brought to other countries such as China (*suona*), India (*shannai*), Malaysia (*serunai*) and Central Asia (*surnai, shanai, zorna*).

The suona is made of wood and the lower end, made of bronze, is shaped like a bell (Figure 5.14). It has seven finger holes in front and one at the back. It has a double-reed which is inserted into the player's mouth with his lips resting against a small metal lip-disk. Air is blown through the reeds and pitches are produced by opening and closing the finger holes. Hence, the suona is always called the Chinese oboe because the principle of producing sound is the same as the oboe. Nevertheless, because the sound of the suona is very shrill (when compared to the tone of the Western oboe), the suona plays a role similar to the trumpet in the Western orchestra. In general, the suona appears in three sizes referred to simply as small suona, medium suona and large suona.

The percussion instruments This section in the orchestra consists of different types of drums, gongs, wood blocks and other membranophones and idiophones that are struck with a wooden beater. These instruments complete the music of the huayue tuan with rhythmic patterns, and they play an important role in producing powerful percussion music. The percussion instruments normally used are listed below:

The *shimian luo* (*shi*: ten; *mian*: face; *luo*: gong) consists of 10 small, flat gongs (Figure 5.15). Each small gong is tied in a metal frame with three strings and struck with a wooden beater.

The *muyu* (*mu*: board; *yu*: fish) is a woodblock in the shape of a fish. In Malaysia many huayue tuan replace this type of struck woodblock with a piece of wood (Figure 5.16).

The *gu* (drum) is a double-headed Chinese drum. The drum head is attached to the wooden body with metal tacks. It is found in two sizes: *xiao* [small] and *da* [large] (Figure 5.17). This drum is placed upright and hit with a wooden stick on the drum head. The wooden beater for the *dagu* (large drum) is padded.

The *shuangyin mu* (*shuang*: pair; *yin*: sound; *mu*: wood) is a woodblock in the shape of a 'T'. A wooden beater is used to hit the two ends (Figure 5.18).

The *ling* (bell) is a small cup made of brass or bronze. The cup is attached to a wooden handle (Figure 5.19). This instrument is held with one hand and struck with a metal beater.

The *maling* (*ma*: horse, *ling*: bell) consists of five bells that are tied together with a metal wire (Figure 5.20). It is called ma ling because it is always used to depict the movement of a horse in Chinese music.

The *luo* (gong) is a flat gong made of bronze. The rim is shallow and the walls are thin. The luo is hung and struck in the middle with a padded, wooden beater (Figure 5.21).

The *bo* (cymbals) consist of two round disks held in the hand and struck together (Figure 5.22). These hand cymbals are made of bronze and have a cup-like knob on the middle, outside surface. The bo is made in various sizes to obtain different pitches.

The *bangzi* (a type of Chinese opera) is a woodblock in a trapezoidal shape that is struck with two wooden sticks. It is called bangzi because it was first used in the bangzi type of Chinese opera.

The repertory and musical features

Much of the music played by the modern Chinese orchestra in Malaysia is imported from Hong Kong, Taiwan and China. Three types of pieces are performed in Malaysia:

1.   Pieces from the regional music repertory that are played in heterophonic style such as *Crazy Dance of the Golden Snake* and *Moonlight Over the Spring River*. In these pieces the musical instruments with different tone colors are played in succession;

2.   Pieces that use triadic harmony such as *Dance of the Yao People*. Most of these are folk tunes or pieces from the above category that have been rearranged; and

3. Concertos such as *A New Song of the Herdsmen* for dizi and orchestra. In the concerto one solo instrument plays with the orchestra. The sections or passages in which the solo player can show his skill are stressed in this kind of piece.

Like the instrumental regional music of China, many pieces for the huayue tuan are divided into several programmatic parts. For example, the piece *Moonlight Over the Spring River* depicts the view of the moonlight that interplays with the rustling river water. The composers for the huayue tuan combine features of Chinese and Western music. As may be seen in this piece, the elements of Chinese melody, scale, and notation combine with Western harmonic triads.

Other than the three categories of music noted above, some Chinese orchestras in Malaysia also play arrangements of patriotic songs or Malay folk tunes such as the pieces *Berjaya, Tanah Air Ku, Air Didik, Inang Cina* and others. In the piece *Tanah Air Ku* (see the score in the Appendix, arranged by Lee Soo Sheng), the Malay melody is colored with chromatic tones such as the sharp 1, 2, and 4 and the flat 7 (bar 7). Several instruments play heterophonically, but simple triads on the tones V (in bar 3) and I (in bar 4) are used.

In addition, some composers have arranged huayue tuan pieces that contain other features of Malay music. For example, in the piece entitled *Malay Dance*, the composer Saw Yeong Chin has used the inang rhythmic pattern and a Malay melody.

In conclusion, the huayue tuan is very popular among the Chinese in Malaysia today because its music sounds modern but still retains some traditional Chinese characteristics. It uses both Chinese and Western musical instruments, and the young Chinese in Malaysia can identify with it. Although the huayue tuan is still an entity of the Chinese people, its repertory is slowly changing and it has already absorbed many local elements.

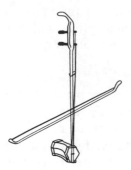

Figure 5.1 *Erhu*

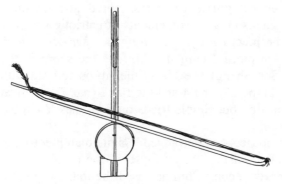

Figure 5.2　*Panhu* (the bow is permanently fixed between the two metal strings).

Figure 5.3 *Gehu*

Figure 5.4 *Beida gehu*

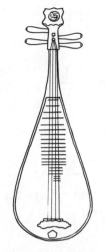

Figure 5.5 *Pipa*

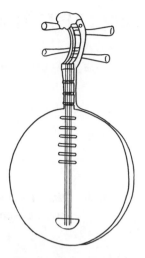

Figure 5.6 *Yueqin*

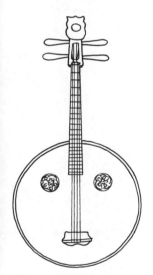

Figure 5.7 *Ruan*

Figure 5.8 *Sanxian*

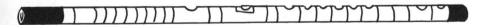

Figure 5.9 *Dizi*

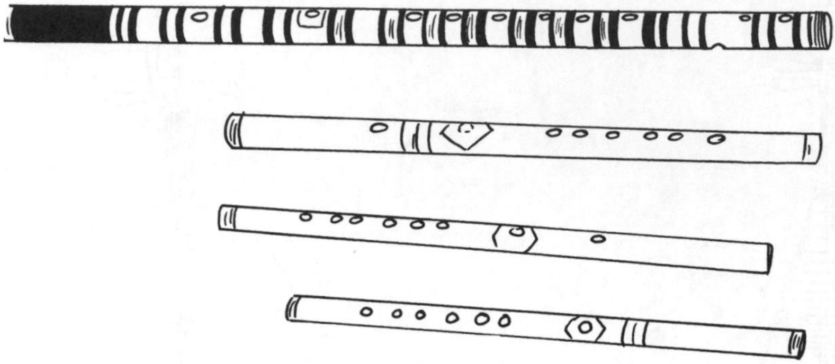

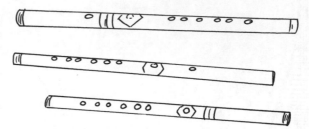

Figure 5.10 *Dizi* **of various sizes (note the membrane that covers the hole between the mouth hole and finger holes***)*.

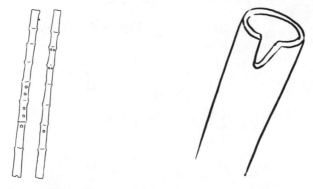

Figure 5.11 *Xiao,* **and mouth hole of the** *xiao.*

Figure 5.12 One bamboo pipe of the *sheng.*

Figure 5.13 *Sheng*

Figure 5.14 *Suona (Sona)*

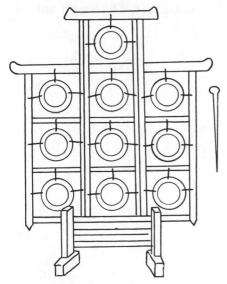

Figure 5.15 *Shemian luo*, the numbers 1-10 arc thc pitches for each small gong.

Figure 5.16 *Muyu*

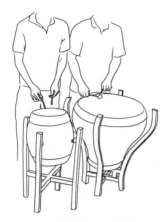

Figure 5.17 *Gu (da/xiao)*

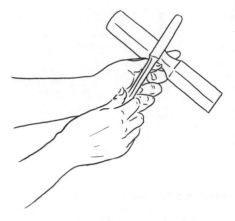

Figure 5.18 *Shuangyin mu*

Figure 5.19 *Ling*

Figure 5.20 *Maling*

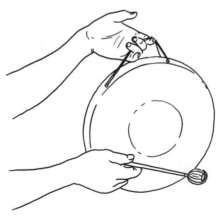

Figure 5.21 *Luo*

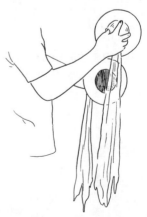

Figure 5.22 *Bo*

Music of the Portuguese Community of Malacca.[6]

Although the Portuguese community has existed in Malacca since the 16th century, the current music and dance of that community only appeared in the year 1952. In that year, Father Manuel Joachim Pintado introduced Portuguese folk music and dance to a group of upper-class Eurasians in his church in Malacca. This group referred to a book about folk dance and costume in Portugal, and the dances studied were performed at a welcoming party for the Commander Manuel Maria Sarmento Rodrigues from Portugal who visited Malacca at that time (Sarkissian, 1993, p. 39).

Since 1952, the dances and tunes introduced by Fr. Pintado have been passed down in an oral tradition to the young people and children of the Portuguese community in the Malacca Portuguese Settlement. At the same time, new, syncretic dances and tunes combining features of Portuguese, Malay, Straits Chinese and Western music were composed. Most of the new pieces used the Kristang language (the Creole language of the Portuguese people of Malacca) and not modern Portuguese. The *branyo* dance (Kristang language for the social 'joget dance') was introduced as the standard, final piece in all performances of music and dance by the Portuguese community. Just as in a joget dance session, the audience is invited to dance with the branyo dancers. The popular tunes from Portugal and other Western countries are adapted and staged by the Portuguese community of Malacca (Sarkissian, p. 41)

Today, the Portuguese dancers and musicians of Malacca perform dances and tunes to entertain tourists who visit the Portuguese Settlement there. They also perform for the general community at celebrations such as weddings and at hotel banquets throughout the country.

The musical instruments

The music ensemble of the Portuguese community consists of the violin, accordion, guitar, rebana drum, tambourine and the triangle. As discussed in the sections on ronggeng (Chapter 5) and bangsawan (Chapter 1), the violin, accordion and rebana were brought to the Malay Peninsula by Portuguese inhabitants in the 16th century. Singers were usually accompanied by violin and accordion players who played heterophonically with the singer; the guitar players strummed basic chords and the rebana, tambourine and triangle players completed the rhythm patterns in a piece.

Today, the number and types of musical instruments change from performance to performance, depending on the musicians available. For example, the rebana can be left out if there is no rebana player in the ensemble, and several guitars may be used to accompany a singer especially for night time shows in the Melaka Portuguese Village. Sometimes a *tambor* (large bass drum) is added. A synthesizer could also be used when musicians are not available.

Music and texts

The pieces entitled *Jinkly Nona* and *Ti' Anika* have become Malacca's Portugese cultural emblems. They are known as 'traditional' songs among the Portugese community.

Ti' Anika (the final vowel of 'Tia', meaning 'Aunty', is usually lost in the elision with 'Anika' or 'Annie') is the best known of all core repertory dances (Example 5.20). It has become a signature tune for the Portuguese Settlement in Malacca. This is a song imported from Portugal in the 1950s, and it is still sung in old Portuguese, which is no longer used as a spoken language today.

This bouncy, duple dance in two sections (*AB*) has become representative of the entire style. Children often imitate their older siblings in circle dances while singing this melody.

Example 5.20 *Ti Anika.*

In contrast, the piece *Jinkly Nona* is a type of branyo song sung in the Kristang language and combines features of Portuguese, Malay and Straits Chinese music. This brief discussion focuses on the piece *Jinkly Nona* (see Examples 5.21 and 5.22).

Just as in the joget dance music, the branyo stresses a rhythm of three notes followed by two notes played by the drum, violin and accordion. This feature is also found in Portuguese and Spanish music.

Example 5.21 *Jinkly Nona* (violin accompaniment).

Just as in a performance of the dondang sayang, an enjoyable ambience emerges when male and female performers sing poetic verses back and forth in repartee. The competition between the two singers is called *mata kantiga* which means 'killing the song'. This same kind of repartee singing is also found in many regions of Portugal.

Each verse consists of four lines as in the verses of *Jinkly Nona* sung by Rosil de Costa and Stephen Theseira in the 1980s (transcribed and translated by Sarkissian, 2000, p. 112):

<u>Chorus</u>: (in unison)

Teng kantu teng	You've got what you've got
Kantu teng fala nunteng	However much you have, you say you have nothing
Amor minya amor	Amor, my love
Amor minya korsang	My love, my dear [lit.: 'my heart'].

<u>Stephen</u>

Jinkly Nona, Jinkly Nona	Jinkly Nona, Jinkly Nona
Yo kere kaza	I want to marry you
Kaza nunteng potra Nona	Your house has no door
Kai logu pasa	How can I enter?

<u>Rosil</u>

Da lisensia Siara meu	Give me your permission
Yo rinta bos sa jarding	That I may enter your garden
Rafinadu sua cheru	Your perfumed smell
Chuma roza menggaring	Is like a jasmine flower.

<u>Stephen</u>

O Nona minya Nona	Nona, my Nona
Ai Nona minya korsang	Nona, my dear
Ai Nona mutu bemfeta	You are very beautiful
Baba ja kai n(a)' afesang	I've fallen for your beauty.

The melody of each verse is divided into two repeated couplets (*AABB*). The chorus part (*CC*) is sung by all present at the performance.

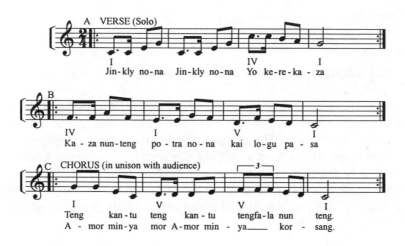

Example 5.22. *Jinkly Nona.*

Today, many singers do not sing the poetry in repartee, but rather they sing the verses from memory. *Jinkli Nona* is often sung with Malay words while other Malay joget pieces such as *Joget Pahang* are also sung by the Portuguese musicians using lyrics in the Kristang language.

Finally, the Portuguese dances and tunes, which have existed for some 40 years, have been accepted as part of the traditional culture of the Portuguese community in Malacca. The similarities between the joget and dondang sayang with the branyo (social dance) and mata kantiga (competitive repartee singing) indicates the musical interaction which has taken place among the Portuguese, Malays and Straits Chinese of Malacca. These dances and tunes are still passed down from one generation to another in an oral tradition, and the small children of the Melaka

Portuguese Settlement study the dances and songs by rote method in their daily music and dance lessons.

Indian classical music and orchestras in Malaysia

Music plays an important role in the religious and social lives of the Malaysians of Indian heritage as it also does of the people of India. Indian immigrants, whose descendents make up some seven per cent of the population today, carried the various traditions of Indian music to Malaysia. Hence, a variety of classical, folk and popular music from south and north India can be heard in Malaysia. Commercial popular Indian music from Tamil and Hindustani movies, such as '*Kuchh Kuchh Hota Hai*', abounds throughout Malaysia on compact disc, cassette tape, record albums and on the radio and television.

Religious music is performed at Hindu temples in various parts of Malaysia at festivals of deities such as Lord Vishnu and Lord Muruga, and other Hindu festivals such as *Thaipusam*, *Chittirai Paruvam* and *Ponggol*. The devotional singing at Hindu temples is mainly accompanied by the harmonium and *mridangam* drum, while instrumental music at temple festivities is provided by the *nagaswaram* shawm and *tavil* drum. *Bhangra*, a popular folk dance of the Punjabis, is performed to celebrate *Vasakhi* (the birth of Sikhism) as well as for entertainment at concerts.

In addition, the classical music traditions continue to be carefully nurtured in private institutions such as the various Indian societies and associations. Because of the south Indian majority in Malaysia, these private institutions are engaged mainly in teaching and sponsoring activities in *Karnatak* (south Indian) music and dance for private as well as public functions and concerts. In particular, the *Sangeetha Abhivirdhi Sabha* [Association for the Propagation of Music], set up in the Brickfields area of Kuala Lumpur, was responsible for training many Malaysian musicians in Karnatak music in the 1950s and 60s. The musicians who came from India, such as S.C. Nagasamy and Thangavelu (from Tamil Nadu) and D. F. John (from Kerala) taught at the association, and Gopal Shetty, a famous *Kathakali* and *Bharatha Natyam* performer, taught dance there. Today, the Temple of Fine Arts, which was set up in 1987, plays a major role in teaching and promoting Karnatak music, with branches in Kuala Lumpur, Johor Bahru and Penang. Although Karnatak music is the prevalent type of Indian classical music in Malaysia, individuals competent in north Indian *sitar* and *tabla* also perform publicly at concerts and restaurants.

The Indian classical music traditions in Malaysia essentially retain the major characteristics of the same musical traditions in India today. Many classical musicians continue to go to various parts of India to study with the masters in *vina, sitar* and *tabla* performance, while musicians from India, including Ravi Shankar, are invited to give performances to the general public in Malaysia. In addition, the Temple of Fine Arts often brings in specialists (from India) to teach specific instruments at the association.

Background to Indian classical music

A musical tradition existed in India from ancient, pre-Christian times, and the earliest religious musical tradition emerging on the Asian sub-continent was known as the *RigVeda*, consisting of chants performed in the temples. This Vedic literature of chanted poetry and hymns dates from around 1500 B.C.E. (Wade, 1979, p. 37) and, at first, existed only in an oral tradition. but was eventually written down by about the 10th century C.E. This early poetry and chant was a vehicle of religious teaching and prayer used by the upper three castes [*jati*, 'birth' group] of Hindu society. The fourth caste learned religion through the famous epics, the *Ramayana* and the *Mahabharata*, and through the *Purana* stories. These stories were often staged in the villages, and were also sung by bards who traveled from village to village.

During the period between the 2nd century B.C.E. and the 6th century C.E. (a precise date is unknown), a manuscript on drama, music and dance was written and entitled *Natya-Sastra* [Treatise on the Dramatic Arts] (Jairazbhoy, 1995, p. 654). With this work, the documentation of musical concepts and terms appeared for the first time. In the *Natya-Sastra*, scale systems were described and the term *raga* appeared. The raga or melody-type was defined as the basis for the creation of melody in Indian music, and remains so to this day. This treatise also explained the concept of rhythm, *tala* (time cycle), beat, tempo, stress and other aspects of music.

Another ancient treatise entitled *Brhaddesi* by the theorist Matanga was written in about the 10th century and further discussed the concept of raga in some detail (Jairazbhoy, 1995, p. 656). Following, in the 13th century, the theorist Sarngadeva produced a treatise on Indian classical music entitled *Sangita-ratnakara* [Ocean of Music and Dance] (Jairazbhoy, *Ibid.*). This work is particularly important, for it describes the state of south central Indian music just before the effect of Muslim influence was strongly felt in the Indian musical arts.[7]

By the 12th and 13th centuries Muslim inhabitants from Central and West Asia (Persia) settled in the northern and central regions of the Indian sub-continent. With the conquests by these peoples, the Moghul empire was founded as an Islamic government that supported and patronized the development of music. During the Mogul empire Muslim musicians created new raga and tala and also introduced new forms and genres of music as well as new musical instruments.

Between the 12th and 16th centuries, two different traditions of classical music emerged (Wade, 1979, p. 20). In northern India the tradition known as 'Hindustani' music developed in the palaces of the Mogul rulers with a strong base in Islamic culture. At the same time, a musical tradition known as 'Karnatak' music was evident in southern India with the strong influence of Hindu religion and culture. Although both of these traditions of music originated from the same theoretical principles, the two styles exhibit different musical forms, raga, tala, musical instruments and other musical details.

Musical instruments and ensembles

The musical instruments in India are many and varied, and the ensembles in which they are found clearly exhibit some of the differences in the Hindustani and Karnatak musical traditions. Western musical instruments are also found in India, and these are sometimes heard in combination with the traditional instruments in film and other forms of music.

Today Indian musical instruments are well documented, and many published works carry excellent descriptions and photographs of them (see for example, Wade, 1979, *The Garland Encyclopedia of World Music*, Vol. 5 'South Asia', and many published sources from India). Only a brief over view of instruments in the classical Indian traditions is given here.

Chordophones The vina, gottuvadyam, violin and tambura are important and typical string instruments in Karnatak music. In India the violin, often providing accompaniment to the voice, is held in a nearly vertical position. The end of the violin neck is supported on the player's foot as he sits cross-legged on the floor while bowing the strings. In contrast, the vina, gottuvadyam and tambura are plucked lutes.

In the Hindustani ensemble the main stringed instruments include the *sitar, sarangi* and *sarod*. The sitar and its large size, called *surbahar*, along with the sarod are all plucked lutes, while the sarangi is a bowed lute. The tone color on these lutes is enriched by sympathetically vibrating strings contained in the respective instruments. A plucked zither used by Muslim singers in Hindustani music is called the *surmandal*.

Aerophones Among the wind instruments in Indian classical music are flute and reed types. The Hindustani flute is called the *bamsri* and has a rather long bamboo body, while the Karnatak flute is called *venu* and features a short body.

The double-reed pipe is called the *nagasvaram* in southern India and the *shahnai* (or *shehnai*) in northern India. In addition to its use in classical music, the nagasvaram is also used to play music in the Hindu temples to accompany processions and other events. This instrument is frequently heard at temple events in Malaysia. An instrument that accompanies the nagasvaram, by playing a drone pitch, is the *ottu*.

The *shahnai* in Hindustani music is usually accompanied by the *sur*, a reed pipe that has only two or three finger holes to play specific drone pitches. Sometimes the *sruti* is used to provide the drone along with the shahnai melody. The sruti is like a harmonium (see below) with a bellows that are pumped with the player's hand. Today the sruti box also takes the form of an electronic instrument able to produce a wide range of pitches that function as the drone in the music.

The harmonium is basically an organ that was borrowed from Western music and introduced to Indian musicians by the British during colonial times in India. It has a bellows that is pumped with one hand and a keyboard that is played with the other hand. The harmonium is often used to play the secondary melody in Hindustani music.

Membranophones The prominent drum found in Karnatak music is the *mridanga* (or *mridangam*). This drum is barrel-shaped and has two drum heads that are struck with the player's hands. The two elaborate drum heads are made from several layers of cow and goat skin with a small layer of paste to tune them (see Wade, 1979, pp. 129-31). Another drum used in Karnatak music is the barrel-shaped *tavil* that usually accompanies the nagasvaram double-reed pipe.

The *pakhavaj* barrel-shaped drum in north India is similar to the mridanga and is usually used to accompany the vocal music known as *dhrupad* in Hindustani music (a form not frequently performed).

Since around the 18th century the drum that is featured in Hindustani music is the *tabla* and *baya*. Both of these small drums are always found as a set and are played by one drummer who hits both drums simultaneously with the hands. On the player's right is the tabla or *dahina* (or *dayan*; meaning 'right'). The term '*bayan*' (meaning 'left') is used for the small drum placed at the player's left hand. The tabla (dahina) is precisely tuned while the baya is tuned one octave lower than the tabla. Each drum has one drum head that is attached with laces (Cf. Wade, 1979, pp. 135-40).

To accompany the music played on the shahnai in Hindustani music, a pair of drums, the *dukar-tikar* or the *naghara*, is played by one drummer. The drums are kettle-shaped and have one drum head each, which is struck with wooden beaters.

Idiophones While the main percussive rhythms in Karnatak music are usually played on the mridangam drum, occasionally an additional instrument may be found playing a rhythmic part. One of these is the tambourine called *kanjira*. Small metal disks, inserted into the wooden frame, jingle when the instrument is struck. The *ghatam* clay pot may also be added to the Karnatak ensemble, on which rhythmic patterns are beaten out with the player's wrists, fingers and fingernails. The *morsing* is a plucked jew's harp sometimes also found in the Karnatak ensembles.

In both Karnatak and Hindustani traditions, the melody may also be performed on a set of approximately 18 small porcelain bowls of different sizes called *jaltarang*. The bowls are filled with different levels of water and tuned to various pitches. They are arranged in a semicircle in order of pitches, with the smaller bowls (higher pitch) on the right hand side and the bigger ones (lower pitches) at the left of the performer. The bowls are hit with two thin sticks.

The Karnatak ensemble In the Karnatak music tradition a typical ensemble consists of a main melody that is usually sung by a solo vocalist. However, if an instrument is used, then the vina, venu, nagasvaram, violin, gottuvadyam, or even the jaltarang would be used. A secondary melody in the given piece is often played by the violin (except when the nagasvaram shawm plays the main melody).

One or two percussion instruments usually provide the rhythmic patterns in a piece. The drums that might be used are the mridangam or tavil, while the idiophones would include the kanjira, ghatam   or sometimes the morsing jew's harp.

One or more instruments produce the drone in a given piece. Examples are the tambura, ottu or the sruti box.

The Hindustani ensemble The Hindustani classical music ensemble sometimes needs to provide for two main melody instruments, while only one percussion instrument provides the rhythmic patterns in the music.

The possible instruments that play the main melody are many and include a singer, the sitar, surbahar, sarangi, bamsri, shahnai, violin and sometimes the sarod.   For the second melody, the sarangi, harmonium or the surmandal might be used.

The percussion instrument or drum that is typically found in a Hindustani ensemble is the tabla/baya.   However, as noted above, the pakhavaj drum usually accompanies the dhrupad, and when the double-reed shahnai is used for the main melody then the dukar-tikar or the naghara drums provide the rhythmic accompaniment.

The drone instrument in the Hindustani ensemble is usually the tambura, but the sur peti or the sur reed pipe are also found.

Elements of classical music

Indian musicologists have written that Indian classical music focuses on melody and rhythm.   Elements such as functional harmony and key changes are not found in this music.   The classical compositions are improvised and the concepts of *raga* or *rag* and *tala* or *tal* are the basis for the improvisation.

Melody   In Indian classical music melody is based on the *rag* (in the Hindustani tradition) or *raga* (in the Karnatak tradition).   The rag or raga is built on a 7-tone scale (the solfege syllables *sa ri ga ma pa dha ni* are used to sing the scale).[8]   It is a scale-like arrangement or 'melody-type' with a specific ascending pattern and a different descending pattern.   All raga have specific names and gender, and all are also associated with particular emotions (*bhava*) and sentiments (*rasa*) and specific times of the day. Many written examples of rag and raga can be found in notes that accompany recordings, such as the album *The Sounds of India, Ravi Shankar, sitar* (Album CBS CS 9296), and in written sources such as *The Garland Encyclopedia of World Music* (Vol. 5, 2000).   Literally hundreds of raga exist and they are classified in various ways in both the Karnatak and Hindustani traditions (Cf. Wade, 1979).

By using a specific raga, melody is composed and improvised upon in a composition during the actual performance of the piece (and not before).

Rhythm   The *tal* (Hindustani music) or *tala* (Karnatak music) refers to the time measure and rhythm in classical music.   The tal or tala is a time cycle that contains a specific number of beats.   The given time cycle used in a performance is repeated throughout the piece.   It is the basis for organizing time in the music and for playing the rhythmic patterns on the drums and other percussion instruments. The repeated tal or tala may be quite short (8 beats, for example), or 30 or more beats long. A given tala is subdivided into units with strong stress on certain beats. For example, in the popular tala called *Aditala* in Karnatak music the time unit is 8 beats long. It is divided into three units with strong stress on beats 1, 5 and 7 (units of 4 + 2 + 2 beats).

In Hindustani music a frequently used tal is called *Tintal*, a repeated cycle of 16 beats, divided into four units, with stress and no stress on specified beats. In the Hindustani tradition, the tal is further defined by the *theka* or syllables that represent specific timbres on the drum to play the basic tal. While divisive rhythm is found in both Karnatak and Hindustani music, additive rhythm is also very common.

In the Karnatak tradition a system for classifying the main tala, a system called the *sulaldi tala*, exists (Jairazbhoy, 1978, pp. 226-9), while the classification of Hindustani tal is not as systematic as in the south Indian tradition.

The raga and tala are the foundation for creating and improvising melody and rhythmic patterns in classical Indian music. Both of these elements are created in the context of particular musical forms.

Musical form In general, musical form or structure in Karnatak and Hindustani pieces involves two main parts. The *alapana* (Karnatak tradition) or the *alap* (Hindustani tradition) is the first part. The music in the alap or alapana is not metered and usually the drums are not played. In this first part the specific raga for the piece is introduced. The player reveals the particular raga slowly, bringing out all pitches and melodic motifs little by little. At this time the rhythm is free and there is no tala present. The alapana or alap usually develops in stages, proceeding to a short section called the *tanam* (in the Karnatak tradition) or the *jor* (in the Hindustani tradition). In this short section the player begins to establish a steady beat or pulse in the music, but there is still no tala present. At the end of the alapana sometimes the performer stops momentarily to re-tune his instrument.

The second main part in a Karnatak or a Hindustani piece consists of the main composition. In this part there is the specific raga and tala, and usually the drummer enters the performance at this time. There are various musical forms that may be used as the basis for the composition. In Karnatak music the forms known as *kritana* or *kriti*, the *varnam* and the *tillana* are favorites, while a very long form called the *ragam-tanam-pallavi* sometimes is played as the only composition on a given program.

In Hindustani music the forms *thumri, khyal* and *gat* are often heard, while the vocal form known as the *dhrupad* is only occasionally performed today.

Light classical music

Besides classical musical traditions, which retain the basic characteristics of south and north Indian music, the Indian musical associations in Malaysia also promote light classical and new music to attract the various ethnic groups from South Asia as well as the Malays and Chinese to their concerts. Shorter melodic themes and faster rhythms are used. Catchy melodies and new instruments are showcased to attract the audience. For instance, the group '*Vadya Sammelanam*' [meaning, 'a gathering of musical instruments'], which performed for Radio Malaysia (Indian Service) in the 1950s and 60s, highlighted the jaltarang as a virtuoso instrument. Many of their compositions used shorter melodic phrases that were easier to hear and understand as well as five tone raga such as *Mohanam* and *Madyamavathi* and the 8-beat *adi tala*. Light classical music was also composed to accompany dance dramas such as the *Ramayana*, complete with sets and props.

In recent years, the Temple of Fine Arts has also contemporized classical music and promoted light classical music to attract the younger generation, as in previous decades. Their new compositions are written for a huge ensemble of some 65 members, and they emphasize shorter melodies and catchy rhythms. The musicians try to bring together the different Indian musical traditions in Malaysia.

The piece *Swaraamritham* [The Essence of Swaras], for example, is a Karnatak musical composition with some Hindustani elements added.[9] It combines the Karnatak vina and mridangam, the Hindustani sitar and tabla and the Western digital piano, keyboard, vocalists and other percussion instruments from north and south India. The piece begins with an alap based on the raga *Charukesi*, improvised by the flute and vocal soloist. The composed piece comprises short melodic sections played by different instruments such as the flute, vina and sitar, using the *Misra Chaapu/Rupak* tala as the basis for the rhythm and time organization in the music. The instrumental sections are interspersed with vocal sections using the traditional Indian solfege syllables (*sa ri ga ma pa dha ni*) instead of texts (that are more difficult to follow). There are also interlocking drumming interludes by the mridangam, tabla and other percussion instruments. The piece reaches a crescendo with a '*jugalbandi*' (common in Hindustani music) where the solo role is shared between the violin, flute, sitar and keyboard.

By way of conclusion, it should be highlighted that Karnatak and Hindustani musical elements have influenced other local music in Malaysia. Hindustani and Tamil film music has found its way into contemporary Malaysian pop through the *lagu Hindustan* in the 1950s and 60s and *dangdut* in the 1980s and 90s. In addition, the tabla, bin, sitar and vina are often employed in contemporary jazz and art music (Cf., Chapter 6).

Notes

1   Ronggeng performed at amusement parks was modernized in the 1950s and became known as *joget moden* [modern joget]. Western musical instruments such as the trumpet, trombone, double bass and Western drum were employed. Modern dances such as the rumba, foxtrot, cha-cha-cha and mambo were later added.

2   From *Siri Lagu-Lagu Rakyat Malaysia*, arrangement by Johari Salleh (Kuala Lumpur: Kementerian Kebudayaan Belia dan Sukan Malaysia [Ministry of Culture, Youth and Sports]), pp. 24-5.

3   From *Siri Lagu-Lagu Rakyat Malaysia*, arrangement by Johari Salleh (Kuala Lumpur: Kementerian Kebudayaan Belia dan Sukan Malaysia), pp. 18-19.

4   See a list of popular *tukang karut* tunes in *Dikir Barat. Siri Mengenal Budaya*, No. 10 (Kuala Lumpur: Kementerian Kebudayaan Belia dan Sukan, 1981), p. 10.

5   *Ibid.*

6   Based on Margaret Sarkissian, *D'Albuquerque's Children, Performing Tradition in Malaysia's Portuguese Settlement* (Chicago and London: University of Chicago Press, 2000). See Sarkissian, 2000, for an in depth discussion of Portuguese Music in Malacca.

7   Concise commentary on the early treatises and the development of raga, tala and other aspects of Indian music may be found in the articles 'South Asian Peoples, Music of' by N. A. Jairazbhoy in *The Encyclopædia Britannica*, 15th ed. (1975), *The New Encyclopædia Britannica* (1995) (Chicago, Encyclopædia Britannica, Inc.) and his article 'Music' in Arthur Basham (ed.) *A Cultural History of India* (Clarendon, Oxford University Press, 1978).

8   In the solfege system, the abbreviated name *sa* originates from the name *shadja*, *ri* from *rishabha*, *ga* from *gandhara*, *ma* from *madhyama*, *pa* from *panchama*, *dha* from *dhaivata*, and *ni* from *nishada*. See further N. A. Jairazbhoy, 'Music' in Arthur Basham (ed.), *A Cultural History of India* (Oxford: Clarendon Press, 1978), pp. 216-19.

9   A recording of *Swaraamritham* is included in the compact disc, *Naad Brahma, Music for the Soul*, Kuala Lumpur: Temple of Fine Arts, 1998.

Chapter 6

Contemporary Art and Popular Music

Over the last century, many innovations have occurred in contemporary Malaysian music. Experimentation has taken two different directions. The first is pioneered by composers trained in formal western classical or traditional music who write art music using music notation in the format of a score. Art music is accessible to an interested, small, educated elite, and is performed in concerts for small audiences. It is disseminated through published scores and recordings in the form of tape cassettes and compact discs, and occasionally aired over radio and television.

The second type of contemporary music is composed by pop musicians who usually have not acquired formal musical training, but whose music attracts audiences of all levels of society. Pop music follows trends in Anglo-American pop and is disseminated through the mass media and live performances in pubs, concert halls and open-air performance spaces catering to huge audiences.

This chapter surveys the main trends in the historical development of both contemporary art and popular music. The latter has a longer history emerging in tandem with the syncretic music of the bangsawan theater and joget dance halls of the early twentieth century. While both kinds of contemporary music are mainly cast in Western-based idioms, attempts have been made to incorporate local elements from Malay, Chinese and Indian folk, classical and syncretic music. This is especially apparent in the post-independence era as local musicians join fellow literary writers and visual artists in search of a Malaysian national identity.

Contemporary Art Music

By the middle decades of the 20th century many Malaysian musicians were well trained in the performance of Western and local instruments, and in the basic theory and elements of Western classical music. Composers during this time, such as Johari Salleh, Alfonso Soliano and Gus Steyn, were attached to Radio and Television Malaysia. They not only played in the RTM Orchestra, but also wrote arrangements of pieces as well as original compositions for this orchestra and other small ensembles. The musical activity by these early composers planted the seeds for the development of a contemporary art music movement in Malaysia.

The early Malaysian composers of this kind of music relied heavily on Western models such as the lyric song, symphony, symphonic poem, and other forms. Their compositions in the 1950s and 60s, utilizing the piano, a full symphony orchestra and Western harmony, symbolized the emergence of a modern nation. At the same time, they attempted to write music that would appeal to all people in a multi-cultural society. Alfonso Soliano, conductor of the RTM Orchestra in the 50s and 60s, wrote numerous arrangements of traditional tunes such as *Dondang Sayang, Jingli Nona* and *Bunga Tanjung* for voice and piano. His original compositions for orchestra used asli rhythms (as in his work *Asli Abadi*) and musical elements from other ethnic groups. Kuala Lumpur-born Tan Chong Yew also wrote arrangements of local melodies for voice and piano, and from the 60s through the 80s he played piano and composed other new works for the RTM Orchestra.

Experiments with the fusion of gamelan instruments and a Western orchestra led to pieces such as *Gurindam Gamelan* by Johari Salleh, while programmatic music using local legends and a western music ensemble by Gus Steyn (his *Si-Tanggung*) exhibited yet another path of interest among composers of this time. While Western musical forms, harmony, lyrical melodies and instruments of the orchestra were essential and predominant features of the music, certain elements from Malay, Chinese and Indian music cultures lent a Southeast Asian and, in fact, a Malaysian flavor to the music of this period. This art music of the 50s, 60s and early 70s was known as 'serious music'[*muzik serioso*].

During the 1980s and 90s young Malaysian performers and composers returned home from their studies abroad at the major international conservatories and universities in the United States and Europe. The composers of these recent decades were trained in 20th century music composition, with particular attention to techniques developing in the post-World War II music world. These techniques include attention to the use of serial composition, atonality, polyrhythm, new formal structures, and electronic and other new tone colours. In addition, these composers reached out to the musical and philosophical elements from traditional Asian music cultures, finding new ways of using and playing traditional musical instruments, using computers and other elements of modern technology. In effect, these young composers have begun the process of developing a new musical style that reflects their own personal taste and, at same time, attempts to maintain a continuity in establishing an Asian and, indeed, a Malaysian identity. Their outlook generally is global, drawing on sound resources and ideas from all cultures of the world, and also looking toward Asian aesthetics and sensibilities as the basis for a piece of music.

Several new compositions reflect this outlook. The work *10 Nyanian Settings* [10 Song Settings] *for Soprano, Alto, Chorus and Two Pianos* (1981-90) by Razak Abdul-Aziz of Penang uses the lyrics of Malay children's nursery rhymes in all of the songs, while the opening of the sixth piece (*'Nyanyi Pinjam Dandang'*) is inspired by rhythmic patterns from the Kelantanese wayang kulit repertory. Razak has also been inspired by the music of the makyung theatre. Traces of this influence can be seen in his *Sketch for MZ* (part of a work in progress), which utilizes the concept of cyclical gong units, microtonal intervals in the vocal and instrumental lines and flexible rhythms. The use of precise microtones and rather flexible rhythm in the orchestral parts are evident in the excerpt from this *Sketch* given in Example 6.1 below. Razak's interest spans both Western and Eastern musical worlds, as seen in one of his most recent works, a set of etudes for piano solo. As shown in the excerpt in Example 6.1, the etudes are pianistically and rhythmically demanding as the composer works with harmonic and melodic intervallic structures in this particular study.

The works of the composer Valerie Ross from Kuala Lumpur also exhibit a strong influence from the Asian musical world. Her piece entitled *Karma*, for example, not only features several Southeast Asian and Indian instruments but also uses a slendro scale system from the Indonesian gamelan and the techniques of overlapping textures as found in traditional Malay music. These Southeast Asian elements in the music are combined with the Indian tala concept for the organization of time in the music. Both new and old ways of playing the traditional Chinese, Indian and Malay instruments are combined in this piece. In other works, such as *Web 2*, Ross has searched for new sound resources including the chirping of crickets and birds from the natural environment as part of the musical continuum. Ross, too, has composed multimedia forms, as in the works *Nadis-Chakra*, a sound sculpture installation, and *Fatamorgana*, a music *cum* dance theater work.

Excerpt from *Sketch for MZ*

Razak Abdul-Aziz

Excerpt from *Etude No. 1 for Piano Solo*   Razak Abdul-Aziz

Example 6.1 Excerpts from *Sketch for MZ* and *Etude No. 1 for Piano Solo* by Razak Abdul-Aziz. (Used by permission of the composer)

Based in Penang, Johan Othman's works also reflect Asian musical influences. For instance, *Kabuki* is a piece for solo soprano and violin based on a Japanese folk tale of love and betrayal, using the narrative structure of Asian story telling. The soprano soloist plays the role of the story teller. In the score she is subjected to detailed instructions on vocal execution, such as the various magnitudes of vocal vibrato found in Japanese and Korean story telling. The violinist employs pizzicato and different bowing techniques imitating the *shamisen* and *koto* instruments of Japan.

Other contemporary Malaysian composers, such as John Yong Lah Boh and Julia Chong from Sarawak as well as Tan Su Lian, Minni Ang and Raymond Kong from Peninsular Malaysia, have maintained close ties to Western forms, including the symphony, concerto, variation form and ballet suite.

For example, the composer Minni Ang Kim Hui, based in the Kuala Lumpur metropolitan area, uses the theme and variations form in her recently composed *Rhythm of Life, for Percussion Ensemble*. This work is scored for tubular bells, concert xylophone and marimba, four timpani, bass and snare drums, congas, tam-tam and sizzle and suspended cymbals, requiring a total of six players. The piece features dialogue between pairs of instruments played over an underlying and constantly repeated 5-beat pulse. While the repeated pulse is meant to represent the heartbeat of life, the Asian influence is limited to the composer's choice of using only percussion instruments that reflect the sounds of tuned bamboo and other instruments indigenous to Asia in general.

The Sarawakians John Yong and Julia Chong have used local musical elements to bring a uniquely Malaysian identity to their generally programmatic works. John Yong's symphonic poem in three movements, entitled *The Mystery of The South China Sea*, is cast for a Western chamber orchestra, basing much of the music itself on atonality but also inserting the typically Chinese pentatonic scale.

The late Julia Chong consistently utilized local motifs in her musical works. The ballet suites entitled *Sang Kancil, Soraya* and *Manorah* derive their inspiration from local legends and theater forms, while the music itself is imbued with local motifs and scale structures. She has also attempted to use Sarawak instruments, as in the work *Rushing Waters*, a programmatic piece depicting the swift, flowing waters of the Rejang River. In this work we hear the suling flute, the engkerurai mouth organ, the sape plucked lute, the jatung utang xylophone, and the engkerumong gong-chime.

In the 1990s, some very old music genres in Malaysia have experienced development in the context of a contemporary art music tradition. The joget gamelan is a case in point. Composers such as Sunetra Fernando, Tan Sooi Beng, Suhaimi Mohd. Zain and Ariff Ahmad have attempted to bring a new Malaysian identity to gamelan music. Large and new formal structures, vocal parts, and adaptations of other Southeast Asian gamelan styles as well as instrumental combinations from Malaysia's diverse cultures have become part of the music vocabulary in this genre.[1]

Sunetra Fernando negotiates harmonic structures with the linear textures and modalities of Malay and Javanese gamelan in the pieces *Sembuh Sudah, Three Pieces for Scorpion Orchid* and *10-sen*. *Sembuh Sudah* (Example 6.2) is a setting of Latiff Mohidin's poem *Jauhi Bibirmu Sayang* for gamelan, voice, Malay and Javanese drums and Javanese sitar. In this piece, Sunetra combines the ostinatos found in the gong ensembles of Southeast Asia, linear textures of the gamelan, Malay poetry and the asli singing style with a harmonic base. Many of these features, especially the use of an ostinato figure and the linearity of the texture, are evident in the excerpt from the piece *Sembuh Sudah* shown in Example 6.2 below. The ornamented vocal part is shown in both the traditional gamelan notation and in staff notation.

In contrast, Tan Sooi Beng's music for gamelan is framed by polyphonic textures and musical structures of Malaysian/Southeast Asian music. Central in her piece *Perubahan*, is the multiple layering of rhythms such as those of the gendang drums of the gamelan and wayang kulit as well as the Chinese *shigu* drums. Melodies with Malay and Chinese elements played heterophonically by the various melodic instruments of the gamelan are superimposed above these interlocking rhythms within the framework of the Malay gong cycle or *gongan* [gong unit].

As shown in *Suasana*, Suhaimi Mohd. Zain's music refers to the rich Malay musical heritage as he juxtaposes excerpts of Kelantanese wayang kulit and makyung, keroncong tunes and kompang/rebana rhythms and gamelan melodies. The different excerpts are linked by a Malay poem about the 'atmosphere' or 'mood' as the title suggests.

The Temple of Fine Arts in Kuala Lumpur has also experimented with new art music based on the Karnatak and Hindustani traditions. Under the baton of Chandrakant Kapileshwari of the Kirana Gharana (School) of Hindustani Music, the Temple of Fine Arts has set up a 60 piece orchestra comprising vocalists who form the major part of the orchestra and instrumentalists who perform on the veena, sitar, flute, keyboard, mridangam, ghatam, tabla and other north and south Indian, Western and Malay rhythmic instruments. The orchestra performs music composed and arranged by Kapileshwari and Swami Shantanand Saraswathi (the founder of the Temple of Fine Arts).

Sembuh Sudah (excerpts)   Sunetra Fernando

Voice		Ja - u - hi_____		bi - bir - mu sa____ yang____	
Voice	: . 3 3 32	3 . . .	. 3 3 32	34.2 1#7.	
	Ja- uh- i--	----	bi-bir-mu	sa--- yang	
Bonang *barung*	33.3 .3.3 ٪ / 22.2 .2.2 ٪	٪	٪	٪	
Bonang *panerus*	: .3 .3 .3 .3 / 2 2 2 2	٪	٪	٪	
Saron/ *Demung/* *Slentem*	: + / 653 653 653 3 / (saron 2nd time only)	٪	٪	٪	
Kenong	: .3 .3 .3 .3	٪	٪	٪	
Gong 0/ *Kempul* *( )*	: 0 . ( ) .	٪	٪	٪	

(repeated 3 times)

1st time: LOUD *f*
2nd time: Chorus sings melody in heterophonic style (like the *makyung*
        chorus), to syllables 'e', 'e', VERY LOUD
3rd time: Singer sings melody octave lower, SOFT
+ damp as played.
* damp at rest on repeats.

(For illustrative purposes, the composer's transcription of the vocal line has
been inserted above the vocal part of the original score for *gamelan* and
voices.)

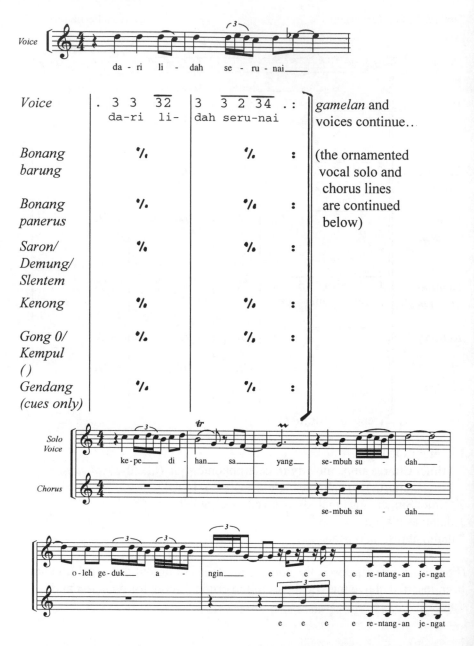

Example 6.2 Excerpts from *Sembuh Sudah* for *gamelan* and voices by Sunetra Fernando. (Used by permission of the composer)

The new music created by the musicians from the Temple of Fine Arts serves as both entertainment and divine offering to the Hindu gods. The human voice is employed as a musical instrument in many pieces. Contemporary compositions blend Hindustani and Karnatak musical styles as well as local Malay and Chinese elements.[2]

Rhythm of the Ocean, for instance, is a percussion piece that features Karnatak and Hindustani question and answer sections and *konukhol* or recitation of drum syllables. The instruments used include the mridangam, tabla, ghatam, ganjira, morsing, pakhavaj, dholak, dholkhi, duff, kompang and western drums. Set in a time cycle of eight beats (*Aadi taal*), the music reflects the movements of the ocean.

Accompanied by multiple keyboards, veenas and sitars playing in heterophony, vocalists of the Temple of Fine Arts sing Malay *puisi* [poetry] texts set to an Indian folk tune in the composition entitled *Timeless*. The piece ends with a modern rap in Malay, English, Tamil and Cantonese with the mridangam and tabla (and other percussion instruments) providing the rhythmic bass. *Timeless* blends tradition with the modern.

All art music today is written using the various types of notation available to composers, types such as the usual staff notation, modified staff, cipher, graph, tablature and other types. While Western music elements may still be seen in the Malaysian art music of the late 20th century, the regional genres, forms, tonalities, and Asian aesthetics have become its foundation.

Popular Music

Local versions of transnational pop sung in Malay, Mandarin/Cantonese, English, and Tamil/Hindustani form the bases of mainstream pop and cater (though not exclusively) to the respective ethnic groups.

This section focuses on the main trends in Malay pop --- the predominant local pop music in Malaysia. Malay pop has Malay texts and encompasses hybridized music with varying degrees of acculturation ranging from pop that is derived from local folk and syncretic music to pop and rock derived from Anglo-American mainstream styles. It is aimed specifically at Malay and other Bumiputera audiences, but Chinese, Middle Eastern, and Indian elements are often added to attract other ethnic groups. Malay pop trends show that pop musicians continuously negotiate between the local, the national and the global, resulting in tensions between homogeneity and heterogeneity.

Popular music of the pre-World War II Era

Malay popular music developed in the early twentieth century when socio-economic and political changes were taking place in Malaya as a consequence of British intervention. It was performed live in the bangsawan theatre (Cf., Chapter 1), and in the dance halls and amusement parks in new urban centers such as Singapore, Penang, Ipoh, and Kuala Lumpur. The urban multi-ethnic population comprising Malays as well as Chinese, Indian, and Indonesian immigrants (engaged in government services, trade, mining, plantations, and construction) emerged with new tastes and provided a potential market for popular music. During the colonial period, Singapore was the center for Malay popular music. However, the center shifted to Kuala Lumpur after Independence in 1957 and especially when Singapore opted out of Malaysia in 1965.

The first recordings of Malay popular music were made by Fred Gaisberg of The Gramophone Company (later known as His Master's Voice or HMV) of England in 1903. Other companies that recorded in Malaya included Columbia of England, Pathe of France, and Beka, Hindenburg, and Odeon of Germany. All these companies merged to form the Electric and Musical Industries Ltd. (EMI) in the 1930s. The Gramophone Company also allowed its local dealers to set up subsidiaries, which produced labels such as Chap Kuching (Cat Label) and Chap Singa (Lion Label). Most of the Malay records made after the 1930s were products of EMI, and singers were recorded at the EMI recording studio in Singapore. The wax matrices were then sent to the Gramophone Company's factory at Dum Dum, India for processing. Recorded and live popular music was also broadcasted by amateur radio societies set up in the main towns of Malaya (Tan, 1993, Chapter 2; Tan, 1997).

Pop music based on Malay folk social dance forms   About half of the gramophone pieces of the pre-War period were derived from Malay folk social dance and entertainment music, such as asli, inang, joget, dondang sayang, zapin (also called *gambos*), masri, and keroncong, which were performed at social occasions such as weddings and at amusement parks in various parts of Malaya. As shown in the earlier parts of this book on ronggeng, keroncong, and zapin, these dance-songs combined Malay, Western, and other foreign instruments and musical elements. The asli, inang, joget, and dondang sayang pieces were accompanied by a violin or accordion, one or two Malay frame drums called rebana and a Malay gong. The musical instruments used in the early recordings of zapin and masri included the *ud* (or *gambos*) plucked lute (originating from the Middle

East), a violin, three or four marwas hand-drums, and a dok cylindrical drum. Each song was associated with a specific local or foreign-derived rhythmic pattern.[3] The syncretism apparent in this music made it accessible to local ears and helped to attract multi-ethnic audiences (Cf., Chapters 2 and 5 of this work; and Chopyak, 1986).

Beginning in the 1920s, the asli, inang, joget, dondang sayang, zapin, and masri styles were transformed into modern popular genres by bangsawan musicians. These genres were adapted to dance band arrangements that became the standard combination in the mainstream recorded repertory of Anglo-American popular music. The early 20th century bangsawan musicians substituted the accordion with the piano and the frame drum with the Western drum kit. The ensemble was enlarged with a plucked bass, extra violins, and other instruments of the Western dance band. However, the newly arranged songs retained their local folk character by using the rhythmic patterns associated with each dance-song, topical texts and the alternation of witty exchange in Malay pantun verse structure. Other folk elements in the popular songs of this time included fairly independent vocal and instrumental lines and a singing style with a narrow range and a tense vocal production (Tan, 1993, Chapter 6). Famous singers such as Temah, Tijah and Dean often incorporated Chinese, Middle Eastern and Indian elements as in the songs *Mas Merah* (Temah, 1920s), *Aladom* (City Opera, 1930s) and *Tandi-Tandi* (Tijah, 1940s), respectively.

Pop music based on Anglo- and Latin-American dance music Popular music based on Anglo-American and Latin American dance music sung in Malay formed the other half of the recorded repertory of the pre-World-War II period. Compared to the modern versions of recorded Malay social dance music, Anglo-American pop elements predominated in this category of songs. The songs had catchy melodies superimposed on waltz, foxtrot, tango or rumba rhythms. They were accompanied by Western dance bands known locally as the orkes Melayu, or Malay orchestra, comprising the violin, trumpet, trombone, flute, clarinet, piano, double bass, guitar, saxophone, drums, maracas, claves, and woodblock. The well known musicians performing these pieces included Soliano, D'Cruz, and Martinez who were, in fact, Filipinos earlier brought to Malaya by the British to form the Selangor State Band. The orkes Melayu performed at dance halls in the amusement parks, in the bangsawan shows, and at other festivities. Besides Latin American dance music, the orkes Melayu also played sub-styles of keroncong such as *keroncong rumba, keroncong slowfox,* and *keroncong Hawaii.*

Local flavor was maintained in the orkes Melayu repertory through the song texts. With the rise of nationalism, songs such as *Malaya* (Ahmad CB, 1940s), which instilled the spirit of harmony and love of one's motherland, were composed. A number of these early recorded songs had topical texts. For example, *Taxi Rumba* [Rumba Taxi] and *Apik Tukang Becha* [The Old Trishaw Puller] (Tarminah and Piet S, 1930s) identified with the common people such as the taxi driver and the trishaw man who had to work hard to earn a living. These topical songs had elements of humor, incorporated different dialects, and portrayed the sentiments of the common people:

Apik Tukang Becha (Tarminah and Piet S, HMV, 1930s)

Diwaktu hari panas	*On a hot day*
Apik tukang becha	*The old trishaw puller*
Berlari tarik nafas	*Runs breathing hard*
Apik tukang becha	*The old trishaw puller*
Apik lari cari wang	*The old man runs to earn money*
Buat beli makan	*To buy food*
Apik kalau dapat no-kak	*If the old man gets twenty cents*
Pergi chyak kopi	*[He] goes to drink coffee.*

As the trishaw man is Chinese, the singer mixes Malay with Hokkien words such as *chyak kopi* [drink coffee], *no kak* [twenty cents] and *apik* [old man]. These comical songs provided an insight into significant social changes in Malaya and formed a tradition that prevailed in the songs of P. Ramlee, Aman Ballon, Mohd Yatim (1950s) and Hang Mokhtar and Rampa (1990s).

Film music of the 1950s and early 1960s

When the Japanese Occupation of Malaya took place in 1942, record production stopped. Only a few labels such as HMV, Parlophone, Columbia, and Pathe survived after the War. During this period, popular music developed in close association with the Malay film that reached its peak in the 1950s. Malay films were produced by Chinese-owned companies such as Malay Film Productions (Shaw Brothers) and Cathay-Keris Productions (Ho Ah Loke and Loke Wan Tho). These companies employed Indian directors who relied on local actors and actresses (Yem, Shariff Medan, Suki, Kasma Booty, and Siput Sarawak) and choreographers from the bangsawan theater. Legends and folk tales from bangsawan as well as new contemporary stories with social themes were filmed. The bangsawan musicians such as Zubir Said, Osman Ahmad, Wandi Yazid, Yusoff B., Ahmad Wan Yet, and Ahmad Jaafar composed and performed music for the song and dance sequences (Baharudin Latif, 1989).

The outstanding film stars who recorded their songs included Asiah, R. Azmi, Lena, Salmah Ismail or Saloma, Momo, Jamaliah Shariff and Jasni. Most of the film music was, however, sung by P. Ramlee who began his film career as a playback singer, slowly taking on small supporting roles to become the leading actor of the 1950s. He is said to have appeared in 63 films, directed a few and sung more than 200 songs (Baharudin Latif, 1989, p. 63). His films and songs had a wide appeal. They attracted both Malay and non-Malay audiences as well as rural and urban folk as they portrayed the lives and problems of ordinary people. P. Ramlee's films made audiences laugh at their own weaknesses, films such as *Penarik Beca* [*The Trishaw Puller*] (1955) *and Bujang Lapok* [Unmarried Trio] (1957). His films and songs are still very popular today.

As in the bangsawan theater, Malay films of the 1950s drew on the Malay asli, inang, joget, masri, zapin, and keroncong as well as the modern Latin American dances for their repertory. Compared to bangsawan music, there was greater stylistic homogeneity since film music and song was composed and arranged by only a small number of studio musicians (who also played in the studio orchestra), and were sung by only a few stars.

The film songs derived from Malay social dance music increasingly used more Western musical elements. Terms such as *joget baru* [new joget] and *masri moden* [modern masri] were often employed by recording companies to differentiate such songs from those of pre-war times. Bandleaders expanded traditional linear lines with brass and reed instruments such as the trumpet, trombone, saxophone, and clarinet as well as the Western trap set. There was also a tendency towards Western instrumentation replacing all traditional instruments. Singers used the crooning style and added more vibrato as they adapted to the use of the microphone. The singers and instrumentalists harmonized with one another while the plucked bass and piano played primary triads. The songs *Rintihan Jiwaku* [Lament of My Soul](P. Ramlee and Saloma, 1950s) and *Serampang Lapan* [name of dance] (Asiah and Abd. Chik, 1950s) are examples of asli and joget songs, which exemplify the film style.

New Latin-American dances such as the *kaparinyo, paso doble, bolero, samba, beguine, conga, cha-cha-cha, baion* and *mambo* were also popularized through film. Songs with jazz-tinged harmonies, which were categorized as swing, were also recorded. Compared to the pre-war days, more instruments were added to the orkes Melayu. Besides the trumpet, trombone, clarinet, saxophone, flute, violin, accordion, piano, plucked bass, drum and other percussion instruments, the electric guitar was introduced at the end of the 1950s. There was a trend towards orchestration and less improvisation. Contrasting instrumental timbres and long instrumental interludes were often employed, and the songs were homophonic in nature. Often, the Malay text was the only Malay element found. The songs *Nasib Di Bunga* [Fate in the Flower] (Lena, 1950s) and *Lihatlah* [Look] (Asiah, 1950s) exemplify the cha-cha-cha and swing styles of the 1950s.

Despite greater stylistic homogeneity, the film style was eclectic. The asli song *Tudong Periok* [A kind of sea fish] (P. Ramlee and Saloma, 1950s) incorporated characteristic phrases using minor 3rd intervals in a typical Chinese pentatonic scale. Middle Eastern-derived rhythmic patterns such as zapin and masri were employed in *Maafkan Kami* [Pardon Us] and *Nasib Si Miskin* ([The Fate of the Poor] (P. Ramlee, 1950s). Songs with a Hindustani flavor (*irama* Hindustan) became popular in film songs. *Tidorlah Nanda* ([Sleep Nanda] (Noormadiah, 1950s) starts with an un-metered introduction like an *alap* and uses typical Indian vocal ornamentations. Some ghazal melodies sung to Malay pantun and accompanied by the Indian harmonium and tabla, Middle Eastern gambos and western violin, guitar, maracas, and tambourine also became popular in the 1950s.

Local flavor was maintained through the song texts. The film songs of the 1950s and early 1960s advised audiences to take care of the poor, especially orphans, as in the song *Nasib Si Miskin* ([The Fate of the Poor] (P. Ramlee, 1950s). Other film songs that encouraged youths to unite and work towards achieving Independence [*Merdeka*] were common:

Pemuda Melayu [Malay Youths] (Ahmad CB and Osman Ahmad Orchestra, 1950s)

Pemuda mesti berbakti	*Youths must be loyal*
Membela ibu pertiwi	*Uphold [our]*
	motherland
Marilah bersama bertegak	*Let us together stand*
bersatu	*upright and unite*
Merdeka tetaplah Merdeka	*Independence [is]*
	definite.

The singers of the 1940s and 50s continued to add humour to their songs. They used colloquial Malay, English, Tamil, Hindustani, and even some Chinese dialects to comment on personal, ethnic, and social problems, or to appeal to the social conscience of the audience. Comical songs such as *Yam Choi Chow* [Drink Alcohol] (Mohd. Yatim, 1950s), *Kling Mabok* [The Drunken Indian] (Aman Ballon and Leiman SS, 1940s), and *Dalam Masa Nipon* [During the Japanese Occupation] (Mohd. Yatim, 1950s) incorporated Cantonese, Tamil, and Japanese texts, and commented on drinking and hardships faced by the Malayans during the Japanese Occupation.

Pop-yeh-yeh, ballads and rock (late 1960s-1980s)

In the late 1960s, Anglo-American-derived pop began to dominate the music scene in Malaysia. Only a few singers such as Orchid Abdullah, Rafeah Buang, and Rosiah Chik continued to record asli and ghazal songs. Paralleling the Beatles craze, a phenomenon called *pop yeh yeh* emerged. Bands called *kugiran* (*kumpulan gitar rancak*) [literally meaning, 'lively guitar groups'] comprising three guitars and a drum gradually replaced the orkes Melayu that accompanied bangsawan theater and social dancing in the 1940s and 1950s. Jeffridin and the Siglap 5, The Hooks, Nirwana, Mutiara Timur, Roziah Latiff and the Jay Hawkers, Les Flingers, Ramlie and the Rhythm Boys and Ahmad Daud and The Swallows were some of the popular bands of the 1960s. Dressed in colorful jackets and tie (or bow), dark glasses and cowboy boots, band singers with outrageous hairstyles delivered songs in the style of the Rolling Stones and Cliff Richard and the Shadows. They played the twist, shake, *a-go-go* and *bosanova* at live concerts. The texts of pop-yeh-yeh songs expressed romantic love or they invited audiences to dance. The famous bands were recorded by EMI and Philips on 45 RPM records. Some groups also appeared on local television (*Bintang dan Lagu*, August, 1966, and October, 1967).

In the 1970s and 1980s, a type of transnationalized music by pop stars (such as Michael Jackson, Boney M and Abba) were marketed throughout Malaysia by giant conglomerates like CBS, EMI, Polygram-Philips, and WEA. (Sony and BMG entered Malaysia in the 1990s.) This music became accessible even to those in remote villages through the introduction of cheaper transistor radios and tape cassette pirating. In the wake of the invasion of transnationalized pop, local mainstream pop concentrated on versions of chart-oriented and easy-listening songs. Central figures such as Sharifah Aini, Khatijah Ibrahim, Latif Ibrahim, Uji Rashid, Noorkumalasari, Azlina Aziz, D.J. Dave, Zalipah Ibrahim and prominent groups such as The Alleycats, Sweet Charity, and Sweet September were known for their formulaic soft rock and sentimental ballads [*balada*] in which minor chords were predominant. The disco beat became hip after the launching of the film *Saturday Night Fever*. Although joget and asli rhythms were incorporated by some of the singers, the music was so heavily synthesized that the asli flavor was lost.

Nevertheless, some innovation took place. Sharifah Aini (1988), Zaleha Hamid (1988), and other singers of EMI popularized a form of Hindustani-influenced pop music called *dangdut*, which first emerged in Indonesia in the 1960s. The dangdut fused the Indian tabla and the Hindustani film vocal style with electric guitars, synthesizers and drums. In addition, Sudirman (1980, 1984) and Kembara (1982) who recorded for EMI and Philips, respectively, included lyrics about the problems of rural-urban migration and the problems faced by Malay youths in the city. Asiabeat (1983), a prominent group advocating jazz fusion in Malaysia, combined the Malay gamelan and the Japanese *shakuhachi* with western electric guitars and drums in their CBS albums.

Smaller independent local companies such as Warnada, Sinar, Suara Cipta Sempurna (SCS), and Suria Records promoted music on the fringe that was disregarded by big foreign companies. The availability of tape cassettes provided a new means for the distribution of songs, especially the underground ones. Hang Mokhtar and Rampa incorporated comments on poverty, corruption and even complaints against the government in their lyrics. Songs that made a parodly of the problems in Malaysian society such as excessive drinking, gambling, motorbike racing, womanizing, and the plight of taxi drivers were composed. Taking after earlier stars such as P. Ramlee and Mohd. Yatim, these singers invigorated their songs with humor in the tone of voice and lyrics and started a trend called *lucu* [comical] songs.

In *Tampal Korek* [Patching Up Digging, 1987], Hang Mokhtar employed a Chinese popular tune, and the Chinese language syntax to sing about the perpetual digging of roads to the frustration of commuters:

Tampal Korek (Hang Mokhtar, 1987)

Lobang, kolek	*Digging holes*
Talikom tampal	*Talikom patches up [one hole]*
LLN nanti kolek	*LLN digs another*
Hali-hali tampal kolek	*Every day [someone] is*
	patching or digging holes
Balu tampal besok atak	*What has been patched up*
Kolek	*is dug up the next day*
[Aya jua-a, banyak susah	*[Aya, it is hot, I am*
hati loh]	*distressed loh]*

Rampa (1988) showed how working people of all ethnic groups in Malaysia (such as Malay shoe makers and Chinese and Indian street hawkers) shared the same fate and aspirations in *Senasib* [Of the Same Fate] (Tan, 1995).

A Malaysian brand of heavy metal emerged in the 1980s. Rock bands such as Search, Lefthanded, Bumiputera Rockers, Bloodshed, and Wings attracted thousands of fans to their live rock concerts. A youth subculture comprising mainly Malays who called themselves 'rockers' or *mat/minah rok* emerged. Mat (short for Ahmad) and Minah are common names for Malay men and women, respectively. The rockers kept long hair, wore corduroy jeans and T-shirts, rode motorbikes, spoke their own language and hung out at shopping complexes. The rock groups promoted two main styles. The first, known as slow rock, resembled the core of mainstream balada except that it was amplified and hardened. The second style, which rockers referred to as heavy metal, featured heavily amplified drums and electric bass providing the beat and bass sound for the voice and lead guitar. The electric guitar played riffs. Although singers shouted in hoarse [*serak*] voices, the melodic component was still prominent. Lyrics invited the audience to 'fight' [*berjuang*] against injustice, greed, power, money and drugs and for rockers' rights. *Hukum Karma* [Condemn Fate] (The Wings, 1988) and *Ringgit* [Money] (Ababil, 1989) were two examples. Above all, heavy metal music helped young people to dance and to release frustrations arising from everyday problems (Tan, 1995):

Dunia Kehidupan ([Living World], Ella, 1989)

Kita berjumpa lagi	*We meet again*
Kita bermesra lagi	*We are absorbed again*
Di pesta muzik malam ini	*At the music festival tonight*
Jangan kau bersedih hati	*Don't be sad*
Dengarlah lagu ini	*Listen to this song*
Lupakan duka lara di hati	*Forget your misery.*

World beat, metal, hip-hop and fringe in the 1990s and the turn of the millennium

With the advent of new electronic technology such as satellite television, digital video discs, compact discs and the internet, transnational popular music promoted by multi-national conglomerates continued to flood the music scene in Malaysia in the 1990s.

Anglo-American pop stars (Britney Spears, Christina Aguilera, Westlife), Hindustani and Tamil film icons (Akshay Kumar, Sunidhi Chouhan, Shah Rukh Khan) as well as Hong Kong, Taiwanese (Andy Lau, Coco Lee), and Japanese or J-pop singers (Ayumi Hanasaki, Hikaro Utada, Smap) mesmerized youths from English, Indian, and Chinese-educated backgrounds, respectively. Likewise, Malay mainstream singers of the 1990s such as Nora, Jesslina Hashim, Siti Nurhaliza, Amy Mastura, Fauziah Latiff, KRU and Sheila Majid continued to favor easy-listening pop such as the Malay balada, soft versions of R & B, and soft rock.

However, due to the exposure of local musicians to world beat and the increased circulation of diverse musics through the media, there has been a resurgent interest in the use of indigenous elements in mainstream pop music since the 1990s. Local musicians initiated new types of hybrid music in which local instruments, musical elements, and concerns were combined with global musical idioms (Tan, 2002). Manan Ngah and Sheqal initiated the *balada nusantara* [ballad of the archipelago] synthesizing Arabic, Hispanic, European, and Asian elements. Traditional instruments such as caklempung, angklung, gamelan, gendang, seruling, tabla, gambus, sitar, and kompang were mixed with electric guitars and synthesizers (Sheqal, 1990).

Zainal Abidin blended different Malay, Indian, Latin American, and African drums (*Zainal Abidin,* 1991). His music emphasized African rhythms, syncopated phrasing, and call and response singing style. The song *Gamal* [Images] (1994) began with an excerpt of a live recording of the gong chime ensemble (engkerumong) of the Iban of Sarawak, evoking images of the activities of the Iban longhouse. M. Nasir experimented with the Sarawakian sape and the Malay seruling, rebab, gong, serunai, and drums such as gendang and kompang in *Canggong Mendonan* [Deserted Strangers] (1993).

World beat also influenced devotional music, namely *nasyid,* a type of Islamic devotional song previously sung without musical accompaniment. Song texts praised Allah, and prescribed universal love and brotherhood in Islam. Groups like Raihan, Hijjaz, Rabbani and Brothers, Hawa, and Solehah sang *nasyid pop* in two or three-part harmony. They were accompanied by the masri rhythm[3] played by percussion instruments such as the Malay kompang and rebana, cowbells, and congo drums (Raihan, 1997, Rabbani, 2000).[4]

The 1990s witnessed the emergence of *Irama Malaysia* [Malaysian Beat], a type of pop music that combined Malay social dance and syncretic music such as asli, inang, joget, zapin, ghazal, and dikir barat with the Anglo-American pop idiom. The composer Suhaimi Md. Zain (better known as Pak Ngah) and singers such as Noraniza Idris, Jamal Abdillah, and Siti Nurhaliza were associated with this genre. *Irama Malaysia* differed from earlier synthesized versions, as the songs stressed the mixture of traditional drums such as the rebana, kompang, tar rodat, *jidor* double-headed barrel drum, marwas, gendang dikir, and tabla. The gambus and accordion were often added, and the lyrics were written in Malay verse form [*pantun*] (Tan, 2002).

World beat also made an impact on local Chinese pop music. To forge a new Malaysian Chinese identity, the BM Boys (an exponent of world beat using Chinese dialects) used drums from China, India and Malaysia in their compositions. They employed Chinese instruments such as the dizi (Chinese flute) and erhu (2-string spiked fiddle). Besides Mandarin, they often used different Chinese dialects such as Teochew, Hokkien and Hakka, and they consciously adapted Malay words and folk tunes in their songs. For example, *Tong Nian Xiong* [*Song for Childhood*] (BM Boys, 1998) was sung in Mandarin using the Malay inang dance rhythm. It incorporated the Malay folk song *Lenggang Lenggang Kangkong.*

Hybrid bands such as Tuku Kame and Sayu Ateng of Sarawak and Seni Kinabalu of Sabah fused various instruments and musical elements of Sarawak and Sabah with the world beat idiom. *Lagenda Gunung Mitos* [The Legendary Mountain of Mitos] (Sayu Ateng, n.d.) welcomed listeners to the mountain of Mitos with sounds of birds of the forest. This was followed by a short melodic motif played on the Iban engkerumong gong chime, two sape plucked lutes of the Kayan and Kenyah and the Iban ketebong single-headed waisted drum. The singer was then accompanied by the electric guitar and electric bass that played a variation of the engkerumong motif.

World beat cut 'n' mix soundscapes were employed to communicate social concerns and responses to modernity. Zainal Abidin expressed concerns about the environment in *Hijau* [Green] (1991):

Hijau (Zainal Abidin, 1991)

Bumi yang tiada udara	*The earth that has no air*
Bagai tiada nyawa	*Resembles having no life*
Pasti hilang suatu hari	*[We] will disappear one day*
Tanpa disedari...	*Without being aware....*

Korupsi, oppressi,	*Corruption, oppression,*
obsessi diri	*obsession of ourselves*
Polussi, depressi, di bumi kini...	*Pollution, depression,*
	on earth now...

In addition, M. Nasir sang about the meaning of life and enlightenment in *Apokalips* [Apocalypse] and *Di Balik Cermin Mimpi* [Behind the Dream Mirror] (1993). The pop nasyid singers encouraged youths to praise Allah and to stay away from social ills (Raihan, 1997), and *Irama Malaysia* singers were concerned about revitalizing traditional Malay music (Noraniza Idris, 1999).

Through *Lagenda Gunung Mitos*, Sayu Ateng welcomed travelers who respected the 'mountain's wealth, peace and tranquility', but warned those who sought the 'rare blue orchid' which grew there. *Rintihan Suara Sungai* [Cries of the River] lamented about the pollution of rivers in Sarawak (Sayu Ateng, n.d.).

In *Nang Si Chit Keh Nang* [We are a Family], the BM Boys (1998) stressed that all Malaysians should live in harmony, tolerate each other, communicate with one another and work hard together as they are a family:

Nang Si Chit Keh Nang (BM Boys, 1998)

The stars are in the sky, people are on earth
It does not matter where you come from
You play the Malay drum, I carry the Chinese lantern
Lighting this earth.

We are one family
It does not matter if you have money
You must work hard to earn money
Only then can one eat and be independent...

Besides interest in local elements and instrumentation, the 1990s also saw the advent of new types of heavy metal music. A new generation of heavy metal fans dismissed the rock singers of the 1980s (such as Wings, Ellie, Amy and Awie) and other hard rock groups as conformists performing *rock kapak* (Malay slang for 'low class rock') --- they had contracts with transnational companies and sang commercial rock ballads. The critics dedicated themselves to punk, thrash metal and other sub-genres of heavy metal such as black/death metal with their high decibel, pace, discordant chords, guitar riffs, and rough pitched or non-pitched vocals.

Under the banner of non-commercialism, these groups went underground [*bawah tanah*] and performed gigs at clubs, pubs and open spaces. They emphasized the DIY (Do-It-Yourself) spirit, organized gigs that brought different bands together, produced their own magazines (*fanzines*) that were often photocopied, and informed fans about the gigs through flyers. Unknown groups produced their own 'demo' tapes for sale, while the more established ones were recorded by independent companies such as Psychic Scream Entertainment, DB Productions, and Strange Culture Records.

Thrash metal groups such as FTG (Freedom That's Gone), Koffin Kanser and Samurai highlighted the alienation of Malay youths from the materialistic and controlled world in which they lived. Black metal (As Sahar, Koma, Sil Khannaz), punk (Carburetor Dung), and alternative (Butterfingers, Subculture) helped Malay youths to release tension at gigs through headbanging and moshing.

Chinese and Indian youths who were anti-mainstream pop from Hong Kong, Taiwan and India (and the local versions) also created their own rock. Mandarin-based Chinese rock bands (Chong Yang, Moxuan, KRMA) performed at the clubhouse run by the independent Huang Huo (Yellow Flame) organization, and at various pubs and community halls. These bands produced pounding music with aggressive lyrics clothed in metaphors. Tamil rock bands such as Lock-Up, The Keys, Darkkey, Apachean, and Vyrus also contested mainstream foreign Hindustani/Tamil film music through their own gigs.

Beginning in the mid-1990s, hip-hop or rap began to make some impact among the Malay youths. Except for a few groups such as Poetic Ammo and Too Phat, which became mainstream, most hip-hop groups such as The Teh Tarik Crew, The Project, and Phlowtron operated the underground DIY way. Clad in oversized T-shirts, baggy pants or jumpsuits, sneakers and baseball/ski caps, they rapped and break danced at outdoor venues to teenage audiences who were too young to enter clubs. These venues included such places as the Sunway Lagoon and Bintang Walk, and at shopping complexes such as the Sungai Wang Plaza in Kuala Lumpur. Although many hip-hop acts performed cover songs from foreign albums using English, some groups began to create their own distinct style. Poetic Ammo's album *It's a Nice Day to be Alive* (1998) encompassed Malay, Tamil, and Cantonese raps and local-flavored samples. In *Anak Ayam*, Too Phat (2001) rapped over the folk song *Kuda Ku Lari* using the zapin beat.

Finally, pubs, cafes, and restaurants, provided fringe singers such as Rafique Rashid, Amir Yusoff and Julian Mokhtar the opportunity to showcase alternative unplugged acoustic songs with social concerns. In particular, Rafique Rashid was known for his slapstick parody and biting commentary. *Shut Up* concerned press censorship, while *Ignorance is Bliss* criticized Malaysians for being complacent. The Halo Café in Kuala Lumpur championed local Chinese music with regular folk-pop evenings and mini-showcases for unsigned acts. Several of Malaysia's Chinese singers who have been successful, such as Michael and Victor, Ah Gu and the BM Boys, first performed in the café.

Government Censorship

Concerned that certain types of foreign and local versions of transnational music could create conflicting cultural trends among youths, and partly because of pressure from Islamic lobbyists, the government attempted to control and censor what it deemed 'undesirable', whatever could 'stimulate one to violence' and was 'too westernized'. A censorship board screened all songs before performances were held. Pop songs had to comply with certain guidelines before they could be played on national radio and television (Tan, 1990).

In particular, attempts to regulate heavy metal rock were significant because of its alleged influence on the values and behavior of Malay youths. Open-air rock concerts were banned in 1986 as the rockers were accused of 'acting wildly' and 'not reflecting the code of ethics' of the people. In 1999, punk music was excoriated for encouraging youths to dye and spike their hair and to spit at each other at gigs. In 2001, black metal became the main target of the State resulting in arrests of cult members. Black metal music allegedly promoted nihilism and anti-Islamic values.

By way of conclusion, throughout the history of popular music in Malaysia, there has been a continuous dialogue between the local, the national, and the global. Malaysian pop singers negotiate with the state bureaucracy as well as transnational corporations, which attempt to homogenize consumption patterns. While local mainstream pop follows trends in transnational pop, some local musicians have been able to innovate beyond the confines of formulaic chart-oriented pop and to establish their own distinctive identities.

Malaysian pop musicians have not broken into the international scene, but there is an emerging market for Malay pop in Singapore, Indonesia and Japan. Nasyid singers are trying to make inroads in the Islamic countries of the Middle East, while Chinese singers are beginning to be recognized in Singapore, Hong Kong and Taiwan.

In September 2002, the Islamic PAS government of Kelantan banned public performances of all rock and pop bands except the Islamic pop nasyid in an effort to check 'moral decadence'. Women are, also, not allowed to participate in concerts or other live entertainment in Kelantan. Nevertheless, gigs of rock and pop continue to be heard at private parties that are not open to the public.

Notes

1 New gamelan compositions analyzed have been recorded on the compact disc *Rhythm in Bronze, New Music for the Malaysian Gamelan*, Five Arts Centre and Actors Studio, Kuala Lumpur, 2001.
2 Live performances of the two compositions analyzed have been recorded and produced by the Temple of Fine Arts, *Naad Brahma, Music for the Soul*, Kuala Lumpur, 1998.
3 The masri rhythm is similar to belly dancing rhythms in the Middle East.
4 *Puji-Pujian* (Praises), the title track of Raihan's album of the same name, included texts praising Allah. As in other world music, the video clip of the Puji-Pujian saw lip-syncing singers playing the Malay rebana in continually changing settings, including mountains and deserts (as though in the Middle East).

Appendix

Sapu Lidi (keroncong asli)

Sapu Lidi *(keroncong asli)*

Sapu Lidi (keroncong asli)

Sapu Lidi (keroncong asli)

Sapu Lidi (keroncong asli)

Sapu Lidi (keroncong asli)

Dikir Barat
(Kelantan, 1994)

Dikir Barat

Dikir Barat

Dikir Barat

Dikir Barat

Dikir Barat

Dikir Barat

Dikir Barat

ber - at ra-sa - nya nak ku ting-gal - kan ting-gal - sa-yang

ker - an a ha-ti_____ ter-ta-wan

hai hai

Dikir Barat

Dikir Barat

Dikir Barat

Dikir Barat

Tanah Air Ku

Arranged by Lee Soo Sheng

				ff	>	>>	>>	>>	
Di zi	–	–	–		1̇	7̇1	67	23	4346
Liu yueqin	–	–	–		1̇	7̇1	67	23	4346
Pipa	–	–	–		1̇///	7̇1	67	23	4346
Zhong sanxian	–	–	–		1̇///	7̇1	67	23	46
Zhong ruan	–	–	–		1̇///	7̇1	67	23	42
	–	–	–		1̇	71	67	23	4346
Yangqin	–	–	–		1	71	67	23	
Gaohu	–	–	–		>1̇	>>7̇1	>>67	>>23	4346
Erhu	–	–	–		>1̇	>>7̇1	>>67	>>23	4346
Zhonghu	–	–	–		>1̇	>>71	>>67	>>23	42
Dahu	–	–	–		>1	>>71	>>67	>>23	42
Gehu	–	–	–		>1	>>71	>>67	>>23	42
Gu	*sf* ⟫ *mp* ⟪ *f*			D/// – – – – – – – – – – –		D/// – – – – – – – – – – –			
Maling	>C/// – – – – – – – – – – –					C	–	–	–

Tanah Air Ku

Tanah Air Ku

Dizi					
Liu yueqin					**and so on...**
Pipa					
Zhong sanxian					
Zhong ruan					
Yangqin					
Gaohu					
Erhu					
Zhong hu					
Dahu					
Gehu					
Gu					
Maling					

Key: dot below a note --- low octave; dot above a note --- high octave; short diagonal lines --- tremolo; single horizontal line --- quaver note; double horizontal line --- semiquaver note; dashed line --- note held for the beats specified.

Bibliography

Abd. Samad Idris (1970), *Hubungan Minangkabau Dengan Negeri Sembilan Dari Segi Sejarah dan Kebudayaan*, Terbitan Pustaka Asas Negeri Sembilan, p. 15.

Abdul Hamid Adnan (1996-97), '*Struktur Muzikal Caklempong sebagai Struktur Sosial dalam Masyarakat Minangkabau di Negeri Sembilan*' [Caklempong Musical Structure as Social Structure in Minangkabau Society of Negeri Sembilan], Honours paper, Music Department, Universiti Sains Malaysia, Penang.

Abdul Razak Hassan (1985-86), '*Persembahan Tumbuk Kalang*' [The Tumbuk Kalang Performance], Honours paper, Malay Studies Dept., University of Malaya, Kuala Lumpur.

Abdullah bin Mohamed (1974), 'The Ghazal in Arabic Literature and in Malay Music', *Malaysia in History*, 14(1), pp. 24-31.

Adibah Amin. (1979), 'Ghazal Music is Becoming Popular Again', *New Straits Times Annual*, Kuala Lumpur.

Affan Seljuq (1976), 'Some Notes on the Origin and Development of the Naubat', *Journal of the Royal Asiatic Society, Malaysian Branch*, 49(1), pp. 141-2.

Ahmad Omar (1984), 'Joget Gamelan: The Art of Orchestral Dance', *Performing Arts*, I(1), pp. 38-41.

Andaya, B. W. and Andaya, L. Y. (1982), *A History of Malaysia*, Macmillan, London.

Ang, B. S. (1997), '*Perkembangan dan Struktur Persembahan Menora di Utara Semenanjung Malaysia*' [Development and Performance Structure of the Menora in Northern Peninsular Malaysia], M.A. thesis, Universiti Sains Malaysia, Penang.

Asmad (1992), 'Seni Permainan Kompang', in *Seni Lagu dan Permainan Tradisi*, Associated Educational Distributors (M) Sdn. Bhd., Melaka, Negeri Sembilan, Malaysia.

Bahagian Hal Ehwal Islam (BAHEIS) (1992), *Panduan Zikir Harian*, BAHEIS, Jabatan Perdana Menteri, Kuala Lumpur.

Baharudin Latiff (1989), 'The Beginning' and 'P. Ramlee: The Living Legend', *Cintai Filem Malaysia*, Perbadanan Kemajuan Filem Nasional Malaysia, Kuala Lumpur, pp. 45-8, 63-5.

Balfour, H. L. (1904), 'Report on a Collection of Musical Instruments from the Siamese Malay States and Perak', in *Fasciculi Malayanses* (Anthropology, IIa), Williams & Norgate for the University Pr. of Liverpool, London.

Becker, J. (1976), 'Kroncong, Indonesian Popular Music', *Asian Music*, VII(1), pp. 14-9.

----- (1984-86), *Karawitan, Source Readings on Javanese Gamelan and Vocal Music*, 3 Vols., Michigan Papers on South and Southeast Asia, University of Michigan Press, Ann Arbor, Michigan.

Bintang dan Lagu (1966, 1967), August (2), October (15).

Blacking, J. A. R. (1954-55), 'Musical Instruments of the Malayan Aborigines', *Federation Museums Journal*, 1(11) (New Series), p. 35.

Camoens, C. L. (1982), 'The Wayang Parsi, Tiruan Wayang Parsi, Komidi Melayu and the Bangsawan, 1887-1895', *Malaysia in History*, 25, pp. 1-20.

Chopyak, J. (1986), 'Music in Modern Malaysia: A Survey of the Musics Affecting the Development of Malaysian Popular Music', *Asian Music*, XVIII(1), pp. 111-38.

----- (1987), 'The Role of Music in Mass Media, Public Education and the Formation of a Malaysian National Culture', *Ethnomusicology*, 31(3), pp. 431-54.

Couillard, M-A., Cardosa, M. E. and Martinez, M. R. (1982), 'Jah Hut Musical Culture and Content', in *Contributions to Southeast Asian Ethnography*, I, pp. 35-55.

Cuisinier, J. (1936), *Danses Magiques de Kelantan*, Gallimard, Paris.

----- (1957), *Le Théâtre d'ombres à Kelantan*, Gallimard, Paris.

Daud Hamzah. (1991), 'Malaysia', in Harrison, R. (ed), *New Music in the Orient, Essays on Composition in Asia*, Frits Knuf Publishers-Buren, The Netherlands, pp. 91-6.

D'Cruz, M. F. (1979), 'Joget Gamelan, A Study of Its Contemporary Practice', M.A. thesis, Universiti Sains Malaysia, Penang, Malaysia.

Frame, E. (1976), 'Major Musical Forms in Sabah', *Journal of the Royal Asiatic Society, Malaysian Branch*, XLIX(2), pp. 156-63.

-----. (1982), 'The Musical Instruments of Sabah, Malaysia', *Ethnomusicology*, XXVI(2), pp. 247-74.

Gamelan Music (1980), Universiti Kebangsaan Malaysia, Kuala Lumpur.

The Garland Encyclopedia of World Music (2000), 'South Asia' Alison Arnold, ed., Garland Publishing, Inc., New York and London.

Ghulam-Sarwar Yousof (1976), 'The Kelantan Mak Yong Dance Theater, A Study of Performance Structure', Ph.D. dissertation, University of Hawaii, Honolulu.

----- (1979), 'Mak Yong', *Dewan Budaya*, Sept., pp. 31-4 and Oct., pp. 37-40.

----- (1981), 'Ramayana Branch Stories in the Wayang Siam Shadow Play of Kelantan', *International Seminar on Variations of the Ramayana in Asia*, New Delhi.

----- (1981), 'Wayang Gedek Dari Utara', *Dewan Budaya*, Vol. 3(11), (November), pp. 24-7.

----- (1982), 'Mak Yong: The Ancient Malay Dance-Theatre', *Asian Studies*, University of the Philippines, Asian Centre, Manila.

----- (1983), 'Mak Yong di Serdang, Sumatera Utara', *Pinang Sirih*, Dewan Bahasa dan Pustaka, Kuala Lumpur.

----- (1986), 'Bangsawan Opera Melayu', *Dewan Budaya*, Nov., pp. 50-4 and Dec. pp. 33-8.

----- (1989), 'A Previously Unknown Version of the Ramayana from Kedah, Malaysia', in Sinha, D.P. and Sahai, S. (eds), *Ramayana Tradition and National Cultures in Asia*, Government of Uttar Pradesh, Lucknow, India.

----- (1992), *Panggung Semar, Aspects of Traditional Malay Theatre*, Tempo Publishing, Kuala Lumpur.

----- (1994), *A Dictionary of Southeast Asian Theatre*, Oxford University Press, Kuala Lumpur.

Goldsworthy, D. (1979), 'Melayu Music of North Sumatra', Ph.D. dissertation, Monash University, Australia.

Gorlinski, V. (1988), 'Some Insights into the Art of Sape Playing', *Sarawak Museum Journal*, Vol. XXXIX(60) (New Series), pp.77-104.

----- (1999), 'Swinging into the Global Music Scene at the Rainforest World Music Festival, Kuching, Sarawak', *Borneo Research Bulletin*, 30.

Gullick, J. M. (1981), *Malaysia: Economic Expansion and National Unity*, Westview Press, London.

Guntavid, J., John-Baptist, J., Pugh-Kitingan, J. and Lasimbang, R. (1992), *Introduction to Sabah's Traditional Musical Instruments*, Department of Sabah Museum and State Archives, Kota Kinabalu.

Gustam Nagara (1954), *Pantun Soal Jawab*, The Royal Press, Singapore.

H. Zainuddin Hamidy and Fachruddin Hs. (eds), (1974), *Tafsir Qur'an*, Klang Book Centre, Klang, Selangor, Malaysia.

H.S.L. (1924), *Penghiboran Hati*, Criterion Press Ltd., Penang.

Hajah Zaiton Ajmain and Hamdan Yahya (1987), 'Definisi, Bentuk dan Fungsi Muzik Rakyat Sabah', in Mohd. Taib Osman (ed), *Muzik dan Puisi Rakyat Malaysia: Kumpulan Kertas-kerja Seminar*, Kementerian Kebudayaan Belia dan Sukan Negeri Sabah, Kota Kinabalu, pp. 8-18.

Han Kuo Huang (1979), 'The Modern Chinese Orchestra: Introductory Notes', *Asian Music*, XI (2).

Hardjowirojo (1968), *Sejarah Wayang Purwa*, Balai Pustaka, Jakarta.

Harmunah S. Mus (1979, 1987), *Keroncong: Sejarah, Gaya dan Perkembangan*, Pusat Musik Liturgi, Yogyakarta and Jakarta, Indonesia.

Harun Mat Piah and Solehah Ishak (1983), 'Rodat', *Pinang Sirih*, Dewan Bahasa dan Pustaka, Kuala Lumpur.

Holt, C. (1967), *Art in Indonesia; Continuities and Change*, Cornell University Press, Ithaca, New York.

Hose, C. and McDougall, W. (1912), *The Pagan Tribes of Borneo*, Vols. I-II. MacMillan and Co. Ltd, London.

Imam Habib Abdullah Haddad (1980), *Nasihat Agama dan Wasiat Iman*. Pustaka Nasional Pte. Ltd., Singapore.

Jairazbhoy, N. A. (1974) 'South Asian Peoples, Arts of', in *Encyclopædia Britannica*, Vol. 17, The Encyclopædia Britannica, Inc., Chicago.

----- (1978) 'Music' in Arthur Basham (ed), *A Cultural History of India*, Clarendon Press, Oxford.

----- (1995) 'South Asian Peoples, Arts of', in *The New Encyclopædia Britannica*, Vol. 27, The Encyclopædia Britannica, Inc., Chicago.

Kahn, J. S. and Loh, F. K. W. (eds) (1992), *Fragmented Vision, Culture and Politics in Contemporary Malaysia*, ASAA Southeast Asia Publications Series No. 22, Allen & Unwin, Sydney, Australia.

Kassim Ahmad (ed) (1973), *Hikayat Hang Tuah*, Dewan Bahasa dan Pustaka, Kuala Lumpur.

Kartomi, M. (1980), 'Kucapi' and Hasapi' in *The New Grove Dictionary of Musical Instruments*, MacMillan, London.

Kedit, Peter Mulok (1976), 'Sambe', in Kumio Koizumi (ed), *Asian Musics in an Asian Perspective*, Heibonsha, Tokyo.

Kementerian Kebudayaan Belia dan Sukan (n.d.) *Siri Lagu-lagu Rakyat Malaysia 1 dan 2* [Malaysian Folk Songs 1 and 2], Kuala Lumpur.

Kementerian Kebudayaan Belia dan Sukan (1980), *Gendang Gendut, Pameran Alat-alat Muzik Tradisional Malaysia*, Kuala Lumpur.

Kementerian Kebudayaan Belia dan Sukan, Bahagian Budaya (1980), *Siri Kebudayaan Kebangsaan: Bil. 18 Permainan Dan Tarian Rakyat Negeri Perak* [National Culture Series No. 18 Games and Folk Dances of Perak], Kuala Lumpur.

Kementerian Kebudayaan Belia dan Sukan, Bahagian Kebudayaan (1980), *Siri Mengenai Budaya Bil. 1 Kompang* [Cultural Series No. 1 Kompang], Kuala Lumpur.

----- (1980), *Siri Mengenal Budaya: Bil. 2 Hadrah* [Cultural Series No. 2 Hadrah], Kuala Lumpur.

----- (1980), *Siri Mengenal Budaya: Bil. 3 Wayang Kulit Purwa* [Cultural Series No. 3 Wayang Kulit Purwa], Kuala Lumpur.

----- (1980), *Siri Mengenal Budaya: Bil. 4 Bangsawan* [Cultural Series No. 4 Bangsawan], Kuala Lumpur.

----- (1980), *Siri Mengenal Budaya: Bil. 5 Boria* [Cultural Series No. 5 Boria], Kuala Lumpur.

----- (1981), *Siri Mengenal Budaya: Bil. 6 Teater Tradisional Jikey* [Cultural Series No. 6 Jikey Traditional Theater], Kuala Lumpur.

----- (1981), *Siri Mengenal Budaya: Bil. 7 Tarian-Tarian Malaysia* [Cultural Series, No. 7 Malaysian Dances], Kuala Lumpur.

----- (1981), *Siri Mengenal Budaya: Bil. 8 Mak Yong* [Cultural Series No. 8 Mak Yong], Kuala Lumpur.

----- (1981), *Siri Mengenal Budaya: Bil. 10 Dikir Barat* [Cultural Series No. 10 Dikir Barat], Kuala Lumpur.

----- (1983), *Siri Mengenal Budaya: Bil. 13 Tarian Saba* [Cultural Series No. 13 Saba Dance], Kuala Lumpur.

----- (1983), *Siri Mengenal Budaya: Bil. 14 Tarian Pulai* [Cultural Series No. 14 Pulai Dance], Kuala Lumpur.

Kloss, C. B. (1906), 'Malayan Musical Instruments', *Journal of the Royal Asiatic Society, Straits Branch*, 46, pp. 285-387.

Knaap, O. (1971), 'A Mahieu' *De Indische Band*, 18 and 25 July, 1903, translated in *Tong Tong*, 16 (1 March) and 21 (15 May).

Kornhauser, B. (1978), 'In Defense of Kroncong', in Kartomi, M. (ed), *Studies in Indonesian Music*, Centre of Southeast Asian Studies, Monash Papers on Southeast Asia, 7, Melbourne, pp. 104-83.

Ku Zam Zam, Ku Idris (1978), 'Muzik Tradisional Melayu dari Kedah Utara: Ensemble-ensemble Wayang Kulit, Mekmulung, dan Gendang Keling dengan Tumpuan kepada Alat-alat, Pemuzik-pemuzik dan Fungsi', M.A. thesis, Universiti Malaya, Kuala Lumpur.

----- (1983), 'Alat-alat Muzik dalam Ensemble Wayang Kulit, Mekmulung dan Gendang Keling di Kedah Utara', in Mohd. Taib Osman and Wan Kadir Yusof (eds), *Kajian Budaya dan Masyarakat di Malaysia*, Dewan Bahasa dan Pustaka, Kuala Lumpur, pp.1-54.

----- (1985), 'Nobat Diraja Kedah: Warisan Seni Muzik Istana Melayu Melaka', in Abdul Latiff Abu Bakar (ed), *Warisan Dunia Melayu: Teras Peradaban Malaysia*, Biro Penerbitan GAPENA, Kuala Lumpur.

----- (1993), 'Nobat: Music in the Service of the King - the Symbol of Power and Status in Traditional Malay Society', in *Tinta Kenangan*, Jabatan Pengajian Melayu, Universiti Malaya, Kuala Lumpur.

----- (1993), 'Tumbuk Kalang, Satu Genera Muzik Kerja Pertanian Padi', in Nik Safiah Karim (ed), *Segamal Padi Sekunca Budi*, Akademi Pengajian Melayu, Universiti Malaya, Kuala Lumpur, pp. 210-13.

----- (1994), 'Alat-alat Muzik Nobat: Satu Analisis Tentang Simbolisme Muzik dan Daulat Dalam Kesultanan Melayu', *Tirai Panggung*, 2, pp. 1-10.

----- (1996), 'Nobat dan Daulat: Satu Perspektif Tentang Lambang dan Manifestasi Kuasa Kesultanan Melayu', in *Tradisi dan Kemodenan*, Universitas Sumatera Utara, Medan, Sumatra, Indonesia.

Laderman, C. (1991), *Taming the Wind of Desire: Psychology, Medicine and Aesthetics in Malay Shamanistic Performance*, University of California Press, Berkeley.

Liang, Mingyue (1985), *Music of the Billion; an Introduction to Chinese Musical Culture*, McCredie, A.D. (ed), International Institute for Comparative Music Studies, Berlin, and Ivan Vandor (ed.), Heinrichshofen Edition, New York.

Lindsay, J. (1992), *Javanese Gamelan, Traditional Orchestra of Indonesia*. 2nd ed., Oxford University Press, Singapore.

Linehan, W. (1951), 'The Nobat and the Orang Kalau of Perak', *Journal of the Royal Asiatic Society, Malayan Branch*, XXIV(3), pp. 60-8.

Lockard, C. (1996), 'From Folk to Computer Songs: The Evolution of Malaysian Popular Music, 1930-1990'. *Journal of Popular Culture* 30(3), pp. 1-26.

Lord, A. B. (1976), *The Singer of Tales*, Atheneum, New York.

Low, K. C. (1976), 'Dondang Sayang in Melaka', B.A. thesis, Monash University, Australia.

Maceda, J. (1962), 'Field-recording Sea-Dayak Music', *Sarawak Museum Journal*, V(19-20) (New Series), pp. 486-500.

----- (1981), *A Manual of Field Music Research with Special Reference to Southeast Asia.* Quezon City, College of Music, University of the Philippines.

Malaysia 2000 Official Yearbook (2000), Kementerian Penerangan [Dept. of Information], Kuala Lumpur.

Malm, W. (1969), 'Music of the Ma' Yong', *Tenggara*, 5, pp. 114-120.

----- (1971), 'Malaysian Ma'Yong Theater', *The Drama Review*, XV(3), pp. 108.

Masing, J. J. (1997), *The Coming of the Gods, An Iban Invocatory Chant of the Baleh River Region, Sarawak*, 2 Vols. Dept. of Anthropology, The Australian National University, Canberra, Australia.

Matheson, V. and Andaya, B. W. (eds) (1982), *Tuhfat al-Nafis* by Raja Haji Ahmad and Raja Ali Haji, Oxford University Press, Kuala Lumpur.

Matusky, P. (1980), 'Music in the Malay Shadow Puppet Theatre', Ph.D. dissertation, University of Michigan, Ann Arbor.

----- (1982), 'Musical Instruments and Musicians of the Malay Shadow Puppet Theater', *Journal of the American Musical Instrument Society*, VIII, pp. 38-68.

----- (1985), 'An Introduction to the Major Instruments and Forms of Traditional Malay Music', *Asian Music*, XVI(2), pp. 121-82.

----- (1986), 'Aspects of Musical Style Among the Kajang, Kayan and Kenyah-Badang of the Upper Rejang River: A Preliminary Survey', *Sarawak Museum Journal*, XXXVI(57) (New Series), pp. 185-229.

----- (1989), 'Alat-alat dan Bentuk-Bentuk Muzik Tradisi Masyarakat Melayu', in Mohd. Taib Osman (ed), *Masyarakat Melayu: Struktur, Organisasi dan Manifestasi*, Dewan Bahasa dan Pustaka, Kuala Lumpur.

----- (1990), 'Musical Styles Among the Kayan, Kenyah-Badang and Malay Peoples of the Upper Rejang River [Sarawak]: A Preliminary Survey', *Sarawak Museum Journal*, XLI(62) (New Series), pp. 115-49.

----- (1992), 'Musical Instruments of the Indigenous Peoples', in Lucas Chin (ed), *Sarawak - A Cultural Legacy*, Society Atelier Sarawak, Kuching.

----- (1993, 1997), *Malaysian Shadow Play and Music, Continuity of an Oral Tradition*, Oxford University Press, Kuala Lumpur, and The Asian Centre, Penang.

----- (1994), 'Music of the Mak Yong Theatre, A Fusion of Southeast Asian Malay and Middle Eastern Islamic Elements', in Ellen Leichtman (ed), *To The Four Corners:A Festschrift in Honor of Rose Brandel*, Harmonie Park Press, Warren, Michigan.

----- (1998), 'Peninsular Malaysia (the rural musical traditions)', 'Island Southeast Asia: An Introduction', 'Borneo', in Miller, T. and Williams, S. (eds), *The Garland Encyclopedia of World Music*, Vol. 4, Garland Publishing, Inc., New York and London.

----- (2001), 'West Malaysia', in Sadie, S. (ed), *The New Grove's Dictionary of Music and Musicians*, Vol. 15, Macmillan Publishers Ltd., London.

----- and Hamzah Awang Amat (1997), *Muzik Wayang Kulit Kelantan*, Akademi Seni Kebangsaan, Kuala Lumpur.

----- and Tan, S. B. (1997), *Muzik Malaysia, Tradisi Kelasik, Rakyat dan Sinkretik*, The Asian Centre, Penang, Malaysia.

Mohd. Afandi Ismail (1975), 'Perkembangan Mak Yong Sebagai Satu Teater Tradisional', *Dewan Bahasa*, 9(6), pp. 363-6.

Mohd. Anis Md. Nor (1986), *Randai Dance of Minangkabau Sumatra with Labanotation Scores*, University of Malaya Press, Kuala Lumpur.

----- (1991), 'Malay Folk Dances of the Straits of Melaka: Traditions and National Aspiration', Manila International Dance Conference, The Philippines.

----- (1993), *Zapin, Traditional Dance of the Malay World*, Oxford University Press, Singapore.

----- (1995), 'Archives and Fields: A Discourse in Dance History in Malaysia' and 'Dance Research in Malaysia: Old and New Interpretations' in *The Challenge and Message in Dance*, Seoul.

----- (1995 'Dance' in *Encyclopedia of the Modern Islamic World*, Oxford University Press.

----- (1996), 'Dance In Malaysia: Major Forces in the Changing Scene', *SPAFA Journal*.

----- (2000) 'Between Myth and History: Reconstructing Traditional Dances in Southeast Asia', ICTM 20th Ethnochoreology Symposium Proceedings-Dans Muzik Kulture, Bogazici University, Istanbul, Turkey, pp. 115-24.

----- (2001) 'Dancing on the Proscenium: Re-constructing, Revitalizing and Appropriating Malay Folk Dances', 21st Symposium of the ICTM Study Group on Ethnochoreology, Institute of Ethnology and Folklore Research, Zagreb, Croatia, pp. 238-243.

Mohd. Anis Md. Nor and Mohd. Nasir Hashim (1994), 'Engkerurai: Organ-Mulut Orang Iban dan Orang Ulu', *Tirai Panggung*, 2, pp. 11-26.

Mohd. Ghazali Abdullah (ed) (1995), *Teater Tradisional Melayu*, Book I, Kementerian Kebudayaan, Kesenian dan Pelancongan Malaysia, Kuala Lumpur.

Mohd. Ghouse Nasaruddin (1976), 'Muzik Ethnik Malaysia', in *Bahasa, Kesusasteraan dan Kebudayaan Melayu*, Kementerian Kebudayaan Belia dan Sukan, Kuala Lumpur, pp. 162-303.

----- (1988), *Tarian Tradisi Melayu*, Dewan Bahasa dan Pustaka, Kuala Lumpur.

Mohd. Taib Osman (1984), *Bunga Rampai: Aspects of Malay Culture*, Dewan Bahasa dan Pustaka, Kuala Lumpur.

----- (ed). (1974), *Traditional Drama and Music in Southeast Asia*, Dewan Bahasa dan Pustaka, Kuala Lumpur.

Mudi, A. (1988), 'Musical Instruments of Sabah, A Perspective on the Sompoton', Paper presented at the Symposium of the International Musicological Society and Festival of Music, 28 August-2 September, Melbourne, Australia.

Mustafa Mohd. Isa (1987), *Awang Belanga, Penglipur Lara dari Perlis*, Dewan Bahasa dan Pustaka, Kuala Lumpur.

Ong, W. J. (1982), *Orality and Literacy, The Technologizing of the Word*, Methuen, London.

Persatuan Silat Seni Ezhar dan Kompang Wilayah Persekutuan dan Selangor Darul Ehsan (1992), *Cara dan Kaedah-Kaedah Bermain Kompang Kesenian EZHAR bersama Khalifan (Jurulatih) Ezhar.*

PT Ichtiar Baru van Hoeve (ed.) (1994), *Ensiklopedi Islam*, PT Intermasa, Jakarta, Indonesia.

Pugh-Kitingan, J. (1987), 'Muzik Instrumental dan Alat-alat Muzik Dusun Tambunan', in Mohd. Taib Osman (ed), *Muzik dan Puisi Rakyat Malaysia: Kumpulan Kertas-kerja Seminar*, Kementerian Kebudayaan Belia dan Sukan Negeri Sabah, Kota Kinabalu, pp. 28-72.

----- (1988), 'Instruments and Instrumental Music of the Tambunan Kadazan/Dusun', *Sabah Museum and Archives Journal*, 1(2), pp. 24-61.

----- (1990), 'Musical Instruments of Sabah', in *Sabah ---- Borneo's Paradise* (Information book for Sabah exhibition at Pesta '90 Malaysia, Kuala Lumpur Plaza), Sabah Tourism Promotion Corporation, Kota Kinabulu.

----- (1990), 'Cultural Dances of Sabah', in *Sabah ---- Borneo's Paradise* (Information book for Sabah exhibition at Pesta '90 Malaysia, Kuala Lumpur Plaza), Sabah Tourism Promotion Corporation, Kota Kinabulu.

----- (1991), 'An Introduction to Sabah's Cultures and Music', *The Sabah Performing Arts Company from East Malaysia*, East-West Center Institute of Culture and Communication, University of Hawaii, Honolulu.

Redfield, R. (1959), *Peasant Society and Culture*, University of Chicago Press, Chicago and London.*ur*

----- (1962), 'The Folk Society', in Redfield, M.P. (ed), *Human Nature and The Study of Society*, University of Chicago Press, Chicago and London.

Roland Abd. Rahman (1979), 'Dondang Sayang: Pembicaraan dari segi fungsi muziknya' (unpublished paper).

Roseman, M. (1991), *Healing Sounds from the Malaysian Rainforest*, University of California Press, Berkeley.

----- (1995), *Dream Songs and Healing Sounds in the Rainforest of Malaysia*, Smithsonian Folkways no. 40417. Compact disc and Booklet.

Ross, V. (1994), 'The "Craft of Karma" – For Chamber Ensemble', *Tirai Panggung*, 2, Universiti Malaya, Kuala Lumpur.

Roth, H. L. (1968), *The Natives of Sarawak and British North Borneo*, Vols. I-II, Truslove & Hanson, London, and University of Malaya Press, Kuala Lumpur.

Rubenstein, C. (1985), *The Honey Tree Song, Poems and Chants of Sarawak Dayaks*, Ohio University Press, Athens, Ohio and London.

Sachs, Curt. (1940), *The History of Musical Instruments*, W. W. Norton and Co., New York.

Sadie, S. (ed.) (2001), *The New Grove Dictionary of Music and Musicians*, 2nd edition, Macmillan Publishers Ltd., London.

Sandin, B. (1974), 'The Iban Music', in Mohd. Taib Osman (ed), *Traditional Music and Drama of Southeast Asia*, Dewan Bahasa dan Pustaka, Kuala Lumpur, pp. 320-6.

Sarkissian, M. (1995-96), '"Sinhalese Girl" meets "Aunty Annie": Competing Expressions of Ethnicity Identity in the Portuguese Settlement, Melaka, Malaysia', *Asian Music*, XXVII(1).

----- (2000), *D'Albuquerque's Children, Performing Tradition in Malaysia's Portuguese Settlement*, University of Chicago Press, Chicago and London.

Sather, C. (2001) *Seeds of Play, Words of Power: An Ethnographic Study of Iban Shamanic Chants*, Tun Juggah Foundation and Borneo Research Council, Kuching, Sarawak.

Seeler, J. DeWitt (1975), 'Kenyah Dance, Sarawak, Malaysia: A Description and Analysis', M.A. thesis, University of Hawaii, Honolulu, Hawaii.

----- (1969), 'Some Notes on Traditional Dances of Sarawak', *Sarawak Museum Journal*, XVII(:34-35) (New Series,), pp. 163-201.

Sheppard, M. (1938), 'The Trengganu Rodat', *Journal of the Royal Asiatic Society, Malayan Branch*, 16(1), p. 112.

----- (1967), 'Joget Gamelan Trengganu,' *Journal of the Royal Asiatic Society, Malayan Branch*, 40(1), pp. 149-52.

----- (1972), *Taman Indera, Malay Decorative Arts and Pastimes*, Oxford University Press, Kuala Lumpur.

----- (1973), 'Manora in Kelantan', *Journal of the Royal Asiatic Society, Malayan Branch*, 16(1), pp. 161-70.

Strickland, S. S. (1988), 'Preliminary notes on a Kejaman-Sekapan oral narrative form', *Sarawak Museum Journal*, XXXIX(60)(New Series), pp. 67-75.

Studies in Malaysian Oral and Musical Traditions (1974), Michigan Papers on South and Southeast Asia, No. 8, Center of South and Southeast Asian Studies, University of Michigan, Ann Arbor.

Sweeney, A. (1972), *Malay Shadow Puppets,* The British Museum, London.

----- (1976), *The Ramayana and the Malay Shadow Play*, Penerbit Universiti Kebangsaan, Kuala Lumpur.

----- (1980), *Authors and Audiences in Traditional Malay Literature*, Center for Southeast Asian Studies, University of California, Berkeley.

----- (1994), *Malay Word Music, A Celebration of Oral Creativity*, Dewan Bahasa dan Pustaka, Kuala Lumpur.

Swettenham, F. (1959), 'A Malay Nauch', *Malaya in History*, 5(1), Feb., pp. 38-41 (reprint of 1878 report).

Tan, S. B. (1980), 'Chinese Opera in Malaysia: Changes and Survival', *Review of Southeast Asian Studies*, 10, pp. 29-45.

----- (1984), 'An Introduction to the Chinese Glove Puppet Theatre', *Journal of the Malaysian Branch of the Royal Asiatic Society*, LVII(1), pp. 40-55.

----- (1988), 'The Thai *Menora* in Malaysia; Adapting to the Penang Chinese Community', *Asian Folklore Studies*, XLVII(1), pp. 19-34.

----- (1989), 'From Popular to Traditional Theatre, the Bangsawan of Malaysia', *Ethnomusicology*, 33(2) pp. 229-44.

----- (1990), 'The Performing Arts in Malaysia: State and Society', *Asian Music* 21(1), pp. 137-71.

----- (1993), *Bangsawan, A Social and Stylistic History of the Malay Opera*, Oxford University Press, Singapore.

----- (1994), 'Moving Centrestage: Women in Malay Opera in Early Twentieth Century Malaya', *Kajian Malaysia*, 1-2, pp. 96-118.

----- (1995), 'Popular Music in Multi-Ethnic Malaysia: Diversity Despite Control,' in Kimberlin, C. and Euba, A. (eds), *Intercultural Music, Vol. 1*, Bayreuth African Studies, 29, pp. 143-63.

----- (1997), 'The 78 RPM Record Industry in Malaya Prior to World War II', *Asian Music*, 28(1), pp. 1-42.

----- (2001), 'Heritage, Spectacles and Packaged Traditions: Georgetown Responds to Modernity at the Turn of the Century', Unpublished paper presented at the World Conference of the International Council for Traditional Music, Rio de Janeiro, July 5-11.

----- (2002) 'Negotiating Identities: Reconstructing the Local in Malaysia through World Beat', *Perfect Beat*.

----- and Matusky, P. (1997), *Muzik Malaysia, Tradisi Kelasik, Rakyat dan Sinkretik*, The Asian Centre, Penang, Malaysia.

Thomas, P. (1986), *Like Tigers Around a Piece of Meat*, Institute of Southeast Asian Studies, Singapore.

Tunku Nong Jiwa (Raja Badri Shah) and Sheppard, M. (1962), 'The Kedah and Perak Nobat', *Malaya in History*, VII(2), pp. 7-11.

Wan Abdul Kadir (1983), 'Pertumbuhan Budaya Popular Masyarakat Melayu Bandaran Sebelum Perang Dunia Kedua', in Mohd. Taib Osman and Wan Kadir Yusoff (eds), *Kajian Budaya dan Masyarakat di Malaysia*, Dewan Bahasa dan Pustaka, Kuala Lumpur.

----- (1988), *Budaya Popular Dalam Masyarakat Melayu Bandaran* [Popular Culture in Urban Malay Society], Dewan Bahasa dan Pustaka, Kuala Lumpur.

Wade, B. (1979), *Music of India: The Classical Traditions*, Prentice-Hall, Inc., Englewood Cliffs, New Jersey.

Winstedt, R. O. (1929), 'The Perak Royal Musical Instruments', *Journal of the Royal Asiatic Society, Malayan Branch*, XII, p. 451.

Wong, A. and Soraya Mansor (1995), *Engkerurai: Alat Muzik Masyarakat Iban Sarawak*, Kementerian Kebudayaan Kesenian dan Pelancongan, Kuala Lumpur.

Yung, B. (1989), *Cantonese Opera, Performance as Creative Process*, Cambridge University Press, Cambridge.

Websites

http://www.theasiancentre.com
http://www.malayculture.org
http://www.music.upm.my/malaysia
http://www.AmirYussof.com.my
http://www.positivetone.com.my

Discography and Videography

Folk, Classical and Syncretic music

Dream Songs and Healing Sounds in the Rainforest of Malaysia (1995), Compact disc, Smithsonian Folkways no. 40417. Recording and Booklet by M. Roseman.

Festival Nusantara 2001 (2003), 12 digital video disc set: 1-2 *Festival Nusantara 2001* (Malay and English), 3 *Wayang kulit gedek*, 4 *Wayang purwa*, 5 *Wayang kulit Melayu*, 6 *Wayang kulit Kelantan*, 7 *Wayang purwa Indonesia*, 8 *Wayang golek Indonesia*, 9 *Wayang wong Indonesia*, 10 *Nang Talung Thailand*, 11 *Wayang kulit Cina Singapura*, 12 *Wayang kulit Filipina*. Accompanying booklet '*Wayang Dalam Bayang*'. Akademi Seni Kebangsaan [National Arts Academy], Kuala Lumpur.

Gamelan Dance Music (n.d.), Compact disc WEA 9031-71107-2.

Ghazal Menyengat, Menampilkan Fadzil Ahmad (Raja Gambus Malaysia), Datin Orchid Abdullah, Aspalela Abdullah, Jamie Chik (1999), Produced by Ahas Productions, Pahang, Distributed by Form Records, Kuala Lumpur.

Johan-Johan Dondang Sayang, Pesta Dendang Rakyat (1988), Cassette tape, Pusat Musikal Mutiara, Seremban.

JVC Anthology of Music and Dance of the World's Peoples (n.d.), Vol. VIII (Malaysia and The Philippines). VHS video cassette, JVC, Tokyo.

Keroncong Malaysia (n.d.), EMI, TC-FM 30093.

Lagu Melayu Asli (1990), Compact disc, Life Records, Kuala Lumpur.

The Mak Yong Dance Theatre of Malaysia (1995), VHS video cassette by Ghulam-Sarwar Yousof (ca. 20 minutes), The Asian Centre, Penang, Malaysia.

Mari Menari (n.d.), Life Records, LMLP 045.

Mekmulung, dabus, sewang, jikey, awang batil, and barongan (n.d.), Digital video discs by Virtual Malaysia.com, Creative Advances Technology Sdn. Bhd., Lot 2-2 Enterprise 2, Technology Park Malaysia, Bukit Jalil 57000, Kuala Lumpur.

Music of Indonesia 2, Indonesian Popular Music, Kroncong, Dangdut and Langgam Jawa (n.d.), Compact disc (with program notes). Smithsonian/Folkways SF 40056.

Muzik Tarian Malaysia (1987), Cassette tape, Life Records, Kuala Lumpur.

Nasib Panjang (1982), WEA, M40-93478.

Semangat Insan (1999), Five VHS videotapes on *wayang kulit, menora, bangsawan, Chinese opera* and *main puteri*. Planet Films Sdn. Bhd., Petaling Jaya.

Unity in Diversity, A celebration of the music of Asia and Europe (2001), Compact disc (Production and booklet by Keith Howard), ASEF CD1-2, Asia-Europe Foundation, Singapore.

Wayang Kulit Siam, The Malay Wayang Kulit (1995), VHS Video cassette by Ghulam-Sarwar Yousof (ca. 20 minutes), The Asian Centre, Penang, Malaysia.

Websites
http://mall.virtualmalaysia.com
http://www.malayculture.org
http: //www.music.upm.my/Malaysia
http://www.theasiancentre.com

Contemporary art music

Classical Archives, Inspirations and Aspirations,   available   at
http://www.classicalarchives.com/aspire.html
Muzik bunyi-bunian (1992), VHS video cassette (Compositions and production by Tan Sooi Beng), Universiti Sains Malaysia, Penang.
Naad Brahma, Music for the Soul (1998), Compact disc, Temple of Fine Arts, Kuala Lumpur.
Rhythm in Bronze, New Music for the Malaysian Gamelan (2001), Compact disc (with booklet), Five Arts Centre and Actors Studio, Kuala Lumpur.

Popular music

78RPM

Ahmad CB (1930s), *Anak* Koe (*kroncong*). Chap Singa QF 89.
Ahmad CB (1940s), *Malaya* (nationalistic song). Chap Singa QF 87.
Ahmad CB and A Jaafar Orchestra (1950S), *Pemuda Melayu*. HMV N 238.
Aman Ballon and Leiman SS (1940s), *Kling Mabok* (comic song). HMV P 22900.
Asiah (1950s), *Lihatlah* (swing). A. Jaafar Orchestra. Film: *Bahagia di Singapura*. Pathe, PTH 181.
Asiah and Abd. Chik (1950s), *Serampang Lapan* (*joget*). Composers: Q. Jaafar and S. Rahman. A. Jaafar Orchestra. Film: *Insaf*. Pathe PTH 173.
Che Norlia (1930s), *Linggang Mak Inang* (*inang*). HMV 15980.
City Opera (1930s), *Aladom* (*masri*). Beka 26408.
Ismael. (1904), *Lagu Djalak Lintang* (*asli*). The Gramophone Co. 2-120008.
Jacoba Regar (1930s), *Kawin Paksaan* (*kroncong foxtrot*). HMV NS 587.
Lena (1950s), *Nasib Di Bunga* (*cha-cha-cha*). Yusof B. Orchestra. Film: *Lupa Daratan*. Columbia GEM 201.

Mohd. Yatim (1950s), *Dalam Masa Nipon* (comic song). HMV P 22945.

Mohd. Yatim (1950s), *Yam Choi Chow* (comic song). HMV NAM 13.

Noormadiah (1950s), *Tidorlah Nanda* (*irama Hindustan*). Osman Ahmad Orchestra. Film: *Merana.* HMV NAM 206.

P. Ramlee and Saloma (1950s), *Rintihan Jiwaku* (*asli*). Composers: Osman Ahmad and Sudarmadji. P Ramlee orchestra. Film: *Batu Bertangkup.* Parlophone DPE 8103.

P. Ramlee and Saloma (1950s), *Tudong Periok* (*asli*). P. Ramlee Orchestra. Film: *Sumpah Orang Minyak.* Parlophone DPE 8073.

P. Ramlee (1950s), *Maafkan Kami* (*zapin*). P. Ramlee Orchestra. Film: *Pendekar Bujang Lapok.* Parlophone DPE 8093.

P. Ramlee (1950s), *Nasib Si Miskin* (*masri*). A. Jaafar Orchestra. Film: *Antara Senyum dan Tangis.* Parlophone DPE 8050.

Tarminah and Piet S (1930s), *Apik Tukang Becha.* HMV P 13171.

Tarminah and Piet S (1930s), *Taxi Rumba* (*rumba*). HMV P 13172.

Temah (1920s), *Mas Merah* (*asli*). HMV GC-12-13169.

Tijah (1940s), *Tandi-Tandi* (*lagu Hindustan*). HMV P 16489.

Tijah and Dean (1930s), *Dondang Sayang.* Chap Kuching NG 2.

45 RPM

Les Flingers (1967), *Sa Hati Sa Jiwa* (*pop yeh yeh*). Philips 437816 PE.

Maimun Hussein and the Dulcet Boys (1967), *Gerhana, Pemergian* (*pop yeh yeh*). Philips 437811 PE.

Orchid Abdullah (1966), *Bertemu Di Dalam Mimpi* (*ghazal*). EMI/Parlophone.

Roziah Latiff and the Jay Hawkers (1967), Aku Ingat *Pada Mu* (*pop yeh yeh*). Philips 437812 PE.

Cassette tapes/Compact discs/Digital video discs

Ababil (1989), *Ababil: 'Ringgit'.* Target Records TRC 8002.

Asiabeat (1983), *Asiabeat: 'Bamboo Groove'.* CBS MC 111.

BM Boys (1998), *Shi Nian Hao Ge: 'Tong Nian Xiong'.* Follow Me Records.

BM Boys (1998), *Shi Nian Hao Ge: 'Nang Si Chit Keh Nang'.* Follow Me Records.

Ella (1989), *Pengemis Cinta: 'Dunia Kehidupan'.* Warner WEA M40-93565.

FTG (1998), (Freedom That's Gone). *Aku Tak Peduli.*

Hang Mokhtar (1987), *Kocik-kocik Jago Kobau: 'Tampal Korek'.* Segar: CL 1001.

Kembara (1982), *Perjuangan.* Polygram-Philips: 7179159.

Koma (2001), *Aftermath.* Muzik Box Production.

M. Nasir (1992), *Saudagar Mimpi.* Luncai Emas, distributed by BMG-Pacific PMC/MAL 1101.

M. Nasir (1993), *Canggong Mendonan: 'Apokalips', 'Di Balik Cermin Mimpi'.* Luncai Emas, distributed by BMG-Pacific 74321 170124.

Noraniza Idris (1999), *Berkaba.* Suria Records SRCD 99-23475.

Poetic Ammo (1998), *It's a Nice Day to be Alive.* Positive Tone: PT 3008 CS (distributed by Sony).

Rabbani (2000), *Intifada.* EMI 07243 5313724 3.

Raihan (1997), *Puji-Pujian.* Warner 0630-17715-4.

Rampa (1988), *Koleksi Emas Rampa: 'Senasib'.* Warnada: WA 1520.

Samurai (2000), *Pendekar Belantara.* Pony Canyon.

Sayu Ateng (no date), *Echoes of Borneo, Mystical Music from the Rainforest of Sarawak.* These Sound Recording.

Sharifah Aini (1988), *Dangdut-Dangdut: 'Masih Ingat Masih Setia'.* EMI TC-BM 32521.

Sheqal (1990), *Balada Nusantara Menampilkan Sheqal.* Ciku Records, distributed by BMG: BMG/CM 01190.

Sudirman (1980), *Lagu Anak Desa.* EMI TC-EMGS 5554.

Sudirman (1984), *Orang Baru.* EMI TC-EMGS 5626.

Too Phat (2001), *Plan B.* Positive Tone. 07243532771 47 (distributed by EMI).

Vrykolakas (2001), *Aftermath.* Muzik Box Production.

Wings (1988), *Hukum Karma.* Antarctic Sound Production: ASP 0048.

Zainal Abidin (1990), *Zainal Abidin: 'Hijau'.* Roslan Aziz Productions, distributed by Warner WEA 9031-74404-4.

Zainal Abidin (1994), *Gamal.* Roslan Aziz Productions, distributed by Warner WEA 4509-97377-4.

Zaleha Hamid (1988), *Dangdut-Dangdut: 'Dangdut Reggae'.* EMI TC-BM 32521.

Websites
http://www.AmirYussof.com.my
http://www.positivetone.com.my

Index